"Martin Accad's is a voice to be heeded by anyone concerned about Christian-Muslim relations. This book offers an important model of how the historical study of long-standing theological debates can inform and inspire fruitful models for theology and practice."

— Ida Glaser,
University of Oxford

"Full of important information for Christians looking for a theological framework to engage with Islam. The book is an invaluable contribution to a Christian understanding of Islam. It is written with a rare mix of critical scholarly attention, practical wisdom, and a deep commitment to reaching across the theological divide between Muslims and Christians. While there are several works addressing various theological themes in Islam from a Christian perspective, *Sacred Misinterpretation* is among the first to offer a thoughtful and comprehensive theological engagement with Islam. I highly recommend it to Christian theological students and specialists interested in Christian-Muslim dialogue."

— John Azumah,
Columbia Theological Seminary

"An extraordinarily thorough and useful survey of the complex history of Muslim-Christian theological misunderstandings. The book is built on Accad's research into the history of Muslim use of the Bible, a history that has been far richer and more varied than even well-informed contemporary Muslims or Christians usually assume. Accad also addresses Christian understandings of the Qur'an, which are often entirely oblivious to the sophisticated Muslim exegetical tradition. His approach is unapologetically theological, and therefore extraordinarily practical, thoroughly surveying every major point of theological interaction between Muslims and Christians. In the end, *Sacred Misinterpretation* is an optimistic and hope-filled book. Informed by his own experience growing up in post–civil war Lebanon and a family history rich with experience of Muslim-Christian interaction, Accad makes the case that removing the roadblocks to mutual understanding is both imperative and attainable."

— Daniel Brown,
Institute for the Study of Religion in the Middle East

"Martin Accad has succeeded admirably in his attempt to write a book respectful enough of Islam that Muslims will want to read it. He draws upon his impressive familiarity with the Islamic sources and his fascinating personal history to propose a new model for interfaith relations. His concept of metadialogue provides a solid framework upon which creative religious discourse can be established. Because it is attentive to the theological sensitivities of each side, this is a work that just might provide a blueprint for moving beyond the stalemate that has usually been the result of even the best-intentioned attempts at conversations between Christians and Muslims."

— JOHN KALTNER,
author of *Islam*

"In the field of Islamic Studies, where Catholics and Orthodox in the Middle East have been active for generations, here is the first substantial contribution from a scholar who is an Arab and an evangelical Protestant. Because he can access centuries of literature in Syriac and Arabic, he is able to understand how Christians and Muslims have engaged in dialogue over many centuries and can appreciate how historical contexts have shaped the gradual development of theological controversies. Being rooted in the Lebanese context and having lived through intense conflict, he understands well the relationship between religion and politics and can see the role that Christian and Muslim leaders should be able to play—even in the conflicts that rage across the Middle East at the present time. This book will challenge the ignorance, fears, and prejudices of many Christians, because it really does stretch the boundaries and force them to rethink their assumptions."

— COLIN CHAPMAN,
visiting lecturer at the Arab Baptist Theological Seminary

Sacred Misinterpretation

Reaching across the Christian-Muslim Divide

Martin Accad

William B. Eerdmans Publishing Company
Grand Rapids, Michigan

Wm. B. Eerdmans Publishing Co.
4035 Park East Court SE, Grand Rapids, Michigan 49546
www.eerdmans.com

Published 2019
Printed in the United States of America

25 24 23 22 21 20 19   1 2 3 4 5 6 7

ISBN 978-0-8028-7414-6

Library of Congress Cataloging-in-Publication Data

Names: Accad, Martin, 1972- author.
Title: Sacred misinterpretation : reaching across the Christian-Muslim divide / Martin Accad.
Description: Grand Rapids : Eerdmans Publishing Co., 2019. | Includes bibliographical references and index.
Identifiers: LCCN 2018060809 | ISBN 9780802874146 (pbk. : alk. paper)
Subjects: LCSH: Islam—Relations—Christianity. | Christianity and other religions—Islam.
Classification: LCC BP172 .A273 2019 | DDC 297.2/83—dc23
LC record available at https://lccn.loc.gov/2018060809

To the people of Syria—the women, children, and men who continue to be victims of the horrors of religious fanaticism, fueled by political egoism, social injustice, and global economic disparity.
May this book contribute healing to the world.

To Jesus, my paradigm of love, compassion, and peace,
I owe all inspiration.

To God be the glory!

Contents

List of Figures

Foreword

In his *Biography of the Messenger of God*, Ibn Isḥāq (died 767) speaks of sixty Christian "riders" who came to visit the prophet Muhammad from the southern Arabian oasis town of Najrān. The leader of these riders was Abu Ḥāritha, who was famous for building churches (with the help of Byzantine subsidies) in South Arabia. According to Ibn Isḥāq, Abu Ḥāritha knew in his heart that Muhammad was a prophet. He refrained from becoming a Muslim only because of the way the Byzantine Christians supported him and his people. Ibn Isḥāq also notes that during the visit of Abu Ḥāritha and his companions to Muhammad's city of Medina (in modern day Saudi Arabia), their time of prayer arrived, and Muhammad graciously allowed his Christian guests to pray inside his mosque.

Notably (and rather improbably) Ibn Isḥāq relates that the Christian delegation was divided over Christ. Some in the group said that Christ is "God," others that he is the "son of God," and still others that he is "the third person of the Trinity." Each group among them developed certain arguments to defend their Christology. He writes:

> They argue that he is God because he used to raise the dead, and heal the sick, and declare the unseen; and make clay birds and then breathe into them so that they flew away. . . . They argue that he is the son of God in that they say he had no known father; and he spoke in the cradle and this is something that no child of Adam has ever done. They argue that he is the third of three in that God says: We have done, We have commanded, We have created and We have decreed.[1]

1. Alfred Guillaume, *The Life of Muhammad: A Translation of Ibn Ishaq's Sirat Rasul Allah* (Oxford: Oxford University Press, 2002), 271–72.

All of these supposed arguments are in fact reflections of Qur'anic allusions to Jesus and to his miracles. Even the idea that the Christians would differ among themselves over Christ (when in fact South Arabian Christians of the time were almost all Monophysites or Jacobites) probably reflects the influence of the Qur'an (al-Mā'ida 5:14 makes discord among Christians a divine punishment).

Ibn Isḥāq goes on to describe the conversation of this group of Christians with Muhammad:

> The apostle said to them, "Submit yourselves." They said, "We have submitted." He said: "You have not submitted, so submit." They said, "Nay, but we submitted before you." He said, "You lie. Your assertion that God has a son, your worship of the cross, and your eating pork hold you back from submission."[2]

Here we see Muhammad portrayed as a debater and missionary. He is not interested in dialogue with the Christians who came to visit him. He is interested in their conversion. At this point the key moment in the disputation unfolds. The Christians of Najrān offer to Muhammad an argument for the divine sonship of Christ. They declare, "But who is his father, Muhammad?" The prophet does not answer right away. Instead he waits for a revelation that God—after some time—presents to him: a section from the third sūrah of the Qur'an (Āl 'Imrān), which includes what is now verse 59: "Surely the likeness of Jesus is, with God, as the likeness of Adam. He created him from dust, [and] then he said to him, 'Be!' and he was." In other words, Jesus's birth is no more miraculous than that of Adam. Neither had an earthly father. They were both created by a simple divine command ("Be!").

A subsequent verse from this section of Āl 'Imrān has God instruct Muhammad to challenge those who disagree with him to a sort of trial (*mubāhala*). According to Ibn Isḥāq this verse too was meant for the Christian delegation from Najrān. Muhammad, seeing that the Christians would not be convinced by his arguments, challenged the Christians to an ordeal (they were each to invoke a curse on the other). The Christians, however, knowing in their hearts that Muhammad was a true prophet, backed down from the challenge, packed up their belongings, and returned home to South Arabia.

2. Guillaume, *Life of Muhammad*, 272.

The story of Muhammad's disputation with the Christian delegation from Najrān is built around the various allusions to Christianity and Christian beliefs in the Qur'an. It may in fact be mostly exegetical and have no firm basis in a historical event. Still the story includes some important lessons for Muslim-Christian relations. Muhammad's willingness to allow the group of Christians to pray in his mosque reminds Muslims and Christians to show magnanimity in their relations with each other.

Yet the story also has an element of polemics. Muhammad is not interested in dialogue with the Christians. Instead he criticizes their doctrine, rejects their apologetic arguments, and challenges them to an ordeal. The polemical nature of this encounter might be seen to symbolize the larger history of relations between Christians and Muslims. When they have not been fighting wars against each other, Christians and Muslims have been engaged in wars of words.

From the time of Islam's origins a long history of apologetics and polemics between Muslims and Christians has unfolded. Today, however, many Christians and Muslims—even those who continue to believe in the value of apologetics—are interested above all in understanding the other. *Sacred Misinterpretation: Reaching across the Christian-Muslim Divide* is a good place to begin that task.

Martin Accad's book offers a serious and clear analysis of the theological issues in Muslim-Christian relations in a style that is free from polemics, but also free from truisms. He does not ignore the complications in the history of Muslim-Christian relations. Indeed, he is concerned with the very christological and theological debates (some of which feature in the Ibn Isḥāq story above) that marked those relations. Yet instead of repeating old apologetic arguments, or focusing only on points of commonality, Accad shows how a Christian can engage with Islam in a respectful yet serious manner.

At the heart of *Sacred Misinterpretation* is Accad's conviction that the goal of interreligious dialogue is not consensus. Certain doctrinal differences between Islam and Christianity are rooted in the sacred texts of each tradition themselves and therefore cannot (and should not) be done away with. Yet there are also false understandings of the other that are rooted only in the misrepresentations that appeared in the works of polemicists through the centuries. Accad addresses these clearly. Along the way Accad is also clear about his own Christian perspective. He does justice to Islam while offering a sincere witness to his belief in Christ and the authority of the Bible.

Accad's concern with authenticity in Muslim-Christian relations is evident in the section on Jesus in the Qur'an and Muslim-Christian tradition. A long history of Christian writing on Jesus in the Qur'an focuses on passages such as al-Mā'ida 5:72 ("Certainly they have disbelieved who say, 'Surely God—he is the Messiah, son of Mary'"; cf. 5:17), which criticize Christian teaching. As Accad shows, however, when *all* of the Qur'anic material on Jesus is appreciated it emerges that the Qur'an is not principally interested in undermining Christian claims, but rather in advancing its own claims. Most Qur'anic verses on Jesus, Accad shows, are actually concerned with *elevating* the status of Jesus. In Āl ʿImrān 3:45, for example, the angels declare to Mary at the moment of the annunciation: "[Jesus] will be highly distinguished in this world and the hereafter and brought near to God."

Accad shows, however, that Muslim scholars often had a different agenda. For example, a reference to "doubt" over Jesus leads the famous Muslim exegete Muhammad b. Jarīr aṭ-Ṭabarī (died 923) to quote a tradition that has four groups form in the days after Christ: three of these are the ecclesial communities known in the classical Islamic period (which in fact took shape only after the Council of Chalcedon in 451): Jacobites, Melkites, and Nestorians. The fourth are none other than Muslims! Thus aṭ-Ṭabarī presents Islam as the true religion of Christ.

Other Muslims scholars went still further and offered Islamic interpretations of biblical passages. A whole host of scholars—from the ninth-century convert from Christianity ʿAlī aṭ-Ṭabarī (died ca. 860) to the eleventh-century Spanish Muslim Ibn Ḥazm (died 1064)—report the statement found in all four Gospels that a prophet is not honored in his own country as a prooftext, an affirmation that the Bible actually confirms Islamic teaching that Jesus was (nothing more than) a prophet. This sort of prooftexting is frequently found among Muslim scholars despite the common teaching that the scriptures of Jews and Christians are textually corrupt.

According to an idea widespread in medieval texts, and in Muslim preaching and proselytism (*daʿwa*) today, Moses and Jesus received divine scriptures from God, scriptures that must have been similar to the Qur'an in both their content and form. Subsequent generations of Jews and Christians, however, altered those scriptures (or destroyed them and wrote new scriptures) and thereby produced the Bible. In chapters six and seven of *Sacred Misinterpretation* Accad shows how complicated this topic truly is. In fact, the Qur'an does accuse Jews (especially) and Christians of being poor stewards of the word of God. However, it never explicitly states that the Hebrew Bible or the New Testament is corrupt. In fact, in one verse (al-Mā'ida 5:47) the Qur'an seems to command Christians to follow what they find in the Gospel. What is more, through the centuries Muslim scholars actually took a diverse range of approaches regarding the reliability of the Bible. Some, including the intellectual and literary critic Ibn Qutayba (died 889) were genuinely interested in how the Bible might contribute to an authentic understanding of salvation history. In fact, Accad makes a compelling argument that Ibn Qutayba did not rely on oral reports about the Bible but read the Bible itself (although the Bible had been translated into Arabic not long before his time). Notably, Ibn Qutayba introduces reports on biblical expressions with the Arabic phrase *qara'tu* ("I have read"), even while he introduces reports from other sources by explaining who "said" such and such a thing.

Accad's analysis of the diversity of Muslim approaches to the Bible raises a real possibility for new paths of dialogue. As I argue in my own work, the Qur'an does not simply mention biblical figures, it alludes regularly to biblical ideas and narratives, and indeed at times it depends on its audience's knowledge of biblical tradition. The Qur'an is in conversation with the Bible as the New Testament is in conversation with the Hebrew Bible. In other words, the Qur'an does not refute or reject the Bible. It provides a distinctive interpretation of the Bible shaped by its claims of divine prophecy. Accordingly these two books should not be kept apart, but must be read together.

The story of Islam's relationship to Christianity is thus more complicated than is often presented. *Sacred Misinterpretation* offers guidance in dealing with all of those complications. Accad presents the perspective of an Arab intellectual who demonstrates mastery of the academic field of Islamic studies, faithfulness to the Christian tradition, and the perspective of someone who has lived most of his life in the Islamic world. In the introduction Accad writes: "My goal is to reinforce positive and constructive relationships between Christians and Muslims of good will through gracious dialogue on sensitive theological issues, as a small contribution to thwarting religious fanaticism." *Sacred Misinterpretation* does just that. It does not threaten the convictions of faithful Muslim or Christian believers. It holds up what is beautiful in both traditions. It does, however, undermine the simplistic, polemical ideas of those who refuse to find beauty in the other.

Gabriel Said Reynolds
University of Notre Dame

Preface

Many books have been written about Islam since September 11, 2001—some by Muslims in an attempt to explain their religion in a positive light and to counter the negative perceptions projected by the media, and others by secular academics or by Christians, including evangelicals. Secular academics tend to have an agenda similar to many books on Islam written by Muslims, offering a more objective presentation, though theirs tend to be more critical, while attempting to be fair and scholarly. Evangelicals often use a negative, reactive approach in their study of Islam, and this sort of study often has the particularity of objectifying and essentializing Islam, highlighting aspects of it that serve defensive or deconstructive agendas. Thus, much has been written about Islam and violence, war and terrorism, Islam's view of women, and Islamic law. Polemical writing against Islam remains a popular genre, covering Islam's early history and conquests. Many books have been written on evangelism of Muslims, some friendly and others rather polemical. But more hopefully and in parallel with the more negative approaches, a number of initiatives have emerged since the 1990s in which Christians and Muslims have sought to understand each other's faiths on each's own terms. These have often been based on the in-depth study of each other's scriptures.[1]

1. Worth noting is the Scriptural Reasoning (SR) movement (http://www.scripturalreasoning.org), of which David Ford at the University of Cambridge has been a principle proponent. The Building Bridges Seminar at Georgetown University's Berkley Center (https://berkleycenter.georgetown.edu/projects/the-building-bridges-seminar) is another example of positive theological engagement for the sake of building peace. Now in its sixteenth year, the seminar was initiated in 2002 by then-Archbishop of Canterbury, the Rev. George Carey, in the aftermath of and in response to the 9/11 attacks. A significant

Theological issues are crucially important in the relationships between Christians and Muslims, not least because they have been central throughout that dialogical history. When one reads the early classical texts of engagement between Christians and Muslims, and then compares them to more recent ones, or listens to a conversation about God, Jesus, Muhammad, or the Bible between members of the two communities today, there is a sense that not enough progress has been made. Have Christians and Muslims given up on such conversations about doctrines and have all possibilities been exhausted? How does one reduce the conflict between Christians and Muslims that is on the rise today without addressing a history of theological concerns and polemics?

To the barren eye, it would appear as though Christian-Muslim tensions and conflicts have always been driven by geopolitical interests, whether it be the early Muslim expansionist wars, the Christian Crusader wars, the *Reconquista* in Spain, the long history of Western colonialism, the Israeli-Arab and Israeli-Palestinian conflicts, the Gulf War, the post–9/11 wars in Afghanistan and Iraq, the so-called Arab Spring, and the rise of ISIS from a marginal guerilla force fighting a liberation war against the Syrian Assad regime to their establishment of an "Islamic State"—albeit short-lived—across the boundaries of Syria and Iraq. But the reality seems to be that Islam has never been either just about politics

---

development can be seen in Jesuit Father Francis X. Clooney's comparative theology approach, which builds on both the comparative religions and interfaith dialogue schools but goes beyond them by adopting a clear and convinced Christian starting point. His attempt to understand other religious traditions on their own terms before offering a Christian critique is also built on the premise that the Christian theologian will be transformed through the study of other religious traditions. For a helpful example, see his *Comparative Theology: Deep Learning across Religious Borders* (Oxford: Wiley-Blackwell, 2010). A number of recent Christian theologians have followed in these traditions, of which I mention the following: Chawkat Moucarry, *Faith to Faith: Christianity and Islam in Dialogue* (Downers Grove, IL: InterVarsity Press, 2001); Ida Glaser, *Thinking Biblically about Islam: Genesis, Transfiguration, Transformation* (Carlisle: Langham Global Library, 2016); Veli-Matti Kärkkäinen's five-volume work (2013–2017), *A Constructive Christian Theology for the Pluralistic World*, the first volume of which I refer to later, *Christ and Reconciliation* (Grand Rapids: Eerdmans, 2013); Justin S. Holcomb and David A. Johnson, eds., *Christian Theologies of the Sacraments: A Comparative Introduction* (New York: New York University Press, 2017); George Bristow, *Sharing Abraham? Narrative Worldview, Biblical and Qur'anic Interpretation, and Comparative Theology in Turkey* (Cambridge, MA: Doorlight Academic, 2017); and Mark Beaumont, *Jesus in Muslim-Christian Conversation* (Eugene, OR: Cascade Books, 2018). I am grateful to Ida Glaser for these helpful pointers.

or just about doctrine. And neither has Christianity, at least since the Edict of Milan in 313.

This book is an attempt to join the positive dialogical conversation by engaging in a text-based study of Christian-Muslim theological dialogue and its relation to the conflict between Islam and Christianity. Most of what the Qur'an has to say is rhetorical (and often polemical) in tone. The entire qur'anic exegetical endeavor is based on the assumption that God's words can be understood fully only when one recovers the original reasons for which they were spoken. This is why *asbāb an-nuzūl* ("the reasons for the [qur'anic] revelations") have always been so important in Islam. Through this hermeneutical principle, Muslim scholars sought to reconstruct the historico-rhetorical context of God's revelations to Muhammad. Therefore, what the Qur'an has to say about Christians and Jews ("people of the book"), the Torah, the Gospel, and Jesus—in the minds of readers and interpreters of the Qur'an—was always triggered by Muhammad's own interaction with these communities, their central figures, and their books. Even if it may be proven that politics, economics, and military strategy were often primary motivators in the history of wars and conflicts between Christians and Muslims, it would be foolish to believe that the Scriptures of both communities had no connection to the conflict, if not as primary motivators then at least as strong justifiers. Muslim preachers during Friday prayers have continually reiterated these reasons as they interpret and apply the qur'anic text in their congregations. Muslims, Christians, and Jews have sought the blessing and support of their religious leaders before going to war against each other. It would be absurd to ignore the centrality of scriptural text when speaking about Christian-Muslim relations, and therefore this book is profoundly hermeneutical in method.

I wrote this book, on the one hand, for the use of professors of Islamic studies at universities and Christian seminaries who want to present their students with the history and story of the Muslim-Christian discourse on key theological doctrines. Seminary students will find in it an introduction to Christian-Muslim dialogue in history, particularly of the theological kind. They will be exposed to the emergence and development of theological arguments about key controversial issues between the two communities. The section at the end of each core chapter will stimulate students to think beyond some of the usual boundaries of Christian thinking. On the other hand, I will make no attempt to summarize comprehensively for the seminary student the theological conversations currently taking place in the West among Christian and evangelical theologians. Students will, instead, be directed to further readings related to each theme at the end of each chapter (chap. 3) or pair of chapters (chaps. 4–5, 6–7, and 8–9) on the key doctrines, should they wish to read further on some of the discussions that have taken place in the West over the past hundred years.

I also direct this book to the educated layperson in the church, who may find in it much material of interest. Though the book may be of some interest to a general audience, it is primarily people of faith who will find it useful and stimulating. The contents will be helpful to readers who want to know more about what the Qur'an and Muslims say about Christian theological issues, as well as how to think through these issues biblically in the current multifaith environment in which most of us live. Through my sharing of personal stories of growing up and living in the rich, multifaith, but also highly conflictual, environment of Lebanon, the general reader will be able to identify with the issues at hand. It is hoped, as a result, that they will be driven to reflect through their own realities, while developing a desire to take courageous action that works for greater understanding and peace between diverse faith communities.

Committed Muslims, both general readers and students of religion, will also be interested in the book. Though they may disagree with some of the outcomes of my theological investigation, most will recognize the legitimacy with which Islam is approached and understood. Hopefully, they will appreciate that the book adopts a respectful and open-minded attitude and that it takes seriously many of the questions Islam has raised about Christianity over the centuries. Some of the way that the book treats these sensitive issues may be inspiring to Muslims who are open to a Christian biblical perspective. It is my hope that this book will inspire renewed creative engagement between Christians and Muslims in our multireligious world.

The opening section of each chapter contains some personal stories from my life, from growing up in the multifaith, war-torn country of Lebanon, to experiencing paradigm shifts in thinking by living cross-culturally for five years in the United Kingdom, to experiences teaching Arab students from all over the MENA (Middle East and Northern Africa) region at the Arab Baptist Theological Seminary in Lebanon, as well as North American and other Western and non-Western students at Fuller Theological Seminary in the United States. These stories will be woven together with key questions that Christians and Muslims are asking each other in these days of conflict and misunderstanding, at times along with varied answers that can be gleaned through recent books of some relevance, written primarily within the evangelical milieu.

A survey of the most important qur'anic verses relevant to the theme will follow, looking concisely at how Muslims interpreted such verses historically in their commentaries on the Qur'an. Some integration of an initial Christian perspective, analyzing and critiquing the Muslim discourse and interpretation, is contained in these sections.

A survey of the historical Muslim exegetical discourse will look at the way that Muslims understood and interpreted the Gospels historically in support of their qur'anic views. My purpose is to look at the Muslim exegetical metanarrative to identify trends, recognize the historical evolution of the narrative, identify significant points of contention that led to the current deadlock in dialogue, as well as more positive and creative trends that could be built upon for a more hopeful future in theological dialogue.

In summary, the overall historical, textual, and exegetical discourse of Muslims on the various theological themes of the book is brought together in dialogue with their Christian intellectual context, within a framework of the history of ideas, under the label "metadialogue." This section in each of the core chapters highlights points in the metadialogue where the conversation encountered major hurdles or even reached a standstill. Some positive keys to the metadialogue are highlighted as opportunities to move out of the dialogical deadlock on the various theological themes.

In a final section to each core chapter, specific issues discussed by Muslims and Christians today, related to the various theological themes of the book, are addressed. This section ties back to the opening personal connections section of each chapter, attempting some form of synthesis and future pointers. For example, whether Christians and Muslims worship the same God, whether Muhammad can be viewed as a prophet, or where the Qur'an's inspiration comes from. This section is likely to be controversial as I attempt to stretch some of the traditional evangelical boundaries, while at the same time likely not going far enough for the less conservative. The goal is to be respectful of Islam while remaining faithful to the biblical tradition as understood by an open evangelical.

The general Christian reader who does not wish to engage with the more technical and historical sections of the seven core chapters (3–9) can still benefit from the book by reading the opening and closing pages of each chapter. For example, in the chapter on God (chap. 3), a general reader could read the first and last quarters. By doing so, they would (1) be drawn into the subject of our understanding of God through personal stories, (2) get a sense of some of the key questions being asked on the topic, (3) hear a brief and simple summary of what a few evangelical theologians today are saying on these questions, (4) get a good summary of the metadialogue on the topic that has occurred between Christians and Muslims through history, (5) gain an understanding of important theological deadlocks that they will encounter on the issue, and (6) have the opportunity to reflect on certain keys that they could use in moving beyond these deadlocks in their own relationships with Muslim friends.

Due to the length and focus of the book, I do not attempt to summarize the twentieth century to the present discussions taking place among Christian and evangelical scholars in the West on the theological themes addressed in the book. My focus is almost entirely on the dialogue that took place between Muslims and Christians in history, while the contemporary reflections are just that: my personal, theological, and missiological reflections on the themes. The reader is directed to additional reading at the end of each of the core chapters, or pairs of chapters, should they desire to set the historical conversation in the context of twentieth-century and twenty-first-century theological discussions. I am grateful to Caleb Hutcherson and Emad Butros for helping me compile these sections.

My objective is to make a positive contribution to the history of theological dialogue between Christians and Muslims by moving the conversation forward. I seek to model the possibility of making progress in theological dialogue between Christians and Muslims, at a point in history when even many moderates on both sides have given up on anything more than coexistence and tolerance. My goal is to reinforce positive and constructive relationships between Christians and Muslims of good will through gracious dialogue on sensitive theological issues, as a small contribution to thwarting religious fanaticism.

The reader will realize that the conversation between Christians and Muslims historically quickly ceased to be a true dialogue, as each community insulated itself, and its discourse became primarily inward looking. He or she will understand that the historical deadlock in Christian-Muslim dialogue came about to a large extent as a result of historical and political factors rather than rational ones. At the same time, the reader will realize that there are enduring theological disagreements between Muslims and Christians that are unlikely to get resolved, due to a long exegetical history of the Qur'an by Muslim commentators who have reaffirmed for centuries the Muslim rejection of core Christian doctrines. With realism, the reader will become aware of new possibilities for doctrinal dialogue between Christians and Muslims, inspired from the dialogical literature already in existence. Christian doctrines will be once more presented to Muslims in a way that is faithful to the Christian tradition, while taking seriously Muslim theology and the history both of interpretation of key qur'anic verses and of Muslim interpretation of biblical texts. Important questions that Muslims and Christians ask each other, related to various doctrinal issues, will be addressed in light of history and in a cordial manner.

I seek to adhere to a set of values in my approach of Islam throughout the book. I attempt to be respectful of Islam and its core concepts, such as the Qur'an and Muhammad, while at the same time retaining a level of critical distance from Islam's traditional narrative, without being destructive. As a Christian theologian, I maintain a high level of loyalty to Christ and the Bible, but not blindly to Christianity. The reader will find here my personal passion for building bridges of peace and understanding in our multireligious world.

Finally, this book would have never seen the light without the gracious support of a multitude of people. Pieter Kwant, the director of Langham Literature, nearly fifteen years ago, encouraged me to begin this undertaking. Despite my extreme busyness as a young PhD graduate returning to Lebanon to serve the church through the formation of leaders for the Arab church at Arab Baptist Theological Seminary, Pieter never gave up on me and exercised extreme patience by offering constant support, both moral and financial. He eventually took me under his wing by becoming my publishing agent and facilitating a relationship with Eerdmans Publishing. I am extremely grateful both to him and to Eerdmans for believing in this project.

The leadership of the Arab Baptist Theological Seminary, President Elie Haddad in particular, was extremely generous toward me by never holding back permission to take time off over the years to focus on my writing. Friends and mentors provided valuable feedback and encouragement at times when I lost hope and courage to persevere in my writing. Of this multitude I mention in particular Colin Chapman, Ida Glaser, Evelyne Reisacher, Riad Kassis, Paul Sanders, Mike Kuhn, and John Azumah.

Many times, I needed isolated havens where I could spend long hours writing uninterrupted. My aunt, Prof. Evelyne Accad, graciously offered her inspirational studio in Paris and rooftop apartment in Lebanon. Faithful lifelong friends, Tony and Dany, offered me hospitality and friendship during politically traumatic times and allowed me to benefit from writing retreats under their roof in Montreal and in the mountains of Lebanon. My brothers and sister, their spouses, and all of my nephews and nieces were incredibly supportive over the past decade and a half. Their enthusiasm for a yet-unborn book in which they seemed to believe, at times more than I did myself, fueled my desire to bring it to light. My mother, Huguette, and my late father, Lucien, deserve more mention than any other for their role in shaping my thinking throughout my life and for passing down to me a passion for living a life that makes a difference in a world of indifference. My grandfather, Fouad Accad, stands as a towering figure both in my conscious and subconscious, as the man who incarnated love and respect for Muslims. Without his genes, I would not be who I am.

Last but not least, Nadia Khouri, my wife and the love of my life, has never protested my long absences, my disappearances for entire nights, my constant ramblings about long-dead scholars and theologians that intruded into our daily family life. Without her tenderness and kindness, her humor and uplifting spirit, this book would have never seen the light of day. If this book ever serves its intended purpose of bringing more peace to our societies and faith communities, then all of those listed above share in the fruit of this labor. If, however, it is misunderstood, or if it falls into the abyss of a world with too many words and thoughts, then the responsibility is mine alone.

Beirut, Winter 2018

1 Introduction

"What was it like growing up as a Christian in Lebanon, with so many Muslims around you?" "How did you handle the pressures of being a minority in a Muslim-majority context?" These are questions that I have been asked many times while traveling in Europe and North America. The first time I was asked this as a teenager, I was taken by surprise. My family had lived for three generations in Hamra, a Muslim-majority neighborhood of Beirut. I was born and raised there and went to a school where most of my classmates were Muslim. When my parents decided to move to the Christian-majority side, due to the relocation of my father's workplace and the constant dangers of kidnappings and sniping, my most striking memory as a thirteen-year-old was the way that my new Christian friends spoke of Muslims, as though they were a different species. Yet as children, my siblings and I often kept the fast of Ramadan in solidarity with our Muslim friends, and once my brother and I asked my parents for permission to go to the mosque with them. I never experienced Muslims or Islam as a threat. They were simply neighbors and friends who worshiped God with a variant on the theme that I was growing up with.

These days, when people ask me about what it was like to be a persecuted Christian, growing up in Lebanon's civil war, I reply with a smile that most of the bombs that fell near me were Christian bombs and that the only snipers we feared were Christian snipers, whose gunsights had a cross dangling from them. The war in Lebanon was a civil war. You feared the fire and violence of the other side, whichever side you lived on rather than belonged to.

Christians were kidnapped and killed by Muslim militias because their identity card said "Christian," and Muslims were kidnapped and killed by Christian militias because their identity card said "Muslim." The violent jihadi group, ISIS (the Islamic State in Iraq and Syria), has killed more Muslims than Christians and Yazidis, and they have destroyed more Muslim shrines than Christian ones. If they had ever made it to Islam's holiest city, Mecca, there is little doubt that their iconoclastic mindset would have had them destroy the Kaaba, which Muslims have venerated for fourteen hundred years as having been set up originally by Abraham and his son Ishmael. The ISIS attacks on Christians and Yazidis get more attention because these are smaller groups than the majority Sunnī population. But the latter also suffered tremendously at their hand.

How do we make sense of all the conflicts around the world that, for the majority these days, have taken on a religious color? One group of people is up in arms against Islam, perceiving it as the root cause of the violence. Another group finds itself continuously on the defensive, having to argue constantly that the violent groups perpetuating these horrors have nothing to do with Islam. And Islam is certainly not the only religion in the dock. In the Israeli-Palestinian conflict, both Judaism and Christianity stand accused as well. The expansionist policies of Israel are seen by some largely as the result of narrow and fanatical interpretations of biblical promises to the Jewish people. In addition to this, many evangelical Christians, particularly in the United States, have championed an ideology for over a hundred years referred to as "Christian Zionism." This ideology is viewed by many as the primary driver of US foreign policy in the Middle East for the past few decades.

Are the conflicts religious, then? Are violent groups inspired by religious texts? Or are the conflicts neither sectarian nor religious in essence, but is religious identity, as some argue, simply "being manipulated and instrumentalised by sectarian entrepreneurs and shrewd political actors"?[1] Any simple yes or no answer to this question should be viewed with suspicion. But if there is no straightforward answer to such a complex question, there can nevertheless be some guiding principles for our thinking, deriving from historically informed observation. Here are a few that come to mind: most conflicts, historically, started not for religious reasons, but rather as a result of clashing visions on economics, culture,

1. Opinion expressed by political analyst and researcher Hayder al-Khoei, "A Sectarian War Unfolding in the Middle East?" Centre on Religion and Global Affairs, February 6, 2017, available online at centreonreligionandglobalaffairs.org/commentary/ (accessed February 7, 2017).

language, land boundaries, power, and control. Often conflicts take on a religious dimension, and once they do they become far more difficult to resolve.[2] Religious texts and beliefs are easy to use by various parties of a conflict in order to defend their ideology, as all meaning derives from a particular interpretation, which is subject to specific contextual factors that change with time and location. Once religion becomes party to a conflict, the resulting intercommunal damage will be deeply rooted and will likely take a long time to heal. Given this intricate relationship between religion and conflict, no religious group can abdicate its responsibility toward it. It is unhelpful to claim that religion has nothing to do with a conflict simply because it was not the root cause of it; if any party at any point claims that it is acting in the name of any religion, then religion has something to do with this conflict.

People of faith have a great responsibility to counter violent ideologies of those who claim to derive them from the Scriptures and traditions of the same religion to which they adhere. The claims of some Muslims, Christians, Jews, or members of any religion that violent people acting in the name of their religion are simply imposters, and that it is therefore not their problem to address, are suspicious. By doing so, they adopt the same tendency as violent extremists who essentialize religion, who claim that they hold the only correct interpretation of their texts, and who anathematize all others. In light of the preceding reflection, I argue that people of faith bear a crucial responsibility in the face of conflict. For the most part, they should not be *held responsible* for the violence of some who claim to belong to their group, but they do *bear responsibility* to fight and debunk these ideologies. Given that they share many scriptural resources with their violent counterparts, they are also the ones best positioned to develop initiatives of change that can be effective in transforming conflict situations.

Christian-Muslim Interaction

A Muslim friend of mine, a cleric, once pointed out how artificial our practice of Christian-Muslim dialogue is. Our usual idea of interfaith dialogue is an officially organized session where one or more representatives

2. P. Barker and W. Muck argue similarly in "Secular Roots of Religious Rage: Shaping Religious Identity in the Middle East," *Politics and Religion* 3.2 (2009): 177–96.

of each religion present their own perspective on a topic before an audience that is generally made up of adherents of each of the religions being spoken for. Instead, he suggested, let us bring our students together and organize a joint outing or picnic. Let our students interact and get to know one another at the human level. The concept was so simple, so relational and human, that I had never thought of it. I was, after all, an Oxford-bred intellectual, an Arab evangelical raised and molded as a transplant of American evangelicalism in the Arab world. I realized that the communal aspect of my faith was weak and that the biblical imperative that God's mission (*missio dei*) was first and foremost about relationship was not always at the forefront of my thinking and practice. Our world has come into its very existence, and we know God as Creator, because of God's initial thrust to create for the sake of relationship. Redemptive history, as reflected in the Bible, is the enactment of God's ongoing initiative to restore humanity and creation to himself by his grace, even as the whole of creation continues to be inclined to move away from him through the exercise of its God-given free will. The ultimate and supreme expression of God's passion for relationship is found in the life and teaching of Jesus of Nazareth, in whom God reaches the pinnacle of relationship-restoration at the cross.

Why is it, then, that as Christians and Muslims in our world today, we so often interact with one another through the cold pages of books and through disengaged dialogue panels? At its worst, our engagement takes place through the cowardly pseudonymous pages of websites, or even by seeking each other's annihilation through armed conflict and suppression.

The Context of My Writing

In December 2010, a Tunisian merchant set himself ablaze in protest against police injustice, leading to mass protests that had a domino effect in Egypt, Libya, and Yemen. The ensuing mass movements throughout the Middle East and North Africa would eventually topple the dictatorial regimes of these countries in 2011, in what the media came to call the "Arab Spring," in reference to the movements that brought down Communism in Eastern Europe in the late 1980s. Events would begin to take a tragic turn with the rise of protests in Syria in March 2011. So long as the uprisings took place in largely uniform Sunnī countries (Tunisia, Egypt, and Libya) and had to do primarily with economics and harsh government policies, they unfolded and led to the downfall of the existing regimes. In Morocco and Jordan, on the other hand, sporadic uprisings were swiftly met with reform initiatives by their monarchs, who were thus able to quell popular anger and save themselves from the fate of the preceding models. No doubt the Syrian debacle that was unfolding in parallel also contributed in convincing Moroccans and Jordanians that reforms were better alternatives to all-out chaos. The uprisings in Yemen and Bahrain took a different trajectory, due to the more diverse Shīʿī/Sunnī populations. As a result of the intervention of strong external powers with interests in these two countries, particularly Saudi Arabia, things took a different twist. These interventions contributed to prolonged conflicts with still no clear outcome in Yemen.

But it is in Syria that the so-called Arab Spring received its final blow. Syria and Lebanon often seem to be the exception to the rule in the Arab world. It is there that the twists of history are the most dramatic, and there that expectations and predictions of political analysts tend to be disappointed. In March 2011, peaceful demonstrations began to emerge in Syria, near the border with Jordan. At Eastertime, my family and I planned our usual road trip to Jordan across Syria, to spend the holidays with my wife's family in Amman. But by April (Easter Sunday fell on the 24th), as more serious turmoil was beginning to brew in Syria, we had the well-advised instinct of traveling by taxi rather than with our own car. As we crossed the border into Syria on our journey back, during the last week of April, our taxi had to stop on the side of the road in order to join a caravan of cars going through small villages to avoid the main roads, where armed groups were beginning to take control. My wartime instinct led me to order the taxi around, and we ended up catching a flight back from Amman to Beirut that year. But as we lingered at the Syrian border, it was clear that popular fear was on the rise, fueled by slogans and propaganda. One border official warned that demonstrators were shouting: "Christians to deportation and Alawites to their graves!" These slogans were likely sparked by government propaganda, but their effect was immediate. The Syrian conflict from then on would turn sectarian, fratricidal, and intractable.

So long as conflicts are sparked by economics and policies of governance, solutions tend to come relatively quickly. But history teaches us that when conflicts turn religious and sectarian, they swiftly break into all-out civil war and can take decades before reaching a resolution. Northern Ireland and Israel/Palestine are dramatic examples. The rise of ISIS in

Syria and Iraq, particularly since the summer of 2014, is a saga that will not be recounted here. Suffice it to say that these regional developments once more revealed the Sunnī-Shīʿī fault lines that have existed since the seventh century in the Muslim world. Christians and other non-Muslim groups once again had to pay a heavy price for this history, begging for new approaches where Christians will be urged to play a more active role of peacemakers, rather than remaining in the position of passive victims.

What Does Theology Have to Do with Conflict and War?

There is little question that religion, if it is rarely the root cause of a conflict, will nevertheless protract it when it becomes a significant dimension of it—which it often does. As Miroslav Volf argues, "sacred things need not be involved for people to fight and go to war. An insult, injury, or act of aggression or treachery may suffice. But when 'holy' things are at stake, conflicts are exacerbated."[3] Why has the world been so slow to recognize, then, the importance of religious dialogue and theology in the resolution of global conflicts?

There is growing recognition globally that religion as a core component of conflict can no longer be ignored. And if it is so, then solutions also need to come from that sector. This is an affirmation that religious actors have a significant role to play in the resolution of conflict now and in years to come. Volf argues that "multipronged approaches are necessary, and engagement with religious convictions and practices." His book *Allah: A Christian Response* is written with that purpose, while recognizing that it is "essential but insufficient in and of itself." Given that extremism on one side of a conflict triggers extremism on the other, he argues that "combating highly negative—and, importantly, inaccurate and prejudiced—Christian views of Muslims is a significant contribution to combating Muslim extremism."[4] The use of theological discourse to resolve differences is a common practice among groups with differing views within a single religion. But the idea that religious discourse can also contribute significantly in working toward peaceful relations between populations with rival ideologies is a relatively recent notion. It is also a primary motivation and belief of the present book.

3. Miroslav Volf, *Allah: A Christian Response* (New York: HarperCollins, 2011), 4–5.
4. Volf, *Allah*, 257–58.

In his book *When Religion Becomes Lethal* Charles Kimball observes that "throughout history, religion and politics have always been intertwined and interdependent," but he affirms in the same breath that "today the volatile mix of the two is more lethal than ever."[5] This reality requires that in the twenty-first century, people of faith draw from their respective traditions inspiration and resources to resolve some of today's most protracted conflicts. Or as Kimball puts it, "Realistic steps forward simply must include ways of understanding and appropriating elements of religion into viable political life and structures in the 21st century."[6]

For people of faith, theology matters supremely in our understanding of reality, of self, and of the other. Our understanding of the character of God is fundamental to our ethics, and our ethics drive our relationships. Our understanding of the way that God interacts with humanity affects our understanding of revelation, and our understanding of divine revelation is fundamental to our doctrine of Scripture. The notions we hold about revelation also affect our understanding of prophethood and hence as well the space that we allow for other faiths within the boundaries of our own.

One premise of the present book, therefore, is that our theologies have been fundamental to our understanding of one another, and our murky relational history seems to indicate that our mutual perceptions have been largely negative. The conflicts that currently mire our world have taken on a decisive religious coloring, and so have a great majority of conflicts throughout history. Given the present shape of things, it matters little whether the roots of these conflicts were originally religious or not. If we want to face the present and its realities, we ought to realize that the burden of history lies largely on people of faith. This book seeks to take stock of this burden by launching into an exploration of theology as a foundation for dialogue. I express my premise, and indeed my motivation for writing, as follows: your *view* of Islam affects your *attitude* to Muslims; your *attitude*, in turn, influences your *approach* to Christian-Muslim interaction, and that *approach* affects the ultimate *outcome* of your presence as a witness among Muslims.

How, then, do we develop a *view* and an *understanding* of Islam that fosters in us the right attitude and approach, in order for our relationships

5. Charles Kimball, *When Religion Becomes Lethal: The Explosive Mix of Politics and Religion in Judaism, Christianity, and Islam* (San Francisco: Jossey-Bass, 2011), 5.

6. Kimball, *When Religion Becomes Lethal*, 9.

to be constructive and fruitful? In the context of reflecting over this question I developed the SEKAP Spectrum of Christian-Muslim Interaction (figure 1).[7] The spectrum emerged in my attempt to identify a diversity of positions and attitudes between the two extremes of syncretism and polemics, of which those engaged in dialogue are often accused. The acronym SEKAP stands for the five positions on the spectrum: syncretistic, existential, kerygmatic, apologetic, and polemical. The five positions move gradually along the dialogical spectrum from D1 to D5, with D referring to dialogue. While the reader may refer elsewhere for a fuller explanation of this framework, I here repeat briefly the main components of the kerygmatic position, as it is foundational to my engagement with Islam and Muslims. The present book is a full-fledged attempt at doing theology with a kerygmatic mindset.

The Kerygmatic Approach to Christian-Muslim Interaction

The kerygmatic level of Christian-Muslim interaction has the potential of being most fruitful for Christ's Gospel as good news, and most conducive to peace in our age of great conflicts. It is through this kerygmatic approach that we will be able to think the most "Christ-likely" about Islam and Muslims. The term "kerygmatic" comes from the Greek word *kērygma*, and the verb *kēryssō* is most often found in the Gospels in the form of the present participle: *kēryssōn* ("proclaiming"). The *kērygma* in the New Testament is both the act of proclaiming and the proclamation itself. It is connected with the proclamation of God's good news, concerning repentance, the kingdom, and Jesus, first by John the Baptist (Matt 3:1; Mark 1:4; Luke 3:3), then by Jesus himself (Matt 4:23; 9:35; Mark 1:14, 39; Luke 4:18; 8:1), and later by the disciples in the book of Acts (20:25; 28:31). One significant characteristic of the *kērygma* in the apostle Paul's usage of the term is that it does not entice through the use of wise human words, but rather relies on the power of God's Spirit (1 Cor 2:4). This is why Paul entreats Timothy to proclaim (*kēryxon*) the message "in season and out of season" (2 Tim 4:2). And when he finds himself before the

7. See my "Christian Attitudes toward Islam and Muslims: A Kerygmatic Approach," in *Toward Respectful Understanding and Witness among Muslims: Essays in Honor of J. Dudley Woodberry*, ed. Evelyne A. Reisacher (Pasadena: William Carey Library, 2012), 29–47.

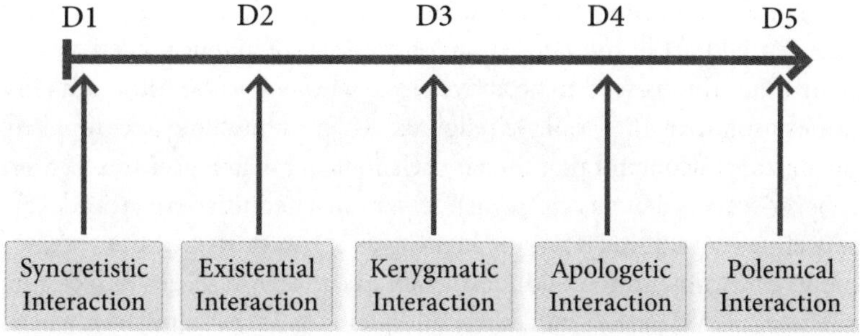

Figure 1. The SEKAP Spectrum of Christian-Muslim Interaction

tribunal in Rome, even though the session is officially supposed to be "his first defense" (*apologia*) (4:16), he considers it an opportunity for "the proclamation" (*kērygma*) to be heard fully by all the Gentiles (4:17).[8]

I want to retain from this Pauline usage particularly the difference between *kērygma* and *apologia*—the difference in attitude that it reflects between an apologetic defense of one's beliefs on the one hand and a positive proclamation of it on the other. The biblical kerygmatic approach to Christian-Muslim interaction is thus devoid of *polemical* aggressiveness, *apologetic* defensiveness, *existential* adaptiveness, or *syncretistic* elusiveness—not because any of these other four approaches is necessarily wrong, but because that is the nature of *kērygma*: God's gracious and positive invitation of humanity into relationship with himself through Jesus. It needs essentially no militant enforcers, no enthusiastic defenders, no smart adapters, and no crafty revisers. If it often seems to be suspiciously absent from standard handbooks of Christian-Muslim dialogue or even from the recorded theater of history, this does not mean that it has not actually existed. The very continuous *presence* of the church in Muslim lands through active participation and contribution in society, and the ongoing proclamation of the church's faith through liturgy, are in themselves part of the church's kerygmatic presence in society. But perhaps the more intentional and proactive articulation of a kerygmatic approach to Christian-Muslim interaction has been lacking.

8. On the various meanings of the concept, both inside and outside of the biblical text, see Gerhard Friedrich, "*Kērygma*," in *Theological Dictionary of the New Testament*, ed. Gerhard Kittel and Gerhard Friedrich, trans. Geoffrey W. Bromley (Grand Rapids: Eerdmans, 1965), 3.714–17.

For the kerygmatic Christ follower, religions are recognized to be an essential part of human psychological and sociological need. At the same time, God is seen to be above any religious system. Although God is the absolute truth, no single religious system is infallible or completely satisfactory. I contend that the Gospels indicate that Jesus himself, who is never seen as denying his Jewishness, incarnated this very attitude. He was at peace with his religious identity as a Jew, practiced the requirements of the law from childhood, entered the Jewish places of worship, and was trained in Jewish theology and method. At the same time, whenever Jesus expressed frustration in the Gospels, it was generally either toward some stratified religious institutional form or toward stubborn institutional religious leadership. His message cut through the safety of the legalistic boundaries of righteousness, and his invitation to God went right to the labeled marginalized and outcast of his society. He even went further and, through carefully crafted parables, proclaimed himself to be the inaugurator of God's kingdom in fulfillment of God's promise to the nations, and he established himself as the final criterion of admission into that kingdom as the way to the Father.

Therefore, in recognition that social organization is a natural human phenomenon toward which we are all inclined, the kerygmatic position and attitude does not consist in rejecting one's religious heritage, for it would unmistakably soon be replaced by another form of ideology. But at the same time, in the kerygmatic position it is Christ himself who is at the center of salvation, rather than any religious system. The kerygmatic person is always dislodging the safety mechanisms and categories of institutional religion. And it is Christ himself who is always proclaimed in the *kērygma*, himself being the suprareligious good news of God's invitation of humanity into relationship with himself. The *kērygma* is never a message of condemnation, but it brings condemnation to those stuck within religious boundaries. The principal difference between this position and the other positions on the dialogical spectrum is that the conversation is removed entirely from the realm of institutionalized religious talk. One theologian who captures this worldview very well is Karl Barth. In an essay appropriately titled "The Revelation of God as the Abolition of Religion," Barth defiantly affirms: "We begin by stating that religion is unbelief. It is a concern, indeed, we must say that it is the one great concern, of godless man."[9]

9. John Hick and Brian Hebblethwaite, eds., *Christianity and Other Religions: Selected Readings* (Philadelphia: Fortress, 1980), 35.

The kerygmatic approach that I advocate is therefore the equivalent of this Barthian revelation of God. The *kērygma* upheld by this approach is nothing less than God's own revelation in Christ. How, then, does a kerygmatic, suprareligious approach to the way of Christ develop a meaningful view and expression of the Islamic phenomenon?

The Islamic Phenomenon

Whereas the kerygmatic position adopts a suprareligious approach to understanding and relating to God in Christ, it recognizes Islam as an institutionalized religious phenomenon par excellence. It can adequately be said that Islamic law, Sharīʿa, is the most authentic manifestation of the nature of Islam. Sharīʿa, like Mosaic law, divides into two main categories: *ʿibādāt* and *muʿāmalāt*. The *ʿibādāt* are prescriptions relating to liturgical law—the regulations concerning prayer, fasting, pilgrimage, and so on. The *muʿāmalāt*, on the other hand, are prescriptions relating to civil law, including criminal law, prescriptions related to the waging of war, issues of inheritance, family law, and so on. The first category can be described as vertical prescriptions, dictating guidelines for a proper human relationship with God; and the second category can be seen as horizontal prescriptions, offering guidance for human beings as they relate to one another. In a very real sense, this strong legal manifestation of Islam places it in the category of a sociopolitical phenomenon dressed up in religious clothing. This does not make the religious manifestation of Islam less real or genuine, at least from the perspective of its adherent believers. As a matter of fact, one could say that Islam was particularly successful because of its strong religious ideological component.

Based on a reading of the Qurʾan itself, the kerygmatic position considers that Islam preserved many important and positive elements from the Judeo-Christian tradition. As such, a Jew or a Christian may affirm that Islam contains much truth about God and his revelation. On the other hand, because the kerygmatic approach seeks to be supremely Christ-centered, a follower of Christ will also consider that Islam lacks many of the essential truths of God's good news as revealed and proclaimed in and by Jesus Christ in the Gospels.

Islam's Prophet in the Kerygmatic Approach

The kerygmatic approach states that Muhammad, Islam's messenger, believed that he received a genuine divine calling to be God's prophet to the Arabs. Muhammad's personality is complex and cannot be defined entirely through one single period of his life. He was a charismatic, prophetic leader, in Mecca and in the early Medinan period, but then became much more of a political, military, economic, and social leader particularly in the later Medinan period. Qur'anic evidence seems to indicate that he saw himself very much in continuation of the Judeo-Christian prophetic line, whose mission was to turn his people away from idolatry and to the worship of the one God.

A kerygmatic approach believes in the finality of Jesus Christ, in whom the fullness of God's Gospel was revealed. But this should not prevent us from admitting the greatness of Muhammad and perceiving him, if not as a prophet, nonetheless as a *messenger* in the more literal sense of the word, a *rasūl*, who carried an important message about God to his people, leading them away from polytheism and drawing them to the worship of the one God (see chaps. 8–10 for more details).

The Qur'an in the Kerygmatic Approach

Numerous verses in the Qur'an seem to reflect the understanding that its message was a genuine attempt to provide the essential elements of the Judeo-Christian Scriptures to Arab people in a language that they could understand, namely in the Arabic dialect of Quraysh (e.g., az-Zukhruf 43:2–3; Maryam 19:97; ad-Dukhān 44:58; and al-Qamar 54:17). The nature of the very word "Qur'an" suggests that it derives from Syriac *qeryānā*, which appears in classical Syriac texts simply in the sense of "lectionary."[10] From this perspective, the Qur'an would originally have been essentially an Arabic lectionary of the Bible, consisting of scriptural passages, with interpretations and expansions from other traditions related to the text.

10. For this view in recent scholarship, see Christoph Luxenberg, *The Syro-Aramaic Reading of the Koran: A Contribution to the Decoding of the Language of the Koran* (Berlin: Schiler, 2007), 70–74. But note that Luxenberg simply agrees in this with most Western scholars, as attested by J. D. Pearson, "Al-Kur'ān," in *Encyclopaedia of Islam*, ed. P. Bearman et al., 2nd ed. (Leiden: Brill, 1954–2005), 1.400–432 at 400.

Many verses in the Qur'an seem to support the view that Muhammad perceived his message to be a continuation of the Judeo-Christian tradition, at least at some point in his life. God encourages his messenger by telling him that if his own tribe of *Quraysh* does not accept his message, he should tell them to ask the "people of the book" (Christians and Jews), who will confirm to them that the message is authentic. There is an assumption in those portions that Christians and Jews will naturally receive his message, since it does not stand in contradiction with their own Scriptures (see in particular an-Naḥl 16:43 and al-ʿAnkabūt 29:47).

Other verses are less optimistic in outlook. They reflect Muhammad's disappointment with the way that Jews and Christians rejected his message, as though it contained some elements that were foreign to their own Scriptures (e.g., al-Baqara 2:101).

In verses placed by Muslim scholars in the later Medinan period, Muhammad begins to dissociate himself from the Judeo-Christian tradition. One of the most striking examples of this is the change in the direction of prayer (*qibla*) introduced in al-Baqara 2:143–45. Initially, the community of Muhammad prayed in the direction of Jerusalem, as did the Jews (Eastern Christians always prayed to the East). Al-Wāḥidī's treatise *Asbāb an-Nuzūl* (The Occasions of the Revelations) mentions with regard to al-Baqara 2:144 that Muhammad received this new instruction sixteen months after his arrival in Medina. This was roughly the time period when Muhammad's relationship, especially with the Jews of Medina, was said to have seriously deteriorated.[11]

In the qur'anic sūrah considered by Muslim commentators as the first that Muhammad received, God commands his messenger: "Recite in the name of your Lord who created, created the human being from a clinging substance. Recite, and your Lord is the most generous" (al-ʿAlaq 96:1–3).

The word *iqra'*, rightly translated "recite" by Kaskas, is more naturally understood in Arabic in the sense "read"—as found in several other translations. Here again, however, the Syriac word *qrā*, which literally means "call out!," makes more sense as the root of the qur'anic word. In any case, this only confirms the oral origins of the Qur'an, about which the Islamic tradition is unanimous. Muhammad's knowledge of the Bible was probably also mainly oral. He must have witnessed the reading of the

11. An English translation of this work can be found at altafsir.com/AsbabAlnuzol.asp?SoraName=2&Ayah=144&search=yes&img=A.

biblical text and its oral homiletic exposition during his travels through Syria on trade caravans, as he took care of his wife Khadīja's business. This helps us make sense of some discrepancies found between the qur'anic accounts of biblical stories and the biblical original. Such inconsistencies, however, need not lead us to the conclusion that any purposeful or deceitful corruption of the biblical message took place in the Qur'an.

Muslims in the Kerygmatic Approach

If we believe the traditional Islamic account of the development of Muhammad's early community, we can conclude that Arabs who received the initial Meccan message essentially found themselves in a similar position as the kinsmen of the biblical patriarch, Abraham, who in the qur'anic narrative are invited to abandon polytheism and to take up the worship of the one God. During the early Medinan period, however, the early community of Muhammad found itself in conflict with those with whom it had sought continuity, particularly the Jews of Medina. Furthermore, not unlike the Jews of Jesus's time, Christians who came into contact with Muhammad's message increasingly had to reckon with a picture of Jesus that conflicted in many respects with the one familiar to them from their own tradition. Due to growing economic, social, and political conflicts with the Medinan Jews, the result was a rejection of that picture and a growing chasm with the Judeo-Christian tradition.

Today, a kerygmatic perception of Muslims says that even though Muslims have as their foremost concern to please God, they lack the ability to enjoy that deep and personal relationship with him, which according to the Gospels is possible only for those who respond to Christ's invitation to approach God as Father through a brotherly sonship with himself. This view of the Islamic phenomenon, including the understanding of where Muslims are in their search and journey toward God, is what motivates a follower of Christ to be a witness, to share this divine *kērygma* with Muslims.

Purpose of Relationship with Islam and Muslims

Against the backdrop of the position developed above, those Christ followers who hold a kerygmatic understanding of Islam will engage with Muslims on two solid foundations: respect and trust. On the one hand, neither the syncretistic attitude to religions that plays down the uniqueness of a person's spiritual experience, nor the polemical attitude that seeks to emphasize the negative aspects of another person's worldview, will foster mutual respect between two people. On the other hand, both existential and apologetic approaches will shy away from true engagement, the first seeking to stay away from God-talk, and the latter raising a defensive wall, rarely engaging creatively and positively. These are of course somewhat generalizations, but they are helpful to identify further the middle way. Followers of Jesus embracing the kerygmatic approach will not shy away from theological engagement. And as they do so, based on a thoughtfully developed framework and understanding of Islam, they will do so respectfully, with a genuine desire to learn through a mutual exchange of perceptions about God and faith. The kerygmatic person remains a Christ follower and therefore cannot be expected to compromise solid biblical truths. Dialogue at this level will therefore likely remain in a space that maintains disagreements. But engagement with Islam at a kerygmatic level will almost always be enriching for all involved.

In the context of this mutually enriching relationship of respect, trust will develop, to the point where meaningful conversation can take place. Meaningful, life-transforming, conversation can hardly take place outside such respect and trust. And the kerygmatic person knows that any meaningful conversation about Christ should be life-transforming, as the uniqueness that Christ brings to our human relationship with God is shared. But it is important to emphasize that this engagement does not go merely in one direction. The relationship of trust and respect developed through the kerygmatic approach should be mutual. Kerygmatic engagement creates an opportunity to listen to what Muslims have to say about religious issues as well, the opportunity to learn and stand corrected, rather than stick to our own perceptions of what they believe, so that misunderstandings and misperceptions may be diminished.

Methods Used in the Kerygmatic Approach to Islam and Muslims

The practice of the kerygmatic approach in Christian-Muslim interaction knows few boundaries. Every occasion is suitable to bear witness respectfully to Christ's good news. A Christ follower using that approach will happily make use of the Qur'an and other elements of the Islamic tradition as a bridge, seeking to do so—as we will see in the next chapter—legitimately.

This approach will not shy away from discussion forums on theological, doctrinal, social, cultural, and other issues. No topic is taboo, since a respectful exchange is prepared and assumed. At the kerygmatic level, dialogue takes place between religious and scholarly leaders who have a deeply rooted faith and are willing to share uncompromisingly with genuine counterparts. As a result, the outcome of such exchange is deep and reaches the grassroots.

Expectable Outcomes

My research in the past few years has focused on the six foundational centuries of Christian-Muslim interaction, the eighth to the fourteenth. The discursive history of that period emerges largely as a history of conflict and hardening of positions.[12] This negative picture is not all due to the Christian and Muslim experiences of engagement, for the political circumstances often also played an important part in the stratification of the discourse. Sadly, history often repeats itself cyclically. The damage caused on Christian-Muslim relations by the cycle of violence between Christian and Muslim empires at the beginning of the second millennium is irreparable. Depending on one's reading of history, some hold that it was the persistent push of the Islamic Empire into central Europe, both from the East all the way from Constantinople to Vienna, and from the West in Andalusian southern Spain, which triggered the violent reaction of the Crusader wars. Others identify the Crusader aggression as the root cause of the cycle of violence that ensued. There is some truth in both perspectives. Whatever one's view, it is a constant of history that violence breeds violence. Unfortunately, the end of the second millennium as well, exacerbated by the dramatic event of 9/11 during the second year of the third millennium, is witnessing the unfolding of ascending violence and wars. Postcolonialism, neocolonialism, Zionism, Islamic radicalism, terrorism, and many more isms, could be and are being blamed on both sides of the conflict. But in reality, it is the diabolic predilection for domination and paranoia—one thing leading to the other in a spiraling downward fall—that leads to never-ending conflicts for which no one ever takes responsibility.

12. For a survey of this discursive history, see my "The Gospels in the Muslim Discourse of the Ninth to the Fourteenth Centuries: An Exegetical Inventorial Table (Part I)," *Journal of Islam and Christian-Muslim Relations* 14.1 (2003): 67-91.

This brings us back to our original assumption: *attitude* determines the path of relationship between two ideologies, all the way down to *expectable outcomes*. The kerygmatic position is all about attitude, understanding, and methodology. A carefully developed kerygmatic approach will lead to the positive transformation of mutual perceptions and relationships, with potential for deep impact into the multireligious and multiethnic societies that form today's world.

From a missional perspective, the nonaggressive and suprareligious nature of the kerygmatic attitude and discourse has the potential to avoid immediate enmity between a Muslim who wishes to explore the implications of God's good news in Christ and the other members of that person's community. This means that this person's extraction—whether induced or self-imposed—from his or her community can be avoided, so that the community as a whole may benefit from Christ's transforming power.

A Legitimate Insider's Knowledge of Islam

Deriving from mutual trust and respect, the kerygmatic Christian-Muslim engagement is driven by an interest in acquiring a legitimate knowledge of Islamic realities and methods. Misperceptions foster the propagation of stereotypes, producing a caricatured version of the other and ending with two separate discourses that never meet. This is the recipe for two separate monologues rather than engaged and committed dialogue. Insider's knowledge is sought, not for the purpose of discovering the weaknesses of the other, but in order to develop what may be called a legitimate discourse.

What I mean by an "insider's knowledge" of Islam is exemplified in the apostle Paul's attitude to the Old Testament and the law of Moses. Scholars argued that Paul's ability to reinterpret (and thus embrace) the law of Moses in light of the Christ event actually preserved the Old and New Testaments together in the canon. And ultimately it was this that preserved continuity within the Judeo-Christian tradition. For Paul, faith preceded the law in the person of Abraham; and afterward, the law served until the time of Jesus. But it had now been superseded.[13]

13. For a fine example of this scholarly perspective, see Hans Freiherr von Campenhausen, *The Formation of the Christian Bible*, trans. J. A. Baker (Philadelphia: Fortress, 1972 [originally 1968]), esp. chap. 2.

The Suprareligious Approach and the "Two-Buildings" Analogy

In Christ, the Christian tradition affirms, God truly came to meet us. He did not merely adapt to our situation by pretending that he was a human being or that he was experiencing joys and sufferings. That, indeed, was the heresy of Docetism, which the early generations of Christ followers quickly identified as an unfaithful expression of the Christ event that they had experienced. The early community of Jesus understood that the calling that they had received was above religion. They understood that "in these last days [God] has spoken to us by his Son, whom he appointed heir of all things, and through whom he made the universe," and that "the Son is the radiance of God's glory and the exact representation of his being, sustaining all things by his powerful word" (Heb 1:2–3). This is why they never attempted to establish a new religion. In fact, even talking about a new religion at that stage would be anachronistic. Early disciples understood Jesus's coming as the fulfillment of all of God's promises through the prophets. They understood Jesus's call to the worship of God "in spirit and in truth" (John 4:23) and had therefore no further need for new or readapted religious forms and institutions. They continued to function with the old Jewish ones, radically reinterpreted through the Christ event.

In Nicodemus's secret night visit with Jesus, the latter affirms this way of thinking. Nicodemus was a learned and respected religious leader, a Pharisee who feared God (John 3:1), much like a good Muslim or a good Christian today, who would perceive themselves as faithful followers of the religious tradition and institution that they were born into. He and Jesus, no doubt, could have had a fascinating theological discussion. Instead, to Nicodemus's affirmation of Jesus's miracles as a sign of his coming from God (3:2), Jesus replies with a surprising statement about the necessity of getting "born again" (3:3). Nicodemus would have believed that he belonged to the kingdom of God by virtue of being born of the "seed of Abraham." But Jesus challenges this notion by affirming that one must rather be born of (the seed of) God's Spirit (3:5–6): "Very truly I tell you, no one can enter the kingdom of God unless they are born of water and the Spirit. Flesh gives birth to flesh, but the Spirit gives birth to spirit."

Jesus further explains this unusual language by using the metaphor of the snake, which Moses "lifted up in the wilderness," just as he would be "lifted up" on the cross. Hence, being born of the Spirit, in Jesus's understanding, signifies a total reliance on faith in the son of man's salvific act of self-giving. As evangelicals, we must be careful not to turn the concept of "being born again," as we often do, into yet another prayer ritual that guarantees our belonging to God's kingdom. Jesus rebuts this sort of reliance on religious forms and expectations, and he declares the Spirit of God free of all bounds when it comes to his work in people's lives (3:8): "The wind blows wherever it pleases. You hear its sound, but you cannot tell where it comes from or where it is going. So it is with everyone born of the Spirit."

In the next chapter of John's Gospel (chapter 4), Jesus has another very similar encounter, but this time with a woman, a Samaritan woman, a Samaritan woman with a bad reputation no less. The repetition of the same message in a way that would have appealed to different audiences is not unusual in the Gospels. In Luke 15, for example, the same message of God's care for the lost, and his rejoicing over the repentance of a single sinner, is expressed three times through three different parables. The first parable concerns a lost sheep, in a way that would have appealed to poor shepherds (15:4–7); the second concerns a lost coin, in a way that would have appealed to middle-class women homemakers (15:8–10); and the third parable concerns the lost son of a wealthy household, in a way that would have appealed to a general religious household (15:11–32). The third parable is the most developed, as it proclaims the further message about the extension of the good news of salvation outside the "household of Israel," to the gentiles who were formerly in rebellion against God (the younger son). It contains, as well, a warning to the Jews (the elder son), inviting them to rejoice and celebrate, rather than hold a grudge, at the universalization of God's grace.

The message of Jesus's encounter with the Samaritan woman in John 4 is a variant on the theme of John 3, in his encounter with Nicodemus the Pharisee. But this time, instead of a righteous Jewish religious man coming to Jesus, it is Jesus who goes to an unrighteous Samaritan woman. He accosts her at the geographical location that would have represented her own hope for salvation, "near the plot of ground Jacob had given to his son Joseph" (4:5). "Jacob's well was there," we are told (4:6). The significance of the well for the Samaritans will be revealed in 4:12, in response to Jesus's bold statement that if the woman had known who was speaking to her, it is she who would have asked him for a drink: "Are you greater than our father Jacob, who gave us the well and drank from it himself, as did also his sons and his livestock?"

In other words, Jesus met the Samaritan woman at the very heart of her religious tradition. But instead of affirming and venerating this tradition, just as he challenged Nicodemus's reliance on being born of the seed of Abraham with the notion that he must be born of the Spirit, he challenges the Samaritan tradition by affirming (4:13–14): "Everyone who drinks this water will be thirsty again, but whoever drinks the water I give them will never thirst. Indeed, the water I give them will become in them a spring of water welling up to eternal life."

It is not that Jesus despised religious traditions. He respected them enough to meet people at the very place where these traditions impacted them. But he affirmed in no uncertain terms that religious traditions in themselves do not save. They can bring people of faith together, but they can also distract them and lead them astray. Puzzled with Jesus's discourse, the Samaritan woman moves to a theological topic that was clearly close to her heart. She now wants to know once and for all whether Judaism or the Samaritan religion—which derived from ancient Israelite faith—had gotten it right (John 4:20). The next few verses reflect one of the most beautiful and most significant revelations proclaimed by Jesus in the Gospels (4:21, 23–24):[14]

> "Woman," Jesus replied, "believe me, a time is coming when you will worship the Father neither on this mountain nor in Jerusalem. . . . A time is coming and has now come when the true worshipers will worship the Father in the Spirit and in truth, for they are the kind of worshipers the Father seeks. God is spirit, and his worshipers must worship in the Spirit and in truth."

It is difficult to read this passage without hearing the echoes of 3:8 from the encounter with Nicodemus ("the wind blows wherever it pleases"). Finally, after the woman decides to defer this whole complicated matter to a later time, when Messiah will come and "explain everything to us" (4:25), Jesus closes with the powerful "I am" saying: "I, the one speaking to you—I am he."

The construction of these narratives is absolutely stunning. The same "I am" who had encountered Moses in the wilderness (Exod 3:14), *Ehyeh Asher Ehyeh*, "I am who I am," was standing face to face with a Samaritan woman. The same "I am" had also challenged Nicodemus's safest religious beliefs, and the same also continues to challenge our own.

14. I skip John 4:22, as commentators generally consider it to represent a parenthetical reflection of the Gospel writer, expressing what Jews would have believed: "You Samaritans worship what you do not know; we worship what we do know, for salvation is from the Jews." The verse certainly flies in the face of the essential message of the passage if it were an affirmation of Jesus's own belief.

To further illustrate this, I use what I call "the Two-Buildings Analogy." Many who call themselves Christians live as though Christianity were just another religious institution. Even though we claim the opposite, we emphasize the centrality of form and language in our religious system. We view Islam and Christianity as two buildings trying to lay exclusive claim on the same plot of land. To those who think this way, Christian mission to Muslims requires *destroying* "the building of Islam" and uprooting its foundations to replace it with "the building of Christianity."

There is, however, another way to look at this for those Christ followers who belong to the *community of the Spirit* inaugurated by Jesus, as revealed to Nicodemus and the Samaritan woman. We may legitimately maintain that Islam, as a religious institution, can be represented as a building. From a *community of the Spirit* perspective, everyone, including Muslims, is invited to become part of this *community of the Spirit*.This is not hard for evangelicals to grasp, because we invite our own children to become part of this community. We do not assume they are part of the kingdom simply because they are our offspring, nor do we need to convince them that they are utterly evil before they willingly become disciples of Jesus. We simply invite them to enter into God's kingdom by proclaiming to them the good news of God's salvation through Christ. In the same way, as a community of the Spirit, we call on the Spirit of Christ to *indwell the building of Islam*, as well as the building of any other religious institution, including Christianity. The *supra-institutional community of the Spirit* has no alternative institution to offer adherents of any religion but invites all to inaugurate the reign of Christ within their own institutions.[15]

Does this reading of Christ's attitude to religion mean that the community he inaugurated was called to be disembodied? Is it devoid of any earthly communal expression? I reemphasize that, though Jesus held what I believe to have been a suprareligious understanding of faith, he never abandoned the Jewish religious fold. Quite the opposite, he maintained a consistent presence at the temple and the synagogue. He never objected to being called Rabbi and Teacher, which shows clearly that he was trained in the methods of teaching and preaching from the Torah in the Jewish tradition. But at the same time, he hit at the root of religiosity, which

15. I have developed further the whole concept of mission within this suprainstitutional framework as finding its source in the natural expression of God's Triune life in my article (with John Corrie) on the Trinity in the *Dictionary of Mission Theology: Evangelical Foundations*, edited by John Corrie (Downers Grove, IL: IVP Academic, 2007).

always attempted to keep at bay the marginalized and those considered as outcasts by the religious institution. He had much compassion for tax collectors, prostitutes, and sinners, yet little patience for arrogant religious leaders who venerated their religious symbols of exclusion, such as the Sabbath and the temple. To those, he said that "the son of man is Lord of the Sabbath" (Matt 12:8) and that "the Sabbath was made for man, not man for the Sabbath" (Mark 2:27). To one of his disciples who observed, as they were leaving the temple, "Look, Teacher! What massive stones! What magnificent buildings!" he responded, "Do you see all these great buildings? . . . Not one stone here will be left on another; every one will be thrown down" (Mark 13:1–2). John reports that Jesus said, "Destroy this temple, and I will raise it again in three days" (John 2:19), and the evangelist observes: "But the temple he had spoken of was his body" (2:21). We know from the Gospels that these religiously offensive words would cost him his life, as they came back to bite him when he stood before the tribunal of the Sanhedrin (Matt 26:61 and Mark 14:58).

I argue that the blueprint of a new perspective on suprareligious ecclesiology, then, needs to find its foundation in the living out of dynamic values, rather than in form and structure. Form and structure are sociologically and ethically neutral. The problem is when form and structure start to replace essence and core values in the life of the community. The two core values for "being church" in a multireligious world, from a suprareligious perspective, are "Christ centeredness" and "the prophetic." I hope to have already argued abundantly the Christ-centered nature of a suprareligious approach to religions. Something needs to be said, in closing, about the prophetic value. I adopt, here, Walter Brueggemann's understanding of the dual role of the prophetic calling as criticism and energizing.[16] Brueggemann argues convincingly that the power of the prophet's role, both in the Old Testament and in the ministry of Jesus, was the ability to criticize the "dominant royal consciousness," on the one hand, and the ability to project a new "alternative prophetic vision" of what is divinely possible, on the other. I suggest that the foundation of a suprareligious ecclesiology lies in the ability of all members of Christ's community to live their life daily as "prophetic living." The prophetic, in this new community, is not the role of a few lone voices crying in the desert. It is the life to which all of Christ's followers have been called. To live

16. See Walter Brueggemann, *The Prophetic Imagination*, 2nd ed. (Minneapolis: Fortress, 2001).

the prophetic life is the ability to create permanent discomfort within the religious forms and structures, as a result of community members' own discomfort with the risk of sliding into the comfort of a dominant royal consciousness. The prophetic life, however, does not stop at criticism of the establishment. It moves into the projection of a vision for an alternative consciousness, with the capacity to be permanently amazed (a word often used by Brueggemann) at the possibilities offered by the reign of Christ amid his constantly transformed and renewed community.

A Book Respectful Enough of Islam for Muslims to Read It

The present book is addressed to both Christians and Muslims, and I therefore hope that it will be accessible to Muslim readers without hurting their religious sensitivities, while at the same time leading both Christians and Muslims to be disturbed at times and challenged to rethink where we are and what we have achieved through our relationships. At the same time, as a committed follower of Jesus, I am aware that my assessment of Islam will, at times, have a Christian bias. I would not claim otherwise. But as a follower of Christ rather than Christianity, I will often be critical both of Christianity and of Islam.

If some consider that I have failed to be objective in certain places, they will probably be right. One cannot claim full objectivity, including (perhaps especially) when one holds strong faith commitments. But what I can affirm with a clear conscience is that everything I say is written in full conviction and transparency—at least at the time of writing, since convictions may legitimately change with time—and with no intended hypocrisy or compromise.

I write this book at a time of world crisis. We live in a post–9/11 world. The impact of the wars in both Afghanistan and Iraq is still very much being felt, and there is no end in view to either conflict. The Israeli-Palestinian conflict is hitting a new level of deadlock, after the Palestinian bid for statehood in September 2011 and the US commitment to use its veto power in due time to prevent this application from going through. The so-called Arab Spring, observed with excitement by some and with deep concern by others, is described by many as having turned into an "Arab Autumn." And the Syrian conflict that emerged from an initially peaceful uprising has already turned seven cycles of autumn leaves into the bloodiest crimson colors.

In any case, the world is anxiously waiting to see what fruit an "Arab Summer" might bring, and it is likely that the fruit will vary between one country and the next. Whatever the outcome, the current unrest in the Middle East and North Africa is making Lebanon look like the most stable and ideal regional honeymoon destination! Cracks of conflict and misunderstanding that appeared in the early years of the new millennium have by now deepened between Shīʿītes and Sunnīs; between Christians, Muslims, and Jews; between Arabs and non-Arabs; between the so-called East and so-called West. As a human partaker in, and observer of, all these realities, and more deeply as a Christ follower living through this particular period of history, whereas my hope is that many Muslims will read this book, my primary responsibility is to be a voice within the community that also associates itself with Christ by calling itself Christian.

I hope that this book will be far more than another intellectual contribution to Christian-Muslim dialogue. I hope that it will address not just the mind, but also the heart, soul, hands, and feet of Christians all over the world. I hope that it will lead Christians, both Arab and non-Arab, to greater and more fruitful interaction with Muslims.

By my Muslim readers, I hope that this book will be received as an innovative approach that genuinely seeks rapprochement between communities of faith in the God of peace who seeks and promotes interpersonal relationships.

I don't expect this book to be received with great fervor by extremists of either community, but I hope that it will be an encouragement and contribution to moderates everywhere who seek to be ever more effective promoters and practitioners of mercy, justice, and humility that alone can lead to greater and more deeply rooted peace.

A Biblical Theme: God's Agenda

In many ways, God's agenda for global peace is encapsulated in a verse from the Hebrew Bible that contains the deepest expressions that should inspire public policy from a Christian point of view:

> He has showed you, O man, what is good.
>   And what does the LORD require of you?
> To act justly and to love mercy
>   and to walk humbly with your God. (Mic 6:8)

Understanding the Importance of Mercy

A great deal of today's conflicts in the world results from the inability of those who hold power to understand the importance of mercy. The tragedy of our reality is that those with power should be expected to act mercifully toward those who are not in a position to do so. Those who lie under the burden of oppression are in a mode of survival and resistance to oppression and will generally be led to violence in their struggle to recover their human dignity. Yet in their effort to quench violence, the powerful are steadfast in their attempt to justify themselves. They possess all the mechanisms necessary to convince the world of their own self-righteousness and of their enemies' evil motivations.

Because they have the natural upper hand, the powerful need to come to a cognitive understanding of their almost exclusive access to initiatives of peace. In a conflict, each side should seek to identify those areas in which they have a very real authority to demonstrate their convictions about mercy, for at that level at least, peace is largely their responsibility.

Because true mercy is more than pity that engenders pride and self-righteousness, Jesus promises that those who resort to genuine mercy will receive a reward both earthly and heavenly: "Blessed are the merciful, for they will be shown mercy" (Matt 5:7). The New Testament Epistle of James further elaborates on that principle by putting forth the following dramatic incentive to mercy: "Judgment without mercy will be shown to anyone who has not been merciful. Mercy triumphs over judgment!" (Jas 2:13). In other words, James affirms that only by understanding the centrality of this principle of mercy and putting it into practice will we be able to please God and escape his judgment.

Adopting an Attitude of Humility

It is only by coming to an understanding of their very real responsibility for peace by the demonstration of a deep sense of compassion and mercy that those with the upper hand in conflict will be able to adopt the humility required to act upon their understanding. Humility, of course, is no easy thing for anybody, and even less so for those who are convinced that they could easily resolve a conflict by resorting to violence and through it quench any dissent with their hegemony and self-righteous convictions. The further complication is that humility, even if adopted, can often become patronizing and thus lose legitimacy by losing any credibility with regard to its authenticity.

But it is doubtful whether any kind of long-lasting resolution to conflict can actually be found without genuine humility. It is doubtful whether even the beginning of a solution to conflict can be found without humility, for only humility will lead the stronger party in a conflict to come to the negotiation table. It will seldom be difficult to convince the weaker party to come to the table, for they often have little to lose anymore and much to gain from negotiating a peaceful solution. Once again, humility is expected on the part of the powerful. But it is precisely there that it is difficult to obtain, because the powerful will fear that humility will be seen as a sign of weakness that will only embolden the adversary. Therefore, when the stronger party of a conflict finally acquiesces to negotiations, they generally do it in a patronizing way and thus doom the conversation to failure from the start. The endless cycle of negotiations between Israelis and Palestinians, which have so far always eventually collapsed, demonstrates this principle abundantly. The United States has in most cases been the broker of such talks, but seldom recognizing its role in exacerbating the conflict as a result of its uncompromising support of Israel. Most likely, peace will come only at the price of humility on the part of the broker, if it is ever able to adopt a more contrite and equitable attitude.

Humility is a deeply rooted attitude that cannot be faked or feigned without revealing itself as it really is: plain arrogance. For humility as an underlying attitude to be genuine, it needs to begin with some sort of repentance expressed at least through some level of recognition of error. Therefore, deep reconciliation arising from genuine humility can only ever be the reward of the truly courageous who are honestly looking for peace beyond the niceties of political rhetoric.

And for those in power who fear that humility will remove from them their legitimacy as rulers, they had better be corrected by hearing the words of Jesus, who describes the characteristic of leadership that stands alone in commanding respect: "Take my yoke upon you and learn from me, for I am gentle and humble in heart, and you will find rest for your souls. For my yoke is easy and my burden is light" (Matt 11:29–30). The paradox of bearing an easy yoke can be understood only on the basis of the leader's genuine and profound humility. Far from rendering leadership illegitimate and weak, humility, because it leads to conflict resolution, has the potential of affirming itself as the key component of effective leadership that leads to peace.

Seeking Ways to Act Justly

Justice, because it moves to the behavioral level, represents the moment of truth in situations of conflict. Justice cannot be faked, because it has immediate bearing on people in communities. Real justice has to be experienced by communities that have suffered injustice before it can pass the test of authenticity. Powerful nations that call for peace quite easily succeed in convincing their own people that their intentions are genuine merely through well-sounding political statements in their national media. They are able to do so only because their own people are outsiders to the actual conflict. But it takes much more than rhetorical niceties to convince the people suffering on either side of any conflict. In order for these "disturbing masses" to be convinced, it always takes an actual implementation of justice that demonstrably works toward the relief of their situation of suffering.

In the late nineties, while I was studying for my PhD at the University of Oxford, I began to take interest in the South African context. I left Lebanon in 1996, half a decade after the end of the Lebanese civil war, and I was looking for answers to understand what comes next in rebuilding a country that had gone through such a bloody internal conflict. I became interested in the Truth and Reconciliation Commission of post-Apartheid South Africa. That situation seemed to have many parallels with the Lebanese case, and the TRC seemed to have gone a long way into demonstrating the primacy of justice in bringing about reconciliation. The TRC offered anyone and everyone the chance to receive forgiveness for practically any kind of crime—in political language it offered them amnesty—in exchange for humble and authentic recognition of guilt.

Thus, a level of justice without precedent in its depth—though also deeply unconventional—was obtained for the victims of crimes on both sides of the conflict. Justice in the South African case did not translate into superficial material compensation, but in the victim being offered an opportunity for release from anger, bitterness, and the desire for revenge, by accepting the confession of crime perpetrators. Authority in the ultimate resolution of the conflict at the human heart level was thus handed over—as it should be—to the decision of the victims, by giving them the opportunity to choose psychological and emotional release over the option of retaliation. Thus, demonstrated humility on the part of the crime perpetrators, based on their conviction that they had failed to show mercy when they should have, was the means by which the true potential for justice was established. Ultimately, it became up to the victim to accept that justice was done or not. But the potential had been created, not by means of financial compensation, which would have done little as a payback for especially the human losses of the victims, but by moral, psychological, and emotional restitution through the confession of guilt.[17]

The expression that most strongly describes being in the will of God in the Gospels is the term "Son of God." Jesus used the expression to describe his own identification with the will of his "heavenly Father," and a very few times he used the expression with reference to human beings whose hearts are in line with the will of God. In these occurrences, God is portrayed as primarily concerned with peace. The most straightforward reference in the Gospels is found in the Sermon on the Mount: "Blessed are the peacemakers, for they will be called sons of God" (Matt 5:9). This first occurrence is indiscriminate in its intended audience. The peacemaker can be either a powerful or a weaker party in a conflict. A second statement is more directly addressed to the victims in a conflict: "But I tell you: Love your enemies and pray for those who persecute you, that you may be sons of your Father in heaven" (5:44–45). Here Jesus goes beyond any conventional human wisdom and actually places potential for peace in the hands of victims. Even when a victim is not in a position of proactive instigation of peace, he or she can nevertheless play an active role in promoting peace in an unlikely situation by loving his or her enemy and praying for them.

Mercy, Humility, and Justice in the Context of Lebanon

The message of the prophet Micah is desperately needed in the context of Lebanon. Much was rebuilt in Lebanon after the civil war, which lasted from 1975 to 1991. In the decade of the '90s, the central district of Beirut was considered to be the largest building site in the world. Bridges, highways, airport, ports, buildings, and entire neighborhoods were all

17. For some good analyses on the Truth and Reconciliation Commission, see Alex Boraine, *A Country Unmasked: Inside South Africa's Truth and Reconciliation Commission* (Oxford: Oxford University Press, 2001); Priscilla B. Hayner, *Unspeakable Truths: Transitional Justice and the Challenge of Truth Commissions*, 2nd ed. (Abingdon: Routledge, 2010); Charles Villa-Vicencio and Wilhelm Verwoerd, eds., *Looking Back, Reaching Forward: Reflections on the Truth and Reconciliation Commission of South Africa* (London: Zed, 2000).

recovered and raised from the ashes in record time, albeit placing this tiny country under massive national debt running into the tens of billions of dollars. Tourists from all over the world came to be entertained, celebrating and musing over the impressive restoration, but little was done for the restoration of a people. Hardly any soul-searching was carried out to try to understand the root causes of the sixteen-year fratricidal conflict. The entire population and the new postwar generation were encouraged to forgive and forget without ever attempting to understand. Instead, we were offered a new powerful diversion, an Arabic pop music industry that achieved its intended job of keeping the entire population under the numbing spell of sensuality, with an impact reaching far beyond the Lebanese borders and deep into the entire Arab world. This has become a travesty substitute for the very real ongoing plea of populations still crushed under the oppression of their own Arab dictatorial regimes and their supportive Western sponsors whose foreign policies are dictated by self-interest and economic gain. The Arab uprisings were popular reactions that brought an end to several of these dictatorial systems. But the Syrian war, particularly now with the heavy involvements of Russia and Iran, has put an end to this popular snowball—for a time.

In Lebanon, the divide has only been on the increase between the wealthier Sunnī, Druze, and Christian social strata concerned with political stability for the sake of economic comfort, and the poorer Shīʿī strata, always kept on the edge by militant political ideologies of resistance and support for causes that will have little if anything to offer them in terms of direct gain. Of course, the large amounts of money invested in fueling these causes would have gone a long way to relieving the poverty of the underprivileged Shīʿa, but history tells us that the masses are fated to be the fuel that keeps ideological causes alive rather than being the eventual beneficiaries of militant struggle.

A semblance of peace was forcefully imposed on Lebanese society so long as the powerful Sunnī figure of Rafic Hariri, in his position as prime minister, was able to tip the balance in favor of economic stability, in the face of Shīʿī militant Hezbollah, with an ideology of struggle and resistance, and with broader regional ideological interests. The balance quickly tipped in the opposite direction upon the tragic assassination of Hariri on February 14, 2005. The deep divide between rich and poor, between favored and underprivileged, between those concerned with economic prosperity and stability and those with greater concern for ideologies of struggle against oppressive dictatorships and neocolonial thrusts, became sharper than at any time before. This divide became immediately obvious in the opposing popular uprisings of March 8 and March 14, 2005, which led to the collapse of the pro-Syrian government and the eventual withdrawal of Syrian military forces from Lebanon in May. The March 8 uprising brought together masses primarily from among the underprivileged Shīʿa, many of them brought in by Hezbollah-organized busloads. Whereas the March 14 uprising brought together the more opulent masses that drove into Beirut in their fancy cars. As both parties, both masses, shouted opposing slogans as expressions of our "democratic" responsibilities, little were we aware that we were expressing the unhealed wounds of the deep divides of war, which none of our politicians had ever cared to tackle, for fear that such a process would lay bare the bloodstains that most of them still carry on their hands.

These sociopolitical realities of Lebanon call for an aggressive effort at tackling deeply social issues of conflict resolution. They indicate that there will be no lasting peace for Lebanon before justice is restored for the underprivileged strata of society, and no justice will be achieved without a real implementation of principles of mercy toward the suffering and the poor. And the implementation of the double principle of mercy and justice will be possible only through a humble national confession by wartime crime perpetrators on all sides of the Lebanese political leadership and a conscious struggle toward social and economic equality through programs of education, community development projects, and perhaps most importantly, the fight against endemic government corruption at every level.

Political Conflict and the Role of Religious Dialogue

The present book is not primarily a political work. It is first and foremost a work of interfaith dialogue and conflict resolution. But if religious dialogue does not carry any political and social implications, it should be rightly dismissed as futile. In the West, where religion is primarily a matter of individual faith preference, dialogue at a purely religious level might be legitimate. But outside the West, and particularly in the Middle East, where individual, family, social, cultural, political, and economic spheres are seamlessly intertwined, the church may not allow itself such luxuries.

What I therefore attempt to do in the following chapters is to tackle the history-long theological conflicts of Christianity and Islam while looking into their immediate social implications. The civil war of Lebanon depicted Christians and Muslims as conventional enemies of one another. And although the enmity has expressed itself primarily in the political and social spheres, the conflict has been fed by mutually false religious perceptions. The hope is that through the examination of a long and complex history of religious conflict, Christians and Muslims in Lebanon will be willing to put a human face on their conventional enemies. For whatever claims our politicians make about the unique model of religious diversity and coexistence that Lebanon offers the world, Christians and Muslims in Lebanon always seem to be lying in wait for their religious counterpart to trip, in order to further their own position of dominance and control over Lebanese politics and society.

The constant political rhetoric about Lebanese religious coexistence begs the question as to our real ability to live together. As Lebanese citizens, both Christian and Muslim, we know better. Whether we like to admit it or not, too many of us have been living in our own religious ghettos, trying to forget about each other's existence. At age thirteen, after having lived the first twelve years of my life in a Muslim-majority part of Beirut, my family moved to the Christian-majority side, and I was struck by the misconceptions and stereotypes that my new Christian friends had about their Muslim co-citizens—even as children. It seems obvious that our sixteen years of civil war were a proof that we do not know how to live together, but facing that reality would be too painful, and our politicians prefer to maintain denial of this fact. It is therefore, no doubt, the role of religious leaders and thinkers to deal with these realities, and we should be aware today more than ever that this question can no longer be ignored. And since it is merely logical that each party in a conflict has the primary responsibility of autoexamination and little if any control over their counterpart's willingness to engage in introspection, my prayer is that the present book will be a Christian contribution to this exercise and the prodding start of a far broader process of conflict resolution, reconciliation, and healing in postwar Lebanon. Recent political events, with potential catastrophic regional consequences, clearly demonstrate that this process can no longer be postponed.

I often say in public speaking engagements in Western countries that Europe and the United States are only now stepping over the threshold of a reality that the Middle East was living for the past fourteen hundred years, namely that of Christian-Muslim coexistence. Islam remained to a great extent an external reality for Western societies until World War I, with the collapse of the Ottoman Empire and the gradual twentieth-century disintegration of the colonial order. These events brought with them the emergence of new geopolitical realities in a majority world that had been for several centuries under colonial rule. The ensuing emergence of new global socioeconomic realities brought with it the substantial migration of previously colonized peoples to the countries of their former masters, and with it the creation of the present patchwork of multicultural and multireligious societies of contemporary Europe and North America.

If the reality of the Islamic presence in these Western regions—for many a disturbing reality—was able to be ignored by many in the political sphere, this new global reality hit home quite violently after the dramatic events of 9/11. Whether that event epitomized the encounter of Christianity and Islam in the West is highly controversial. Such an interpretation would be too painful to fathom, so both political and religious leadership in the mainstream usually prefer to downplay the religious significance of the clash, attributing it to some extremist groups that are unworthy of their religious affiliation. I will not entirely dismiss this interpretation since I very well know the complexity of any religious reality, and particularly—as will emerge from the present study—the complexity of the Islamic religious reality. At the same time, since it is not possible entirely to dissociate political and religious ideology in Islam—and arguably the same could be said about some expressions of contemporary North American Christianity—the events of 9/11 and their aftermath cannot—should not—be dissociated from their religious roots and implications.

In that context and from that perspective, therefore, it is my hope that the present book will also be of assistance to Christian and Muslim leadership in the West—both political and religious—if they should care to listen to the voice of history and learn from the experiences of religious communities coming into direct encounter in the Middle East, beginning in the seventh century of the Christian era.

The end of the Cold War era had already brought Islam far closer to the center of world attention to replace Communism as the next threat to an ideological free world, but 9/11 brought it center stage. There is enough literature demonstrating the direct correlation of the 9/11 tragedy with the foreign policies of Western nations to justify not going into any detailed analysis of these political realities.[18] These works, even if considered to be

18. For example: Noam Chomsky, *Hegemony or Survival: America's Quest for Global Dominance* (London: Penguin, 2004); Chomsky, *Failed States: The Abuse of Power and*

too far on the political left by some, had better be heard by all inside and outside the church, as they trace the rise of militant Islamic radicalism clearly and directly back to the Palestinian-Israeli conflict. Here again, the fundamental problem is the issue of justice, that the international community has allowed several generations of Palestinians to grow up in conditions of appalling poverty both inside Gaza and the West Bank and outside of their homeland in the conditions of extreme poverty of refugee camps especially in Syria, Lebanon, and Jordan.

Here again, if the implementation of principles of mercy, justice, and humility can rarely be expected of political leadership driven by political and economic self-interest, the universal church will never be forgiven for abandoning these principles, neither in this world by history nor in the next by divine justice. This is why it is crucially important today for the church to engage in a radical reexamination of its assumptions with regard to its understanding of Islam, which the rulers of the present world have portrayed to us as the ultimate conventional enemy. To this end I hope that the present book will make a meaningful contribution.

After establishing a hermeneutical framework to understand the roots of much of our theological discourse and mutual presuppositions in chapter 2, chapters 3–9 engage in an exploration of some of the key theological themes of our dialogical history. Chapter 3 explores our dialogical history on the doctrine of God, and chapters 4 and 5 on the doctrine of Christ. Chapters 6 and 7 look at the doctrine of Scripture, the way that Muslims have viewed the Bible, and the implications for our own understanding and communicating of scriptural truths. This is followed by chapters 8 and 9, reflecting our dialogical history on the person of Muhammad. Finally, chapter 10 looks at the implications of our theology for the construction of a more peaceful future.

---

the Assault on Democracy (New York: Metropolitan, 2006); Robert Fisk, *Pity the Nation: The Abduction of Lebanon*, 4th ed. (New York: Nation Books, 2002); Fisk, *The Great War for Civilization: The Conquest of the Middle East* (New York: Knopf, 2005).

2 Hermeneutics and Dialogue

John (not his real name) was a missionary known for his boldness and strong sense of initiative, and he had just obtained a special permission from a top Shīʿī cleric in south Lebanon to hold open debate sessions in the *ḥusayniyya*, the meeting halls annexed to local Shīʿī mosques. It was a great achievement, and he was thrilled. He invited his young Lebanese Christian friend Martin (his real name!), a budding theology student, to come and argue the reality of Jesus's crucifixion to a large number of Muslims assembled in the hall. We had Christian friends praying both nationally and internationally for the event, and a dozen Christian young men and women accompanied us to support the event.

I had prepared an airtight argument, based on the Qur'an. When the time came, I began with the qur'anic verse that seemingly denies the crucifixion (an-Nisā' 4:157): "And [they] said, 'We have killed the Messiah Jesus, son of Mary, the messenger of God.' However, they did not kill him, nor did they crucify him, though it was made to appear as if it had been so."

I then proceeded to appose to the verse other qur'anic verses that affirm that ʿĪsa actually died and that he will return at the end times as proof that on several occasions the Qur'an acknowledges the death of Jesus, such as Maryam 19:33–34: "'And [God's] peace was upon me the day I was born and the day I will die and it will be upon me the day I am raised alive.' Such is Jesus, the son of Mary—the word of truth about which they are in dispute."

I dutifully anticipated the Muslim argument that this last verse is often interpreted as referring to Jesus's death *after* he returns at the end of time by pointing out that the same words are spoken of John the Baptist in Maryam 19:12–15 and that it cannot therefore be taken as a reference to an end-time occurrence. Rather, I argued, it is the single denial verse that requires reinterpretation, in order to be brought into line with other qur'anic evidence and with the historical biblical account. After this, I pointed out that the literary context allows conjecturing that the verse does not actually deny the reality of 'Īsa's death by crucifixion, but rather is a denial of the Jewish claim that they had killed him. In reality, crucifixion was the Roman method of execution, whereas the Jews would have used stoning. Alternatively, I offered that the verse could also be understood as a denial that Jesus had died definitively at the cross since, according to the biblical account, he had ultimately risen from the dead.

With approving smiles from my Christian friends and inward satisfaction and gratefulness that God had helped me carry out my argument with a concise power of conviction, I stepped down from the pulpit. I had barely reached my place, however, before I heard with deep disappointment the swift and tacit rebuttal of my argument by the local sheikh. "Although we appreciate your effort and amicable approach," Sheikh Yūsuf said defiantly, "it is arrogant on your part to claim the right to interpret our Holy Text. Only our trained *'ulamā'* [scholars] are permitted to do this, in line with the legitimate principles taught us by our tradition!"

The audience was satisfied and pleased as they stood up at the closing of the evening, except for me and my puzzled missionary friend and the others accompanying us. On our way out, friendly Muslims smiled at us kindly, with a hint of pity. A young man named Omar patted me on the back and told me that he would be happy to get back together with me to show me how Jews and Christians had historically corrupted their Scriptures, leading to all sorts of doctrinal heresies!

This anecdote from the early nineties represents the ongoing story of Christians and Muslims coming face to face, whether at official debate and dialogue sessions or in day-to-day encounters between friends. A parallel story could easily be written reflecting misinterpretation of the Bible by a Muslim. I still think that my argument was valid from a rational outsider's point of view, but to Muslims for whom the Qur'an subscribes to specific norms of interpretation, the argument did not even begin to communicate. At the heart of the issue are two very different approaches to scriptural interpretation that, if left unraveled, will continue to lead to misunderstanding and miscommunication between Christians and Muslims.

Christian Misrepresentation: Reading Christian Thinking into the Qur'an

As I now think back on this experience, I realize that the first error that I committed was to presume that I had the right to interpret verses from the Qur'an by using sheer personal logic. Historically, this approach was known and used by some Muslims in qur'anic interpretation, referred to as "interpretation based on opinion" (*at-tafsīr bi ar-ra'y*). But it was not the more generally accepted approach, and certainly it was not to be performed on its own. But more fundamentally, my mistake was to presume that I, as a layperson and a Christian, could allow myself this undertaking. Not only is qur'anic interpretation (*tafsīr*) regarded as an advanced science restricted to trained Islamic scholars, but the exercise itself abides by strict principles, developed over the first centuries of Islam, to which I will turn later in this chapter.

Christians through the centuries have repeatedly undertaken the interpretation of qur'anic passages in a way that fits their Christian worldview, reading Christian doctrines into the Qur'an in the manner of prooftexting, rather than approaching the text in its own right. And they have done so usually by adopting an apologetic or polemical approach. This is not the only approach to dialogue with Islam adopted by Arab Christians, as will become clear throughout this book. Methods range from apologetic to philosophical to exegetical at various points of that history of interaction.

More recently, this method can be observed in several contemporary authors who base their apologetic approach to Islam on the Qur'an, not least by my own grandfather, Fouad Accad.[1] To be fair to my grandfather, however, I add that he felt that Arab Christians were not ready for his approach. He therefore insisted on publishing the work in English rather than in Arabic, a language in which he would have been much more at ease. He adapted and simplified his approach to suit a Western readership with little knowledge of Islam, and he meant for his book to help non-Arabs come to a deeper appreciation of Islam that would encourage them to adopt a more sympathetic and friendly approach to Muslims. But Fouad Accad spent his entire life studying Islamic writings, including the extensive *tafsīr* literature. I have inherited several of his qur'anic

1. Fouad Accad, *Building Bridges: Christianity and Islam* (Colorado Springs: NavPress, 1997).

commentary series, and they are replete with tiny handwritten notes on almost every page. His knowledge of Islam was among the most profound that I have encountered, and his understanding and love for Muslims was a rare gem that one would wish to find more often among Christians today. From my private conversations with him, I know that what is found in his book is but a meager digest of the vast knowledge and data that he collected throughout his life.

But to come back to my earlier point, many verses in the Qur'an, for a Christian reader, beg to be interpreted in such a way. Among these are verses that describe Jesus as "a word from God" (āl-'Imrān 3:45) and as "God's word" (an-Nisā' 4:171); verses that speak of God's Spirit, or the Holy Spirit, as being "sent by God to support/confirm 'Īsa" (al-Baqara 2:87, 253; al-Mā'ida 5:110); verses that represent Jesus as being "a spirit from God" (an-Nisā' 4:171) or having come to Mary through "a breath of God's Spirit" (al-Anbiyā' 21:91; at-Taḥrīm 66:12). As tempting as it might be to read Christian Trinitarian thinking into such verses because of the Word and Spirit connotations, however, and as well-intentioned as those who have used this method might be, the problem is that a quick read through the Muslim commentaries on these verses shows that they have not lent themselves traditionally to such interpretation, and therefore from a Muslim's perspective, such readings are considered illegitimate. Yet, just as I used such methods on numerous occasions at the beginning of my ministry of engagement with Muslims, they continue to recur again and again in day-to-day conversations between Christians and Muslims.

Christian Misrepresentation: Giving Primary Attention to Literary Context

The other important issue to which we must turn, and which is also reflected in my story in south Lebanon, is the temptation of Christians to read and interpret the Qur'an in its primary literary context. What led me to draw the conclusion that an-Nisā' 4:157 is not actually a denial of the crucifixion, but rather a denial that the Jews were the ones that crucified Jesus, is the immediately preceding context of the verse. Beginning at verse 153, we read about the Jewish people with whom God established his covenant. Yet in spite of God's favors toward them, they consistently rebelled against him, broke his commandments, and prided themselves on killing all his prophets. I interpreted verse 157 as the Qur'an's victorious proclamation rejecting this claim of the Jews, and I offered two possible alternative interpretations. Either the verse is an affirmation that it was not the Jews who managed to kill him, since their method of execution would have been stoning, whereas crucifixion was the method used by the Romans. Or the verse was an affirmation of Jesus's resurrection, since the Jews only *thought* that they had gotten rid of Jesus, but his resurrection was a clear victory over their claim. In either case, the Jews could not boast about this additional murder as they had done with preceding prophets.

Some familiarity with the mainstream Islamic exegetical tradition concerning this verse would have quickly shown me how far my interpretation was from legitimate *tafsīr*. The verse itself, as we will see in chapter 4, is ambiguous and does not lend itself to a straightforward understanding, as is clearly reflected in the wealth of traditions that developed around it. From a historical critical perspective, some even see in this verse a reflection of Docetic beliefs, denying the *reality* of Jesus's death in order to emphasize his immutable divinity. In this line, Andrew Rippin asserts that this qur'anic verse "would seem to reflect a strange amalgam, on the one hand supporting the argument for the truly divine nature of Jesus and thus denying the reality of his death, while on the other hand denying that Jesus was anything other than a human being."[2] From the perspective of a Christian understanding and methodology of textual interpretation, my exegesis in the *ḥusayniyya* was not farfetched, but from the perspective of Islamic methodology it was not acceptable.

Muslim Misrepresentation: Reading the Bible Muhammado-centrically

Similarly to the way that I read Christian ideas into the Qur'an, Muslims often read (and have read throughout history) their own Islamic thinking into the text of the Bible. Most Christians who have Muslim friends will remember the times when their friends tried to persuade them that Muhammad was in fact the promised "comforter" (*paraklētos* in Greek), the *Fāraqlīṭ*, whom Jesus promised the world near the end of his ministry. More sophisticated Muslims—or rather those better trained in polemics!—will bring up a multitude of other verses from both the Old and

2. Andrew Rippin, *Muslims: Their Religious Beliefs and Practices*, 2nd ed. (New York: Routledge, 2003).

New Testaments that testify that all biblical prophets were expecting the coming of the Prophet of Islam. Chapters 8–9 of the present book will be entirely dedicated to this theme, but I mention this here in order to draw the parallel between the Christian approach to the Qur'an and the Muslim approach to the Bible, namely the reading of our own wishful thinking into the Scriptures of others.

Interestingly, this process on the part of Muslims is very similar to the one that Judaism and the Hebrew Scriptures underwent at the dawn of Christianity. Christian theologians speak of a Christocentric reading of the Old Testament. In the New Testament, the Gospel writers and Paul himself reinterpret the entire Hebrew Bible through the Christ event, with Christ as the center and key for interpretation. Early Christians did that principally because Jesus was a Jew, a rabbi, who in fact always saw himself as an interpreter of the Torah and the Prophets, never as an overthrower of them. In addition, Jesus himself had gradually revealed to his disciples that he was the awaited Messiah of Jewish expectations, a fulfillment of biblical prophecy. After Christ's resurrection and ascension, the early disciples naturally began to search the Scriptures for the prophecies that Jesus had fulfilled. We have an early example of Jesus doing this himself with the two Emmaus disciples (Luke 24:25–27, emphasis added): "He said to them, 'How foolish you are, and how slow of heart to believe all that the prophets have spoken! Did not the Christ have to suffer these things and then enter his glory?' *And beginning with Moses and all the Prophets, he explained to them what was said in all the Scriptures concerning himself.*"

A similar process takes place during the early period of Islam, for which the following is the rationale. First of all, the Qur'an contains numerous verses that speak very positively both about the Bible and about Jesus. Muslims often feel quite vexed that whereas they acknowledge the Judeo-Christian Scriptures as sacred and have a very high view of all the major biblical figures, Jews and Christians persist in their rejection of both the Qur'an as sacred and of Muhammad as God's messenger. The Prophet of Islam himself experienced the same disappointment, as is reflected in the following verse from the Qur'an (al-Baqara 2:101): "And when a messenger from God comes to them confirming what they have, some recipients of the book throw God's book behind their backs as if they knew nothing of it."

From this verse, we can draw a very interesting inference, namely that Muhammad perceived—at least initially—his own message as a confirmation of the Judeo-Christian Scriptures ("people of the book" refers to

Jews and Christians in the Qur'an), containing a message that Jews and Christians should have been already familiar with. At least at that point of the qur'anic revelation, the verse betrays no awareness in Muhammad's mind that his message might contain anything unacceptable to the people of the book.

Second, we presently have no evidence—either from archeology or from history—that any portion of the Bible existed in the Arabic language before Islam. And from certain indications within the Qur'an, we are unlikely to ever find any evidence to this effect. Hence, there are strong indications in the Qur'an itself that Muhammad originally viewed his mission to a great extent as a remedy to this situation. Consider, for example, the following verse (al-Aḥqāf 46:12): "Yet before it, was the book revealed to Moses, a guide and as a mercy. And this a book confirming it in Arabic tongue to warn those who are unjust and to bring good news to those who do good."

This second verse, according to the Islamic exegetical tradition, belongs to a sūrah that was revealed during the early period of Muhammad's life. It reflects some optimism that Jews and Christians will recognize and accept his message. The former verse, on the other hand, belongs to the later period of Muhammad's life and is more pessimistic. Somewhere between these two time periods, the Prophet of Islam went through a process of disappointment. He was disappointed that, whereas Jews and Christians possessed all the criteria to recognize the accuracy of his message, they nevertheless rejected it. He was disappointed that whereas he expected them swiftly to recognize that he was truly a messenger (*rasūl*) from God (and at that stage it is doubtful that there would have been any particularly high doctrine of Muhammad's prophethood), they mocked him instead and accused him of plagiarism. This disappointment is also the incentive that has led Muslims through history to come to the defense of their prophet by searching in the Bible for indications that Muhammad was expected and had to come in the line of Judeo-Christian prophecy.

Comparative Observations on Textual Interpretation

Hermeneutics (or interpretation theory) has gained considerable sophistication in the last few centuries since the emergence of the science of textual criticism. Primarily outside of the Eastern world, sophisticated discussions have been taking place around the question of meaning. Today, Western scholars generally agree that the classical claim that a text stands alone in revealing its own meaning accurately is at best far too optimistic. At least since the eighteenth century, it has become common understanding that the *meaning* of a text lay not solely within that text, but somewhere within the dynamic relationship of a *text*, its *author*, and the *reader* that accesses it at any point in history.

If the question of the locus of meaning is complex for the understanding of any text, it becomes even more complicated when we come to the interpretation of a sacred text. If the meaning of a text derives from the complex interaction between text, author, and reader, where does the role of divine inspiration come in? And if much of modern literary theory developed in the primarily individualistic cultures of the West, what about the contribution of the believing community in collecting, preserving, and safeguarding the meaning of the sacred text that defined and continues to define the identity of that community in the theological, pastoral, and ethical realms? These are questions that apply not only to the Christian Scriptures but also to the Jewish and Muslim Scriptures as well as to any other sacred text, all of which are primarily meaningful for the faith community to which each is linked.

In Christian biblical studies, most scholars have been applying literary hermeneutical theory on the Bible for several centuries now. Although most of those scholars who call themselves Christian recognize divine involvement in the inspiration of the Bible, they nevertheless have been benefiting—to various degrees of success—from literary theory, in deriving constructive theological and practical meaning from the text. In Christian theological circles, it has become normal to read the Bible as literature before moving to any level of theologizing based on the text.[3]

In the Islamic world, such Western approaches are still regarded with a considerable degree of suspicion. Whereas, as we will see later in this book, some Muslim scholars have often been happy to make rather brash use of the findings of critical Bible scholars in order further to emphasize their suspicions regarding the reliability of the Judeo-Christian Scriptures, few have been willing to consider applying such approaches to the Qur'an, and those who have made this attempt—such as Nasr Hamed Abu Zayd—

3. See, for example, Leland Ryken, *How to Read the Bible as Literature* (Grand Rapids: Zondervan, 1985); Jeanie C. Crain, *Reading the Bible as Literature: An Introduction* (Cambridge: Polity, 2010); John B. Gabel, Charles B. Wheeler, et al., *The Bible as Literature: An Introduction*, 5th ed. (Oxford: Oxford University Press, 2005).

have been viewed at best with suspicion and at worst as unbelievers by many of their coreligionists.[4]

On a recent occasion, I attended a public lecture in Beirut whose title promised to treat the question of textual criticism as applied to sacred Scripture. Two clerics (a Christian and a Muslim) had been invited. After the Christian cleric gave a well-structured scholarly exposition of the dynamic between contemporary literary theory and biblical interpretation, we were served a short presentation by the Muslim cleric, who quickly set the context to his own presentation. After establishing the immutable principle of qur'anic *tanzīl* (God's "bringing down" or "dictation" of the qur'anic revelation on Muhammad), where the text of the Qur'an is viewed as the exact literal representation of a divine original revealed to Muhammad, he affirmed that any critical study of the Qur'an as literary text is illegitimate from an orthodox Islamic perspective. He went on to lay down the traditional Islamic principles of qur'anic interpretation that we will further examine in the next section. I know the Muslim lecturer very well and he is not a fundamentalist in ideology, but as a cleric he was not able to break away from the traditionalist approach to the Muslim sacred text and viewed modern literary theory as coming into clash with the dogma of qur'anic *tanzīl*. As far as he was concerned, submitting the Qur'an to critical literary scrutiny means admitting that some human agency was involved in the process of revelation. If that has become commonly accepted by Christians with regard to the inspiration of the Bible, it is not so for Muslims, who maintain the theory of dictation with regard to the revelation of the Qur'an.

It may appear as though qur'anic exegesis is an extremely static exercise, where the meaning of verses has been stratified and simply repeated from the beginning and over the centuries. But that is not the case, as is obvious from the immense corpus of *tafsīr* ("interpretation/exegesis") literature that developed over time. If one looks at the place of *tafsīr* within the overall corpus of Islamic religious sciences, it is clear that the pur-

4. See, for example, Nasr Hamed Abu Zayd, *Ishkāliyyāt al-Qirā'a wa Āliyyāt at-Ta'wīl* (Problems of Reading and Methods of Interpretation) (Casablanca/Beirut: al-Markaz ath-Thaqāfī al-ʿArabī, 1994); and Abu Zayd, *An-Naṣṣ, as-Sulṭa, al-Ḥaqīqa: al-Fikr ad-Dīnī bayna Irādat al-Maʿrifa wa Irādat al-Haymana* (Text, Authority, Truth: Religious Thought between the Desire for Knowledge and the Desire for Hegemony) (Casablanca/Beirut: al-Markaz ath-Thaqāfī al-ʿArabī, 1997). Abu Zayd was charged with apostasy in 1995 in front of the Egyptian Family Court and his marriage was annulled, and as a result he and his wife had to flee the country.

pose of qur'anic exegesis is primarily the practical life and behavior of the Muslim community. Indeed, it could be argued that the defining feature of Islam is the field of law (Sharīʿa). Jurisprudence (*fiqh*) is the science of deriving legal decisions from the Qur'an through the lens of tradition (*sunna*), which is the collection of sayings and deeds of Muhammad and his early companions that have been deemed authentic over the centuries. As such, *fiqh* is by nature very dynamic, as it needs to adapt to the ever-changing contexts of time and place.[5] As is the case with the Mosaic law, Islamic legal decisions, derived from the exercise of *fiqh*, fall into two broad categories: liturgical *ʿibādāt* and relational *muʿāmalāt*—respectively the prescriptions concerning how humans should relate to God and those concerning how humans should relate to each other. How such meaning is derived from the Qur'an and tradition for both worship and everyday life is complex and does not fit within the purpose of the present book. I have, however, developed a diagram (figure 2) that represents very simply the various elements used by Muslim scholars to move from qur'anic text to Islamic law—including the principles of consensus (*ijmāʿ*) and analogy (*qiyās*)—and how these various elements relate to one another. We will look particularly at some of the processes involved in the practice of *tafsīr* in the next section. The point to retain here, however, is that the locus of *meaning*, as concerns the Qur'an, emerges as belonging *within* the community of faith par excellence and, at least until the present day, it is not a text that is open to interpretation simply as a scientific exercise of literary analysis.

Some people may of course object to this and argue that it is their right to carry out qur'anic exegesis using modern critical methods and ignoring the boundaries set by the Muslim faith community. It is quite possible that they will be able to reach a very accurate and enlightening exegesis, but the question is, will it be legitimate? This is the question to which I turn to in the next two sections of the present chapter. What I call legitimate interpretation is the kind of interpretation that is admitted by the community of faith to which a sacred text belongs. Just as Christians consider it illegitimate for people of other faiths or sects (even groups within Christianity) to interpret the Bible without paying due attention to the various contexts of a passage, Muslims also consider it illegitimate for people of other faiths to interpret the Qur'an without paying due attention

5. An excellent recent work on this dynamic process is Rumee Ahmed's *Sharia Compliant: A User's Guide to Hacking Islamic Law* (Stanford: Stanford University Press, 2018).

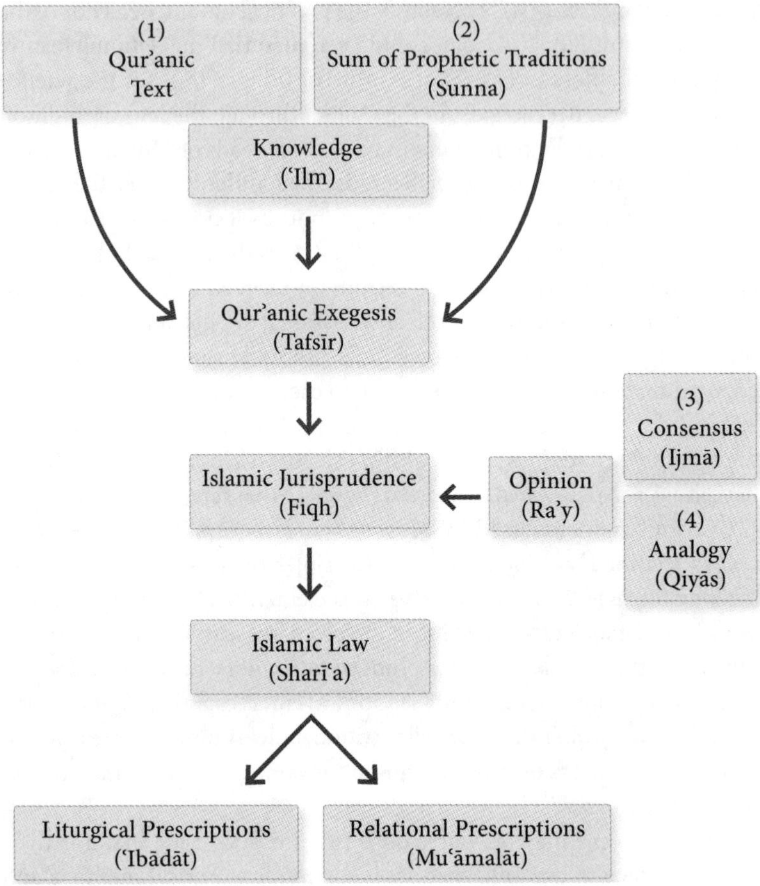

Figure 2. The Hermeneutical Emergence and Development of Islamic Jurisprudence (*Fiqh*)

to the various Islamic traditions that have accompanied the meaning and implications of the text through history.

The Legitimate Interpretation of the Qur'an

The purpose of the present section is to present the most important elements of Islamic *tafsīr* that have developed through history and continue to be viewed by Islam as the elements necessary to a correct and legitimate reading of the Qur'an. The reader will discover that these principles, though unfamiliar at first, are not impossible to come to grips with. And with some further exposure to Islamic *tafsīr*, many will discover that approaching the Qur'an in an Islamically legitimate way will help them establish their understanding of Islam on more solid ground, and as a result this will facilitate their communication with Muslims.

The role of Qur'anic exegesis is quite different from that of biblical exegesis for Christians. To some extent, Christians read their Bible primarily to learn how to be more faithful followers and disciples of Jesus. But especially since the Reformation, Bible reading has become very much a private exercise of devotion. Even in the Middle East today, where roughly until the middle of the twentieth century Eastern Christians were in many cases still prevented from accessing the biblical text for themselves, the Bible recently has become the focus of lay group and individual study. Even though Christian believers may have respect and interest for how other Christians have understood the text of the Bible over the centuries, they generally believe that it is their right—even responsibility—to understand the meaning and implication of the Bible for themselves today, and they rely on the agency of the Holy Spirit to assist them in the process, hopefully on good guidelines that they have learned through their community of faith. Of course, various traditions of Christianity have had their major thinkers and theologians who have written influential volumes on how to relate to God and neighbor based on the Bible, but no collection of legal prescriptions has resulted in a legal corpus that Christians are required to obey.

The case of Islam is very different. Because from very early on, the lifestyle of the Prophet of Islam became the model to be emulated by all Muslims, as paradigm for every age and place, the relationship of the Qur'an to the *sunna* became sealed. There would be little interest for Muslims in qur'anic *tafsīr* if it were not to derive theological and pragmatic teaching from the Qur'an. Even what Christians call theology, including the Five Pillars—the profession of faith (*shahāda*), prayer (*ṣalāt*), fasting (*ṣawm*), almsgiving (*zakāt*), and pilgrimage (*ḥajj*)—belong to the discipline of *fiqh* in Islam. Correct understanding and teaching about these is derived from the Qur'an through the eyes of tradition, and the outcome of such study is found in the great collections of Islamic jurisprudence.[6]

6. For a diagram representing the complex relationship between Qur'an, *Tafsīr*, *Sunna*, and Sharīʿa, through the sophisticated process of jurisprudence (*fiqh*), see figure 2.

Numerous Islamic commentary collections have made their way to us. Besides the more classical corpuses, such as those of aṭ-Ṭabarī (died 923), az-Zamakhsharī (died 1144), Ibn Kathīr (died 1373), ar-Rāzī (died 1209), al-Qurṭubī (died 1273), al-Bayḍāwī (died 1286?), and al-Jalālayn (lit., "the two Jalāls": Jalal ad-Dīn al-Maḥallī [died 1459] and Jalal ad-Dīn as-Suyūṭī [died 1505]), we also have more recent Sunnī ones, such as those of ash-Shaʿrāwī (died 1998) and aṭ-Ṭanṭāwī (died 2010). Important to a study of qur'anic exegesis is the reformist commentary of Rashīd Riḍa (died 1935), *Tafsīr al-Manār*, which is largely a compendium of exegetical traditions he received from his master, Muhammad ʿAbdo (died 1905), the central figure of Islamic reformism in the transition to the modern period. Indispensable as well is the commentary of Sayyid Quṭb (died 1966), *Fī Dhilāl al-Qur'ān*, with its unique political and social critique and agenda. On the other hand, we have a number of important Shīʿī commentaries, such as those of aṭ-Ṭabarṣī (died 1153) and aṭ-Ṭaba'ṭabā'ī (died 1981). Dozens of other commentaries exist, but the ones listed above are considered the most important, and they are the main ones consulted in the present book. The makeup of these commentaries is by no means uniform, but a number of principal elements in them may be regarded as the main tools of Islamic exegetical methodology. It goes without saying that the following exposition does not intend to be exhaustive or entirely comprehensive. It is simply a quick survey of the main elements of Islamic *tafsīr*, several of which will recur in the ensuing chapters.

Language and Grammar

The linguistic complexity of the Arabic Qur'an is such that it required of the interpreters a first stage of explanation of the language. Language and grammar (*al-lugha wa al-iʿrāb*) were also the first stage of interpretation in the classical Greek school system. Before moving to the moral, rhetorical, or philosophical interpretation of a text, the Greeks considered it crucial to establish the text linguistically and ensure the reliability of what was about to be interpreted. This method was adopted by early church fathers in their approach to the Bible, and the same feature is found in much of Islamic *tafsīr*, where the exegete (*mufassir*) starts by establishing the correct reading of the text before proceeding to its interpretation. This is all the more important in view of the place that memorization and chanting hold for students of the Qur'an. The main difference is that in the case of the Qur'an, not only was the text examined in light of established Arabic grammatical rules, but the text itself became the ultimate foundation of Arabic grammar.

The importance of grammatical analysis as the first stage of qur'anic *tafsīr* proves particularly important when we keep in mind that the earliest manuscripts of the Qur'an were transmitted in the *ḥijāzī* script of the seventh and eighth centuries, which contained neither diacritical points nor vocalization. The history of the textual transmission of the Qur'an is extremely complex and, from a modern text-critical perspective, still in its infancy. The normative reading, which is today largely taken for granted, is the result of a standardization of the printed text undertaken in Egypt under the patronage of King Fu'ād I in 1924. This version of the standard text is considered to be the transmission of a particular way of reading the Qur'an, referred to as that "of Ḥafṣ, of the reading of 'āṣim."[7] According to the classical Islamic account of the Qur'an's development, a major codification of the text took place on the order of the third caliph, 'Uthmān, who reigned 644–56. At the present stage in the study of the history of the qur'anic text, it is not possible to know the extent to which this canonical version reflected the Qur'an that circulated orally (and possibly partially in writing) during Muhammad's lifetime. Nor is it possible to know the shape of other authoritative versions that circulated among the companions after Muhammad's death, which the traditional narrative claims the 'Uthmānic recension came to replace after the third caliph destroyed all competing versions. The version we therefore currently have is only one out of numerous possible readings considered legitimate in Muslim history, deriving from 'Uthmān's text.[8]

Occasions of the Revelation

The "occasions of the revelation" (*asbāb an-nuzūl*) has been viewed as the single most important principle in classical qur'anic *tafsīr*. At first view, it has something in common with the historical-critical method,

7. Keith E. Small, *Textual Criticism and Qur'an Manuscripts* (Lanham: Lexington Books, 2011), Kindle location 3269.

8. For an excellent summary of what can currently be known from a text-critical perspective, see especially the concluding chapter of Small, *Textual Criticism*, Kindle locations 3089–3643.

which seeks to reconstitute the original historical context of an ancient text, seeking better to understand its primary intended audience, so that a more accurate original meaning of the text can be arrived at. The main difference is that in the case of historical criticism, the historical setting of a text is to a large extent derived from other elements within that text. So, for example, New Testament scholars acknowledge that with the epistolary genre, it is crucial to reconstruct the historical setting, so that we might understand and identify the issues that Paul was addressing through his letter. A letter by nature preserves only one side of a two-way conversation. The only way we can hope to understand the side that we have received as accurately as possible is to try to reconstruct what the other people in the conversation are saying, questions that they are asking, problems that they are posing and that need resolution, and so on. In order to help in this process, students of the New Testament will read the letter overall, extract information about the people, problems, questions, themes that can be inferred from the rest of the letter, including information about previous interaction that Paul had with these same people, and attitudes being expressed on both sides. In addition, we try to learn about the history and geography of the city or region, whose people are being addressed in the letter, through outside sources, which may help us understand some of the realities that the community in question was facing in everyday life. For this second stage, the New Testament student generally needs to make use of secondary material and existing commentaries, whereas in the first stage, any reader with a little guidance will be able and encouraged to undertake on their own, by paying careful attention to the details of the text.

Here is the fundamental difference with qur'anic *tafsīr*. The stages of interpretation of a Pauline epistle described above, though having to do with the reconstruction of a historical setting, in reality emphasize the importance of the literary context of any passage. For it is from the literary context, broad and narrow, that the normal reader will be able to draw much information that will enlighten a passage of Scripture. In the case of the Qur'an, the individual reader is not allowed to carry out this exercise. Instead, others have done this for them in the past, and they are required to make use of that data in their own reading. Because of the nature of the qur'anic text, which is to a large extent a collection of disconnected narrative accounts, encouragements, warnings, legal prescriptions, and so on, no information inferred from the surrounding literary context of a passage can be taken for granted as shedding light on a particular verse.

So, in the case of my experience narrated at the beginning of this chapter, I looked at the immediately preceding literary context of the verse that denies the crucifixion of Jesus, inferred that the denial related to the claim of the Jews that they had killed all of God's prophets, and then imposed on the text an interpretation that fits my own Christian assumptions, while at the same time making sense of the verse's denial by offering a couple of alternative solutions to its claim. From a biblical exegetical perspective, such alternative conclusions would be quite right, but from the perspective of Islamic qur'anic exegesis, every historical reconstruction of the context of a verse has to be supported by tradition, in this case *asbāb an-nuzūl.*

Muslim scholars claim a great deal of accuracy in reconstructing that historical setting. Every Ḥadīth tradition that they draw upon in support of *tafsīr* consists of two main parts: (1) the actual saying, called *matn*, and (2) the line of reporters that are supposed to have transmitted that saying, called *isnād*. Every saying going back to the time of Muhammad and his early companions, which shed light on a qur'anic passage, will need to be supported by a reliable *isnād*. In theory, that sounds like a solid process. The problem is that, as many Western scholars point out, *isnād* seems to have developed considerably especially during the second and third centuries of Islam.[9] Critical Western scholars observe, for instance, that in their earliest occurrences, many *aḥādīth* (plural of Ḥadīth) ascribed to Muhammad stand alone as *matn* without *isnād*. Whereas later *aḥādīth* reflect a sort of obsession with *isnād*, incidentally at a time when it became assumed that a traditional saying without a reliable chain of transmitters carried no authority. The tens of thousands of traditions that were collected, especially in the course of the ninth century (second/third century of Islam), by the six collections considered reliable (al-Bukhārī, Muslim Ibn al-Hajjāj, Ibn Mājā, Abū Dāwūd, at-Tirmidhī, and an-Nasā'ī) reflect this tendency of *isnād* to "grow backward."

In addition, many individual traditions reflect the attempt to support one side or another of a dispute taking place in the ninth century and would have been clearly anachronistic in the first decades of Islam. The following example illustrates quite well this tendency of Ḥadīth to justify its foundations of authenticity by fabricating traditions. At the same time, it offers a good model of the structure of Ḥadīth for those unfamiliar with

9. On this problem, see especially Ignaz Goldziher, *Muslim Studies*, 2 vols. (London: Allen & Unwin, 1971 [originally 1890]); and Joseph Schacht, *The Origins of Muhammadan Jurisprudence* (Oxford: Clarendon, 1950).

the genre (the *isnād* ["line of transmission"] is in regular font and the *matn* ["prophetic saying"] is in italic):

> Abū Bakr Ibn abī Shayba told us that Ghundār told him, on the authority of Shuʿba, and also that Muhammad Ibn al-Muthannā and Ibn Bashshār told him, that Muhammad Ibn Jaʿfar told him, that Shuʿba also told him, on the authority of Manṣūr, on the authority of Ribʿī Ibn Hirāsh, who heard ʿAlī, may God be pleased with him, giving a sermon in which he said that the messenger of God, may the prayers and peace of God be upon him, said, "*Do not spread lies about me! Whoever spreads lies regarding me will enter the fires of hell.*"[10]

It would be logical to infer that the above Ḥadīth was itself fabricated, since it would make little sense for Muhammad to have preempted the fabrication of his sayings during his own lifetime, when there would have been no reason to do so. Although students of Islam need to be aware of this problem with regard to Ḥadīth material, it still remains that the entire *tafsīr* literature relies on *asbāb an-nuzūl* for the reconstruction of the original historical settings that gave occasion to the qur'anic revelations. For the most part, these reconstructions offer interesting information about the Islamically accepted occasion, or reason, for the revelation of a certain verse or chapter (sūrah) in the Qur'an. But their historical reliability is, to say the least, questionable. Nevertheless, given that these are considered by Muslims to be the necessary starting point of *tafsīr*, they also become the principal legitimate starting point for Christian-Muslim interaction on qur'anic questions.

A final issue derived directly from *asbāb an-nuzūl* is the question of the provenance of each sūrah, and often of various verses within a certain sūrah. Muslim exegetes, most of the time, begin their interpretation of a sūrah or verse with a discussion of whether the passage was revealed while Islam's messenger was in Mecca (*makkiyya*) or Medina (*madaniyya*) after the migration (*hijra*) of Muhammad and his early companions from Mecca to Medina. As will be seen later, the Meccan or Medinan provenance of a sūrah has considerable impact on its tone and message, which is important for our understanding of the diversity within Islam. Within the second period in the life of Muhammad, exegetes often differenti-

10. Citation from Rippin, *Muslims*, 47 (emphasis added). A short but good summary of this problem in Ḥadīth literature can be found at 46–48.

ate between early Medinan verse and later Medinan verse, as reflecting rapidly changing circumstances in the life of the early Muslim community during that period. Finally, it should be said that there is no general consensus between Muslim scholars with regard to the "occasions of the revelation." Different scholars and interpreters select different traditions to set the historical context of a verse or passage, and each favors a particular account over others.

Interpretation Proper

The next section, often entitled *al-maʿna* ("meaning") in a qur'anic commentary, is usually the longest section in the exegesis of a passage. It can consist of a verse-by-verse exposition of the meaning of the text or the interpretation of an entire cluster or pericope of verses. *Tafsīr al-maʿna* will make use of any helpful information derived from the grammatical exposition and from the explanation of the occasions of the revelation. Here a commentator generally transmits exegetical material from predecessors, often in massive cumulative amounts, before stating his agreement with one particular existing opinion. These sections elaborate on narrative passages by bringing in information from other sources, the expression of legal opinions both personal and from different legal schools, dealing with difficulties and obscure readings, and any other elucidating material.

Stories of the Prophets and the Biography of Muhammad

The elucidation of narrative passages in the Qur'an often draws from parallels in non-Islamic sources. The Qur'an often seems to assume that its reader is familiar with much of the Judeo-Christian scriptural tradition, in addition to other traditions that were specific to the Arabian context. Qur'anic narratives about biblical prophets are usually recorded outside their original literary context. They are brief and sketchy, and when it comes to important characters such as Abraham, Moses, or Jesus, the Qur'an can be quite repetitive, as different portions of their lives are dispersed across different sūrahs. In order to remedy for the gaps created by this literary style, qur'anic exegetes had to make considerable use of narrative reconstruction. Independent narratives—told and transmitted by well-known storytellers (*quṣṣāṣ*)—about the lives of various prophets circulated from very early on within the Islamic community. These often contained popular and apocryphal material, reflecting an oral transmission rather than the canonical text of the Bible. Especially in the early commentaries, these versions of the stories of the prophets (*qiṣaṣ al-anbiyā'*) are primarily used in *tafsīr*.

In addition to *qiṣaṣ al-anbiyā'*, the other material often used in *tafsīr* is various events from the life of Muhammad, drawn particularly from *As-Sīra an-Nabawiyya* (The Biography of the Prophet) of Ibn Isḥāq, as transmitted by Ibn Hishām. Both the lives of the Prophet of Islam and those of the biblical prophets are viewed as an important paradigm of pious life, which is to be emulated by Muslims everywhere and in every generation.

Identification of the Obscure

Again, due to the often-eclectic genre of the Qur'an and the assumptions it often seems to make about the background knowledge of its readers, many places and people's names quickly became obscure as Islam spread outside of the Arabian Peninsula and further away from the Judeo-Christian context. It took only a few decades for Islam to spread westward to North Africa and Spain and further east into the Persian Empire and beyond. The exegetes realized that data in the Qur'an was familiar to the Arab reader but obscure to the non-Arab. This is what became known as "identification of the obscure" (*ta'yīn al-mubham*). It consisted particularly in the identification of unfamiliar places and people, as well as *tafsīr gharīb al-Qur'an*: "the explanation of the difficulties [or unfamiliar elements] of the Qur'an," information that would have no longer been familiar to later generations of Muslims.

The Theory of Abrogation

One more important issue needs to be discussed in relation to qur'anic *tafsīr*, that is the famous—and often infamous nowadays—theory of abrogation. This is an issue that many politically motivated non-Muslims have abused especially since 9/11. The "theory of abrogation" (*an-nāsikh wa al-mansūkh*) is a Muslim principle of qur'anic exegesis used by the *mufassirīn* over the centuries as a tool to help resolve emerging contradictions between verses of the Qur'an. The principle dictates that if two verses seem to contain contradictory statements, the verse that was revealed later chronologically is considered to "abrogate"—that is to cancel, correct, or replace—the earlier revelation. The relationship between this principle and the "occasions of the revelation" (*asbāb an-nuzūl*) is immediately obvious. The method used to decide which verse was revealed later chronologically is precisely the specific occasion of its revelation. The principle of abrogation is inferred from the Qur'an itself:

> Yet, whenever we sent a messenger or a prophet ahead of you, and he was hoping [that his warning would be heeded], Satan would cast [doubt] on his hopes. But God destroys that which Satan insinuates, and God confirms his messages, for God is all knowing and all wise. He makes what Satan spews forth a temptation only to those whose hearts are sick or hardened—surely the unjust are profoundly opposed to the truth. (al-Ḥajj 22:52–53)

The word "destroys" in Kaskas's translation reflects the Arabic *yansakhu* (hence *an-nāsikh wa al-mansūkh*—"the canceller and the cancelled"). What the verse is saying is that Satan has always been at work to inspire messengers with words that are not from God, but that God ensures that none of these insertions remain without correction. Al-Ḥajj 22:53 asserts that such "satanic verses" will in fact remain in the text as a test for "those whose hearts are sick or hardened," but that other verses will be also there to be heard by the believers, which will correct the verses that are not from God. One famous example of a passage inspired by Satan, which has been preserved and transmitted in the Islamic tradition, though not in the Qur'an in its current form, is the so-called satanic verses connected to an-Najm 53:19–23:

> So have you considered al-Lat and al-'Uzza? And Manat, the third, the other one? Why do you choose for yourself male offspring and assign to God the female? That, then, is an unfair distribution. These [allegedly divine beings] are nothing but names, which you [who worship them] and your forefathers have invented. God sent no authority for them. They [who worship them] follow nothing but guesswork and their egotistical whims, although guidance has come to them [your people] from their Lord.

In his commentary, az-Zamakhsharī conveys the following "occasion of the revelation" in al-Ḥajj 22:52–53, cited above:

> As the members of the tribe of the messenger of God turned away from him and took their stand in opposition to him, and as his relatives also opposed him and refused to be guided by what he brought to them, then, as a result of extreme exasperation over their estrangement, and of the eager desire and longing that they be converted to Islam, the messenger of God hoped that nothing would be revealed to him that would make them shy away. . . . Now this wish persisted until the sūrah called "The Star" [Sūrat an-Najm 53] came down. At that time he [still] found himself with that hope in his heart regarding the members of his tribe. Then he began to recite [53:19–23 are cited here].
>
> When, however, he came to God's words "And Manat, the third, the other," Satan substituted something else conformable to the wish that the messenger of God had been harboring, that is, he whispered something to him which would enable the messenger to fulfill his wish. In an inadvertent and misleading manner his tongue hurried on ahead of him, so that he said: "These [goddesses] are exalted cranes. Their intercession [with God] is to be hoped for. . . ." Yet the messenger of God was not clear at this point until the protection [of God] reached him and he became attentive again.[11]

It is quite striking that the Islamic tradition preserved such an account, that on an occasion when Muhammad was desperate for his tribe to accept his message, he allowed Satan to interfere in the revelation and made a compromise by allowing the polytheist members of his tribe to preserve their goddesses as intercessors between them and God. This satanic version of the verse, however, did not eventually make it into the Qur'an and, according to tradition, was set straight after the angel Gabriel pointed out the error to the messenger. Whether the tradition of the satanic verses was itself a fabrication in order to support the principle of *an-nāsikh wa al-mansūkh*, or whether the account is the historically reliable occasion for the revelation of the abrogation principle of Sūrat al-Ḥajj 22, it is impossible to say for sure. But the result is the same, and the solution that the *tafsīr* tradition of Islam chose in order to resolve contradictory verses in the Qur'an is that principle of abrogation. As with the case of *asbāb an-nuzūl*, there

11. Translation from F. E. Peters, ed., *A Reader on Classical Islam* (Princeton: Princeton University Press, 1994), 177–78.

is no general consensus between Muslim scholars and exegetes with regard to which verses are abrogated.

An Argument against the Claim of Medinan Abrogation

The principle of abrogation has often been misused. A number of non-Muslim writers on Islam these days try to paint a very negative picture of Islam as a purely violent religion. Moderate Muslims object by saying that the Qur'an calls for peace and moderation. The truth is that the Qur'an contains both, verses that call for moderation and verses that call for violence. (I treat this problem more extensively in chapters 8 and 10.) The problem, which anti-Islamic voices are quick to point out, is that most of the violent verses in the Qur'an are found in the sections that *asbāb an-nuzūl* places in the later Medinan period of the qur'anic revelation. Based on the principle of abrogation, therefore, those who wish to serve a polemical agenda point out that all the peaceful verses of the Meccan and early Medinan periods, which call for moderation, have been abrogated by the later verses that call Muslims to violence and *jihād*. This, however, is a brash oversimplification of the matter.

The two hermeneutical principles of *asbāb an-nuzūl* and *an-nāsikh wa al-mansūkh* form, in fact, what is termed in biblical hermeneutics a "hermeneutical circle." But a third hermeneutical principle is often brought into this circle, which Muslim exegetes refer to as *al-ʿām wa al-khāṣṣ* ("the universal and the particular"). According to these three principles, when Muslim commentators come across two verses or passages in the Qur'an that stand in (apparent) contradiction—for example, one that calls to nonviolence and the other that seems to legitimize violence—they first study the occasion of each verse's revelation. They do this for a dual purpose: to establish their chronology and to establish whether elements in the historical setting justify considering one or both of the verses as being historically relative. If the violent verse is viewed by a commentator as being historically relative, then they consider that the peaceful verse abrogates the violent one, the qur'anic call to peace being, in this view, a universal principle. This is what moderate Muslim scholars often do. If, on the other hand, a radical Muslim wishes to ignore the possibility that the implication of some verses might be limited to a specific past history and context, then they can easily draw the conclusion, based on chronology alone, that the violent verse abrogates the peaceful one. I argue that we must strive for an understanding of qur'anic exegesis that takes seriously the complexities of hermeneutics. Should we not listen to the moderate voices of Islam, and encourage the school of thought that calls for a peaceful Islam, rather than succumb to the narrative of Muslim extremists who are always looking for ways that legitimize their violent interpretation of Islam?

Tradition versus Opinion

Historically there has been a tension within Islam between "interpretation according to tradition" (*at-tafsīr bi al-ma'thūr*) and "interpretation according to opinion" (*at-tafsīr bi ar-ra'y*). The controversy between tradition and reason in Islam was, for many centuries, considered a matter of the past—an ancient controversy between the *Muʿtazilī* current and Sunnī Islam. However, it came back to prominence about a century ago in the context of Islam's rich and diverse attempts to come to terms with modernity. The *Muʿtazilī*, who reached the peak of their influence under two ʿAbbāsid caliphs of Baghdād during the ninth century, remained influential for several centuries even after they lost official power. They called for a rational interpretation of the Qur'an (Arabic *ijtihād*, "rational effort"). The approach was based on the doctrinal belief that the Qur'an was created, whereas the view that eventually won the day and became orthodoxy is that the Qur'an is eternal or uncreated. From the latter perspective, the words revealed to Muhammad were dictated by the angel Gabriel from the original Qur'an, preserved in heaven as God's eternal word.

Another feature of *Muʿtazilī* thinking was the theological belief in human free will. Eventually, however, in this sphere as well, the orthodox Sunnī belief in radical predestination won the day and is today the standard view. As pointed out earlier, qur'anic *tafsīr* has yet to come to terms more seriously with the historical-critical method and with the various theories of literary criticism that have developed over the past couple of centuries outside the Muslim world. Where such theories have had an impact, this has led some Muslim scholars to venture back into *at-tafsīr bi ar-ra'y*. The continuing interaction between these two currents needs to be followed closely, but it is primarily an intra-Muslim dynamic. As far as Christians are concerned, or for that matter anyone else interested in entertaining a healthy dialogue with Islam, we need to become familiar with the accepted principles of qur'anic interpretation primarily and make use of them when we use the Qur'an in our interaction with Islam and Muslims. In order for one's discourse to be heard, it needs to be viewed as a legitimate discourse by the person whose listening ear one hopes to capture.

Legitimate Christian Interpretation of the Qur'an

A legitimate approach to the Islamic text does not necessarily mean that one needs to accept the traditional conclusions of Islam with regard to a specific issue. But it does require that we adopt the Islamic method in using the tradition in qur'anic exegesis, even if we reach unconventional conclusions. Quite often, we will discover that the Islamic tradition is so rich in narrative options that finding a common starting point for constructive dialogue is not as difficult as Christians and Muslims often assume in today's conflictual reality.

On both the Trinity and the crucifixion, two articles written by Joseph Cumming exemplify very well the approach that I advocate.[12] Cumming seeks to promote better understanding between Christians and Muslims by showing how they might have misunderstood each other through history. He engages in no denial of history. On the contrary, his assumption seems to be that perhaps the contemporary relational context offers a better chance for Christians and Muslims to listen to each other's thinking with greater openness.

On the doctrine of the Trinity, he demonstrates that in the standard Sunnī understanding of God's "attributes of essence" (*sifāt adh-dhāt*), as elaborated particularly in the writings of Abū al-Ḥasan al-Ashʿarī (died 935), one of the most respected figures of Sunnī Islam, one can find an understanding that is very close to the Christian understanding of the three divine hypostases of Father, Son, and Holy Spirit. As Cumming rightly points out, this parallel is by no means new, as it had already been discussed by brilliant Arab Christian theologians of the medieval period. But perhaps the fourteen centuries of history that separate us from the

12. Joseph L. Cumming, "Ṣifāt al-Dhāt in al-Ashʿarī's Doctrine of God and Possible Christian Parallels" (May 2001); and Cumming, "Did Jesus Die on the Cross? The History of Reflection on the End of His Earthly Life in Sunnī Tafsīr Literature" (May 2001). Both articles available online at faith.yale.edu/reconciliation-project/resources (accessed January 3, 2017).

beginnings of Christian-Muslim interaction might allow us to capitalize in new ways on these points of agreement.

On the crucifixion, Cumming illustrates very convincingly that the wholesale rejection of Jesus's crucifixion by most Muslims today is by no means justified in light of the Islamic *tafsīr* tradition. Based precisely on that tradition, there is ample room for Muslims today to admit the historicity of Jesus's crucifixion. What should be the topic of exchange and dialogue between Christians and Muslims today is not whether the crucifixion occurred, but rather the *significance* of this death on the cross and its connection to salvation.

He concludes his article on the Trinity by stating: "I think, though, that a deeper analysis of both doctrines shows that they are much closer to one another than is commonly supposed."[13] In his article on the crucifixion he concludes: "Among the varied answers which Muslims have given through the centuries, I believe that there is much more room to find common ground with Christians than is generally supposed by either Muslims or Christians today."[14] In some ways, Cumming reaches similar conclusions as Fouad Accad (my grandfather) with regard to both the Trinity and the crucifixion. But his approach is now more legitimate from an Islamic point of view because he draws heavily on Islamic sources—both Qur'an and tradition—to demonstrate this closeness in doctrinal thinking.

In my 2003 article on *taḥrīf*, I took a very similar approach to Cumming's with regard to the Muslim accusation that Jews and Christians have corrupted their Scriptures. Drawing from over a dozen respected Muslim theologians of different theological and intellectual convictions, from the seventh to the fourteenth centuries, I argued that the Muslim accusation was, up to the eleventh century, almost exclusively one of misinterpretation (*taḥrīf al-maʿna*, "corruption of meaning") rather than an accusation of textual falsification (*tahrīf al-lafẓ*, "corruption of text").[15] Through this survey, my purpose was to offer alternatives to the current deadlock on the issue, which can be used in today's Christian-Muslim dialogue. Abdullah Saeed came to the same conclusion by surveying primarily the exegetical

13. Cumming, "Ṣifāt al-Dhāt in al-Ashʿarī's Doctrine of God," 52.

14. Cumming, "Did Jesus Die on the Cross?" 35.

15. Martin Accad, "Corruption and/or Misinterpretation of the Bible: The Story of the Islamic Usage of Taḥrīf," *Near East School of Theology Theological Review* 24.2 (2003): 67–97.

tafsīr literature of the Islamic tradition.[16] Others before Saeed and myself had already pointed out that the eleventh century marked a turning point on this issue, but no extensive study had been done up to that point.[17] In chapter 7 below, which is dedicated to the question of *tahrīf*, I present an even more exhaustive study of this question, based both on Islamic *tafsīr* and on the dialogue literature of the seventh to the fourteenth centuries. The present book is an attempt to reapply this methodology to a number of other key doctrinal issues.

The Importance of Context

Grant Osborne, a Christian scholar of biblical hermeneutics, affirms in his book *The Hermeneutical Spiral*: "I tell my classes that if anyone is half asleep and does not hear a question that I ask, there is a fifty per cent chance of being correct if he or she answers 'context.'"[18] This statement is an excellent reflection on the crucial importance of context in our understanding and interpretation of the biblical text. It is impossible for us to understand words and phrases outside their literary, intellectual, and logical contexts. Anyone with some experience in the study of the Bible knows very well that the interpreter ignores that fundamental principle at his or her own risk, exposing the text, the reader, and the broader receiving community of the biblical message to the dangers of doctrinal fallacy. Examples of this type of error are not lacking in Christian history. For example, some taught marriage abstinence for all Christians, based on the recommendation of the apostle Paul in his first letter to the Corinthians: "It is good for a man not to marry" (1 Cor 7:1), or his other saying: "Are you unmarried? Do not look for a wife" (7:27). Standard commentaries on 1 Corinthians point to the historical context of the time as a key to understanding these verses. Once we learn that the city of Corinth went through several famines during the same period that Paul was writing, then we can better understand the apostle's concern for the additional burden that marriage would have placed on a man

16. Abdullah Saeed, "The Charge of Distortion of Jewish and Christian Scriptures," *Muslim World* 92 (Fall 2002): 419–36.

17. See, for example, Thomas Michel, *A Muslim Theologian's Response to Christianity* (Tehran: Caravan, 1985), esp. 89–90.

18. Grant R. Osborne, *The Hermeneutical Spiral* (Downers Grove, IL: InterVarsity Press, 1991), 21.

called to provide for his family. With that contextual knowledge, we then understand why Paul says a few verses later: "I would like you to be free from concern" (7:32).

On a different topic, some classical sources report that one church father, Origen, castrated himself, based on Jesus's words in the Gospel of Matthew that some "have made themselves eunuchs for the kingdom of heaven's sake" (Matt 19:12, King James Version). The report is not entirely reliable, as its provenance is polemical, since Origen was later considered heretical especially due to his Neoplatonic views about the eternity of souls. The point remains, however, that a more accurate translation of the Matthean passage, such as the one found in the New International Version, which pays closer attention to the literary context of Jesus's teaching in that verse, reads, "Others have renounced marriage because of the kingdom of heaven." We know that the church, throughout its history, opposed such extreme teaching, and we thus find among some of the church fathers a more balanced teaching concerning these issues based on an interpretation that pays greater attention to contexts.

I draw the relationship of the various contexts to each other in figure 3. The fixed point of reference for any reader of the Bible in every age is the text of the Bible itself. Bible scholars attempt to draw up a theology of each book of the Bible and as a result we can properly speak, for example, of a theology of the Psalms or a theology of the book of Job or of a Matthean, Johannine, or Pauline theology. Out of these various views emerges a biblical theology of the entire canon. Dogmatic theologians then seek to systematize all these views in what is referred to as systematic theology, and neither biblical nor dogmatic theologians ever escape the influence of contemporary philosophical thinking on their own analysis of the biblical text. Finally, I place Christian praxis at the center of figure 3 to indicate that all of this hermeneutical operation in the end of the day affects our practice of biblical faith, and that praxis in turn has a major influence on all of our hermeneutical endeavor.

Interpretation and the Emergence of Doctrine

Many a doctrinal battle was fought by the early church against theological currents that were thought to be extreme and not faithfully reflecting the biblical witness as a whole. Based on a narrow interpretation of select Bible passages, for example, Adoptionism taught that God adopted Jesus

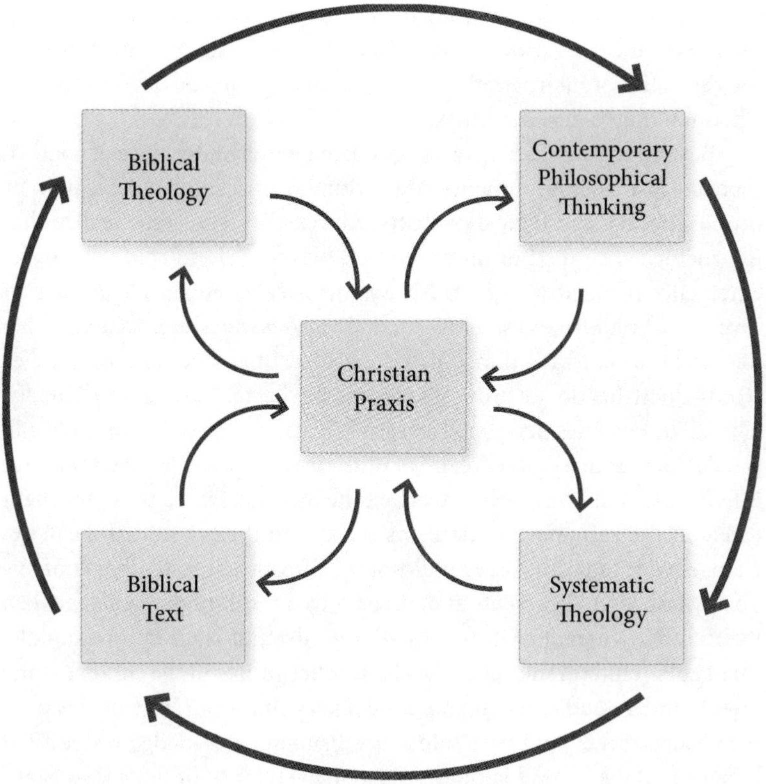

Figure 3. The Hermeneutical Emergence and Development of Christian Thought and Praxis

as his Son only at the point of his baptism. Docetists taught that Christ only in appearance suffered at the cross, since God cannot really suffer. Arians, and with the same logic of the impossibility of divine suffering, taught that Jesus was a supreme angelic being but not God. Donatists taught that a member of clergy who rendered himself impure by denying the faith under persecution could not be readmitted into the clergy, as he would render the whole mass invalid. All of these examples—and one could give many more—demonstrate how a biased reading of certain biblical passages can lead to incorrect theology with regard to the doctrine of God, Christ, salvation, and other fundamental Christian doctrines. In each case, church fathers countered such doctrines by referring the biblical passages to their narrower and broader logical contexts and to their literary contexts both immediate and broader. Besides emphasizing the importance of various contexts, these simple examples demonstrate the centrality of interpretation, or hermeneutics, in the development of Christian theological doctrines.

Beyond these negative warnings related to the importance of context, there are also positive dimensions resulting from a study of texts in their proper literary and logical contexts. Above all, we need to realize that the rhetorical context of interpretation played a significant role in the emergence of Christian doctrines. By rhetorical context I mean the rich diversity of philosophies, religions, and various literatures that combine to create the context within which the history of ideas develops. In other words, doctrines do not grow out of some intellectual vacuum. Originally, Christian doctrines developed as early Christians related to the cultural, intellectual, and religious realities of their societies. We may therefore infer that Christian doctrines reached the forms in which we know them today, at the primary level, only as a result of the broad dialogical exchanges with Judaism, Greek philosophy, Gnosticism, and other contemporary intellectual currents and, second, as a result of dialogue between the different currents within Christianity itself. It is clear, for example, that Paul's reinterpretation of the Hebrew Scriptures in the context of the Jewish understanding of them played a very important role in this doctrinal development. It is also safe to say, from our knowledge of doctrinal history, that the Greek Platonic philosophical understanding of God's absolute oneness on the one hand and the more popular Greek polytheistic views on the other, with their developments in the Arian interpretation of certain passages, had an important influence on the Christian expression of the doctrine of God and the incarnation. Since the present book is not a work on doctrinal history, I will not go into further details beyond the principles just laid out. But these principles form the foundation of much of what is pursued in this book.

Historical Context

The influence of contemporary thinking on the formation of any idea in any age cannot be overemphasized. This assumption is the starting point of the present book. Just as the worlds of Jewish absolute monotheism and Greek polytheism were the two pressure points at either end of the spectrum within which Christianity originally found and defined its theological expression, the way that Islam and Muslims viewed the Bible and Christian doctrines from the seventh century onward created the matrix within which Arab Christianity defined and expressed itself, beginning at that period in history. Because the Muslim culture is a fairly traditional culture, especially when it comes to approaching sacred Scripture, this history should form the fundamental context of a Christian interpretation of the biblical text even today. This rhetorical context is also the context from which all of our hermeneutics, theology, and praxis should emerge. And since today we are all living in a postmodern, multicultural, and multireligious global world, this rhetorical context should also become an important basis for the construction of contemporary theological thinking whether in the Middle East or in the rest of the world. Rather than allowing this context subconsciously and negatively to shape a reactionary theology and behavior, I call for a positive and proactive approach constructed out of a conscious awareness of this rich history of dialogical interaction.

Sacred Misinterpretation and the Emergence of Religious Monologue

Our first question, therefore, is: How did Muslim thinkers use the Bible during the main centuries of Muslim-Christian interaction, that is, between the seventh and fourteenth centuries? In order to examine that question, I focus our attention on their interpretation of the Gospels only, not of the whole Bible, and that for several reasons. First, it is simply necessary to limit our quest within the space available. Second, Muslim writers focused their attention particularly on the four Gospels in their interactions with Christians, and therefore our attention to their treatment of the Gospel text is a sufficient representative of their approach to the biblical text in general. And third, since our purpose is to construct the rhetorical context for a contemporary Christian theological discourse, characterized by an awareness of Christian-Muslim realities, it is only natural that we focus on the Gospels, since they are the foundation of Christian doctrine.

I examined two dozen texts written by over twenty-one Muslim writers between the seventh and the fourteenth centuries.[19] What is immedi-

19. An inventory of my findings can be found in "The Gospels in the Muslim Dis-

ately striking is the vast number of citations that the Muslim authors refer to from the four Gospels alone. I gathered approximately thirteen hundred Gospel citations, each of which consists of between one and twenty verses, and examined the way that Muslims approached and used these texts. Our first expectation would be to find in these Muslim interpretations a reflection of the disputes that are widespread today, such as the accusation of *taḥrīf*, or the rejection of Christ's crucifixion, or the favorite contemporary claim that the Gospel references to the Paraclete in the Johannine passages about the Holy Spirit are a testimony to the Prophet of Islam. The reality, however, is quite different. In spite of these themes featuring in the classical discourse, we find that the Muslim writers display in their study of the Gospels a much broader thematic creativity, be it by simply drawing from the text objective historical information, all the way to much more subjective disputative allegations. Some of these themes approach the Gospels with an impressively objective scientific approach, while others approach it with a pure disputative tone and purpose, often forcing bits of text out of their literary contexts. I want to emphasize, however, that the disputative tone was in no way the most widespread in that past. On the contrary, the aggressive logic that we often find today in Muslim writings that claim to belong to the genre of comparative religions (*muqāranat al-adyān*) is in fact quite far from the tone of most of the classical texts that I studied.

As a Christian theologian, I seek to avoid any apologetic or polemical tone in my own study. What is striking, however, is that we Muslims and Christians tend to read each other's sacred texts in the exact way that we do not wish our own Scriptures to be read. This is a crucial issue. The fundamental Islamic principle of qur'anic exegesis is that the meaning of the text should always find justification from traditional precedent, from the *sunna* and earlier *tafsīr*, not from personal intellectual effort (*ijtihād*). On the other hand, I strongly affirm the importance of contexts, and particularly the literary context in the interpretation of any biblical passage. That is how each of the two communities arrives at what it considers to be the legitimate interpretation of its texts. The problem arises when, as Christians, we read qur'anic verses in their literary context and interpret them as we would the Bible, bringing the

---

course of the Ninth to the Fourteenth Centuries: An Exegetical Inventorial Table (Parts I–IV)," *Journal of Islam and Christian-Muslim Relations* 14 (2003): 14.1: 67–91, 14.2: 205–20, 14.3: 337–52, 14.4: 459–79.

Qur'an in line with Christian thinking. With this approach, some of us are able to demonstrate that the Qur'an affirms the Trinity, the divinity of Jesus, and the reality of the crucifixion. On the other hand, Christian exegetes have a word for the Islamic approach to the Bible, which theology students are taught to avoid very early on in their studies—proof-texting. This approach consists in starting from a preconceived idea and then searching for those verses that confirm our position, ignoring that Christian biblical interpretation pays primary attention to literary context. As well intentioned as anyone from either of the two communities might be, they end up with meanings that are considered illegitimate by the other community.

Figure 4 diagrams the striking feature observed in Christians reading qur'anic verses in their literary context as they are taught to do with the Bible, and Muslims reading biblical verses outside their literary context as they are taught to do with the Qur'an. When teaching Islam in Christian institutions, it should be minimum courtesy that Christian professors teach their students to read and understand the Qur'an according to the hermeneutical principles that Muslims use to approach it. If Muslim teachers and writers also, and all Muslims for that matter, tried to read and interpret the Bible the way that Christians approach it, primarily in its literary context, then again both communities would have a much more serious platform on which to make progress in dialoguing and relating with one another. And if we both fail, we will at least have tried, and in the process, we will have gained more respect for one another, which is what our modern complex world desperately needs.

To summarize, interpretation is central to the development of any theological discourse. Sacred texts do not emerge from a vacuum, nor do they live in a vacuum. They emerge from and within a community, and their interpretation lies primarily with that community. Mere assumptions about how the sacred texts of others are to be read lead to two religious discourses that never meet: religious monologue, plain and simple. It is only by learning and applying the principles that each community considers as legitimate when approaching their sacred text that interfaith dialogue can hope to be fruitful and eventually help to break out from the grasp of agelong conflicts.

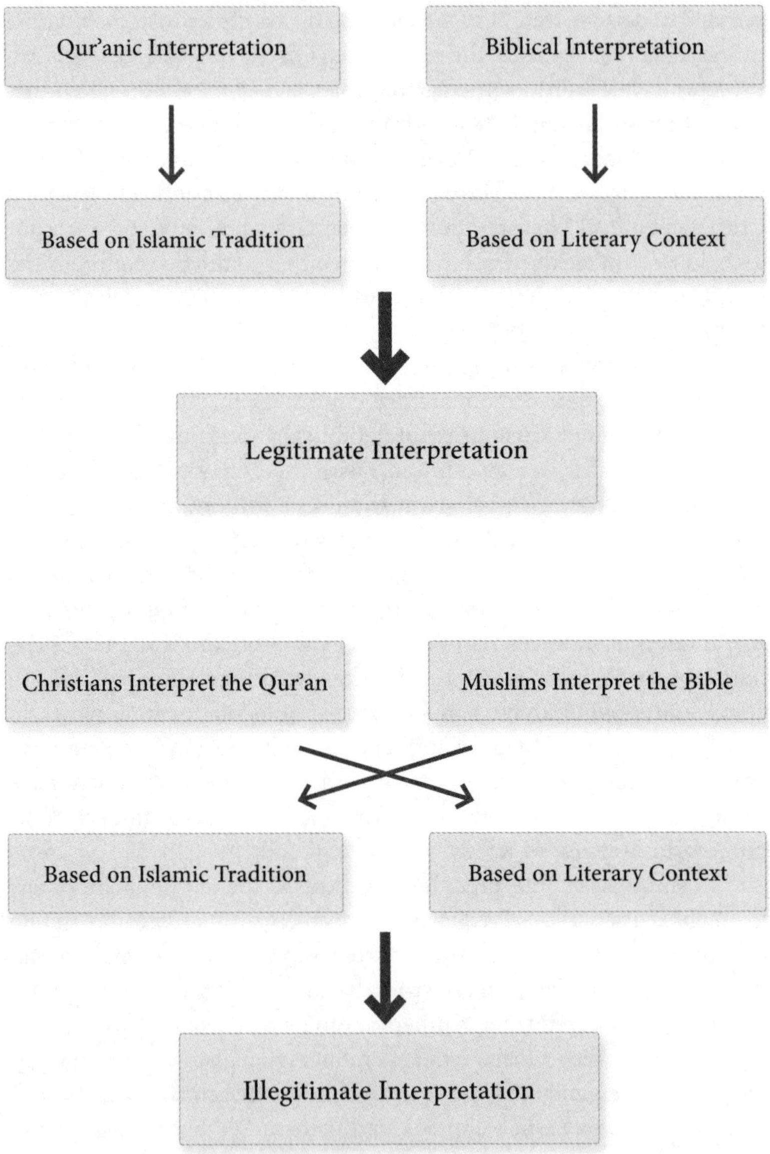

Figure 4. Interpretation and Misinterpretation

Establishing a Hermeneutical Method for Christian-Muslim Theological Dialogue

Having labored to establish some of the fundamental differences between Muslim exegesis of the Qur'an and Christian exegesis of the Bible, I propose a new hermeneutical method for Christians engaged in theological dialogue with Muslims. This is the methodology I employ throughout the remaining chapters of this book. It consists first in establishing the rhetorical context of the Muslim-Christian discourse on a particular doctrinal issue, by discovering the way that specific passages from the Gospels have been understood and used by Muslim theologians over the centuries. This is done by journeying through two kinds of literature; first the *tafsīr* literature written by Muslims primarily for consumption by Muslims, and second the dialectical literature written by Muslims in dialogue with Christian ideas, both to teach Muslims how to think about Christian theology and to refute and correct Christians in their theological convictions. Through the exploration of this Muslim historical rhetorical context, Christians today can begin to develop a new theological discourse that may help both our communities to break out of some of the persisting deadlocks of history.

The Promise of Hermeneutics in Christian-Muslim Dialogue

Historically, much of the Christian-Muslim theological discourse moved around in circles for many centuries. The result is that, today, Christians and Muslims often prefer to stay away from doctrinal conversations in their engagement. I have participated in numerous dialogue initiatives that have usually preferred to avoid theology and focus instead on coexistence and the "dialogue of life." These are absolutely crucial in helping us build community cohesion and good neighborliness in the multicultural and multifaith societies of the twenty-first century. But they can go only so far in reducing our prejudices and quite often unspoken suspicions and negative assumptions about each other.

I personally long for opportunities where Christian and Muslim theologians will establish long-term roundtables of dialogue on theological issues that will help reduce the gap between our presuppositions with regard to one another's theologies and core beliefs. The dialogue of life will help a Muslim be more tolerant toward a Christian because of the love and friendship that will develop between them, but Muslims will remain largely convinced that Christians are "associators" (*mushrikūn*), rather than real believers in monotheism (*tawḥīd*), the fundamental confession of Islam. Likewise, the dialogue of life will help a Christian feel safer with a Muslim as a result of their growing trust and friendship, but Christians will remain convinced that Islam is fundamentally a violent religion that does not tolerate social diversity because of the way that we have usually read the Qur'an. Our history is burdened with conflicts and wars that have been legitimized by religion. It will take more than a few good interfaith friendships for Christians and Muslims to lay new foundations for the future that begins today, and for them together to set the tone for the history to come. If our past is riddled with mutual theological misconceptions, is our future not therefore in desperate need of a theological dialogue that will mend our mutual prejudices? This book yearns to be a meaningful step in this direction. Each of the next chapters will thus examine one particular core belief of the Christian faith in accordance with the structure described below.

Study the Internal Muslim Understanding

The purpose of these sections in each chapter is not to offer an exhaustive presentation of Muslim doctrine. This would be an impossible task in the space afforded by the purpose of the present book, for the subtle differences that exist between the different schools regarding Muslim doctrines are at least as diverse and rich as they are between the various schools of Christian thought across the ages. I will limit discussion to the broad lines of Muslim doctrinal understanding, primarily based on a limited exploration of exegetical works on key qur'anic verses. I focus on the theology that derives from qur'anic exegesis in order to keep with the spirit of the present work, which seeks primarily to be exegetical and textual in nature. This should not limit our conclusions, moreover, since, as we have seen, all theology is primarily derived from scriptural exegesis. It must be remembered, furthermore, that theology is developed in apologetic hermeneutics. Doctrinal affirmations are made in order to rebut and correct what is seen as heterodox thinking. Muslim exegetes exposed these apologetic contexts in what they referred to as the "occasions of the revelation" (*asbāb an-nuzūl*).

All references to qur'anic commentaries in this book are from the online resource provided by the Aal al-Bayt Institute for Islamic Thought, in Amman, Jordan, which can be found at altafsir.com. All commentaries, except Sayyid Quṭb's *Fī Ḍhilāl al-Qur'an* can be accessed freely through the dropdown menu on the front page of the website. The latter commentary is found elsewhere on the same website (altafsir.com/MiscellaneousBooks.asp). Page numbers in commentaries are not provided, given their electronic format, but the reader can easily go back to the original by searching the relevant sūrah, verse, and commentator on the website. The commentaries are in Arabic, and all citations and paraphrases reflect my own English renderings.

Study the Historical Dialogue

A second step in each chapter will be to unravel the dialogical discourse on a particular doctrine. In order to achieve this, we will journey through the story of the Muslim discourse on Christianity's core beliefs through important texts of Muslim theologians of the eighth to fourteenth centuries, the fundamental period that established the basis of Muslim-Christian relations throughout history until the present day. Much of this discourse derived from the way that key qur'anic passages were understood and applied in the early period. From both the exegetical and the dialectical sections in each chapter will emerge what I call the metadialogue on a particular doctrine, which in turn represents the hermeneutical context out of which a new constructive Christian theological discourse will be able to grow.

Identify Historical Deadlocks

Having discovered the metadialogue on a particular doctrine, we will then be able to identify some of the historical deadlocks that have emerged on specific theological issues. Dialogical texts individually often present only a narrow, and somewhat biased, understanding of the way that Muslims and Christians were talking together about theology. But once the metadialogue is established, greater historical coherence emerges, and this helps us understand better why we have reached where we currently are in the conversation. This new understanding derives from the emergence of particular issues that have become deadlocks in today's dialogue and relationships.

Search for Hermeneutical Keys to Break the Deadlock

The fourth section in each chapter takes up the principal milestones in the metadialogue and addresses the various deadlocks in light of history, proposing new approaches in the development of an alternative theological discourse for the twenty-first century. It will be possible to see these solutions, or hermeneutical keys, only thanks to the more holistic dialogical landscape that will have emerged, and the particularities of our time may promise new hope for progress in interreligious relationships and conversations. It is on this basis that we will be able to propose a renewed Christian theological discourse in dialogue with Islam.

Globalizing the Theological Conversation

My primary interest is to establish the historical metadialogue of the theological discourse between Christians and Muslims in the East. I choose, for the most part, not to engage with writings of contemporary Western Christian scholars who have picked up the dialogical engagement with Muslims with various degrees of success. This was a conscious choice on my part, as doing otherwise would have amplified the present volume to an impossible size. I therefore chose to provide a doctrinally comprehensive volume, rather than a historically comprehensive treatment of any single doctrine. My purpose is to provide a historical starting point that establishes a helpful framework for those who will want to engage in greater and more comprehensive depth on specific doctrines. By doing so, I seek to remedy a significant gap that exists in the contemporary literature of Christians' engagement with Islam over the past hundred years of postcolonial writing.

The colonial enterprise began to provide modern Western Christian scholars, often referred to as "Orientalists," the opportunity to engage with Islam as a result of unprecedented interaction between Western and Eastern thinkers. Though the context of this opportunity was the unfortunate result of military conquest, driven by economic ambition, the resulting intercultural cross-fertilization called for evaluation, correction, and progress, rather than regret. The postcolonial era (from the 1920s onward) offered new opportunity for engagement as a result of the reactionary reverse migration of previously colonized peoples to previously colonizing nations. This resulted in what we might view as an unprecedented creative environment, where Christian and Muslim scholars and theologians engage with one another, both in the East and in the West, as never before in history.

The depth and creativity of understanding of the other that Kenneth Cragg (on Islam)[20] or Mahmoud Ayoub (on Christianity)[21] attained in the twentieth century has hardly been matched by anyone else so far. Cragg was reproached for not engaging sufficiently with other contemporary Christian writers on the subjects he treats in his books, and Muslim scholars sometimes considered his work to be overly forceful in drawing Islam into a Christian mold. The same critique may be leveled at Ayoub's attempts to understand Christian doctrines authentically as a Muslim. But such transgressions are inevitable when we are courageous enough to undertake the study of a faith tradition other than our own.

Other recent theological writings, such as Miroslav Volf's attempt to write on the doctrine of God in a way that takes seriously his Muslim counterparts,[22] as well as Veli-Matti Kärkkäinen's dialogical theology series with sections engaging with Islamic doctrines,[23] do a better job at integrating their writing within the broader contemporary Western Christian conversation. But the inevitable result is that their engagement with the historical Muslim discourse on these doctrines remains limited and somewhat lacking in historical depth.

Every book, then, inevitably must make choices, and ends up with some strengths and some weaknesses. In the present book, the depth and focus will be found in the comprehensive nature of the historical metadialogue that will emerge on the most pertinent theological topics of Christian-Muslim dialogical engagement. But as a result, my engagement with conversations currently taking place among Western Christian theologians on the same topics will inevitably suffer. But I believe that this

20. Kenneth Cragg, *The Call of the Minaret*, 3rd ed. (Oxford: Oneworld, 2008 [originally 1956]); Cragg, *Muhammad and the Christian: A Question of Response* (Oxford: Oneworld, 1999); and Cragg, *Jesus and the Muslim: An Exploration* (Oxford: Oneworld, 1999 [originally 1985]), in particular.

21. Mahmoud Ayoub, *Redemptive Suffering in Islam* (Berlin: De Gruyter, 1978); and *A Muslim View of Christianity* (New York: Orbis Books, 2007), in particular.

22. Miroslav Volf, *Allah: A Christian Response* (New York: HarperCollins, 2011).

23. Veli-Matti Kärkkäinen, *A Constructive Christian Theology for the Pluralistic World*, vol. 1: *Christ and Reconciliation* (Grand Rapids: Eerdmans, 2013); and Kärkkäinen, *A Constructive Christian Theology for the Pluralistic World*, vol. 2: *Trinity and Revelation* (Grand Rapids: Eerdmans, 2014).

book will fill a crucial gap in the conversation, and therefore this weakness is necessary. My hope is that, with this choice, I provide Christian theologians and students of Islam with an important body of information, which will then allow our theological enterprise to go deeper in its engagement with global Muslim realities.

Finally, to somewhat remedy for this weakness, I provide brief annotated bibliographies at the end of each doctrinal theme. These sections will guide students of Islam and of Christian theology who desire to read and write further about the theological topics of this book, as they seek to engage in conversation with both their Christian and Muslim counterparts.

Closing Considerations: Continuity Rather than Discontinuity

In closing this chapter, I ponder on an important question that struck me as I journeyed through the theological metadialogue between Muslims and Christians. I came to wonder why Islam should have bothered to preserve the sanctity of Jesus within the Muslim tradition rather than dismiss him altogether, since they disagreed quite radically with the way that his memory had been handed down through the Christian tradition. This, of course, is part of the bigger puzzle about the reason why Islam located itself in continuity with the Judeo-Christian tradition rather than affirming itself as a completely independent tradition. One can understand why the early church affirmed its continuity with Judaism, as the Jewishness of Jesus is an essential part of his story. Thus, when the early Christian leader, Marcion of Sinope (circa 85–circa 160), attempted to dismiss the Old Testament and the God of Israel as lesser than the Father of Jesus Christ—in embarrassment with some of the Old Testament narratives—church fathers were quick to dismiss him as a heretic. It is much harder to dislocate Jesus from the Judeo-Christian tradition than it is to maintain him within it.

But the case of Muhammad and the Qur'an is quite different. There is little evidence in the Muslim tradition to support the affirmation that Muhammad was either a Jew or a Christian, certainly not in a mainstream orthodox sense. One can indeed understand why a ninth-century convert to Islam such as Alī b. Rabbān aṭ-Ṭabarī, whose works we will study extensively, would have wanted to find continuity between his newly adopted faith and his previous faith, in a natural instinct of self-justification. But why the Qur'an itself spends so much time insisting on the continuity with Judaism and Christianity with such passion, along with their Scriptures and prophets, remains largely a mystery to the external observer. If Muhammad originated from a pagan tribe in the pagan environment of Mecca, as the Muslim tradition generally affirms, then Islam's insistence on the vindication of what it considers to be the pure versions of Judaism, Christianity, and the biblical prophets does not make much sense. Such matters and others cause us to question the traditional Muslim narrative about Islamic origins. It seems to argue for far more connectedness and continuity between Muhammad's own socioreligious origins and the Judeo-Christian tradition.

Nor are these questions simply contemporary ones. From the very early beginnings of Islam's encounter with the largely Christian world of the Eastern Mediterranean, key Christian figures such as John of Damascus in the eighth century tried to make sense of the new conquerors' ideals and place their ideology within the larger intellectual and theological framework that they knew. One of the earliest perceptions that comes across through John of Damascus is that Islam was a new form of Christian heresy. Both communities gradually became more aware of each other's mutual perceptions, and the ensuing Christian-Muslim metadialogue is a direct outcome of the intellectual interaction that resulted from this emerging awareness.

For example, Muslims became aware that some Christians objected to the qur'anic claim that they considered Mary to be God alongside Jesus and to the claim that they had replaced the "true God" with Jesus and Mary. In response, Shīʿī exegete aṭ-Ṭabarṣī (died 1153) reports a tradition implying that in the early days there were Christians called "Maryamites" (*al-Maryamiyya*) who believed that Mary was divine. The interesting point about such exegetical material is that it shows how sterile some of these doctrinal conversations have been between Christians and Muslims. Even as Christians continue to claim that the Qur'an is often attacking a straw man when it accuses Christians of believing that God is Jesus, or that Christians believed in three gods, or that they believed in a Trinity that included Mary, it is clear that Muslims have known of this Christian riposte for a long time historically. Yet, as we clearly see in such exegetical material, Muslim commentators found their way around this Christian rebuttal. They could not, of course, be expected to come to the conclusion that the qur'anic revelation contained errors, nor would most accept the Christian suggestion that perhaps the Qur'an was attacking another form of belief that was found in Arabia in the days of Muhammad. Instead, Muslim exegetes until today continue to hold on to the traditional understanding that the qur'anic message contains a strong refutation of Christian doctrines as taught by mainstream Christianity, and they find ways of holding on to the literal text to reaffirm the qur'anic polemic.

Today, however, as we stand at the receiving end of a long debate on this issue, the passions may have somewhat abated, and it may be possible for Muslim theologians to listen again to a more authentic expression of the Christian doctrines of the Trinity and of the divine self-revelation in Christ. By reclaiming the continuity of Muhammad and the Qur'an with the Judeo-Christian tradition, which appears prominently through the sūrahs of the Qur'an, Christians and Muslims can come together on firmer common ground as they explore the cardinal theological themes of their respective traditions.

3 God in Christian-Muslim Dialogue

Shortly after I left Lebanon to study in England in the mid-nineties, a Christian friend asked me who I thought that the *Allāh* of Muslims was, when compared to God in the Bible. He probably thought that, since I had grown up in a country where there were many Muslims, I was an expert on Islam. But, to my own surprise, the question brought me close to tears. For twenty-three years, living in a Muslim-majority country, neither I nor my Muslim friends had ever thought of asking each other this question. *Allāh* was the word I had used to address God in Arabic since my childhood. My Sunday school teachers told us stories of biblical heroes and their relationship to *Allāh*. My pastor read aloud from his Arabic Bible with repeated references to *Allāh* before he began to preach. My English friend's question seemed to undermine the legitimacy of my own lifetime of worship.

I still feel the same gut reaction whenever someone asks me this question or when I read about Malaysian Christians being forbidden to use the word *Allāh* in their own literature, hymns, and worship. Is this really an intellectual matter that can be decided based on texts and theological truth claims? Or is it a far more subjective matter, one to be reflected upon in humble meditation and worship?

Do Christians and Muslims Worship the Same God?

So, who is this God that Muslims worship? Is he different from the one Christians worship? So many books have been written on this topic in recent years that it would be futile to try to review all of them. But it seems to me that the more balanced writings on the topic refrain from offering a categorical answer to the question. I chose three recent books to look at in more detail.

Timothy George

In 2002, Timothy George wrote a book with the title *Is the Father of Jesus the God of Muhammad?* This rhetorical question seems to invite the answer no. Yet, George's answer is not that simple. He affirms the monotheism common to both Islam and Christianity, while also giving an extensive explanation of the Christian Trinity. He emphasizes the distinctiveness of the "Father of Jesus" by considering implications that the biblical understanding of the Trinity has for the Christian understanding of God's character.

"Bare monotheism," he affirms, "divorced from the rich content of biblical faith is not enough. The doctrine of the Trinity is not peripheral but essential to our understanding of the character and nature of the one true God." The Bible affirms that God *is* love, rather than simply *loving*, which he believes would be the extent of what can be attributed to God in Islam. This affirmation challenges Unitarianism, explains the reason for creation, reveals the nature of God's essentially relational being, and helps us understand why he came to us in Christ. Love as *divine essence*, George affirms, is possible to understand only if God lives in eternal triune community.

George's book is effectively a presentation of various aspects of Islam, which adopts a comparative approach from an evangelical Christian perspective. His approach is respectful and sympathetic, even though at times somewhat reductionist. But in the end, he remains somewhat conflicted about the answer to the question that gave the book its title. On the one hand, he seems to answer his question in the negative as a result of his thoroughly Trinitarian starting point. At the end of the day Muslims are not worshiping the true God since they reject the Trinity. And given that they reject the fundamentals of Christ's divinity and of the incarnation, their belief in the Jesus of the Qur'an is really no help to them. Finally, since they reject the reality and implications of the cross, they stand outside God's salvation.

Nevertheless, George never closes the door to Muslims. Jesus stands at their door and knocks, waiting for them to open for him, and George believes that they are more likely to open for him than the average person because of their genuine search. Thus, on the other hand, reaffirming his belief in the possibility of only one God, George closes his book with a prayer uttered at the Keswick Convention in 1915: "O God, *to whom the Muslim world bows* in homage five times daily, look in mercy upon its people and reveal to them thy Christ."[1]

Miroslav Volf

Miroslav Volf is more straightforward than Timothy George in his answer to our question in his book *Allah: A Christian Response*, published in 2011. His answer is shaped by his experience growing up in Yugoslavia, a country that no longer exists, and by his work on conflict resolution, forgiveness, and peace. He strongly believes that the recognition that Muslims and Christians worship the same God is not just a matter of theology. "Muslims and Christians will be able to live in peace with one another," he affirms,

> only if (1) the identities of each religious group are respected and given room for free expression, and (2) there are significant overlaps in the ultimate values that orient the lives of people in these communities. These two conditions will be met only if the God of the Bible and the God of the Qur'an turn out to embody overlapping ultimate values, that is, if Muslims and Christians, both monotheists, turn out to have "a common God."[2]

Volf does not make this affirmation lightly, and he spends most of his book qualifying the notion of "common."

For Volf, because a people's belief in God is the source of ultimate values, the answer to whether Christians and Muslims worship the same God can be not only a source of conflict, but it can also be a powerful source of healing and peace. He points to the significance of Abraham Lincoln seeing both North and South worshiping the *same* God as an argument for the resolution of the civil war. Even though they held mutually opposed moral positions on slavery and each side prayed for victory,

1. Timothy George, *Is the Father of Jesus the God of Muhammad?* (Grand Rapids: Zondervan, 2002), 138 (emphasis added).

2. Miroslav Volf, *Allah: A Christian Response* (New York: HarperCollins, 2011), 8.

it is still possible to maintain that they were praying to the same God. It is impossible for this God to be in agreement with both positions at the same time, and both groups' prayers could not be answered as they wished. Yet by affirming that both groups are worshiping the same God, Lincoln affirmed the possibility that the conflict and disagreement could be overcome and peace brought in.[3]

Volf also cites Rick Warren's prayer at Barack Obama's inauguration as president of the United States in 2009:

> Almighty God, our Father, everything we see and everything we can't see exists because of you alone. It all comes from you. It all belongs to you. It all exists for your glory! History is your story. The Scripture tells us, "Hear O Israel, the Lord is our God, the Lord is one!" And you are the compassionate and merciful one toward everyone you have made.[4]

Warren refers to God not only as the God of the Judeo-Christian Scripture, but also as the God of the Qur'an, when he refers to him as the "compassionate and merciful one." The affirmation of a common God in our worship and prayer will no doubt continue to be a source of healing, understanding, and peacemaking.

Imad Shehadeh

A precious example of a gracious, respectful, yet evangelically convinced systematic theology of God, which also takes Muslim thinking about God seriously, is Imad Shehadeh's book on the Trinity, published in 2009.[5] It is strongly rooted in the Eastern tradition, both Christian and Muslim, as well as in the broader global theological conversation on the topic. That the book is written in Arabic makes it a rare gift to the Arabic-speaking church and student of theology.

Chapter 6 in Shehadeh's book is entitled "One God or Two Gods?" After adducing textual, linguistic, historical, and theological arguments,

3. Volf, *Allah*, 9–10.

4. Volf, *Allah*, 5.

5. Imad Shehadeh, *Al-ʾāb wa al-ibn wa al-rūḥ al-qudus ilāhun wāḥid, āmīn: ḍarūrat at-taʿaddudiyya fī al-wiḥdāniyya al-ilāhiyya* (The Father, Son and Holy Spirit, One God, Amen: The Necessity of Diversity in Divine Unity) (Beirut: Dar Manhal al-Hayat, 2009).

Shehadeh arrives at the emphatic conclusion that the God preached by Muhammad and reflected in the Qur'an is the one God of Judaism and Christianity.[6] The author, nevertheless, distinguishes between, on the one hand, the "historical starting point" of the Muslim understanding of God, which he sees as agreeing with the Judeo-Christian starting point, and on the other hand "the nature of God as it is described in Islam." In other words, he asserts that though Christians, Muslims, and Jews agree on the divine subject of their faith, they differ on his attributes (Arabic *ṣifāt*; lit., "descriptors").[7]

Shehadeh divides God's attributes into essential and relational attributes. In opposition to the classical Muslim *Ash'arī* differentiation between the *eternal* "attributes of essence" and *temporal* "attributes of accident," he affirms that Christians believe that all the divine attributes, whether absolute (*asāsiyya*—lit., "fundamental") or moral (*adabiyya*), are perfect and eternal. In this, he follows the scholastic Christian classification that distinguished between absolute, incommunicable attributes and relative, communicable attributes. By rooting his discussion of the divine attributes in a solid belief in the triune nature of God, Shehadeh is able to affirm that the relational attributes also exist eternally within the triune Godhead, rather than having come into existence as a result of God's relationship to his creation at a specific point in time. In contrast, based on the same concern of avoiding the possibility of introducing change in the absolute God, the official Muslim position derived from *Ash'arī* thought had to arrive at a more agnostic conviction. For Islam, the essential attributes of God are a necessary part of his essence, but they add fideistically in *Ash'arī* fashion that these attributes are "neither his essence, nor anything except his essence." Islam adopts a position of convinced agnosticism by refraining from going any further in the exploration of this question. The limited nature of the human mind means that Muslims affirm the reality of the divine attributes because of the witness of the Qur'an, but they stop short of further elaboration by affirming it *bilā kayf* (lit., "without how"), in other words unquestioningly.[8]

6. Shehadeh, *Al-'āb wa al-ibn wa al-rūḥ*, 105–12.
7. Shehadeh, *Al-'āb wa al-ibn wa al-rūḥ*, 112–13.
8. Shehadeh, *Al-'āb wa al-ibn wa al-rūḥ*, 122–27.

Summarizing Reflection

Given the centrality of the attributes related to "power" in the Qur'an, and their derivatives of "justice," "wrath," and other such "muscular" attributes, Christians tend to overemphasize the contrast between the *loving* Christian God and the *just* and *wrathful* Muslim God. But is it really the case that the God of Islam and the God of Christianity differ fundamentally in their attributes? First of all, we would do well to follow the example of the prominent evangelical theologians just examined, avoiding the use of language "our God" versus "their God." It is far more constructive and more sound theologically, to speak of "our *understanding* of God" and "their *understanding* of God."

I am personally convinced that the difference between the Christian and Muslim understandings of God is far more a matter of emphasis than one of nature. In a course I teach on the Muslim understanding of God, I ask my Arab students to select one of the so-called ninety-nine beautiful names of God in the Qur'an and to do a word study on it. They have to identify every verse in the Qur'an that contains a reference to the name or attribute that they have chosen. They thus begin to uncover the breadth of meaning of the attribute in its various qur'anic contexts. They then proceed to explore the way that the attribute has been understood through the exegesis of these verses in the Muslim exegetical tradition. Finally, they are asked to compare the qur'anic attribute that they chose with the biblical attributes closest in meaning with it.

Invariably, my students, Arab men and women from all across the Middle East and North Africa, who often come with strong reservations about Islam and Muslims, report that they have found little difference between the way that the attribute of God that they have studied occurs in the Bible and in the Qur'an, and the way it has been understood and interpreted by Christian and Muslim theologians. The primary conclusion that we reach every time is that Christian and Muslim understandings of God differ far more in *emphasis* than in *nature*. To take one example, the love-justice axis is prominent both in the biblical as well as in the qur'anic witness. The popular Christian belief that Islam's God does not possess the attribute of love appears to be somewhat misguided. The qur'anic attribute *wadūd* translates best as "warmly loving." But in addition to this, the formula *bismillāh ar-raḥmān ar-raḥīm* (the so-called *basmala*) is found in the opening statement of all but one of the 114 sūrahs of the Qur'an (Sūrat at-Tawba 9).

The two divine attributes *raḥmān* and *raḥīm*, due to their semantic connection with the word *raḥm* ("womb"), have intimate connotations of maternal compassion, mercy, and love. The qur'anic context, the Muslim exegetical tradition, as well as the Syriac/Aramaic linguistic root RḤM of the two attributes, all point to the dual meaning of *mercy* and *love*. It is not, therefore, that one God is loving whereas the other is wrathful, not that the one is merciful while the other is just. Rather, due to the centrality of the cross in Christianity, which speaks of the self-givingness of God and derives from his essential triune relational essence, the entire biblical tradition is read and understood through this act of ultimate sacrificial love. As a consequence, the more muscular attributes of God, though quite prominent in the Old Testament, lose their sharp edge when they are reinterpreted in light of the cross. But the cross itself is at the heart of the Christian theology of atonement, which presupposes a strong understanding of God's justice against the background of the Old Testament sacrificial system. Conversely, in Islam, though God's power, justice, and wrath are prominent theological concepts, and though the Islamic understanding of absolute monotheism suggests a God who is wholly other and untouched by the daily human condition, the Qur'an also affirms about humans that God is "closer to him than his jugular vein" (Qāf 50:16) and that God is the "all merciful and all compassionate."

So why, then, have we now come to the point in history when Muslims and Christians are questioning whether we worship the same God? It is this matter that I explore in the remainder of this chapter, as we journey through the story of God through centuries of Christian-Muslim interaction.

Islam and the One God

As we listen to the overall Muslim discourse in its engagement with Christianity, we are under the firm impression that absolute monotheism was a given, an axiom never called into question. Through this radical monotheistic worldview, Muslims approached all Christian doctrines, including Christology, soteriology, and pneumatology. Through it also Muslims evaluated the Bible and judged the way that Jews and Christians read it. Eventually, this approach delineated Islam's relationship to Judaism and Christianity and determined the future of Muslim-Christian relations, but was this necessarily the starting point? What factors motivated Muslims in their engagement with Christians, and how did the Muslim doctrine of God influence the way that Muslims viewed Christianity?

The Qur'an's Vindication of Jesus

Notable for Christian-Muslim relations is that nowhere in the Qur'an or in the entire Muslim tradition do we encounter any slander of Jesus. Whatever opinions developed regarding the disciples, the early Christians, or priests and monks later on—and the opinions are diverse—Jesus himself always remains blameless. In the next two chapters, I explore in detail how Muslim scholars aggressively retained the blameless icon of Jesus. But here, I focus mainly on one particular verse (al-Mā'ida 5:116) and on the way that qur'anic interpreters have used it both as a means of affirming Islam's pure monotheism and as a way of incriminating Jesus's followers.

One principal affirmation of the present book is that all theological discourse is born in tension between apologetics and polemics. The emerging discourse finds its vindication and justification in past theological discourse and uses this as a platform for dismantling rival narratives. Just as over the first four centuries of the Christian era the doctrinal expressions that came to be recognized as distinctly Christian emerged in tension between Jewish and Greco-Roman understandings of the divine, the distinctly Muslim understanding of God emerged in tension between what the Islamic tradition describes as the polytheistic world of Mecca and the Judeo-Christian elements strongly present in the broader environment of the Arabian Peninsula and beyond. I am not saying that the doctrines themselves were born in this tension. What I am saying is that the *expression* of these beliefs, the theological discourse that sought to understand and explain these doctrines, was born in these largely apologetic and polemical matrixes.

Given this, it is understandable why the character of Jesus is often the starting point for the Qur'an's expression of some of Islam's chief doctrines. The Qur'an views its own message as being both in continuity with the Judeo-Christian tradition and a fulfillment of it. But it also seems concerned with distinguishing itself from that tradition and correcting it. So, Jesus becomes the prototype of piety and monotheism, in the spirit of continuity and fulfillment. But the qur'anic portrayal of him also becomes the antitype that corrects the Christians' representation of Jesus.

The following brief dialogue between God and Jesus in al-Mā'ida 5:116 illustrates this process. Here, Jesus is questioned by God on whether he ever taught people to worship him and his mother instead of God. Jesus vehemently denies this accusation and renders to God the knowledge of all things that belong to him:

> God said, "Jesus, son of Mary, did you say to people, 'Worship me and my mother as gods instead God'?" [Jesus] answered, "May you be exalted in your limitless glory. It is not for me to say what I have no right to say. Had I said this, you would have known it. You know all that is within me, whereas I do not know what is in you. It is you alone who has full knowledge of unknown things."

In a single verse, the Qur'an challenges Christianity's two core doctrines: the Trinity and the divine nature in Christ. But it is worth keeping in mind that many Muslim writers understood the original intention of such verses in the Qur'an as an attempt at *rapprochement* with Christianity. The qur'anic principle of continuity and fulfillment left an indelible mark on early Muslim scholars and was particularly cherished by Christian converts to Islam such as Abū al-Ḥasan 'Ālī b. Sahl Rabbān aṭ-Ṭabarī (circa 782–860). In his *Book on the Refutation of Christians* (*Kitāb ad-Radd 'ala an-Naṣāra*) he sought to realign Jesus's person and teaching with the logical and sound teaching of Islam. He explains that the reason he wishes to bring Christians to agree with Islam is in order to fulfill āl-'Imrān 3:64: "People of the book, 'Come to a common word between us that we will not worship any but God, and we will not ascribe partners to him, nor will we take each other as lords in addition to God.' If they turn away, say, 'Bear witness that we have submitted to God.'"[9]

Aṭ-Ṭabarī then enumerates twelve points of agreement between Muslims and Christians, which he would like to see become a bridge between the two religions. All twelve points focus on the oneness of God and his radical otherness. But although these are supposedly points of agreement with Christianity, they deny implicitly some of the most important ideas of the Christian doctrine of the incarnation.

Aṭ-Ṭabarī also points out that Moses, Jesus, and all the prophets confessed God's unity.[10] He challenges the Christian doctrine of the Trinity,

9. Cf. 'Alī b. Sahl Rabbān aṭ-Ṭabarī, *Kitāb ar-Radd 'ala an-Naṣāra*, in I. A. Khalifé and W. Kutsch's "Ar-radd 'ala-n-nasārā," *Mélanges de l'Université Saint Joseph* 36.4 (1959): 115–48 at 128.

10. Aṭ-Ṭabarī, *Radd*, 121.

pointing out that it amounts to the proclamation of a "quaternity": Father, Son, Holy Spirit, and finite man Jesus Christ. The Islamic tradition strives hard to depict Jesus as a faithful Muslim prophet. Jesus becomes a significant qur'anic mouthpiece to affirm the cardinal elements of the Muslim doctrine of God.

"I Would Never Say What Is Not Rightfully Mine to Say!"

Al-Mā'ida 5:116 (quoted above) is used by Muslim commentators to reaffirm God's greatness and superiority over Jesus—with the implied dismissal of his equality with God. Some even suggest that these words were spoken to Jesus while he was still on earth and were intended as a warning against making any claims to divinity. But the majority of Muslim exegetes think that this dialogue took place either on the day when God raised Jesus to himself (that is, in the past but at the end of his ministry) or on the day of judgment (i.e., in the future). The verse is then interpreted as God's way of informing Jesus that his followers went astray after he left them. Thus, this verse becomes Jesus's disclaimer with regard to his followers' teachings about him. Qur'anic interpreter Ibn Jarīr aṭ-Ṭabarī (died 923) also uses this as an opportunity to reaffirm Jesus's inferiority to God in knowledge, saying that Jesus knew only what God chose to make known to him. Qur'anic exegete al-Qurṭubī (died 1273) affirms that Jesus's rejection of the words attributed to him by his followers means that Jesus was saying: "I am under lordship and am not a lord; I am a worshiper [*ʿābid*] and not one who is worshiped [*maʿbūd*]."

Az-Zamakhsharī (died 1144), however, argues that this conversation would take place on the day of judgment. He points out that in the qur'anic rendering, Jesus does not really answer God's question. He did not simply respond: "No, I did not teach my followers to consider me and my mother as gods instead of you." Instead, he saw the question as rhetorical. God, being all knowing, already knew the answer to his own question, and so Jesus simply reaffirmed his position by answering: "I would never say what is not rightfully mine to say!"

Az-Zamakhsharī also notes that some may object to this verse's implication that Christians consider Mary to be God alongside Jesus. This point has indeed been made by many Christians. Some wonder whether Muhammad was perhaps refuting a marginal sect of Christianity rather than orthodox Christianity. Shīʿī exegete aṭ-Ṭabarṣī (died 1153) is aware of such Christian objections already in his days and seems open to their suggestion that the Qur'an may have been refuting a heterodox Christian group. He reports a tradition that, in the early days, there were Christians that were called Maryamites (*al-Maryamiyya*), who actually believed that Mary was divine. But az-Zamakhsharī responds by arguing that when Christians claim that Jesus and Mary performed miracles by their own authority rather than by God's, they are ascribing to them the power to perform miracles, a quality that applies only to God. This harder position endures to the present day.

For example, Muhammad Rashīd Riḍa (died 1935), a famous Muslim reformer whose qur'anic commentary, *Tafsīr al-Manār*, had an enduring influence on the shaping of Islamist ideology in the twentieth century, engages with the text from the perspective of his contemporary reality. His exegesis represents an incisive critique of the Middle Eastern Christianity he knew. He was a well-traveled scholar born in the small coastal town of Qalamūn, near Tripoli (in today's Lebanon), but then spent the most productive years of his adult life in Egypt. He points out that the Orthodox Christians of his day (as he had observed personally at the Balamand monastery in Lebanon), as well as the Jesuits, the Armenians, and the Copts, all offered worship (*'ibāda*) to the Virgin Mary. And therefore, he saw this qur'anic verse as an absolutely fitting rebuke.

Jesus Affirmed That "There Is No God But God"

For later Muslim writers, the vindication of Jesus in al-Mā'ida 5:116 becomes a template and the starting point for their portrayal of Christianity's central figure as a pious Muslim. They do so not only through their treatment of the qur'anic text, but also based on verses from the Bible. One passage from the Gospels that lent itself ideally to support the vindication argument was Jesus's response to the man who called him good in Matthew 19:16–17: "Why did you call me good [*khayyir*]? Is not God alone *khayyir*?"[11]

This is the quotation as found in Ibn Rabbān aṭ-Ṭabarī's *Refutation of Christians*. According to him, through this statement, Jesus denied

11. One should read *khayyir* instead of *ḥabr* found in the edition of Khalifé and Kutsch. In Arabic, the misreading occurred simply as a result of the misplacement of two diacritical points.

himself the title that belongs only to the divinity, proclaiming instead "an absolute and clear monotheism" (*at-tawḥīd al-maḥḍ al-muṣarraḥ*).[12] Thirteenth-century Egyptian scholar Shihāb ad-Dīn al-Qarāfī (1228–85), who habitually borrows arguments from aṭ-Ṭabarī, uses the same passage twice in an anti-Christian polemical treatise entitled *Glorious Answers to Brazen Questions*, in the following form: "Do not call me good/just [*ṣāliḥ*]. There is no *ṣāliḥ* except God (May he be exalted!) the one [*al-Wāḥid*]."[13] Al-Qarāfī's version replaces "God alone" (*Allāh waḥdahu*) with "God the one" (*Allāh al-Wāḥid*). This form serves well the purpose of portraying Jesus as an authentic and confessing Muslim prophet.

Another favorite passage from the Gospels among Muslim writers was Jesus's prayer to God for his disciples in John 17, particularly 17:1 and 17:3. Both aṭ-Ṭabarī and al-Qarāfī cite these verses in order to demonstrate that Christ held an absolute monotheistic belief:

> Aṭ-Ṭabarī: Jesus raised his eyes to heaven and interceded to God and said: "Eternal life is for people to know [*yajib li an-nās an yaʿlamū*] that you are the one true God, and that you sent Jesus Christ."[14]
>
> Al-Qarāfī: Christ said, having raised his eyes upwards: "My God, eternal life belongs to people if they know [*tajib li an-nās idhā ʿalimū*] that you are the one [*al-Wāḥid*], the true [*al-Ḥaqq*], who sent the Christ."[15]

Though aṭ-Ṭabarī is clearly the textual source of al-Qarāfī, it is striking that in the course of the four hundred years separating them, Muslim writers had lost interest in understanding the biblical text in and of itself. Al-Qarāfī's quotation is entirely subjected to his polemical purpose. This double confession of Jesus is, for both authors, a confession of God's unity and of Christ's pure servanthood. By quoting the verse as "the one true God" (*Allāh al-Wāḥid al-Ḥaqq*), rather than "the only true God" (as is the more straightforward sense of both the Greek and the Syriac biblical versions), they are able to make Jesus's statement sound much more like the standard Islamic monotheistic statement of faith.[16]

12. Aṭ-Ṭabarī, *Radd*, 121–22.

13. Shihāb ad-Dīn al-Qarāfī, *Al-Ajwiba al-Fākhira ʿan al-As'ila al-Fājira*, ed. Bakr Zakī ʿAwaḍ (Cairo: Wehbeh Publishers, 1987), 219, 296.

14. Aṭ-Ṭabarī, *Radd*, 122.

15. Al-Qarāfī, *Al-Ajwiba al-Fākhira*, 296.

16. The same wording occurs in al-Qarāfī with the same exegetical intention.

Lastly, famous fourteenth-century Muslim scholar Ibn Qayyim al-Jawziyya also cites this passage (especially John 17:3) on three different occasions in his anti-Christian treatise entitled *Guiding the Confused in Answering Jews and Christians.*[17] In the first and third instance, he points out that Christ's statement contradicts the Christian claims, as the Gospel indicates clearly his belief in the one God and his consciousness of being sent. Ibn Qayyim al-Jawziyya's comment on the citation in his first reference to the verse indicates how strongly he strives to align Christ and the Gospel witness with the Islamic faith. He presents it flatly as a paraphrase of Islam's "first pillar," the *Shahāda*: "And this, in truth, is [also] the testimony of Muslims: That there is no God but God [*anna lā ilāha illa Allāh*], and that Muhammad is God's prophet/apostle [*anna Muhammadan Rasūl Allāh*]."

Jesus Affirmed and Practiced the Worship of God Alone

Beyond Jesus's affirmation of monotheism, Muslim scholars point out his exclusive worship of God as the manifestation of his exemplary piety. In the Gospel account of the temptation of Jesus, one of the three temptations (Matt 4:8–10 and parallel in Luke 4:5–8) quickly became a favorite to that end. In the context of his survey of biblical passages from both the Old and New Testaments that reflect the orthodoxy of biblical prophets, ʿAlī aṭ-Ṭabarī cites Christ's rebuttal of the devil's invitation that he worship him in return for all the riches and glories of the world: "It is written that you should worship none but the Lord your God, and bow down to nothing besides him."[18]

Two later authors—al-Ḥasan b. Ayyūb (a tenth-century convert to Islam) and the previously mentioned Egyptian al-Qarāfī—take over the same biblical reference directly from aṭ-Ṭabarī, and with the same rhetorical intent. The nature of their borrowing indicates that they must have come under the direct influence of his writings.[19]

17. Shams ad-Dīn Muhammad b. Abī Bakr Ibn Qayyim al-Jawziyya, *Hidāyat al-Ḥayāra fī Ajwibat al-Yahūd wa an-Naṣāra*, ed. Aḥmad Ḥijāzī as-Saqā (Cairo: al-Maktaba al-Qayyima, 1980), 272, 275, 294.

18. Aṭ-Ṭabarī, *Radd*, 122.

19. Ibn Ayyūb, *Risāla ila Akhīhi ʿAlī* (Letter to His Brother ʿAlī, Explaining to Him Why He Converted to Islam), preserved in Taqī ad-Dīn Aḥmad b. Taymiyya, *Al-Jawāb aṣ-Ṣaḥīḥ li-man Baddala Dīn al-Masīḥ* (Cairo: Nile Press, 1905), 1.2.325; and al-Qarāfī, *Al-Ajwiba al-Fākhira*, 217.

Similarly, in his *Refutation of Christians*, a ninth-century Zaydī Shīʿī imam from the Yemen, al-Qāsim b. Ibrāhīm ar-Rassī (785–860), draws the portrait of a Jesus that sounds like a deeply devout Muslim, absolutely categorical about God's worship. He refers to the same temptation account in the following terms: "So Christ cursed him [Satan] and shamed him and said: 'It is not right to worship anyone but God. God forbid! You enemy of God.'"[20]

The account in question features as Christ's third temptation in Matthew's Gospel and as his second in Luke's. Following neither of the two evangelists, seemingly to add to the rhetorical effect, ar-Rassī reorders this temptation as the first of the three in his own account. Another Shīʿī scholar, ninth-century historian Aḥmad b. Abī Yaʿqūb, better known as al-Yaʿqūbī (circa 825–905), reproduces the temptation account quite literally in his *Tārīkh* (a history of the world from Adam to his own time). Christ's confession of absolute monotheism in Matthew 4:10 is once again stressed with particular emphasis. The author tacitly skips 4:8–9, which provided the context where the devil takes Jesus to a high mountain and offers him all the riches of the world. Al-Yaʿqūbī simply provides Christ's *reply* to the devil's third temptation, which in this form stands as an absolute confession, unrelated to any particular context: "Then he said to the devil: 'Go away! For it is God that I worship and him whom I adore.'"[21]

Nor did Muslim writers necessarily respect the canonical Christian version of the biblical text when they needed to use a particular verse to serve a rhetorical end. For example, ʿAlī aṭ-Ṭabarī uses a version of John 5:43–44 that has undergone substantial change from its original form: "Christ said to the Jews: 'You do not believe, and you seek praise from one another—the praise [that belongs] to God who is worshiped—and you do not follow me.'"[22]

Jesus is represented as reproaching the Jews for seeking praise for themselves, the praise that he confesses as rightfully belonging to God. Aṭ-Ṭabarī's version of the verse certainly serves his purpose of representing an orthodox Muslim Jesus's view of worship, and the reproach he addresses to the Jews in the Gospel citation is easily transferrable as a

20. Ar-Rassī, Ar-*Radd ʿala an-Naṣāra*, in Ignazio Di Matteo's "Confutazione contro I cristiani dello zaydita al-Qâsim b. Ibrâhîm," *Rivista degli Studi Orientali* 9 (1922): 324.

21. Al-Yaʿqūbī (Aḥmad b. Abī Yaʿqūb), *Tārīkh*, ed. M. T. Houtsma (Leiden: Brill, 1883), 1.76.

22. Aṭ-Ṭabarī, *Radd*, 129.

critique of Christians. However, the quotation is inexact. The canonical version reads as follows: "I have come in my Father's name, and you do not accept me; but if someone else comes in his own name, you will accept him. How can you believe if you accept praise from one another, yet make no effort to obtain the praise that comes from the only God?" (John 5:43–44 New International Version).

Aṭ-Ṭabarī's version differs from both the Greek and the Syriac translations that would have been available to him, particularly as a former Christian who no doubt read at least Syriac. The Syriac Peshitta and Old Syriac versions read: "And praise from the one God [*d-men Ḥādh Alāhā*] you do not seek." The Harklean Syriac translation, following the Greek text more closely, reads: "And the praise from the only one God [*d-men Ḥādh balḥūdāw*[*hy*] *Alāhā*] you do not seek." What is intriguing, and may indicate that this misreading was not intended, is that the standard text, where Jesus is calling God "the one God," would seem to have lent itself much better to aṭ-Ṭabarī's argument. Other reasons, however, may have led to this alteration. For example, the standard reading could have been interpreted as reinforcing the divinity of Christ, if Jesus was understood to be referring to *himself* as "the one God." The present reading also reinforces aṭ-Ṭabarī's particular exegetical argument about God's oneness and singleness in worship.

Alternatively, however, his quotations could have come from a standard collection intended for Muslim-Christian polemics, and the verses would have been fashioned to suit the exercise. This sort of collection was common in classical polemical writings, and it is clear that many later Muslim writers used such collections rather crudely. It is enough to note to what extent the text is reshaped to suit the argument of the polemicist. The end of the quotation is also out of context, since it seems to paraphrase a segment from the previous verse (43): "And you do not receive/accept me" (in aṭ-Ṭabarī: "you do not follow me").

Another truncated passage is cited by aṭ-Ṭabarī and later taken over as is by Ibn Ayyūb. John 8:48–50 is used as a further testimony by Jesus himself regarding the worship of God alone and the illegitimacy of worshiping or praising him:[23] "The Jews said: 'Aren't we right in saying that you are a Samaritan and that you have a devil?' He said to them: 'I am not possessed, but I honor my Father. And I don't like to praise myself, but to praise my Father.'"

23. Aṭ-Ṭabarī, *Radd*, 130; and Ibn Ayyūb, *Risāla*, in Ibn Taymiyya, *Al-Jawāb aṣ-Ṣaḥīḥ*, 1.2.337.

Aṭ-Ṭabarī truncates the end of the verse and interprets it unambiguously after removing it from its context. The canonical version reads: "I do not seek to praise myself, but there is one who seeks it." This could be understood as: "There is one who seeks to praise his own self [or to be praised; i.e., the Father]," and this is obviously how aṭ-Ṭabarī understood it. However, based on John 8:54 ("if I praised myself, my praise would be nothing; it is my Father who praises me"), it is clear that the canonical intention of 8:50 is quite the opposite: "There is one who seeks to praise me" (that is, the Father seeks to praise the Son). Overall, we can see that little exegetical effort is displayed on the part of the Muslim writers. The argument is prepared beforehand, and the Gospel citations are mostly used as prooftext.

God in Islam

Having established the qur'anic foundation of the critique of the Christian doctrine of God in the desire to absolve Jesus from later ascriptions to him, we now come to the heart of Muslim *tawḥīd* (proclamation of the one God) by approaching it through the paramount verse on God's unity: "Say: 'He is God who is uniquely singular, who is eternal, (the uncaused cause of all that exists), who has not given birth nor is he born and there is no equivalent to him'" (al-Ikhlāṣ 112:1–4).

Islam's Doctrine of Absolute Monotheism

Though Islam's affirmation of God's oneness is not the only way that Muslims speak of God, among the many names—or attributes—affirmed by the Qur'an and the tradition it is nevertheless a crucial confession. It is also the primary focus of the Muslim theological engagement with the Christian understanding of God, as well as the measuring rod in their treatment of Christology. God's oneness is therefore the focus of this section, which is naturally not intended to be an exhaustive treatment of the Muslim doctrine.

Sūrat al-Ikhlāṣ 112 (cited above) is, according to Muslim theologians, the most powerful affirmation of Islam's monotheism, despite its being made up of merely four verses. Fakhr ad-Dīn ar-Rāzī (died 1209), in his commentary on the Qur'an, refers to traditions that portray Muhammad as saying that reciting Sūrat al-Ikhlāṣ even once is like reciting a third of the Qur'an. Another tradition affirms that whoever recites this sūrah once will receive the same reward as the one who believes in God, his angels, his books, and his apostles, as well as the reward of a hundred martyrs. The Qur'an is not primarily a systematic treatise, and consequently one does not find in it a systematic treatment of theological doctrines. It is fundamentally a repository of affirmations about God and about right conduct for believers in God. Prophets, including Muhammad, are described as preachers (*mubashshirūn*) and warners (*mundhirūn*) (e.g., al-Baqara 2:213; an-Nisā' 4:165; al-An'ām 6:48; Yūnus 10:2). As such, it is the source both of theological discourse and of Islamic law and jurisprudence. The message of the Qur'an is often referred to as *dhikr* (remembrance) and the messenger Muhammad is repeatedly called to remind (*dhakkir*) people about God's teachings and warnings (e.g., al-An'ām 6:70; ar-Ra'd 13:5). Consequently, innumerable times, believers are entreated to *remember* (*udhkurū*) God and his name and to remember God's grace and covenant (e.g., al-Baqara 2:198, 231, 239; āl-'Imrān 3:103, 191; an-Nisā' 4:103; al-Mā'ida 5:4, 7, 11). It is, therefore, more important for a Muslim to recite Sūrat al-Ikhlāṣ than to analyze it or derive theology from it. At the same time, the recitation of God's unicity (*tawḥīd*) is a theological affirmation of great significance and influence on the mindset of a Muslim and a powerful drive for his or her relationship to the world.

The cardinal verses of Sūrat al-Ikhlāṣ 112 were, according to the earliest exegetical traditions, affirmed in response either to polytheists or to the Jews who sought from Muhammad an explanation of God's origins.[24] Much of the sūrah is self-explanatory. It is an affirmation of God's absolute oneness (*Allāhu aḥad*) and of his eternity, being unborn and having given birth to none. There is considerable emphasis among Muslim exegetes on the significance of the word *aḥad* in al-Ikhlāṣ 112:1. They generally reject the synonymous identification of *aḥad* ("unique") with *wāḥid* ("one"). Most reject that the two words are interchangeable. Fakhr ad-Dīn ar-Rāzī refers to a tradition transmitted by al-Azharī to the effect that "nothing can be described with *unicity* [*al-aḥadiyya*] except God." Consequently, *al-Aḥad* has become one of the attributes or "beautiful names" of God.

Two terms are less clear in the passage: *aṣ-ṣamad* and *kufuwan*. Muhammad b. Jarīr aṭ-Ṭabarī (died 922), in his commentary, surveys a number of interpretations from the Islamic tradition regarding both

24. According to aṭ-Ṭabarī's *Tafsīr*. https://www.altafsir.com.

terms. *Aṣ-ṣamad* is defined as one who is not hollow, in other words who needs nothing. He is one who neither eats nor drinks, from whom nothing emerges, who is absolute in lordship, honor, greatness, patience, meekness, richness, power, knowledge, and wisdom, the eternal one who does not die. *Kufuwan* is explained as "likeness." The verse affirms that nothing is like God or comparable to him.

The oldest traditions, as reported by aṭ-Ṭabarī, make no mention of Christian doctrines as a reason for the revelation of this sūrah. Beginning in the twelfth and thirteenth centuries, however, the Christian rhetorical context becomes important. Evidently, by that time Muslim scholars had become quite familiar with the Christian doctrines, including the diverse interpretations between the various Christian groups. Whether it be in Sunnī commentaries, such as ar-Rāzī (died 1209) and Ibn Kathīr (died 1373), or in Shīʿī commentaries, such as aṭ-Ṭabarṣī (died 1153), the affirmation that God "begot none, nor was he begotten," is by then seen to a large extent as a rebuttal of the Christian claim that Jesus is the Son of God. The same can be observed in the commentaries of more recent exegetes, such as aṭ-Ṭanṭāwī (died 2010) and Shīʿī aṭ-Ṭabaʾṭabāʾī (died 1981). Consequently, a good proportion of the medieval to modern exegesis of Sūrat al-Ikhlāṣ is dedicated to a critique of the Christian view of God.

The Qur'an's Rebuttal of the Christian View of God

Several Muslim polemical treatises against Christianity begin with an extensive exposition of God's oneness and uniqueness based on the Qur'an. God's uniqueness is so fundamental to Muslim thinking that it becomes the basis and starting point for all further arguments against Christian doctrines. As we will see in the next chapter, it is on the basis of God's absolute uniqueness that Muslims cannot conceive of Jesus being more than human. In the Muslim worldview, acknowledgment and affirmation of God's oneness, otherness, and uniqueness set the context for an accurate understanding of the world in all of its parts. Even though Christ may be ascribed the highest prophetic status, his purely human reality is required by God's absolute uniqueness.

In fact, Muslim scholars find support for their view of God in Jesus's own attitude and affirmations in the Gospels. Throughout the history of Muslim-Christian interaction, Muslims did not limit themselves to a rational philosophical critique of Christian doctrines, but they have ventured to reinterpret large portions of the Judeo-Christian Scriptures in an effort to bring them into alignment with the qur'anic message. The qur'anic view of God as absolutely transcendent and without equal is the norm and hermeneutical key behind this new exegesis that Muslim scholars apply to the text of the Bible. And early Christian leaders and theologians come under criticism as having allegedly done a terrible job of biblical interpretation, primarily due to their attachment to power and leadership.

Despite the numerous verses in the Qur'an that speak positively about Christian clergy and monks (e.g., al-Baqara 2:62; al-Mā'ida 5:69, 82–83; al-ʿAnkabūt 29:46), there is also plenty of qur'anic support for harsher criticism, particularly in accusing them of misleading their people. We will see later in this book that even the early disciples get mixed reviews. But until the eleventh century, they are not central to the Muslim critique of Christianity. From the eleventh century onward, especially beginning with Ibn Ḥazm, the corruption of Jesus's message will be traced back all the way to the early disciples (*ḥawāriyyūn*), and the apostle Paul will occupy the prominent place as *corrupter* of original Christianity.

Beyond the strong affirmation of monotheism elaborated on the basis of Sūrat al-Ikhlāṣ 112, a number of verses in the Qur'an have been interpreted by Muslim exegetes through history as a direct rebuttal of the Christian doctrines of God and Christ. Several such affirmations are found in al-Mā'ida 5, notably verses 72–73, with a preview to verse 72 also in verse 17 of the same sūrah:

> Those who say, "God is the Messiah, son of Mary," have defied God. The Messiah himself said, "children of Israel, worship God. He is my Lord as well as your Lord." If anyone associated others with God, he will not permit them to enter heaven. Their destiny will be hell. No one can help such unjust people. Those who say, "God is the third of a trinity"[25] are denying the truth because there is only one God. Unless they stop saying this, a painful punishment will happen to those of them who are determined to deny the truth.

25. Kaskas's translation perpetuates an inaccurate rendering of the Arabic text, which literally reads: "Those who say that God is the third of three [gods] [*thālithu thalātha*] are denying the truth." The belief that the Qur'an is attacking would be better described as tritheism than as Trinity.

These two verses are interpreted in Muslim commentaries as two sides of the same coin, one being a denial of Jesus's divinity and the other a denial of the Trinity, both having a significant impact on the Muslim view of God. The seriousness of the heretical views generally attributed to Christians is highlighted by the punishment promised to those who hold them: fire with no hope for intercession and a "painful punishment."

Although most of the Muslim exegetical and theological tradition through history understood these verses as a rebuttal of Christian doctrine, neither of the two abhorred beliefs described in al-Mā'ida 5:72–73 accurately describes orthodox Christian doctrine. It is true that the church affirmed that Christ was fully God, but no orthodox Christian would make the converse assertion that "God is Christ," the claim rejected by al-Mā'ida 5:72. The affirmation of Christ as the incarnation of God builds on the Pauline assertion that "he is the image of the invisible God" (Col 1:15). And if the church has always endorsed that "God was pleased to have all his fullness dwell in him [Christ]" (1:19), there is also a sense that God cannot be entirely *contained* by a physical recipient. So, when we read in Colossians 2:9 that "in Christ all the fullness of the deity lives *in bodily form*," we must perhaps read "bodily form" (*sōmatikōs*) as a qualification of that particular indwelling. While affirming Christ's divine nature, the verse also recognizes the limitation of our ability ever to know God's fullness so long as we are looking at a physical being.

As for al-Mā'ida 5:73, it is clear that the Christian doctrine of the Trinity has never affirmed that "God is the third of three" gods, which is literally what the Arabic text rejects. Rather, the church has always affirmed the oneness of God, who has made himself known through his self-revelation as Father, Son, and Holy Spirit. Whether one agrees with the official doctrines of the Christian church or not, the fact of the matter is that the theological critique contained in al-Mā'ida 5:72–73 does not deconstruct orthodox Christian doctrine, but rather rejects what the historical church has always rejected.

This is important from the perspective of dialogue, to the extent that Christians and Muslims are able to return today to their holy texts when they seek to understand each other and to revisit the age-old theological disagreements between them. It would be ideal if Christians and Muslims were able to start from a blank slate, approaching their respective views of God, as it were without bias, by exploring together relevant biblical and qur'anic verses. But it is unfortunately never possible to rid ourselves of the burden of history. Therefore, before attempting to explore new horizons in dialogue on the doctrine of God, it is necessary to see how the two verses mentioned have been understood by qur'anic commentators through history.

The first striking feature is that Muslim commentators do not seem to pay much attention to the actual affirmations of al-Mā'ida 5:72–73. They are so familiar with the Christian claim that "Jesus Christ is God" that they immediately assume verse 72 to be a rebuttal of that affirmation, whereas it is the converse affirmation that the Qur'an is rejecting: that "God is Christ son of Mary." In the same way, they are so aware of Christians believing in the Trinity that they assume that verse 73 is a rejection of the Christian doctrine, whereas the qur'anic verse would be better read as a rejection of tritheism, the belief in three gods. No text is read in a vacuum, but is always subject to the prior assumptions of its reader. This is not to say that Muhammad and the Qur'an would have approved, either of the affirmation that Jesus Christ was God in the flesh or of the Christian doctrine of the Trinity in its most orthodox expression. But it does seem intriguing that the Qur'an at the time of its earliest appearance did not seem aware of these.

Had the earliest community of the Qur'an never been exposed to the orthodox version of Christianity? That certainly often seems to be the verdict when one reads the Qur'an without allowing too many presuppositions to interfere with the reading. Having appeared, it would seem, in a thoroughly scriptural, yet sectarian and heterodox Jewish-Christian community, the Qur'an gets quickly deprived of its original scriptural setting. The Qur'an soon went off on its own as the Scripture of a new, highly politicized and militarized community. That community would conquer a new empire from the western edges of North Africa and southern Europe, all the way to modern-day Pakistan, in the space of a few decades—and soon after even further. When the Qur'an's emerging community eventually gets exposed to Christian orthodoxy, much of the early critique initially directed against a specific sectarian milieu from a strong monotheistic Jewish-Christian starting point is redirected toward a Christian orthodoxy that seems never to have been known to the early text. Both the original audience and the original literary setting of the qur'anic text would seem to have been lost to official Muslim exegetes of the Qur'an, to the point that much of what the Qur'an says about Christians and Jews can sound rather obscure and its interpretation may sound at times fanciful.

Thus, all qur'anic criticism of Naṣāra is redirected at Christianity as encountered by the early Arab conquerors of the Levant. Already one of the earliest surviving commentaries, that of Muqātil b. Sulaymān (died 767), affirms that the statement referred to in al-Mā'ida 5:72 reflects the views of the Christians of Najrān, whom he further describes as "Jacobites." Commentator Muhammad b. Jarīr aṭ-Ṭabarī (died 922) makes the same identification, and in every following classical commentator, the identification remains either with the Christians of Najrān or the Jacobites or gradually simply with all Christians (which the word Naṣāra is by then understood to refer to). The association of the belief of verse 72 with the Jacobite position is interesting in itself, for on the one hand it indicates that Muslims of the time were aware of different christological views among Christians. But on the other hand, it also reflects that their knowledge of Christian doctrinal distinctives was stereotypical and superficial rather than accurate, and that it increasingly became so through the classical period. For even though Jacobites rejected the Council of Chalcedon (451) and emphasized Christ's divine nature over his human nature, they nevertheless would not have claimed that "God was Jesus." Furthermore, the Jacobites would not have been the only ones claiming that *Jesus is God*. All Christians by the time of Islam's emergence would have made the same affirmation.

As for al-Mā'ida 5:73, aṭ-Ṭabarī explains that all Christians believed in this tritheism before they split into the three groups of Jacobites, Melkites, and Nestorians—a reference once again to the Council of Chalcedon in 451 and its aftermath. The commentator affirms that it was reported to him (*balaghana*) that in those days, Christians believed that the eternal God was one essence, known in three hypostases (*aqānīm*): "A Father who begets but was not begotten, a Son who was begotten but does not beget, and a [female] spouse located between the two." These affirmations are obviously riddled both with false information and with anachronisms. It may be that there were tritheists in Arabia at the time of Muhammad who believed in a Trinity that included the Virgin Mary, but certainly in the Christian mainstream, no Christian group either before or after the Council of Chalcedon had ever believed in such a Trinity.

As we move forward chronologically through the Muslim qur'anic commentaries to the modern period, Sunnī traditionalist exegetes (such as aṭ-Ṭanṭāwī, died 2010) continue largely to repeat the same things that had been said about these verses during the classical period. Other more reformist exegetes, such as the Islamist and politically engaged Sayyid Quṭb (died 1966), demonstrate greater awareness of Christian beliefs as they are motivated to engage Christians in conversation. By the modern period,

Christians generally altogether become associated with the affirmation that "God is Jesus" in al-Māʾida 5:72, and still no exegete questions the actual qurʾanic attribution of the statement to Christians. Furthermore, the rebuttal in verse 73 continues to be understood by some as a rebuttal of some tritheism involving Mary (see aṭ-Ṭanṭāwī and ash-Shaʿrāwī [died 1997]) and by others (such as Sayyid Quṭb and Shīʿī scholar aṭ-Ṭabaʾṭabāʾī [died 1980]) as a refutation of the actual Christian belief in the Trinity.

The Qurʾan's Rebuttal of Christ's Divinity

The Qurʾan presents a rationalization of the reason why Christians have not held faithfully to monotheism: "They have taken their rabbis and their monks, and even Christ, the son of Mary, for their lords instead of God, when they were commanded to worship only one God. There is no god but him. May he be exalted in his glory above all the partners they may ascribe to him" (at-Tawba 9:31). Although Christians were called to worship the one God, the verse argues, they obeyed their priests and monks instead of obeying God. The Qurʾan, then, incriminates neither Jesus nor the Bible for the false beliefs of Christians. But rather, it incriminates the religious leaders and Christians holding them as "lords besides God." Muhammad b. Jarīr aṭ-Ṭabarī provides multiple exegetical traditions that explain what the Qurʾan means by the accusation that Christians have taken their priests and monks as lords. These all interpret the accusation as a description of the attitude that Christians have toward their religious leaders, an attitude of blind obedience to teachings that are contrary to God's will and commands.

The second part of the verse reaffirms the absolute monotheism of Islam, against the "associations" (*shirk*) of Jews and Christians, by proclaiming the first part of the *shahāda*—"there is no God but God" (*lā ilāha illā huwa*). Muhammad ash-Shaʿrāwī (died 1998), once Egypt's minister of religious endowments and respected author of a qurʾanic *tafsīr*, launches on a long discussion of the expression at the end of the verse: *subḥānahu ʿammā yushrikūn* ("he is exalted far above what they join with him"). For him, the word *subḥānahu*, which is very difficult to translate into any other language, summarizes his understanding of the fundamental difference between God's attributes and the same adjectives when applied to human beings. For example, when God creates, he creates perfectly; whereas when humans create or invent something, they think that they have resolved a problem, only to discover later that they have compounded the earth's problems.

Other contemporary exegetes take this verse as a springboard to push through further agendas. Muhammad ash-Shawkānī (died 1834), a Zaydī Shīʿī Yemeni turned Sunnī scholar, after reproducing most of the classical interpretation, uses this verse as a foundation for his criticism of Islamic *taqlīd* ("imitation"). Ash-Shawkānī was a fervent advocate of *ijtihād* ("rational scholarly method"), and he saw in at-Tawba 9:31 a warning to his own coreligionists as well. He invites them to base their religion, not on their imams, but on the Qur'an and the Sunna—the model of Muhammad.

Sayyid Quṭb's exegesis of the verse, which he reads within the overall section of at-Tawba 9:29–35, is dark in its promise. With its usual political and Islamist engagement, it does not bode well for the future of Muslim-Christian relations. He sees in this passage the inauguration of a new order to guide the Muslim community's relationships with Christians. He had seen the preceding verses (at-Tawba 9:1–29) as a guide to the relationships of Muslims with polytheists. But now, he argues, Christians and Jews are to be seen as polytheists as well, since they have joined with God other persons to be worshiped (verse 31). In the Quṭbī interpretation, then, at-Tawba 9:31 marks the turning point in the relationships between the Muslims and the people of the book, as it incriminates them definitely and decisively with the sin of *shirk*.

Summarizing the Metadialogue on the Doctrine of God

Our journey through the historical Muslim-Christian discourse about God reveals a peculiar metadialogue on the issue. The journey begins with a strong Muslim desire to exonerate Jesus from any false accusations of heretical beliefs about God (al-Māʾida 5:116). It is motivated by a qurʾanic mandate to seek good relations with Jews and Christians (āl-ʿImrān 3:64). It comes to a deadlock due to the projection of Arabian sectarian heretical beliefs on the mainstream orthodox Christians of the Levant (al-Māʾida 5:72–73). The entire metadialogue is thoroughly framed within the powerful Islamic mantra of God's oneness (al-Ikhlāṣ 112:1–4). It is steeped in a scathing critique of Christians (at-Tawba 9:31), reflecting the deteriorating relationship between Muslims and Christians. And the entire metadialogue is further aggravated through polemical texts written by Christian converts to Islam, who were keen to demonstrate their loyalty to the new religion that had gained their allegiance.

As we stand at the receiving end of this metadialogue, it seems rather important to note the positive starting point of the Muslim writers. First of all, it is never assumed that Jesus introduced and taught a heretical understanding of God. In fact, the entire critical endeavor of Muslim writers regarding the Christian doctrine of God seems to be built on an affirmation of Christ's orthodoxy and a denial of the ideas that later Christians are assumed to have ascribed to him. This leads us to the suggestion that in the Qur'an, the Christian doctrine of the Trinity is not attacked in and of itself. Rather, it is the qur'anic concern for the absolute oneness of God that is the driving force behind the Muslim critique. Nevertheless, the Muslim discourse historically continues to build on the likely misled assumption that the Qur'an is attacking the mainstream orthodox Christian doctrines of Christ's divine nature and of the Trinity, rather than engaging with the actual ones.

Furthermore, as noted particularly in the writings of ʿAlī aṭ-Ṭabarī, at least some Muslim writers, notably in the early period, carried out their work in an attempt to bring Christian thinking in closer alignment with Muslim thinking. Unfortunately, they did this by trying to pour Christian thinking into a Muslim mold, effectively objectifying it, rather than trying to understand Christian thinking and interacting with it as a worthy counterpart.

Muslim authors not only usually removed the Gospel citations from their wider contexts to apply to them their exegetical presuppositions, but also often transformed their citations and reshaped them so that they would lend themselves perfectly to their own theological argument. Whether these inaccurate citations were done intentionally or not, they certainly played a crucial part in the shaping of the general method and character of Muslim anti-Christian polemics. ʿAlī aṭ-Ṭabarī, whose Gospel text was one of the earliest emerging in the Muslim polemical genre, became quite influential in the later tradition, and therefore his work was foundational for the whole discourse. He seems to be editing his biblical quotations to suit the need of his argument. The text is excised and altered in order to comply with Muslim dogma. Any words that might have implied greatness for Jesus were removed or altered. Jesus was made to proclaim an Islamic type of monotheism, reinforced by a humble Islamic portrait of himself, and bits of different Bible verses were often collated in order to fit into the intended agenda.

Whereas the positive motivations of Muslim writers and their desire for interfaith rapprochement reflect the positive context of this metadialogue on the doctrine of God, the most obstinate historical deadlocks, preventing progress in this discourse, are the result of some Muslim writers' misled assumptions about key qur'anic verses, as well as the attempt by Christian converts to force the biblical text into a Muslim doctrinal mold.

Hermeneutical Keys in Building Bridges beyond Conflict

Against such a historical background and in such an ongoing relational context, can any keys be found to help unlock the historical deadlocks of the Muslim-Christian metadialogue? I venture that the metadialogue that has emerged from tracing the history of the dialogical exchange about God between Muslims and Christians provides us with some clues that may help us move beyond the deadlocks. One may argue that if the interfaith exchange has been so intense and so extensive, why should we hope to escape the deadlock today? But my view is that one new variant today did not exist over the past fourteen hundred years—the variant of history. The realities of our postcolonial, globalized, post–9/11, twenty-first-century world are new factors in the present conversation. And though at some level there is "nothing new under the sun," at the same time every day is a new opportunity with new possibilities that were not there for us before.

Using Deadlocks as Assets

The *vindication of Jesus* (al-Mā'ida 5:116) remains the most powerful asset in conversations about God between Christians and Muslims today. It is the most stable and promising element of our common ground. The position of Jesus, as a powerful manifestation of divine spirit and teaching ("his word conveyed to Mary and a spirit from him"; an-Nisā' 4:171), will never be undermined, precisely because he is at the heart of the Qur'an's testimony. Though some, from the perspective of the philosophy of religion, may argue that we should find our dialogical starting point in the common denominator of God's unity, I hold to the conviction that our best starting point is Jesus. This conviction is not only based on the qur'anic witness, but it is also profoundly biblical and theological. Jesus, the Bible and Christian theology tell us, is where God started with us on the journey of his fuller self-revelation. Without wanting to undermine the value and power of natural, prophetic, and scriptural revelation, I venture that followers of Jesus affirm that God, in his self-revelation, ultimately did not become a book, nor did he stop at revealing himself through his creation, nor was he satisfied with sending messengers who would testify about him. Followers of Jesus can continue to affirm with the New Testament that Jesus was the most comprehensive and authentic manifestation of God, *in bodily form* (Col 2:9). The witness of the Qur'an and the overarching Muslim view about Jesus concur with this view, though it does hold some reservations about how to understand this, and this therefore remains a great starting point.

Second, the qur'anic mandate that calls Muslims to *find "a common word"* with Jews and Christians (āl-ʿImrān 3:64) is an unmatched foundation for interfaith engagement. That it was given central place in recent years, through the *A Common Word* initiative (see acommonword.com), renews the authority of this qur'anic call on a global scale. Some point out that this verse is a polemic against Christian doctrines and that contrary to the claim of the initiative, it is not a call to love God and neighbor. It is true that the verse warns against associating anything with God. And given that the warning is addressed to the people of the book, who are usually identified as the Jews and the Christians, it is likely a rebuke at least of a certain understanding of the doctrines of the Trinity and of Christ's sonship. But in reality, these are somewhat irrelevant to my argument. In Islam, if a particular qur'anic interpretation achieves consensus (*ijmāʿ*) among Muslim scholars, then it represents a legitimate precedent on whose basis one is invited to act. This particular interpretation of the verse, as a result of the *A Common Word* initiative, has achieved to-date consensus (and that is just officially) among 405 prominent religious and scholarly Muslim leaders globally. When one browses through the names of the signatories, found on the initiative's website, one can only recognize that this consensus is nothing short of remarkable. In this particular context, it is sufficient to confirm āl-ʿImrān 3:64 in its position as a solid foundation for positive and creative interfaith engagement in the contemporary world.

The third stage in the metadialogue, the *projection of heretical beliefs on Christian orthodoxy* (al-Mā'ida 5:72–73), is a more sensitive one. If one continued to affirm that the Qur'an, in such verses, was attacking heretical beliefs found in the sectarian milieu from which it emerged, one would probably be close to the truth from a historian's perspective. It would ensue that when Muslims use these verses to critique Christian orthodoxy, they are merely attacking a straw man. But it is largely useless to stop there. The reality is that, as soon as Muhammad's early followers left their original sectarian milieu and were projected into the rich and diverse environment of the territories they rapidly conquered, they immediately applied this qur'anic criticism to the Christians they encountered in their new environment. The previous argument becomes therefore a moot point. It is now this reality that we need to work with, and simply repeating old arguments will not do. If Muslims are able to accept that the doctrines attacked by the Qur'an are not simply the orthodox doctrines of the church, and if Christians are willing to admit that the linguistic expression of their doctrines is open to a certain degree of reframing with language that is more accessible to both Muslims and Christians today, then we may find a firmer foundation on which to hold constructive conversation.

The fourth stage in the metadialogue, the *powerful Islamic mantra of God's oneness* (al-Ikhlāṣ 112:1–4), also seems to be steeped in polemics. From the perspective of classical Islamic chronology that places this sūrah in the Meccan period, there may be good justification for reading it primarily as a refutation of Arabian pagan cultic beliefs. But in light of other qur'anic verses (such as the ones in al-Mā'ida cited above), and allowing for qur'anic verses to be the primary key to the interpretation of other verses (*tafsīr al-Qur'an bi al-Qur'an*), the affirmation may be understood to be an emphatic rejection, once again, both of Christ's sonship and of his divinity. Sūrat al-Ikhlāṣ 112 is not simply an affirmation of God's oneness. Through a sort of ABB'A' construction, it affirms that (A) God is unique, (B) he is self-sufficient; therefore (B') he had need for neither giving birth nor being born, and (A') he has no equal. As in the case of stage three, there is no point ignoring the straightforward implications that this sūrah has on the Muslim view of core Christian doctrines. But the boldness of these verses should intimidate neither Christian nor Muslim to prevent them from talking to each other.

Christians are very comfortable affirming, along with Muslims, the straightforward confession of God's oneness and uniqueness. They are also comfortable affirming that he is self-sufficient, in the sense that none of his actions derive from any sort of need, nor do they add to or retract anything from him. Everything he does derives from his essence, and as far as we can tell in our limited human comprehension, he does it out of sheer pleasure, more like a creative and accomplished fine artist than in pursuit of some personal need. With Muslims, we can affirm that though he created everything, he could just as well have not created anything. But Christians add that *love*, being his essence, creation was, and continues to be, the natural expression of his self-givingness, the most natural manifestation of love. And it is from that same angle that Christians understand Jesus. Followers of Jesus today, like his disciples who walked with him in the past, need not be stuck on static dogmatic formulas to express their understanding of God. Having lived with Jesus, his disciples later realized that they had experienced *Emmanuel*, "God with us." His followers today still want to express *Emmanuel* just as strongly, whom they experience through the presence of the Holy Spirit with them and in them. This "other Comforter/Advocate/Counselor" (John 14–16), like Jesus, continues to be the presence of God with them. This reality—experienced, felt, and perceived—is what followers of Jesus should care to talk about with Muslims. And they should be happy to do so alongside the affirmation of God's oneness and uniqueness, his unchanging nature, that he neither was born nor gave birth in any crude physical way, and that absolutely nothing is comparable to him, our loving, gracious, and self-giving God.

In the fifth stage of the Muslim-Christian metadialogue, *the scathing critique of Christians by Muslims* based on at-Tawba 9:31 reflects their deteriorating relationship. On the one hand, the relationship between Christians and Muslims today may be viewed as being at an all-time low. Christians in the Middle East are being wiped out by violent religious fanatics claiming to be acting on Islam's command. Muslims in the West complain about extreme Islamophobia. Every time a senseless person behaves violently in the name of Islam, Muslims experience attacks on their persons and places of worship and discrimination against them by governments practicing profiling and driven by fear. On the other hand, the opportunities presenting to us today may be seen as unique in history. As heirs of the colonial era, we inherited the phenomenon of massive population migration. As a result, previously colonial countries are being shaped by previously colonized peoples today at least as profoundly and decisively as colonial powers shaped their colonies during the colonial era. Muslims today are an integral part of virtually every society in the world. The diversity that exists within Islam, as well as within Christianity, as a result of all of this cross-fertilization, offers unprecedented opportunities. Furthermore, the ongoing and relentless globalization of our lives, of our means of communication, of our human values, is forcing all of us to question who we are, who we want to be, what we want to stand for, how we want to relate to each other, and what kind of world we want to contribute as a legacy as we move on. As we also recognize that we are heirs of fourteen hundred years of uneasy relationships, as Christians and Muslims we have the choice not to perpetuate the mistakes of the past.

And sixth, polemical texts written by Christian converts to Islam left a *rather detrimental legacy* in the early stages of Muslim-Christian engagement, which largely set the negative tone of the next twelve hundred years in the metadialogue. The danger that can be seen by those who listen to the lessons of history is that history seems to be repeating itself. The question that we must ask ourselves as twenty-first-century Christians and Muslims is whether there exist languages of communication between us beyond polemics. Can we grow closer together? Can we be less triumphalistic? Can we view our diversity as an asset rather than a threat? Every generation's books, movies, news reports, media, and artistic expressions of all sorts set the tone for Christian and Muslim relationships of the next generations. Are we aware of the responsibility that is laid on our shoulders?

Concluding Thoughts

The building of minarets in Western countries has led to many complaints about the calls that issue from them. But for me, when the call to prayer begins to mount at dusk, in a cumulative overlay of *Allāhu Akbar* ("God is great!"), my whole being is drawn back to the nostalgia of childhood, and my spirit feels like responding in prayerful devotion to God. I tend to believe, therefore, that the question of whether Christians and Muslims worship the same God is an emotional question rather than a rational one. Objectively, there is only one God, to whom all pious hearts turn in their search for the truth, and whose favor all worshipers long to receive in response to their sincere worship.

But on a more subjective level, we need to remember that all human worship is somewhat idolatrous. When we address our worship to God, we each have a different mental image of the recipient of our worship. As Christians, it is even more difficult for us to worship God without our minds being overwhelmed by a myriad of images of Christ that come to us from a rich, image-filled Christian artistic tradition. It is little wonder that the Eastern Christian tradition prefers apophatic (negative affirmations about God) rather than kataphatic (positive affirmations about God) theology. By affirming what God is not, Christian mystics such as Basil the Great, Gregory of Nyssa, Maximus the Confessor, and many others taught that we can strive to move out of the idolatry of our minds and move along the path of true worship, as we train ourselves to avoid forming mental images of God in our prayer.

In addition, however, the message of the Gospel is that in Christ, our worship becomes acceptable to God, not by merit but by grace. So, I close this chapter by affirming that it is not by some merit of our own that we worship the true God, nor by some conviction that we possess the correct intellectual understanding of God. If our worship is viewed by God as anything other than idolatry, it is only by his grace and mercy that he accepts it. This is a sobering thought that should help us approach our Muslim brothers and sisters with humility, as we share about the God that we worship.

Further Reading and Research

Cragg, K. *The Call of the Minaret*. 3rd ed. Oxford: Oneworld, 2008 (originally 1956). Cragg represents a turning point in Christian theologizing in the context of Islam that sought mutual understanding without neutralizing doctrinal differences between Christianity and Islam.

Griffith, S. H. *The Beginnings of Christian Theology in Arabic: Muslim-Christian Encounters in the Early Islamic Period*. Burlington VT: Variorum, 2003. Griffith studies the attempts by Christians living in the early Islamic world to do theology in the context of Islam. He explores the modes of argumentation (*kalām*) that early Arab Christian apologists adopted in order to explain Christian doctrines using Muslim patterns of reasoning. This book is only a doorway into the extensive publications by Griffith, David Thomas, and others in this area.

Kärkkäinen, V.-M. *Trinity and Religious Pluralism: The Doctrine of the Trinity in Christian Theology of Religions*. Burlington VT: Ashgate, 2004. In this overview of contemporary Christian approaches to the role of the Trinity in religious pluralism, Kärkkäinen lays the groundwork for future study of the construction of Christian theologies of religion.

Kärkkäinen, V.-M. *A Constructive Christian Theology for the Pluralistic World*, vol. 2: *Trinity and Revelation*. Grand Rapids: Eerdmans, 2014. Emerging out of the contemporary interest in religious pluralism,

Kärkkäinen develops a constructive Christian theology in the context of religious diversity. He argues compellingly for the significance of the doctrine of the Trinity in relating to other religions, including Islam.

Volf, M. *Allah: A Christian Response*. New York: HarperOne, 2011. Volf offers a contemporary exploration of the doctrine of the Trinity in the context of Islam, drawing on two historical approaches (Nicholas of Cusa and Martin Luther). While missing any discussion of the history of Arab Christian and missionary encounters with Islam that support his argument for similarities in the concept of God between Christianity and Islam, his exploration provides a reference point for minority-world theologians to consider for engaging with non-Arab Islam.

4 Who Jesus Is Not according to Muslims

My father worked for the Bible Society in Lebanon for most of his life, serving as its general secretary for over twenty-five years. Growing up, several of my summers were spent in the distribution of biblical literature and in organizing viewings of the Jesus Film in Christian, Muslim, and Druze villages. I have mostly fond memories of drinking lemonade and mulberry juice and listening to pleasant and hospitable conversations about religion and about Jesus in the atmosphere of friendly home gatherings. I grew up in a home that had deep respect and love for the Bible and an ethos strong with the teaching and example of Jesus. I never thought about my relationship with God as religion, but as a life centered on Christ, in whom I experienced God's compassion and love for humanity. Those Bible distribution camps had something ecumenical about them, bringing together followers of Jesus from various backgrounds. Their purpose was not to make converts to Christianity as such, but to introduce people to the Bible, talk to them about Jesus, and invite them to become his disciples.

One of the funny anecdotes that were told as the various teams gathered back together in the evening had been experienced by more than one team involved in showing the Jesus Film. As the story of Jesus unfolded on the screen and came to the scene of the crucifixion, silent sobbing could often be heard from some sections of the audience. And on one occasion, young men suddenly stood up and started shooting their AK-47s in the air. These were the years of the Lebanese civil war, when light and heavy weapons were normative in most village homes. The religious affiliation of those passionate youth did not matter. As they watched the film, whether Christian, Muslim, or Druze, their sympathy for Jesus would grow, and they could not accept the tale of betrayal and injustice that ensued. Just as Peter had sworn allegiance to Jesus's protection, those young men exclaimed that if they had been Jesus's companions, they would never have allowed anyone to lay hands on him and put him to death.

Peter swore: "Lord, I am ready to go with you to prison and to death" (Luke 22:33). He pledged: "Lord, why can't I follow you now? I will lay down my life for you" (John 13:37). But Jesus knew about human weakness. "Before the rooster crows today, you will deny three times that you know me," was his response (Luke 22:34; John 13:38). Elsewhere, having just confirmed to his disciples that he was "the Christ, the Son of the living God," Jesus had to readjust their expectations, and he went on to reveal to them that this same Son was to go to Jerusalem, suffer at the hands of religious people and leaders, be killed, and rise back to life after three days (Mark 8:27–38; Matt 16:13–28). At this paradox of the suffering of God's chosen one, Peter had the audacity to take Jesus aside and rebuke him for his statements. It is this same gut reaction that gripped the young men watching the Jesus Film in the villages of Lebanon. Instead of trying to comprehend the divine logic of power in weakness, forgiveness in persecution, love in response to hatred, life out of death, true love as self-sacrifice and the laying down of one's life for others, we still strive to be God's heroes according to the instinctive human understanding of power.

More recently, I sat with a godly Muslim man in his living room, talking about Jesus. He adequately explained to me the symbolic and relational meaning of the affirmation that Jesus is "the Son of God." He could even grasp the depth of the affirmation that "in Christ all the fullness of the deity lives in bodily form" (Col 2:9). He did not see that the Qur'an in its overall message necessarily denied that Jesus had died on the cross. But what he could not comprehend was how that death could actually bring life and salvation to those who put their trust in this divine initiative.

It is indeed neither easy nor natural to our human thinking to acquire the mind of God in what brings peace to this world. In situations of human conflict, whether interpersonal or international, each party attempts to gain the upper hand on the ground in order to be in a position of power at the time of peace negotiations. Weapons of war, destruction, and invasion are dispatched by powerful nations in an effort to impose peace. Or at best we preach a morality of peace, love, and forgiveness as the tools that we hope might lead to peace and reconciliation. But in the midst of our most concerted human efforts, the words of Jesus to Peter still ring true for us: "You do not have in mind the things of God, but the things of men." He calls us aside, along with his disciples, and instructs us: "If anyone would come after me, he must deny himself and take up his cross and follow me. For whoever wants to save his life will lose it, but whoever loses his life for me will find it" (Matt 16:23–25; Mark 8:33–35). The historicity of the cross is not the most difficult to agree on in the Christian-Muslim conversation. But what remains notoriously hard to grasp, not just in the interfaith context, but also for Christians, Muslims, Jews, and other human beings, is how life and salvation can emerge from death and apparent failure. That is an implication whose truth begins to unfold only as we get drawn into the divine logic about the functioning of power.

The Two-Stage Islamic Approach to Christology

As one reads the Qur'an, what transpires is that the clearest meaning of its narrative sits most comfortably alongside parallel biblical narratives, but not before the latter has been filtered through the unfaltering Islamic affirmation of the unicity of God.

Sooner or later, the Christian who may wish to discuss the doctrine of Christ in a day-to-day conversation with a Muslim will come across the argument implied in the statement of Christian convert to Islam ʿAlī aṭ-Ṭabarī (circa 782–860): "Whoever speaks concerning Christ in accordance with what he spoke concerning himself is the [true] believer in him. And whoever speaks concerning him differently from how he described himself is the proud contradictor."[1] A good Muslim will pride himself/herself not only on holding a more accurate understanding of the nature of Christ's person than a Christian, but also of loving him more because he/she rejects the possibility that God might have allowed him to die on the cross, betrayed by the Jews of his time.

As began to emerge from our exploration of the Muslim discourse with Christians about God in the previous chapter, the Islamic exegesis of Gospel passages does not really consist in demonstrating the absurdity of the Christian doctrines through a fresh reinterpretation of the Gospel texts. Rather, it assumes this absurdity, since the Christian doctrines are

1. ʿAlī b. Sahl Rabbān aṭ-Ṭabarī, *Kitāb ar-Radd ʿala an-Naṣāra*, in I. A. Khalifé and W. Kutsch's "Ar-radd ʿala-n-nasārā," *Mélanges de l'Université Saint Joseph* 36.4 (1959): 115–48 at 122.

seen as disagreeing so flagrantly with Islam, and sets out to correct the Christian interpretation retrospectively. Muslim scholars sought to purge the blessed ʿĪsa from all the heresies attributed to him by Christians. ʿAlī aṭ-Ṭabarī provides an explicit expression of this motive at the beginning of his *Radd*, where he exclaims: "And I do not intend for what I have argued and what I am proving in my present book to be a refutation against Christ (Peace be upon him!) or against the people of his truth, but against those types of Christians who have contradicted Christ and the Gospels, and have changed the meaning [*ḥarrafū*] of the words."[2]

It is the disagreement of the qur'anic picture of Christ with the common Christian belief that motivates the whole exegetical undertaking. Muslim authors felt the need to go back to the same writings, which Christians claimed as the source of their doctrines, and to confirm for themselves the correct way of understanding them. The conclusion that aṭ-Ṭabarī draws from his survey of the relevant verses he emphatically affirms in the following lines: "And we are the ones in agreement with God and with Christ, and they are the ones in disagreement with God and with his Christ."[3]

In the present chapter and the next, we encounter the Muslim attempt to realign the testimony of the Gospels with the qur'anic portrait of Jesus. From the Islamic perspective, we seem to be witnessing a project of restoration. The icon of Christ is being stripped of its corrupt layers, and fresh paint is restoring its authentic traits. In our discovery of this process, we start by examining the negative efforts of the Muslim writers, who work on ridding Jesus's image of its *extra* Christian layers of *sonship* and *divinity*, before beginning to restore his portrait progressively from *man* and *servant*, to *prophet* and *apostle* in the next chapter.

Jesus the Prophet of Islam?

I pointed out in the previous chapter the puzzling attachment of the Qur'an—our earliest and no doubt most reliable source on Islam—to

2. Aṭ-Ṭabarī, *Radd*, 120. It is obvious that aṭ-Ṭabarī is not referring to a *textual* corruption here, since he accuses some Christians of having "contradicted Christ and the Gospels." He is using the word *ḥarrafa* in its weaker meaning of "erroneous *ta'wīl*," or misinterpretation.

3. Aṭ-Ṭabarī, *Radd*, 125.

the Judeo-Christian tradition. If the city of Mecca, Muhammad's shaping context according to the Muslim tradition, were really as pagan and *Jāhilī* ("steeped in ignorance") as the standard traditional narrative would have us believe, why is it that the Qur'an is so intent on affirming continuity with the preceding monotheistic revelations? The same question begs to be answered when it comes to the Qur'an's veneration of Jesus, a prominent figure in the sacred text. Though the Muslim tradition outside the qur'anic text claims to preserve a number of significant historical encounters between Muhammad and Christians, one gets a sense that these were largely incidental.

There is the narrative about a Christian monk, Baḥīra, who recognized the "seal of prophethood" between young Muhammad's shoulder blades as he journeyed on a trade caravan through the desert of Syria with his uncle Abū Ṭālib.[4] We are told about Waraqa b. Nawfal, the Christian cousin of his first wife, Khadīja, who testified about the authenticity of Muhammad's revelations when he began experiencing supernatural encounters with a divine messenger.[5] Later, the accuracy of the qur'anic revelations about God and Jesus is confirmed by Negus, the Christian king of Abyssinia in modern-day Ethiopia, when Muhammad's early converts recited parts of Sūrat Maryam at the Abyssinian court during the first migration from Mecca.[6] But the clear function of all of these narratives seems to be more closely linked to an affirmation of Muhammad's prophethood than to encouraging some sort of cultic veneration of the person of Jesus.

Since the Islamic tradition affirmed the Qur'an as a revealed Scripture emerging purely from divine origins, it is not surprising that Muslims do not attempt to ascribe to these encounters any *causative* role in the Qur'an's positive portrayal of Jesus. Yet, through the Islamic hermeneutical principle of uncovering the *occasions of the revelations*, such encounters are viewed as the historical context within which the qur'anic revelation is embedded. The most significant such occasion for the qur'anic discourse about Jesus, as we will see, was the visit of a prestigious delegation of Christians from Najrān near the end of Muhammad's life. Many of the Qur'an's verses that seem to engage polemically with Christian doctrines (e.g., the first ninety verses of Sūrat āl-ʿImrān 3) were set in the context

4. Alfred Guillaume, *The Life of Muhammad: A Translation of Ibn Ishaq's Sirat Rasul Allah* (Oxford: Oxford University Press, 2002), 80.

5. Guillaume, *Life of Muhammad*, 83.

6. Guillaume, *Life of Muhammad*, 146–53.

of this encounter by the bulk of the Islamic exegetical tradition. That encounter was not nearly as positive as the earlier ones just mentioned. Rather than a confirmation of the authenticity of his prophethood, that late encounter is described as the occasion of a questioning by the Christian leaders of the legitimacy of his religious authority in his new status as the emerging political ruler of Arabia.

Quite aside from a discussion on the historicity of these encounters, we must ask ourselves what function these narratives contributed to the shaping of the religious consciousness among the emerging community of Muhammad. Both the positive portrayal of Jesus in the Qur'an and the mostly positive portrayal of Christians in both the Qur'an and the tradition seem to convey that Muhammad's social origins were not as disconnected from the Christian tradition as the classical Muslim picture would have us believe. This, combined with the departure of the Qur'an and the tradition from the received theological portrayal of Christ, leaves us with a deep sense that Muhammad may have belonged to a sectarian Judeo-Christian milieu in Arabia that was never at peace with the imperial mainstream of Byzantium.

As we approach the Muslim discourse about Christ over the centuries, therefore, it is not surprising that we find ourselves before a very complex sociopolitical metadialogue, rather than before a dispassionate theological discourse. Such a realization does not bode well at first for those who, like me, hope that theological dialogue could help attenuate the conflict between the various monotheistic traditions. On second thought, however, if we are able to recognize the largely political and reactionary nature of the metadialogue from its emergence to the present, this might perhaps clear the way for a fresh start on fairer theological grounds today. The way forward, then, would be for each of our communities to approach the other with a greater openness to understanding the starting point and internal logic of each of our traditions, rather than imposing each our own lens on the other.

No theme brings out the rhetorical nature of the qur'anic text more sharply than the theme of Jesus's identity. It is a rhetoric that wavers mostly between polemics and apologetics. As a result, it often feels as if the Qur'an is more interested in clarifying who Jesus is not, rather than affirming who he is. There is much polemical material against the Christology of Christians in al-Mā'ida 5:72, 116 and at-Tawba 9:30–31. I chose to deal with them in the previous chapter, in connection with the doctrine of God, as these qur'anic verses were used by Muslim exegetes primarily to critique the Christian understanding of God. In the present chapter, I focus on verses primarily from Sūrat āl-ʿImrān 3 and Sūrat an-Nisāʾ 4.

Even some of the most positive affirmations about Jesus in the Qurʾan seem to have an axe to grind. For example, it is difficult to read the qurʾanic affirmation in āl-ʿImrān 3:59 without hearing a critique of Christian claims that Jesus was divine: "To God, Jesus is like Adam, whom he created from dust, then he told him, 'Be!' and he was."

Classical Muslim scholars sought to make sense of such qurʾanic affirmations by searching for the historical context of their revelation, *asbāb an-nuzūl.* About the ninth year after Muhammad led his community of followers out of Mecca and into the city of Yathrib, later al-Madīna (circa 631), and perhaps a year before his death in 632, the main biographer of Islam's prophet (Ibn Hishām [died 833], on the authority of Ibn Isḥāq [died 768]) narrates that a prestigious delegation of Christians from Najrān in Yemen paid an official visit to the rising ruler of Arabia. They wanted to discuss with him theological matters of common interest and, one would assume, learn of his intentions toward those who would not pledge allegiance to his leadership in the peninsula.

In a striking anecdote preserved by the Muslim tradition, when the time of afternoon prayer came—Eastern Christians prayed seven times daily, turning their faces toward the East—the Christian delegation are said to have entered what the tradition refers to as the mosque (*masjid* or place of prayer) of God's apostle, to the dismay of the latter's followers. When they came to him complaining, however, he simply ordered them to leave the Christians alone and allow them to perform their prayers in the *masjid*. Following this, Ibn Hishām tells us, Muhammad entered into a long theological debate about Jesus with the Christian delegation. The gist of the Muslim argument can be found in the first ninety verses of the third sūrah, āl-ʿImrān.

The commentary tradition sets the rhetorical context of these verses in the claim that the Yemeni Christians tried to base their belief in the divinity of Christ on his virgin birth. This is reflected in the earliest, accumulated traditions reported in Muhammad b. Jarīr aṭ-Ṭabarī's commentary (died 922) and in the Shīʿī tradition, as represented in the more recent commentary of aṭ-Ṭabaʾṭabāʾī (died 1981). The latter considers āl-ʿImrān 3:59 to be the basis for two arguments that serve to deny Jesus's divinity. The first argument is found in the use of the verb *khalaqahu* ("he created him"), which affirms Jesus's created nature, even though he was created without the participation of a father. The second argument is that the way that Jesus was created does not surpass in greatness the way that Adam was created, and therefore does not justify the inference of divinity, just as Christians do not confer divinity on Adam as a result of his coming into being without father or mother.

If Jesus's birth took place without the participation of a father, āl-ʿImrān 3:59 affirms, and if Christians use this as proof that he was divine, then the Qur'an argues that Adam's birth was greater than Jesus's, since he was born without either father or mother. Aṭ-Ṭabarī reaffirms the *Sīra* traditions according to which the Christians tried to convince Muhammad that Jesus's virgin birth made him greater than any of God's creations, and that he should therefore be perceived as more than a servant of God. Muhammad would have then received this God-given, irrefutable argument against their claims.

In the later Sunnī tradition, such as in the medieval commentary of ar-Rāzī (died 1209), as well as in the more contemporary traditional Sunnī commentaries of ash-Shaʿrāwī (died 1998) and aṭ-Ṭanṭāwī (died 2010), the views of the Christians of Najrān become representative of the theology of all Christians. Christians are understood to be saying that, since Jesus was born without a father, this proved that his father was God himself. These commentaries continue in the traditional exegesis, setting āl-ʿImrān 3:59 primarily in the qur'anic rhetorical setting of an affirmation of God's unity and rejection of the Trinity, as well as of Christ's sonship and divinity.

The Salafī exegetical tradition of Rashīd Riḍa (died 1935) and Sayyid Quṭb (died 1966) continues in the same vein. However, Quṭb in his usual style does not simply endorse the stories of the past. He does not deny the plausibility of the Najrān delegation as the occasion of the verse's revelation, but he focuses instead on the overall theme of the sūrah, which he identifies as the question of *tawḥīd*—the proclamation of God's unicity. In this context, the story of ʿĪsa, Quṭb affirms, is a confirmation of *tawḥīd* and a rejection of sonship (*al-walad*) and companionship (*ash-sharīk*) in connection with God.

Despite the polemical rhetoric, one recent exegetical commentary on the Qur'an uses the verse in a positive manner. Ash-Shawkānī (died 1834) affirms that the comparison of Jesus's birth to Adam's in this verse was given by God as an argument against those who questioned Jesus's virgin birth. God reminds those people that if he was capable of bringing Adam into existence out of clay, with no intervention from a mother or a father, why would he not bring Jesus into existence simply without the participation of a father?

The Virgin Birth and Christ's Divinity

In reality, it is doubtful that the virgin birth was ever the main argument for Christ's divinity among Christians of the time. That is certainly not what we find in the early Eastern Christian tradition. Among the church fathers, the virgin birth *confirmed*, rather than *proved*, God's agency in the birth, ministry, death, and resurrection of Jesus. At some points during the medieval period, the virgin birth may have been used as a tool to support the claim of Jesus's sinlessness in an increasingly dualistic Neoplatonic worldview. But predominantly in the Christian tradition, it was part of a soteriological, not christological, argument.

It is striking that the earliest New Testament witnesses, both Paul and Mark, seem to have shown little or no interest in the virgin birth. When Paul, in his epistle to the Galatians (4:4), affirms that "God sent his Son, born of a woman," it is not the virgin birth with which he is preoccupied. The chapter is "a tale of two women." Paul is developing a typology where he warns his readers not to revert to their former slavery to the Mosaic law, when they were the children of the "slave woman" (Hagar), but to live out their freedom in Christ, as children of the "free woman" (Sarah). While we were once slaves to the law, as children of the slave woman, "when the time had fully come, God sent his Son, born of a woman, born under law, to redeem those under law, that we might receive the full rights of sons" (4:4–5). The accounts of the virgin birth in the Gospels of Matthew and Luke are not gynecological claims; they are affirmations of God's redemptive initiative in Christ. Together with the apostle Paul, they are affirming that "God sent his Son." In the same way, when Jesus or one of the Gospel writers affirm that Jesus was the "Son of God," they are not making physical genealogical claims; but rather they are affirming with Paul that "God sent his Son . . . that we might receive the full rights of sons."

To the affirmation that Jesus's virgin birth need not lead to the conclusion that he was more than a normal human being, Muslim exegetes adduced a number of other qur'anic verses. With the support of an-Nisā' 4:172, the exegetical tradition affirmed Jesus's humility and that he himself would not have seen it as beneath him to worship God and be his servant: "The Messiah was never too proud to be God's servant, nor were the angels who are near to him. He will gather before him the arrogant and all those who are too proud to worship him."

If even the angels, those beings closer to God than any of his other creatures, says Ibn Jarīr aṭ-Ṭabarī, were not ashamed of their status as servants of God, surely Jesus would not have claimed a higher status. The cherubim, such as *Jibrīl*, *Mīkā'īl*, and *Isrāphīl*, adds az-Zamakhsharī (died 1143), are higher in status and greater in power than Jesus. Therefore, this verse is a refutation of Christian exaggerations in their raising of Jesus's status above servanthood to God. As with the opening ninety verses of Sūrat āl-ʿImrān, the *occasion of the revelation* of this cluster of verses from Sūrat an-Nisā' is described by az-Zamakhsharī and others to be that same encounter between Muhammad and the Christians of Najrān. According to that tradition, the Christians would have rebuked Muhammad for denigrating Jesus. When Muhammad asked them in what way he had denigrated their master, they answered: "You say that he is God's servant and apostle." To this Muhammad responds: "There is no shame in being a servant of God." The qur'anic verse is then revealed to affirm his statement that there is no shame in being God's servant.

The Biblical Narrative of the Incarnation among Civilizational Myths

One of the deepest misunderstandings perpetuated throughout much of the Islamic tradition is that the doctrines of the Trinity, Christ's sonship, and the incarnation were invented or developed in the fourth century, namely at the Council of Nicea (325).

Muslim exegete Ibn Kathīr (died 1373), in his commentary on an-Nisā' 4:171, reports mockingly that Christians gathered in the days of Emperor Constantine, at a time when every twenty, fifty, seventy, or one hundred bishops held a different belief about Christ. When the emperor saw that 318 of them had agreed on the same statement, he adopted and supported it, and those became the Melkites. Then at a second council, the Jacobites were born. And at a third council, the Nestorians emerged. All three groups, he claims, agree on the three hypostases in Christ (Ibn Kathīr is confusing the doctrine of the Trinity with Christology), but they diverge on how the three relate. An-Nisā' 4:171 warned Christians against *ghuluw* ("exaggeration") with regard to Christ's true nature:

> People of the book, do not be excessive in your beliefs, and do not say anything about God except the truth. The Messiah, Jesus son of Mary, is the messenger of God; his Word conveyed to Mary and a Spirit from him. Believe in God and his messengers and do not say "Three." Stop

> this for your own good. God is only one God. So exalted is he, in his glory, from having a son. Everything belongs to him that is in the heavens and on earth. None is as worthy to trust as he.

Many a Christian through history has used this verse to argue that the Qur'an affirms the same Trinitarian thinking as the Bible: "The Messiah . . . his Word . . . and a Spirit from him." Just over a century after the death of Muhammad, John of Damascus (died 749) made that argument in book two of his monumental *Fount of Knowledge*, dedicated to the treatment of heresies. He refers to heresy number 101 as "the heresy of the Ishmaelites," by which he was referring to Islam. It is a highly polemical work, most of which is quite offensive to any Muslim—and indeed to any Christian who respects Islam and Muslims. But this is the way that such works, on both the Christian and the Muslim side, were written in those times. With reference to Sūrat an-Nisā' 171, he disputes:

> And again we say to them: "As long as you say that Christ is the Word of God and Spirit, why do you accuse us of being Hetaeriasts [i.e., associators—Arabic *mushrikūn*]? For the Word, and the Spirit, is inseparable from that in which it naturally has existence. Therefore, if the Word of God is in God, then it is obvious that he is God. If, however, he is outside of God, then, according to you, God is without Word and without Spirit. Consequently, by avoiding the introduction of an associate with God you have mutilated him.[7]

The argument is of course based on the affirmation in the Gospel of John that Christ was the eternal Word of God (John 1:1) and on the New Testament affirmation that, together with the Holy Spirit, the Father and the Son express the triune nature of God. I have used forms of this argument at various points in conversations with Muslims. But I now consider that, to be fair to the qur'anic text, there is in this verse too explicit a rejection of the Trinity to allow for that sort of interpretation.

In chapter 3 I suggested that the Qur'an may have been arguing against a different sort of Trinitarian belief than the one held by mainstream Christianity—a belief that may have been widespread in Arabia at the time. Here too, an-Nisā' 4:171 appears to be rejecting a form of tritheism rather than orthodox triune Christian thinking when it warns:

7. See orthodoxinfo.com/general/stjohn_islam.aspx.

"Do not say 'Three.' Stop this for your own good." The verse's affirmation that "God is only one God" is what the Christian tradition has always affirmed. But the Muslim tradition has not always acknowledged it and has rarely been willing to listen to how Christians sought to balance their belief in God's oneness alongside the biblical testimony of his triuneness.

As with other qur'anic verses that reject tritheism, the Muslim exegetical tradition is unanimous in assuming that the doctrine that the Qur'an is rejecting is the standard Christian belief in the Trinity. Muhammad b. Jarīr aṭ-Ṭabarī opens his interpretation of this verse by affirming that in addressing the people of the book, God was targeting the "people of the Gospel," that is, Christians. He paraphrases: "Believe, O people of the book, in God's unicity and lordship, and that he has no child. And believe his messengers who brought you God's message, and in what I have told you concerning God being one without associates, without a partner, and without a child. And do not say Three; meaning: do not say that there are three Lords."

Ibn Kathīr, in his commentary, reports a tradition on the authority of Shādh b. Yaḥya, who explained that "his word conveyed to Mary" does not mean that "the word became 'Īsa," but that "by the word, 'Īsa came into being." On the qur'anic warning "do not say Three," Ibn Kathīr comments: "In other words, do not make 'Īsa and his mother into associates with God."

The same accusation seems to be implied in the Qur'an's at-Tawba 9:30. Here again, Jews and Christians are accused of inheriting unorthodox beliefs about Ezra and Jesus from "unbelievers" (*al-ladhīna kafarū*): "Some Jews say, 'Ezra is God's son,' while some Christians say, 'The Messiah is God's son.' This is what they say with their own mouths. They repeat the assertions made before by unbelievers. 'May God destroy them.' How perverted are their minds."

According to Ibn Jarīr aṭ-Ṭabarī, "the unbelievers who preceded them" is a reference, according to some traditions, to the Christians who followed the Jewish claims concerning Ezra, in their assertion that Jesus was the Son of God. According to other traditions, this is a reference to pagans, who preceded Jews and Christians with their belief in gods who had sons and daughters, a belief that made its way into Judaism and Christianity.

The *Salafī* commentaries of Rashīd Riḍa (died 1935) and Sayyid Quṭb (died 1966) continue to perpetuate this accusation, but now they are able to benefit from a new panoply of arguments offered to them by a certain stream of Christian theological inquiry. Thanks to their extensive awareness of text-critical studies on the Bible undertaken by their European contemporaries, they argue that these doctrines emerged under the influence of pagan myths. Both take an-Nisā' 4:171–74 as one cluster, and in the context of their exegesis, they spend a good deal of space compiling evidence about the Hindu, Buddhist, Egyptian, and Greek mythological origins of the core Christian doctrines. Riḍa and Quṭb, as we have seen, were not the inventors of this argument. They based it on the foundation of the qur'anic verses just surveyed, as well as being compilers of rather liberal New Testament scholarship that had created these arguments.

Jesus Was Not God

It remains that Islam does not admit too close a connection between the divine and the human realms. As a man without reproach, Muslims affirmed, Jesus knew where he stood before God and never claimed the absurdities later bestowed upon him by his followers. He was a true Muslim and professed the one God of the Qur'an. According to the understanding of the Muslim writers, every detail in Jesus's life stood in diametrical opposition to divine life and to the absurd Christian allegations of divinity made about him. The Qur'an was once again the precursor of this argument. Al-Mā'ida 5:75 contains it very simply and clearly: "The Messiah, son of Mary, was only a messenger. All [other] messengers had passed away before him, and his mother was one who never deviated from the truth. *They both ate food.* See how clear we make these messages for them and how deluded their minds are."

"They both ate food," affirms the Qur'an. What clearer testimony to Jesus's humanity do Christians need? Muhammad b. Jarīr aṭ-Ṭabarī asserts in his commentary, and he is followed by most of the exegetical tradition to the present day, that this statement of God concerning Jesus and his mother affirmed that they possessed bodies that needed food and drink, just like other human beings. Aṭ-Ṭabarī exclaims, "And one who is like this is different from one who is divine, for the one who needs food is sustained by another. And the fact that he needed to be sustained by another is clear proof of his impotence. And the impotent cannot be a Lord, but rather is under lordship."

If we understand the importance of the *kenōsis* (the self-emptying), then the true humanity of Jesus that everywhere comes across in the text of the New Testament becomes natural. Indeed, the opposite would be surprising and unnatural. Yet the human characteristics of eating, hunger, sleep, and tiredness are all repeatedly brought up by Muslim polemicists as proof against Christian doctrines. The point is that Christians would never dream of denying the human characteristics of Christ that are obvious throughout the Gospel text. On the contrary, against Docetic ideas that since the second and third centuries had attempted to deny the real humanity of Jesus—or his full humanity according to later Apollinarians—church father and theologian Gregory of Nazianzus affirmed relentlessly the fullness of Christ's humanity with his now-famous dictum: "What was not assumed was not healed." The patristic concern is clearly soteriology, or the doctrine of salvation: "For what has not been assumed has not been healed; it is what is united to his divinity that is saved. . . . Let them not grudge us our total salvation, or endue the Savior with only the bones and nerves and mere appearance of humanity."[8]

Docetists, then, attempted to deny the real humanity of Christ, sharing the same concern as Muslims for God's absolute otherness. Yet in sharp contrast with the Muslim tradition, they maintained that, in Christ, God had come to achieve human salvation. Church fathers, conversely, maintained that God had visited us in Christ, yet affirmed Christ's full humanity precisely for the sake of the salvation of the entire human person. When Islam entered the stage of history in the seventh century—a predominantly Christian stage—these controversies within the Christian world had already been largely settled. Without the prerequisite theological background, Qur'an exegetes and Muslim theologians alike began on a mission to nitpick the text of the Gospels in order to prove what the Christian tradition had always affirmed as an indispensable component of its soteriology: Christ was fully human!

Choice evidence used by Muslims against Christian doctrines were the Gospel verses where Jesus addressed a divine being outside of himself, or simply where he mentioned God in his discourse, or even where one of the evangelists spoke of Jesus in relation to God. These were seen as ideal proof that Christ himself was not God. Alternatively, as I point out in the next chapter, the concept of divinity could occasionally be preserved

8. "Gregory of Nazianzus," in *New World Encyclopedia*, available online at newworldencyclopedia.org/p/index.php?title=Gregory_of_Nazianzus&oldid=977736 (accessed February 19, 2016), cited from Alister E. McGrath, *Historical Theology: An Introduction to the History of Christian Thought* (Oxford: Blackwell, 1998), 54.

and the term "god" reinterpreted in a symbolic meaning when applied to Christ. In that sense, the evidence presented by Muslim writers in this deconstruction was primarily internal to the text of the Gospels themselves.

ʿAlī aṭ-Ṭabarī (circa 782–860) was quite prolific in developing this argument about Christ. He quotes Luke 2:40, considering it a clear testimony that the Gospels spoke of God distinctly from Jesus: "The boy was growing and was being strengthened with the Holy Spirit and was being filled with wisdom. And the grace of God was clearly upon him."[9] That Jesus was being strengthened by another, was being filled with wisdom, and had God's grace upon him is sufficient evidence for aṭ-Ṭabarī that the one spoken of could not have been God and that the one who related to him in such a way was other than himself.

Other favorites in building this argument were the verses where Jesus's human vulnerability was the most obvious during the time of the passion. The agonizing cry of Jesus on the cross is high on the list of such citations. For aṭ-Ṭabarī, it was clear evidence that he was wrestling with another above him (Mark 15:34 and Matt 27:46). He cites the incident twice in his refutation treatise, the second time as he ventures to examine the different arguments that Christians might use in order to claim divinity for Jesus. Finally, he exclaims: "If you say that you have called him a god because he claimed it, then you have annulled what he [actually] said. For he proclaimed that he had a god in what he said while he was crucified: 'My God, my God, why have you abandoned me?'"[10]

Numerous writers cite this same verse from the narrative of Jesus on the cross. And it appears that the Muslim argument was developed partly in refutation of a Christian claim during that same period, to the effect that while prophets had to intercede to God in order to perform miracles, Christ on the other hand performed miracles by his own authority and without prayer. For example, in his discourse before the Muslim commander ʿAbd ar-Raḥmān al-Hāshimī, which took place in Jerusalem around 820, the monk Ibrāhīm aṭ-Ṭabarānī asserted:

> But what a great difference there is between the signs performed by the prophets and those performed by Christ! For when a prophet wanted to perform an act, he fasted and prayed and implored and petitioned and intensified his prayer, after which he interceded. As for Christ, he

9. Aṭ-Ṭabarī, *Radd*, 124.
10. Aṭ-Ṭabarī, *Radd*, 124, 144.

was not in this position. Rather, he walked in public places and among people, and performed signs and miracles through a command issuing from his own person.[11]

Ibn Ayyūb, in the tenth century, develops a refutation of precisely such a claim: "Christ's case is exactly the same as all other prophets. He used to pray [*yadʿū*], intercede [*yataḍarraʿ*], acknowledge [*yaʿtarif bi-*] God's lordship, and confess [*yaqurr*] servanthood to him."

One of the pieces of evidence that Ibn Ayyūb provides to support his claim is Jesus's cry on the cross, following ʿAlī aṭ-Ṭabarī: "My God, my God, why have you abandoned me!"[12] This argument is later taken over as well by the well-known Muslim scholar and jurist of the tenth and eleventh centuries Abū Bakr Muhammad b. aṭ-Ṭayyib al-Bāqillānī (died 1013). In a book dedicated to the refutation of Muslim sects and other religions and to the demonstration of Muhammad's prophethood, after citing the words that Jesus cried as he was on the cross, al-Bāqillānī adds: "And this is [even] greater than the praying [*duʿāʾ*], intercession [*taḍarruʿ*], and supplication [*ibtihāl*] of Moses!"[13]

Slightly later in the eleventh century, in his book on sects, Ibn Ḥazm makes the same observation regarding the crucifixion narrative and asks in frustration: "[Is] a god betrayed by [*yusallimuhu*] another god? Is there greater foolishness than this?"

With his well-documented comprehensive knowledge of Christian doctrines and arguments, Ibn Ḥazm expects that Christians would reply that such words should be attributed to the humanity in Christ and not to his divinity. He would respond, however, that these words are attributed to Christ (not just to Jesus) and that Christ is believed by all Christians to be made up of both humanity and divinity.[14]

11. Ibrāhīm aṭ-Ṭabarānī, *Le dialogue d'Abraham de Tibériade avec Abd al-Raḥmān al-Hāshimī à Jérusalem vers 820*, ed. G. B. Marcuzzo (Rome: Institut Oriental et Université Pontificale du Latran, 1986), 387.

12. Ibn Ayyūb, *Risāla ila Akhīhi ʿAlī* (Letter to His Brother ʿAlī, Explaining to Him Why He Converted to Islam), preserved in Taqī ad-Dīn Aḥmad b. Taymiyya, *Al-Jawāb aṣ-Ṣaḥīḥ li-man Baddala Dīn al-Masīḥ* (Cairo: Nile Press, 1905), 1.2.335.

13. Abū Bakr Muhammad b. aṭ-Ṭayyib al-Bāqillānī, *Kitāb Tamhīd al-Awāʾil wa Talkhīṣ ad-Dalāʾil* (The Book of Establishment of First Principles and Summary of Proofs), ed. R. J. McCarthy (Beirut: Bibliothèque Orientale, 1957), 99.

14. Abū Muhammad ʿAlī b. Aḥmad Ibn Ḥazm, *Kitāb al-Fiṣal fī al-Milal wa al-Ahwāʾ wa an-Niḥal* (Cairo: Al-Qahira Publishers, 1900), 2.61.

This biblical citation, in refutation of the Christian claim that Jesus performed miracles without resorting to prayer and intercession, continued to travel through the works of Muslim polemicists across the centuries. Notably, it is found again in a work of the late eleventh or early twelfth century, traditionally attributed to the famous Ṣūfī Abū Ḥāmid al-Ghazālī,[15] and in any case a good representative work of the period, *Ar-Radd al-Jamīl li-Ilāhiyyat ʿĪsa bi-Ṣarīḥ al-Injīl* (The Excellent Refutation of Jesus's Divinity through the Plain Text of the Gospel).[16]

The cry of Jesus from the cross is used three times in this work. The first time, it is used to emphasize the widespread evidence in the Gospels regarding Christ's human weakness.[17] The second time it is used simply as proof of Jesus's otherness from God, since he addresses him in prayer. Aṭ-Ṭabarī, as we saw above, already made that argument three centuries earlier. In al-Ghazālī's third mention of the verse, he points out that the juxtaposition of both the persons of Christ and of God in a single sentence makes it impossible to understand it as a reference to the same person. The work calls such occurrences *mughāyara* ("dissimilation" or "differentiation").[18] The author exclaims: "And what God is this . . . that raises his voice, questioning his God [about] why he abandoned him?"

This cry of Jesus from the cross seems so shocking for Muslim theologians that it is not only viewed as unfit for the one that Christians claim to be God in the flesh, but it is not even fathomable coming from a prophet of God. Evidence for this appears in the thirteenth century, in Shihāb ad-Dīn al-Qarāfī's dialectic treatise against Christians entitled *Glorious Answers to Brazen Questions* (*al-Ajwiba al-Fākhira ʿan al-As'ila al-Fājira*). The argument that he builds on the basis of this verse is different from any of those found in the previous writers and is worth mentioning for its peculiarity. Al-Qarāfī is setting about to demonstrate that the Qur'an is more reliable than the Torah and the Gospels in its record of prophetic narratives. Whereas the Gospel writers recorded in good faith that Jesus had been crucified, the Qur'an later revealed

15. This attribution is questioned by some scholars, most famously by Hava Lazarus-Yafeh, *Studies in al-Ghazzâlî* (Jerusalem: Magnes Press, Hebrew University, 1975).

16. Abū Ḥāmid al-Ghazālī, *Ar-Radd al-Jamīl li-Ilāhiyyat ʿĪsa bi-Ṣarīḥ al-Injīl* (Une réfutation excellente de la divinité de Jésus-Christ d'après le texte même de l'évangile), ed./trans. Robert Chidiac (Paris: Librarie Ernest Leroux, 1939), 36.

17. Al-Ghazālī, *Ar-Radd al-Jamīl*, 17–18.

18. Al-Ghazālī, *Ar-Radd al-Jamīl*, 23.

that the man crucified was not Jesus. Al-Qarāfī wants to prove that the qur'anic verse denying the reality of the event is in fact corroborated in the Gospels.

I first cite the qur'anic verse for reference: "And [the Jews] said: 'We have killed the Messiah Jesus, son of Mary, the messenger of God.' However, they did not kill him, nor did they crucify him, though it was made to appear as if it had been so" (an-Nisā' 4:157).

Al-Qarāfī relates that when the supposed Jesus was on the cross, he asked the Jews for a drink. And when they handed him some vinegar, he disliked it and cried out, "My God, my God, why have you abandoned me?" The author then wonders how, while knowing that Jesus stayed forty days and forty nights without eating or drinking, Christians could still believe that he would have been thirsty after spending just one day without drink. Second, al-Qarāfī reads in those words a lack of trust and submission to God's will and predestination on the part of their speaker. And such an attitude, he notes, is unworthy of 'Īsa. One can only conclude from this, he affirms, that the man who was crucified was other than the blessed prophet.[19]

Finally, 'Alī aṭ-Ṭabarī refers to a Paraclete passage in his *Kitāb ar-Radd 'ala an-Naṣāra* that fits in the present category. I look into these Paraclete passages in greater detail in chapter 9, but I mention it here in connection with aṭ-Ṭabarī's agenda to discredit the claim to Jesus's divinity. In an argument that began on the previous page, the writer had asked whether Christ was the "eternal Creator" (*al-Khāliq al-azalī*) in line with the Christian creed, "a chosen human being" (*insān muṣṭafa*) in line with the Muslim creed, or both "God and man" (*ilāh wa insān*) as some Christian sects claim. After affirming that the Muslim creed is the right one and that any other opinion on Christ's identity contradicts the very claims of the Gospel, aṭ-Ṭabarī cites a number of New Testament passages that prove his point. Among these is his passage mentioning the Paraclete. The citation is a combination of several passages often difficult to trace back to their originals (it roughly combines John 14:16a; 16:13; 15:26c–27a; and 16:25). The main point that aṭ-Ṭabarī seems to be making from the quotation is concentrated in the opening clause (14:16a), which reads: "I will ask my Father to give you another Paraclete." That Christ admitted

19. Shihāb ad-Dīn al-Qarāfī, *Al-Ajwiba al-Fākhira 'an al-As'ila al-Fājira*, ed. Bakr Zakī 'Awaḍ (Cairo: Wehbeh Publishers, 1987), 187–89. The issue of the Qur'an's denial of Christ's crucifixion is dealt with again in chap. 8.

that he would ask the Father seems sufficient for aṭ-Ṭabarī to prove that he could not himself have been God.[20]

Jesus Was Not Son

Those who study doctrinal history and who are familiar with the writings of the apostolic fathers and the apologists (first to third centuries) know that these doctrines were not the output of a group of theologians or philosophers sitting back and writing abstractly about God. Rather, the doctrinal formulations of the Trinity, incarnation, and Christ's nature emerged from dynamic conversations that took place between hundreds of sharp minds, who were also for the most part godly men and women, over several generations. Their chief concern was not to invent a religion. What they cared about was faithfully to make sense of the teaching, life, and companionship of Jesus in light of his radical and transforming resurrection from the dead, which had received unanimous support from the earliest eyewitnesses as well as from biblical prophetic expectations.

It is crucial continually to affirm this as we delve into the Muslim project of *deconstruction* and *reconstruction* of Christ's identity. While it is still often assumed by non-Christians that the attributions of the titles "Son" to Jesus and "Father" to God were Nicene innovations that took place in 325, it must be affirmed that the utilization of these titles was part of the community's doxological language from the very beginning, as early followers of Christ were baptized in the name of the "Father, Son, and Holy Spirit." The early church had long strived to avoid introducing foreign, nonbiblical terminology into the Christian creeds. So, for example, when the term *homoousios* ("of the same substance") was suggested as the most apt descriptor of the nature of the relationship of the Son to the Father in the Nicene creed, many initially objected to it, not because they deemed it inappropriate, but because it did not occur in the biblical text.

Homoousios was eventually accepted and became essential in explaining the nature of Christ's relationship with the Godhead. When Islam appeared, however, the church found itself once again in a defensive position, where it had to explain its foundational doctrines to a worldview that was unfamiliar with the history of the development of its theology.[21] In the

20. Aṭ-Ṭabarī, *Radd*, 125.

21. I argue this hermeneutical regression in my "Did the Later Syriac Fathers Take

case of Father and Son, Christians affirmed that they had not innovated these titles, but that they used them simply because Jesus had used them with reference to his relationship with God.

Christians of the Muslim period thus embraced anew a principle that had also become an essential Muslim theological principle. Namely, when speaking about God, it is only legitimate to use inspired language from the Scriptures. But it should be held, conversely, that scriptural language is to be accepted as a legitimate way of speaking about God, even if it makes no sense from a human rational perspective. The vastly influential ninth-/tenth-century Muslim theologian Abū al-Ḥasan al-Ashʿarī (died 936) deeply ingrained this principle in the Muslim theological tradition in his fight against the *Muʿtazilī* current in Islam. For example, he opposed their primary emphasis on rational logic in their interpretation of the Qurʾan and gave primacy to the Ḥadīth. He argued that qurʾanic terminology was to be used exclusively in describing God and his attributes, and this without questioning—*bilā kayf* (lit., "without how").[22]

When it came to their encounter with Christian theological thinking, however, most Muslims passionately rejected the title "Son of God" for Jesus from very early on, in line with their understanding of such qurʾanic verses as at-Tawba 9:30. But in doing so, they required Christians to apply on their Scriptures a principle different from the one they applied on theirs. We will see in the next chapter that not all Muslims were unanimous on this, but the ninth-century theologian Abū ʿUthmān b. Baḥr al-Jāḥiẓ already did not concede even a *figurative* fatherhood for God. After citing the opening of the Lord's Prayer in Matthew 6:9 and mentioning that some people accept that Jews and Christians may have been authorized to use such terminology about God, he concludes: "As for us, we do not allow that God might have a son, neither from the perspective of [natural] begetting [*al-wilāda*] nor from the perspective of adoption [*at-tabannī*]."[23]

Ibn Ayyūb, in the same line, engages in a critique of the Christian usage of the titles "Son" and "Father" based on Matthew 1:1, compar-

---

into Consideration Their Islamic Context When Reinterpreting the New Testament?" *Parole de l'orient* 23 (1998): 13–32.

22. For an excellent treatment of al-Ashʿarī's approach, see Joseph L. Cumming, "Ṣifāt al-Dhāt in al-Ashʿarī's Doctrine of God and Possible Christian Parallels" (May 2001), available online at faith.yale.edu/reconciliation-project/resources (accessed January 3, 2017).

23. Abū ʿUthmān ʿAmr b. Baḥr al-Jāḥiẓ, *Al-Mukhtār fī ar-Radd ʿala an-Naṣāra*, ed. M. A. Sharqāwī (Beirut/Cairo: Dar al-Jil, 1991), 102–3.

ing Gospel testimonies with traditional proclamations of the standard (Nicene-Constantinopolitan) Christian creed. His conclusion is a rejection of Christ's sonship to God. He begins by picking on the Christian statement of faith that Christ was "born eternally" of the Father. He points out that the combination "born eternally" is absurd, musing that one can either be *born* or be *eternal*, for eternity inherently implies a lack of either beginning or end, just as birth implies the occurrence of an accident, and hence a beginning.[24] Further, Ibn Ayyūb moves to the titles "Father" and "Son": "Why have you called the Father a 'Father' and the Son a 'Son'?"

He argues that if Father is a reference to eternity, then the Son as well should be called Father, since according to the Christian creed he is eternal too. And if the title "Father" is ascribed to the Father because he is omniscient (*ʿālim*) and omnipotent (*ʿazīz*), then the same should be said of the Son, since the Christian creed ascribes to him the creation of all things and the bringing of salvation. Ibn Ayyūb's conclusion is that, as it stands, the Christian creed on the fatherhood of God and sonship of Christ does injustice to the Son, placing him in a position of obedience and submission to the Father, all the while claiming that he is equal to him in knowledge, power, and eternity. Rather, he advocates, one should recognize the futility of that Christian claim and reject the language of Christ's sonship to God altogether. It is in this connection that Ibn Ayyūb quotes Matthew 1:1 as proof that the disciple Matthew recognized Jesus's true identity: "[He called him] the son of David, son of Abraham, tracing him back to his actual root. And he [Matthew] did not say that he was the Son of God, or that he was God from God, as they [the Christians] say."[25]

With Ibn Ḥazm, in the eleventh century, we encounter again the same argument that we saw two centuries earlier in al-Jāḥiẓ. Like him, he seems to know people who argue that Christians have the right to use the titles "Son" and "Father" about Jesus and God based on the Gospel's testimony. To this Ibn Ḥazm responds based on the opening verses of the Lord's Prayer that when Jesus taught his disciples to pray to God as *"our* heavenly Father," he showed that there was no difference between them.[26] Later in the second part of his *Kitāb al-Fiṣal fī al-Milal* he gives Christians two options: either they should accept that Christ was Son in the same way that the disciples were, and hence that God was their Father in the

24. Ibn Ayyūb, *Risāla*, in Ibn Taymiyya, *Al-Jawāb aṣ-Ṣaḥīḥ*, 1.2.359.

25. Ibn Ayyūb, *Risāla*, in Ibn Taymiyya, *Al-Jawāb aṣ-Ṣaḥīḥ*, 1.2.359–60.

26. Ibn Ḥazm, *Kitāb al-Fiṣal fī al-Milal*, 1.56.

same way that he was Christ's Father, or they should realize that they are contradicting the testimony of the Gospels, and they should then concede that their Scriptures are corrupt. As far as he is concerned, Ibn Ḥazm has already opted for the second option, on the basis that it is wrong to call God anybody's "Father," or to call anybody "God's son."[27]

By the fourteenth century, the opening verses of the Lord's Prayer had become central to the Muslim argument against Christ's divine sonship. Ibn Qayyim al-Jawziyya explains that such verses should be used as the hermeneutical key to understanding what is meant by Christ's sonship.[28]

The Qur'an and the Cross

If we understand the importance of self-giving in God's economy of love and reconciliation, and its centrality in God's ordering of human relationships between each other and with him, then the implication of the cross begins to take new meaning, beyond simply a conversation about whether it happened historically. This brings us to the most critical qur'anic verse on Christianity's core doctrine of Christ—namely his death on the cross. The only verse in the Qur'an that mentions Jesus's crucifixion is an-Nisā' 4:157: "And [the Jews] said, 'We have killed the Messiah Jesus, son of Mary, the messenger of God.' However, they did not kill him, nor did they crucify him, though it was made to appear as if it had been so. Those who disagree are confused, having no [real] knowledge to follow, only supposition. They certainly did not kill him."

Jesus Was Not Crucified but Replaced by Another

Though a primary reading of an-Nisā' 4:157 need not necessarily have led to the conclusion that Jesus was not crucified, particularly in light of a number of other qur'anic verses that affirmed that Jesus died, the main argument that we encounter in the Muslim exegetical tradition on this verse is that Jesus only appeared to have been crucified on the cross. With

27. Ibn Ḥazm, *Kitāb al-Fiṣal fī al-Milal*, 2.24.

28. Shams ad-Dīn Muhammad b. Abī Bakr Ibn Qayyim al-Jawziyya, *Hidāyat al-Ḥayāra fī Ajwibat al-Yahūd wa an-Naṣāra*, ed. Aḥmad Ḥijāzī as-Saqā (Cairo: al-Maktaba al-Qayyima, 1980), 290.

time, an entire theory emerged whereby Jesus was believed to have been replaced by another man who was crucified instead of him.

Muhammad b. Jarīr aṭ-Ṭabarī (died 922), in his commentary, uses this verse to expand on this replacement or substitution doctrine. In his usual cumulative style, he cites numerous traditions that explain how the substitution of Jesus took place. The first tradition claims that one of the disciples volunteered to die in Jesus's place. As Jesus was gathered with seventeen of his disciples (other traditions mention nineteen, twelve, or thirteen) in a home, a group came to arrest him. At that point, God made all seventeen disciples to look like Jesus. When those who came to arrest him saw this, they threatened to kill them all. Jesus then invited one of them to volunteer to die in his place in exchange for guaranteed salvation. One of them did, and Jesus was then raised by God to heaven.

Aṭ-Ṭabarī cites other traditions that claim that a man named Sergius volunteered to be crucified in his place, and others that it was Judas who, after plotting against Jesus, was made to look like him and was then arrested and crucified in his place. Having cited the various traditions, aṭ-Ṭabarī states his own belief. His conclusion is that the qur'anic verse implies that both the Jews and the disciples were convinced that Jesus had been crucified and that it is not possible that the disciples became aware at any point of God's substitutionary scheme. All Jews and Christians continued to believe that Jesus had been crucified until the truth of the matter was finally revealed in the Qur'an.

One important point is that aṭ-Ṭabarī did not believe that any of the companions would have lied about the true identity of the crucified, had they known the truth. Though he cannot accept that a disciple of Jesus would have lied about something he knew, aṭ-Ṭabarī has no qualms about affirming that God and Jesus themselves had no moral problem in performing this stratagem knowingly.

The influence of aṭ-Ṭabarī's reports and his preference for the theory of substitution continue until today in some of the mainstream exegetical tradition, and the substitutionary claim remains the most widespread at the popular level among Muslims. In most day-to-day conversations between Christians and Muslims about the cross, Muslims perpetuate the claim that someone other than Jesus died on the cross and that therefore the testimony of the Gospel was either corrupt or ignorant until it was corrected by the qur'anic revelation. But though the majority of Muslim commentators eventually came to agree on the substitution, a significant number of them nearly rejected the theory for both linguistic and moral-theological reasons.

Ar-Rāzī (died 1209), in his treatment of the verse, sets it clearly in the context of a qur'anic polemic against the Jews, which began at an-Nisā' 4:153. Thus, in verse 157, when the text denies them the reality of their claims that they have killed Jesus, the primary intention of the Qur'an is to ridicule the Jews rather than to deny the reality of the crucifixion. Having established the context, ar-Rāzī then approaches the subject from two angles: linguistic and theological. Linguistically, he affirms that the qur'anic statement *shubbiha lahum* cannot be a reference to Jesus, since it was not Jesus who was "made to appear" like someone else, but rather the likeness of another would have been transformed into that of Jesus. On the other hand, affirms ar-Rāzī, it could be a reference to the substitute who would have actually been killed, for even though the text does not explicitly refer to that person, he can be thus introduced and then become the subject of the sentence. Even though ar-Rāzī can admit the latter reading linguistically, he seems to prefer to read *shubbiha lahum* as a passive verb referring to an impersonal subject, similarly to the way that Kaskas translates it: "It was made to appear as if it had been so." In other words, though in ar-Rāzī's mind it is possible to read the substitution theory as being implied in this verse, it is better to read it simply as God's polemical affirmation against the Jews: Though you think that you have killed Jesus, in reality you have not!

The idea that Jesus was replaced by another on the cross raises some serious concerns for ar-Rāzī. In his view, if we admit the substitution theory, we risk opening the door to sophistry (*as-safsaṭa*). Indeed, if we cannot rely on the reality of what we see, then everything becomes questionable. For if we say that "we have seen Zayd," the exegete argues, "then perhaps he is not truly Zayd!" All legal affirmations regarding marriage, divorce, and property would then become at best tentative for, he argues, "a transmitted report informs knowledge so long as it leads in the end to something that is perceptible to the senses [*almaḥsūs*]." Ar-Rāzī's fear is that if we allow that this sort of confusion could have affected a perceptible event such as the crucifixion, we are exposing the entire notion of reliable transmission to being discredited (*tawajjaha aṭ-ṭaʿn fī at-tawātur*). Ar-Rāzī realized that, given that all Islamic law, as well as other Islamic sciences, traditionally rely on *tawātur* ("transmission"), Islam would be opening itself up to all manner of deconstruction if the theory of substitution is allowed without solid proof from tradition.

Ar-Rāzī does not come to a conclusion on this matter in his exegesis of this verse, but he does in connection with āl-ʿImrān 3:55, as we will see below. At this point, he simply enumerates five different traditions regarding the substitution stratagem, notes that several are mutually contradictory, and concludes: "And God knows best the facts of such matters!"

With comparable attention to the verse's context, Rashīd Riḍa (died 1935) is not primarily interested in either proving or disproving the crucifixion of Jesus. He considers that the purpose of this verse is to highlight the unbelief of the Jews, since they were killers of the prophets and they aimed at killing Jesus as well. He affirms that proving or disproving the reality of the crucifixion changes nothing in the status of the Jews, since they are known to be evil and unbelievers with or without it. However, he points out that since Christians have given such a central place to the crucifixion of Jesus in their doctrine of salvation, it is nevertheless important to discuss the issue, and he therefore dedicates many pages to it. In the Christian Gospels, he points out, Judas had to agree on the sign of the kiss to confirm to the soldiers which man was to be arrested. He sees this as proof that those who had come to arrest Jesus did not actually know him, and therefore he views this as supporting his affirmation that it was not Jesus who was crucified. He also points to the Gospel of Barnabas as a second proof, which states explicitly that God cast on Judas the likeness of Jesus and that it was he eventually who was crucified instead of Jesus.

Riḍa adopts a somewhat different focus from the traditional one. Beyond rejecting the historicity of the crucifixion on the basis that it has weak *isnād*, the remaining space is dedicated to a rejection of the Christian claim that salvation resulted from this crucifixion. In the process, Riḍa argues strongly against the reliability of the Christian Scriptures. He engages in a long polemical diatribe against the reliability of the Gospels and against the Christian doctrines, in particular soteriology. In that section, it is clear that Riḍa was exposed to many experiences of Protestant evangelism and that he spent a good deal of time rejecting their narrative of salvation through the cross. He engages in this refutation both with Muslim traditional arguments and with material that he gleans from critical biblical studies written by Europeans, whom he calls "liberated/liberal Christians."

The deepest disagreement between Christianity and Islam, then, is not so much the doctrines of the Trinity, Christ's sonship, or his divinity, in and of themselves. Rather, it is the connection of these doctrines with the understanding of salvation. Islam's view of God, who lives in absolute aloneness (*tawḥīd*), independent and separate from any human need, provides salvation quite simply to those who believe in radical *tawḥīd*. It is proper belief that saves you, and your ability to abstain from committing the sin of *shirk* (ascribing partners to God).

Sayyid Quṭb (died 1966), like Rashīd Riḍa, is not interested in elaborating on the details of Jesus's death and resurrection beyond the plain testimony of the Qur'an. Like his predecessor, he affirms that the Qur'an said nothing about these matters and that they are therefore irrelevant. The plain meaning of the Qur'an implies that the Jews did not kill or crucify Jesus and that God raised him to himself, without specifying whether he raised him in the body and in the spirit while still alive or whether he raised him in the spirit after he had died. Nor does the Qur'an specify when that death took place or where. Like Riḍa, Quṭb refers with apparent conviction to the Gospel of Barnabas's account of Judas being transformed into the likeness of Jesus as he came to hand him over to the Romans, and that as a result he was crucified in his place. As for the fate of Jesus himself, Quṭb explicitly avoids coming to a conclusion, given that he sees no finality of opinion in the text of the Qur'an.

Jesus Was Raised Up to God, But When?

In parallel with an-Nisā' 4:157, which seems to affirm that Jesus had not died, Muslim exegetes had to reckon with three other verses in the Qur'an mentioning his death: āl-ʿImrān 3:55; al-Mā'ida 5:117; and Maryam 19:33. Much of the qur'anic exegetical discourse on the cross is also connected to āl-ʿImrān 3:55 in particular, which speaks about Jesus's death and ascension to God:

> God said, "Jesus, I will cause you to die and raise you up to me, and purify you from those who denied the truth, and I will exalt your followers over those who deny you until the resurrection day. Then you all will return to me, and I will judge between you in matters about which you disagree."

Muhammad b. Jarīr aṭ-Ṭabarī (died 922) reports many traditions concerning the affirmation that God caused Jesus to die, most of which are a discussion of the meaning of the verb *tawaffa*. Five interpretations are associated with this verb in the tradition:

1. *Wafāt an-nawm*—the "death" of sleep, in the sense that God caused Jesus to sleep before raising him to himself. These traditions go back to ar-Rabīʿ and al-Ḥasan.
2. *Wafāt al-qabḍ* (*'stawfaytu*—"to exact payment")—as God extracted Jesus from among unbelievers while he was still alive. These traditions go back to Maṭar al-Warrāq, al-Ḥasan, and others.
3. *Wafāt al-mawt*—actual physical death.
4. A tradition going back to Wahb b. Munabbih, which is supposed to have been transmitted from an irreproachable source (*mimman lā yuttaham*), affirms that God caused Jesus to die for three hours of the day and then raised him up to himself.
5. A tradition ascribed to Christians, transmitted originally by Ibn Isḥāq, affirms that God caused Jesus to die for seven hours before he raised him back to life.

Notably, exegetes distinguished between traditions that affirmed that Jesus was raised to God alive (#1 and #2), and those that affirmed that God caused him to die before raising him up to himself (##3–5). In much of the classical exegesis, there is an inclination to favor the former in order to make room for a fairly developed Islamic eschatological narrative. The meaning advanced for this verse is that one day God will send Jesus again to call and preach and invite people to worship God alone. The occasion of its revelation, according to these traditions, is when Jesus reported to God, informing him about how many people had disbelieved in him and the few that had followed him. God consoled him by telling him: "I will cause you to die and raise you up to me." God then promises him that, in the end days, he will send him against the antichrist (*dajjāl*) so that he might kill him, after which he will live twenty-four more years on earth, and then God will cause him to die a normal human death. These traditions are very influential on Asian Islam, as they are at the core of Aḥmadī eschatological beliefs.

Many traditions connect the verse to this classical eschatological doctrine in order to make sense of al-Māʾida 5:110, where the Qurʾan narrates that God confirmed Jesus with the Holy Spirit so that he could teach people both in the cradle (*fī al-mahdi*; i.e., as a baby) and as an old man (*kahlan*). If Jesus had died in his early thirties, as the Gospels affirm, then he would not have reached the older age implied by the word *kahl*. A tradition going back to Ibn Zayd, via Ibn Wahb, thus affirms that God raised Jesus to himself before he had become a *kahl*, and that he will send him again to earth as a *kahl*. The implication of this belief is, in all of these traditions, that Jesus is currently alive with God and close to him.

Aṭ-Ṭabarī favored the interpretation of *tawaffa* that affirmed that Jesus was extracted from the earth and raised to God. His preference is guided by the strength of the Ḥadīth traditions that transmit from Muhammad his affirmation that "Jesus son of Mary will come down and kill the antichrist [*dajjāl*]." After this act, these traditions affirm, Jesus will then stay on earth for a certain length of time (about which there is no unanimity), then he will die, and Muslims will pray over his body and bury him. Traditions that confirm his choice are traced back to Abū Hurayra (via Ḥanẓala b. ʿAlī al-Aslamī), who claims that he heard Muhammad say that God "will establish Jesus son of Mary a just judge and a righteous leader [*imām*] who will break the cross, kill the swine, impose the *jizya*, cause money to flow to the point that recipients for it will no longer be found. He will travel through *Rawḥāʾ* [an area between Mecca and Medina], performing *ḥajj* and *ʿumra* and all other religious duties."

In a similar tradition, also traced back to Abū Hurayra (but this one via ʿAbd ar-Raḥmān b. Ādam), the companion claims he heard Muhammad say that all prophets are brothers because they propagated the same religion, even though they came from different mothers. Muhammad, Abū Hurayra claims, affirmed that he was closest to Jesus because there were no other prophets historically between them. Here too, it is said that Jesus will break the cross, kill the swine, cause money to overflow . . .

> and he will fight people in the name of Islam, until God exterminates all other religious groups during that time. God, during his time, will also kill the lying and false messiah of perdition, until security is established on earth, to the point where lions will be raised with camels, tigers with cows, wolves with sheep, and young boys will play with snakes, not harming one another. He [Jesus] will remain on the earth for forty years, after which he will die and Muslims will pray over him and bury him.

Based on the former traditions that he embraces as authentic, Abū Jaʿfar aṭ-Ṭabarī further supports his choice (that God did not cause him to die during his first lifetime on earth) by affirming that if God had caused Jesus to die the first time, he would not cause him to die a second time after he comes again, as God would never cause Jesus to die twice. For God promised his creation that he would create them, cause them to die, and then bring them back to life, as the Qur'an affirms in ar-Rūm 30:40: "It is God who created you, then provided for you, who will cause you to die and then will give you life again. Can any of your 'partners' do any of those things? May he be exalted in his glory and high above anything they associate with him." Aṭ-Ṭabarī affirms that, although this verse narrates information about Jesus, it actually serves in the Qur'an as a further argument against the Christian delegation from Najrān, who tried to argue against Muhammad's assertion that their claims about Jesus's crucifixion and death were lies. This verse, then, is supposed to confirm that Christians and Jews conspired against Jesus and issued lies about him.

As for God's affirmation that "I will exalt your followers over those who deny you until the resurrection day," aṭ-Ṭabarī conveys traditions that affirm that Christ's "followers" here refers to Muslims, whereas "those who denied the truth," from which God will purify Jesus, is a reference to Christians, Jews, and Magi. Other traditions, however, that aṭ-Ṭabarī refers to affirm that the "followers" of Jesus is a reference to Christians, whereas "those who denied the truth" is a reference to Jews.

Fakhr ad-Dīn ar-Rāzī (died 1209) does not offer much that is new beyond what we find in aṭ-Ṭabarī regarding the interpretation of the various issues in this verse. However, he also takes the opportunity of this exegesis to address the question of God's replacement of Jesus with another on the cross after he raised him to himself. Ar-Rāzī apparently knew of six counterarguments that were raised against the Muslim substitution theory. After enumerating all six arguments, he then proceeds to refute them one by one.

First, Christians argued that accepting the possibility that the likeness of one could be placed on another leads at best to a Sophistic view of the world and at worst to the annihilation of all prophecies, given that we could never one hundred percent assert that words spoken by any prophet were actually spoken by him, rather than by some other imposter who bore his likeness! Ar-Rāzī responds that everyone agrees that God is capable of creating an exact representation of any person, which does not mean that he would do it all the time.

Second, Christians claimed that God placed Jibrīl at Jesus's side at all times, and only the edge of one of Jibrīl's wings would have been sufficient to protect Jesus from his aggressors. Furthermore, given that Jesus raised the dead and healed the sick, how could he not have protected himself against the Jews who came to kill him, had he wished to do so? Ar-Rāzī responds that these claims mean that Jesus could actually have become invincible, breaking natural law, or if God had allowed Jibrīl to protect Jesus, he would have also rendered him invincible, which is an impossibility.

Third, given that God could save Jesus from death simply by raising him up to heaven, Christians argued, what would have been the point, then, of sending a lookalike instead of him to his death? Ar-Rāzī responds that if God had simply caused Jesus to disappear by raising him to himself, without replacing him with a lookalike, that would have been in breach of nature for all the onlookers, and once again this is not the way that God works.

Fourth, Christians advanced that if God replaced Jesus with another without the knowledge of his disciples, leaving them in ignorance about the matter, this would have been unfair to them and an action unworthy of God's wisdom. Ar-Rāzī's answer is that the disciples of Jesus were aware of what God was doing.

Fifth, Christians observed that, given that all Christians in East and West, who are so excessive in their love of Jesus, claim to have seen him crucified and dead on the cross, if we still assert that Jesus did not die, we would be seriously harming the reliability of the principle of transmission of knowledge (*tawātur*), a principle on which Muslims also affirm the prophethood and the very existence of Muhammad, Jesus, and all other prophets! Ar-Rāzī's response is that those who were present at the site of the cross were few in number, therefore the situation does not qualify as scientific transmission, for when the transmission of a story leads back to a small group of people, it is not solid from a scientific perspective.

Sixth and finally, objectors argued that Christians affirm by consensus that Jesus remained alive on the cross for several hours before he died. So, if that had not been Jesus, surely the man would have weakened and informed people that he was not Jesus, and for sure we would have heard of such a matter. Ar-Rāzī suggests that it is possible that the man who took the likeness of Jesus was a Muslim and that he did so willingly. Therefore, he would not have revealed the stratagem to the people standing around.

By the time of ash-Shawkānī (died 1834), mainstream commentators were rather unanimous that Jesus did not die at the hands of his contemporaries. Rather, God raised him to himself for a future mission. Ash-Shawkānī uses the divine attribute *mākir* from the preceding verse as a key to his interpretation of āl-ʿImrān 3:54: "And they [the unbelievers] plotted [*makarū*] [against Jesus] but God caused their schemes to fail [*makara*], for God is the best of all plotters [*khayru al-mākirīn*]."

Makr in Arabic normally carries negative connotations in the sense of "cheating" or "deception." But the exegetical tradition is careful to apply a particular interpretation to the term with reference to God, as can be seen from the English translation above as well as others. Ash-Shawkānī points out that the term is used about God's response to Jesus's enemies simply for rhetorical balance in response to the behavior of the unbelievers, as this adjective could not otherwise be applied to God. God's plotting is then revealed in āl-ʿImrān 3:55 in God substituting another for Jesus on the cross and raising Jesus to heaven so that he will be able to assign him the important mission of coming back to kill the antichrist in the end times, after which he will die a natural death.

The attribute of *mākir* constitutes a moral dilemma for exegetes when it is associated with God. In this particular context, the question that the Muslim commentators are struggling with is whether God would use plotting in order to cause the death of an innocent substitute for Jesus. As we move through the commentary traditions, therefore, substitute candidates such as Peter, a disciple named Sergius, some volunteer from among the disciples, or even some random passerby begin to fall from favor. There develops increasing agreement that the person crucified instead of Jesus must be someone who deserves it because of their sin.

For Abū Bakr al-Jazāʾirī (died 1921), God's *makr* appears in that the person he substituted for Jesus on the cross was the commander of the group of Roman soldiers who had come to arrest him.

Al-Bayḍāwī (died 1286?) also points out this moral dilemma in his commentary. He argues that *al-makr* can be predicated of God only with reference to judgment and punishment, if it concerns a person who is actually guilty. God would not harm an innocent person simply as a means to accomplish a ruse. By laying down this principle, al-Bayḍāwī excludes most of the traditional substitutionary narratives, notably those *aḥādīth* ("traditions") that his predecessors considered to have the strongest *isnāds* ("lines of transmission"). The main possibility that remains from that perspective would be that Judas was the one on whom Jesus's appearance was cast and that he was the one who was then arrested and crucified. However, such narratives in the exegetical tradition were those with the weakest *isnāds*.

Rashīd Riḍa (died 1935) rejects the traditional interpretation that claims that Jesus was raised alive to God, in order to return in the end days, rule by Islamic law, and eventually die a normal death, as found in most of the exegetical tradition. He follows, in this, the exegesis of his teacher, Muhammad ʿAbdo, whom he always refers to as *al-ustādh al-imām* ("the *imam* teacher"). As far as he is concerned, he believes that *mutawaffīka* should be interpreted in its literal sense of "cause you to die," and the conjunction *wāw* ("and") should be understood in its normal function of expressing chronology. In other words, God caused Jesus to die and then raised him to himself. He further interprets the raising as a raising of his spirit to himself, not his body.

Concerning all of the Islamic traditions that claim that Jesus will come back and rule by Islamic law, Riḍa cites his teacher ʿAbdo as saying that the traditions on which these narratives are based are not strong. They are mostly lone traditions (*ḥadīth āḥād*) that can be used only for moral benefit, but not as actual facts. He thus gives an allegorical interpretation to those traditions about Christ's return and ruling on earth. He will in fact return spiritually, and his way of mercy, love, and peace will rule over people.

Just as Jesus was a reformer to the Jews by drawing them to the heart of the law of Moses, the time has come when the Muslim community needs an *ʿĪsawī* reform, where they will be rescued from all the myths of tradition that have diluted the power of God's Sharīʿa and be brought back to the spirit of the law as well. It seems clear that the reference to this *ʿĪsawī* reform is a reflection of Riḍa on his own mission to reform Islam, following in the line of his teacher, Muhammad ʿAbdo, who in turn continued in the line of reform of his teacher Jamāl ad-Dīn al-Afghānī.

He concludes this exegetical tradition from ʿAbdo with the affirmation that "imitation" (*taqlīd*) is the enemy of religion in every age and that the "time of Jesus" (*zaman ʿĪsa*) is the time when people come back to "the spirit and law of the Islamic religion," putting aside superficial forms and application.

Sayyid Quṭb (died 1966) has no interest at all in the entire mass of traditions about Christ's death and rising to God in this passage. If his close predecessors Muhammad ʿAbdo and Rashīd Riḍa rejected the traditional interpretations in order to give the verses a moral value, he on the other hand affirms explicitly that there is no profit in trying to understand the manner of Christ's death and ascension. He affirms again the central point of Sūrat āl-ʿImrān as he sees it, which is the affirmation of pure monotheism.

The Cross in Biblical Salvation History

In its near-unanimous denial of the historicity of the crucifixion of Jesus, the Muslim exegetical tradition stands largely alone. It also stands in rejection of the entire purpose of biblical salvation history. Given the way that an-Nisā' 4:157 has been traditionally understood by qur'anic commentators and Muslim scholars through history, it is nearly impossible to understand the place of the verse in the overall qur'anic discourse about Jesus. Why would the Qur'an want to deny the death of Jesus by crucifixion or by any other means, since it affirms everywhere his finitude and humanity?

In the immediate as well as broader canonical contexts of the Qur'an, if it were not for the extensive exegetical tradition of Islam, the verse would be understood simply as another piece of polemic against the Jews, who in an-Nisā' 4:155 were accused of breaking their covenant with God and killing his prophets. In that context, the denial of their achievement in killing Jesus two verses later would make sense, but not to the extent of affirming that Jesus had not died at all. Verse 157 would then be arguing that the Jews did not succeed in killing Jesus, and it could be conjectured from the immediate literary context itself that this was so because God "raised him up to himself," as in verse 158. This would be a convenient affirmation of the biblical narrative that confirms that the Jews had not actually succeeded in killing Jesus, since he had risen from the dead three days later.

But the extensive exegetical material of the Muslim tradition does not allow for such a straightforward alignment of the qur'anic and biblical texts. Instead, an-Nisā' 4:157 becomes the springboard of an entire religious tradition that denies the most fundamental claim of the Christian faith, namely, the centrality of Jesus's death on the cross and the importance of his death for human salvation.

Other parts of the Qur'an, as we have seen, appear to be more affirming of the alignment narrative than of its denial. Far from confirming the suspicion toward Jesus's death elicited by an-Nisā' 4:157, āl-'Imrān 3:55 seems to confirm that it was in God's divine plan to cause Jesus to die (*mutawaffīka*) in order to raise him up to himself (*rāfi'uka ilayya*) and rescue him (literally "purify you," *muṭahhiruka*) from those who disbelieved in his message. Another affirmation of this narrative is found in Maryam 19:33, where this time it is Jesus who affirms that he would die and be brought back to life: "And [God's] peace was upon me the day I was born [*yawma wulidtu*] and the day I will die [*yawma amūtu*], and it will be upon me the day I am raised alive [*yawma ubʿathu ḥayyan*]."

The immediately ensuing verse (Maryam 19:34) affirms that this (or Jesus, per Kaskas's translation) is "the word of truth" (*qawla al-ḥaqq*) "about which they are in dispute." "They" is presumably a reference to the Jews, who in the preceding narrative accused his mother of immorality as she was found pregnant outside of wedlock. Confirming this interpretation is the assertion of the exact same words a few verses earlier with respect to John the Baptist in Maryam 19:15: "[God's] peace was upon him on the day he was born and the day of his death, and it will be upon him on the day he is raised alive."

An-Nisā' 4:157 thus stands alone in the qur'anic witness in its questioning of the crucifixion and death of Jesus, not based on its primary straightforward meaning, but as a result of fourteen hundred years of qur'anic exegesis to that effect. The question that we must ask, then, is why did the Muslim tradition find it so important to deny a doctrine so central to the Christian tradition?

What transpires from an exploration of this question is that Muslim commentators and theologians were not so much concerned with the historicity of Jesus's death as they were with the salvific implication that Christians ascribed to it.

Summarizing the Negative Metadialogue on Christ

There is nothing that the Qur'an affirms positively about Jesus that a Christian would want to take issue with. Yet, the Muslim tradition's portrayal of Jesus has been complex from the start. The qur'anic version of the lives of biblical prophets, including Jesus, seems to be a rich intertwining of two streams of tradition: the canonical version transmitted through oral channels from Christian and Jewish circles, and the apocryphal version that was transmitted and widespread within the multireligious Arab culture of pre-Islamic and early Islamic times.

What compounds the evidence is that up until now, there is no indication from archeology that the Bible had been translated into Arabic before Islam. On the other hand, the storytelling oral tradition of the Arab Bedouin culture meant that the stories of biblical prophets proliferated in the early decades of Islam. These stories, known as *isrā'īliyyāt* and *masīḥiyyāt* (Israelite and Christian stories), contained numerous apocryphal accounts and sayings that were never part of the official version of the prophets' lives as transmitted by mainstream Judaism and Christianity.[29] The resulting qur'anic portrait of Jesus is one that departs from the Christian portrait of Jesus in certain dimensions and confirms it in others. Overall, when Islam denies anything about Christ, it seems to be the Christian *doctrinal* interpretation of the Christ event that it is rejecting rather than the portrait reflected by a primary reading of the Gospels. The outcome of that starting position was a long history of Islamic *exegetical* discourse on the Gospels (the primary topic of this book) that presumed as its primary purpose to correct Christian doctrines through a correction of the Christian reading of the Bible.

When it came to the doctrine of Christ, Muslims approached their corrective project in two stages: first, they set out to strip off what they viewed as the corrupt layers of Christ's identity tagged on to him by Christians who had been misled in their reading of their Scriptures; and second, they sought to restore the true identity of Christ through a rereading of the Bible from the perspective of a qur'anic corrective. The first step was deconstructionist, whereas the second was reconstructionist. In the next chapter I look at the second stage, while the present chapter focused on the first stage of this dual project.

In sum, the two-stage process of Muslim Christology reflects a significant body of presuppositions, particularly on the part of Christian converts to Islam. The primary concern of the Qur'an was to emphasize Jesus's humanity, as in āl-ʿImrān 3:59's comparison of Jesus with Adam. Muslims affirm that the virgin birth does not prove Jesus's divinity (an-Nisā' 4:172) and that the servanthood of Jesus is a sign of his humility and lack of arrogance. Some recent commentaries, influenced by Western textual criticism affirm that the doctrine of the incarnation was nothing more than a paganization of Christianity, embracing existing civilizational myths. The Qur'an and Muslims continuously deny the divinity of Jesus (Sūrat al-Mā'ida 5) and his sonship to God, affirming the equality of sonship between him and his disciples. Concerning Jesus's crucifixion, they assert that he was not crucified (an-Nisā' 4:157), but that he was replaced by another. He was then raised up to God, but it is not clear at what point (āl-ʿImrān 3:55; al-Mā'ida 5:117; and Maryam 19:33).

29. For a significant collection of narratives and sayings preserved in the Muslim tradition, see Tarif Khalidi, *The Muslim Jesus: Sayings and Stories in Islamic Literature* (Cambridge: Harvard University Press, 2003).

Hermeneutical Keys in Building Bridges beyond Conflict

The centrality of Jesus in the Muslim system reveals more closeness of Muhammad with the Judeo-Christian tradition than the traditional narrative usually allows for. The *Sīra* reflects this closeness, yet attempts at the same time to affirm the independence of the Muslim tradition. How do these observations help us bridge the gap in this history of conflict and disagreement?

Using Deadlocks as Assets

Christians and Muslims engaged in dialogue need to allow the Gospels to speak for themselves, as testimonies about Jesus from people who lived with him. It is to be celebrated that Christians and Muslim together can affirm the reality of the virgin birth. Christians need not use the virgin birth as proof of Christ's divinity, but instead they can affirm with Muslims the importance of his full humanity. At the same time, when it comes to a discussion of Christ's lowliness, Christians need to focus on the church having always affirmed this lowliness, but for the purpose of salvation rather than simply to point out his humility, even though the humility has always been affirmed as a model for unity, as in its Pauline usage in Philippians 2.

Regarding the findings of textual criticism, Christians do not want to throw out the baby with the bath water. At the same time, however, this school of thought, which was popular in the late nineteenth and early twentieth centuries, has proven its limitations, and Christians would affirm today that they need to move beyond it and allow instead the Scriptures to speak for themselves. Christian theologian Veli-Matti Kärkkaïnen points out that there is a fundamental difference between the ancient civilizational myths and the New Testament account of the incarnation, which liberal New Testament scholars rarely acknowledge. In the Near Eastern and Hellenistic myths, the concept of a god-man is always linked with some form of sexual intercourse and/or marriage between a divine and a human. He argues that, in contrast, "in the NT there is no hint of sexual impregnation by a male deity as in the myths." Quoting Raymond E. Brown, Kärkkäinen agrees that there is in the ancient world "no clear example of virginal conception" comparable to the New Testament claims.[30]

30. Veli-Matti Kärkkäinen, *A Constructive Christian Theology for the Pluralistic*

When compared to the mythical accounts of surrounding civilizational traditions, the New Testament affirmation that in Christ God was "with us" (Aramaic *emmanuel*) distinguishes itself completely in both core and detail. The proclamation of *emmanuel* in the Gospels is an extension of God's history of salvation with his people as reflected in the Old Testament, affirming his desire to live among his people. This may not make the incarnation more palatable to a Muslim, or more acceptable to anyone, but it certainly sets it apart as the possibility of a unique divine revelation and initiative.

Furthermore, the "God with us" concept of the New Testament and the ensuing doctrine of the divinity of Christ are intricately connected with the notion of God's *kenōsis*, his self-emptying, which is crucially important in the Christian understanding of soteriology. Christians continue to affirm with the early fathers that "what is not assumed is not healed." This understanding is the flip coin of the affirmation of Jesus's full humanity.

The sonship issue, for the church, reflects faithfulness to the biblical text, which is full of usage of the Son title. We affirm the messianic nature of the title, but we also embrace the New Testament investment of new meaning into the title in light of the resurrected Christ. The early church was reticent to use any language foreign to the New Testament in its doctrinal statements, and therefore *homoousios* was resisted for a while, before being accepted into the Nicene confession. But today, nothing prevents Christians from revising and updating such language in a way that fits better contemporary notions, so long as theologians remain aware of the issues at stake, which were the primary concern of church fathers. This in itself should provide rich space for dialogue between Christians and Muslims.

As evidenced in the complexity of the Muslim exegetical tradition on the question of the cross and who was crucified, it is clear that there is room for further dialogue and conversation. It seems that the qur'anic exegetical tradition has not pronounced its final word on it, so why not reopen this question and discuss it with more tolerance and openness?

World, vol. 1: *Christ and Reconciliation* (Grand Rapids: Eerdmans, 2013), 188. He refers to Raymond E. Brown's *Birth of the Messiah: A Commentary on the Infancy Narratives in Matthew and Luke* (Garden City, NY: Doubleday, 1977), 523.

Concluding Thoughts

The cross is absolutely crucial in the biblical model of salvation history. It is not an afterthought or a matter of whim. The cross is the New Testament response to the necessity of the Old Testament sacrificial system, as a means to address and deal with the gravity of sin. Christians would not object to reopening the conversation with Muslims about soteriology, which will have at its core a discussion of the seriousness of sin, the sinful reality in which we currently live, as we have throughout history, and what God's response is to this reality.

An emphasis on God's perpetual desire to give himself may be more fruitful in a dialogical conversation about soteriology than simply a focus on the historical event of the cross. Christians and Muslims together can affirm God as creator and sustainer of his creation. They can affirm him as *ar-Raḥmān* ("the compassionate") and *ar-Raḥīm* ("the merciful"), who will go to any lengths to restore human beings into relationship with himself. It is true that Islam's answer to this dilemma was the affirmation that God, when he wills something, simply speaks it into being (*kūnī fa kānat*—"Be! And it comes into being"). However, surely the long line of prophets sent by God to achieve his purposes, and the perpetual qur'anic affirmation of God as *Raḥmān* and *Raḥīm* are testimonies as well about the importance of this theme in the Qur'an and in the Muslim understanding of God's attitude to humanity. Surely there must be room for reopening this conversation creatively in dialogue.

On reading the words in an-Nisā' 4:172 that "the Messiah was never too proud to be God's servant," those familiar with the biblical text can hardly help being reminded of the apostle Paul's words in Philippians 2. Using what seem to be the words of an early Christian hymn, Paul affirms that although Jesus Christ was "in very nature God," he did not consider equality with God "something to be grasped. . . . And being found in appearance as a man, *he humbled himself and became obedient* to death" (emphasis added).

In a sense, both the Qur'an and the New Testament affirm that there is no shame in being God's servant. But the Qur'an begins from the conviction that the radical unicity of God affirms that Jesus, as a faithful prophet of God, would not have seen it as beneath him to be called a servant of God. Whereas the New Testament, beginning from a conviction that in Christ we encountered Emmanuel—God with us—affirms that Jesus's embrace of servanthood to God was the result of God's *kenōsis*, his self-emptying for the sake of our salvation. Whereas the New Testament's starting point is God's initiative of salvation, the Qur'an's starting point is the apostle Jesus's faithful submission to the one God.

Whereas the Qur'an considers from a human perspective that it would be proud for Christ to claim to be more than a human servant, the New Testament affirms that by becoming a servant, God humbled himself by coming to us in Christ for the sake of our salvation. In the New Testament, the reason why Christ became a servant had nothing to do with not being proud and everything to do with God's plan of salvation, as he modeled self-givingness as a means of reconciliation and peace with God and with one another.

This comparison of an-Nisāʾ 4:172 and Philippians 2 leads to a reflection on the context of Paul's discourse and back to the opening section of this chapter. God coming to us *in Christ* raised a unique challenge to the human understanding of power. The New Testament teaches us that it is not through violence that God brings in his kingdom on earth. But rather, it was by making himself vulnerable and suffering violence at human hands that he overturned our human understanding of power.

We commit injustice toward this crucial message when we confine the narrative of the incarnation and the cross to mere intellectual speculations and debates about the historicity of the cross and its salvific implications. The biblical narrative can be understood in its full glory only when applied in our interpersonal relationships. It is when we practice the incarnation and the cross in our own lives, when we humbly apply them to heal our conflicts, both interpersonal and international, that the necessity of such doctrines will come to life in its full power. Muslims may object to the incarnation as unfitting of God, and they may object, like Peter, that the crucifixion was unfitting of God's apostle Jesus. And Christians might argue forcefully or even violently for the truth of their doctrines. But in the end of the day, the conviction that God's choice of self-emptying to suffer violence at the hands of human power was the only way to subvert the human understanding of power and violence will come about only through imitation. It is by embracing and imitating God's humility that the Gospel witness to Muslims will stand most powerful. So we stand with Paul, listening again as he entreats us with this earliest Christian hymn (Phil 2:5–11):

> Your attitude should be the same as that of Christ Jesus:
> Who, being in very nature God,
> *did not consider equality with God as something to be grasped,*
> but made himself nothing,
> taking the very nature of a servant,
> being made in human likeness.
> And being found in appearance as a man,
> *he humbled himself*
> *and became obedient to death—*
> even death on a cross!
> Therefore God exalted him to the highest place
> and gave him the name that is above every name,
> that at the name of Jesus every knee should bow,
> in heaven and on earth and under the earth,
> and every tongue confess that Jesus Christ is Lord,
> to the glory of God the Father. (New International Version, emphasis added)

Further Reading and Research

See bibliography at end of chapter 5.

5 Who Jesus Is according to Muslims

My friend Peter believes that the qur'anic portrayal of Jesus stands in complete contradiction with the New Testament witness. He was once called Ahmad, but when he converted to Christianity after consistently watching polemical programs about Islam on satellite television, he became convinced that in order to follow Jesus he had entirely to deny his former Islamic faith, even give up his birth name. The violent social repercussions that he experienced as a result of this decision further convinced him that Islam was entirely evil and did not align in any way with the God of the Bible and his message of love.

Samia, on the other hand, after much inner struggle about certain Islamic practices and behaviors in her society, which she felt strongly conflicted with her personal values, immersed herself in an extensive comparative study of the Bible and the Qur'an. It was primarily as a result of her meditation on the qur'anic portrayal of Jesus that she felt so attracted to him, to the point that she eventually decided to become his disciple. She was more attracted to Jesus than she was to Christianity, and she was able to express this newfound allegiance without alienating her family. Today, she and her brother, and one of their cousins, are discreetly part of a small group that studies the Bible in a home. She is convinced of all Christian doctrines, but does not feel she needs to attack Islam or the Qur'an to elevate Jesus in her life.

Amir is my third friend. He believes that many of the disagreements between Muslims and Christians were historically the result of misunderstandings. As far as he's concerned, the Bible and the Qur'an do not contradict each other in their portrayal of Jesus. Although he considers that certain Christian doctrinal beliefs have historically been excessive in their assertions about Jesus, he does not feel that this is sufficient reason for conflict and mutual exclusion. In fact, he has little patience for some of his Muslim coreligionists who speak aggressively against Christianity and Christians and has been able to carve for himself a group of likeminded friends. He considers himself a follower and disciple of ʿĪsa, even as he feels comfortable attending both church and mosque. He feels called to be an ambassador of peace and unapologetically invites Muslims to become Jesus's disciples.

Sumayya, my fourth friend, is quite feisty when it comes to Jesus! She is convinced that the Christian understanding of Jesus has entirely missed the mark and she regularly has lively arguments with her next-door neighbors, who are Christian missionaries. She hosts qur'anic studies in her home, where she trains Muslim young people on how to debate effectively against Christian doctrines. To her, Islam is the only true religion and all others are in error. She feels called to invite people to Islam in order to save them from the fire of hell.

All four of my friends have a certain understanding of Jesus that has formed as a result of their reading of both the Qur'an and the Bible. But their beliefs are not simply the outcome of their own scriptural exegesis. They also derive from the interaction of their readings with their life experiences and social contexts. Though all four of them were born to Muslim families, they grew up as members of communities that were the recipients of diverse interfaith histories and narratives. Theologies always belong in multilayered contexts, and it is at the intersection of all of them that our commitments and loyalties emerge.

In this second chapter on Christ, I explore the affirmative discourse about Jesus in the Muslim-Christian metadialogue. Beyond the straightforward denial of Christian doctrines about Jesus, what do the Qur'an and the Muslim theological tradition affirm concerning him? Not only are beliefs about Jesus today diverse, but traditional beliefs concerning him do not necessarily lead to loyalty for his teaching and life. Conversely, it does not automatically follow that those who claim to be his disciples hold biblical beliefs concerning his true identity. It is with this awareness that we approach the historical Muslim-Christian positive discourse about Jesus, as we seek to derive from it a coherent metadialogue that we can then evaluate, assess, and build upon.

Jesus in the Qur'an and Islamic Tradition

Christians often focus their attention on the negative Islamic critique of the Christian doctrine of Christ. But the positive portrait of Jesus that emerges from the Qur'an also needs to be emphasized. Although the previous chapter produced a qur'anic portrait of Jesus largely bereft of the fundamental tenets of Christian Christology, such as the divine incarnation in Christ and his salvific work, the negative witness of the Qur'an is in fact not the principal one.

Muslim polemics against Christianity, based on the verses about Jesus, must be examined within their particular historical context, which is driven more by political power struggles than by disinterested theological overtures. But while there are less than a dozen verses in the Qur'an upon which a polemical discourse against Christians can be built, nearly twice as many serve as an affirmation of Jesus's greatness, which stands as a confirmation of Muhammad's message.

One of the premises of textual hermeneutics is that a text does not exist in a vacuum. The author of a text always has an audience in mind. Good authors usually have a considerable knowledge of the realities that will affect their audience's understanding of their message. They are often part of the same context as their audience, and therefore that context also affects their style of writing, their motivation in writing, and their purpose for writing. When one speaks about sacred Scriptures, the question of authorship can be more sensitive, as a community of faith usually believes that God had at least something to do with the authorship of their Scriptures. Such principles are today taken for granted by the majority of Christian scholars who read and interpret the Bible by paying particular attention to literary genre.

On the other hand, we often make huge assumptions about the Muslim view of the Qur'an. Because of the doctrine of *tanzīl* (the coming down of the Qur'an upon Muhammad) and of the mainstream Islamic belief in the "eternity of the Qur'an," we often assume that Muslims have no place for context in their understanding of the Qur'an's revelation. Nothing could be further from the truth, however. One of the most important principles of qur'anic exegesis, as we saw in chapter 2, is the primary attention given to *asbāb an-nuzūl* ("the occasions of the revelation"), which represents par excellence both the historical and rhetorical context of the Qur'an's verses. That qur'anic verses have a primary historical purpose of a specific nature, therefore, is not alien to the Muslim understanding of their Scriptures.

A second issue (already hinted at in the previous chapters) begs to be asked as one immerses oneself into the text of the Qur'an: why is Jesus such a central figure in the Qur'an? The contents of sacred Scriptures are so taken for granted by their receiving communities that we often fail to ask the most basic, yet potentially most crucial, questions. Why did Muhammad not simply proclaim his message of monotheism, calling pagan Arabs to the worship of the one God, leaving the Judeo-Christian tradition alone? If the Prophet of Islam felt the burden, like Abraham, to break away from the religion of his fathers and venture into new territory in response to God's call, why did he have to do so at the expense of the preceding covenants that he claimed to continue and complete?

The extensive qur'anic references to Jesus were not primarily meant to be polemical, even though in historical retrospect they appear to be so. The qur'anic narrative about Jesus only *incidentally* emerges at the expense of the Christian narrative. In its primary purpose, the Jesus metanarrative in the Qur'an was designed as proof of Muhammad's prophethood and only incidentally became a counternarrative, not to the Gospels themselves, but to the Christian interpretation of their texts. There is therefore ample justification for beginning our detailed textual analysis in the present chapter from the angle of the Qur'an's usage of Jesus verses for the purpose of proof of prophethood.

The affirmative references to Jesus in the Qur'an therefore provide the framework of the present chapter, although we will also see how Muslim writers have used even these verses for polemical purposes. In a second step, we will look at the starting point of the Muslim theological reconstruction of Christ's identity, namely the affirmation of his human servanthood. At the end of the chapter, we will look at the soteriological implications of the Muslim theologians' stripping and restoration of the icon of Christ.

Jesus Is Part of a Continuous Divine Prophetic Line

Many verses about Jesus in the Qur'an emphasize the continuity between the Abrahamic revelations, leading up to God's revelation to Muhammad. We will study this process in greater detail in chapter 8, when we look at

Islam's Muhammado-centric reading of the Bible. My purpose here is to highlight one of the most important functions that the Qur'an ascribed to Jesus as a central link in this continuous revelation. Just as Jesus played a central part in the confirmation of previous divine revelations, the Qur'an wants to establish the centrality of Muhammad in the confirmation both of Jesus and of preceding prophets. We read in al-Mā'ida 5:46: "We sent Jesus, the son of Mary, to follow in the footsteps of those earlier prophets, confirming what was available of the Torah. We gave him the Gospel. It has guidance and enlightenment, confirming what was available of the Torah. It has guidance and an admonition for those who are mindful of God."

The meaning of this verse is rather straightforward. Jesus stood in continuity with the message revealed in the Torah, and Muhammad would continue in this line as well. Rashīd Riḍa (died 1935), in his commentary *Tafsīr al-Manār*, agrees with this traditional view, affirming that Christ's law (Sharīʿa) was the Torah, adding that Christians "abrogated" this law (*nasakhūhā*) because of their allegiance to Paul the apostle. About Jesus, however, Riḍa affirms that he not only confirmed the guidance and admonition of the Torah, but that he himself brought the *Injīl*, which also was guidance and enlightenment for those who followed it. He defines the guidance and enlightenment of the Gospel in terms of Jesus's spiritual teaching and ethical exhortation that shook the materialistic sluggishness of the Israelites. It was this earthshaking message of the Gospel, Riḍa affirms, that prepared the people of the book in Syria, Egypt, and Mesopotamia to receive Islam with such openness and at such a rapid rate in the centuries that followed its emergence.

In the Salafī commentary of Sayyid Quṭb (died 1966), *Fī Ḍhilāl al-Qur'an*, the continuity and discontinuity of the three revealed Scriptures is even further emphasized. Jesus endorsed the Torah completely, except for any elements that he explicitly abrogated, and Muhammad and Muslims are to embrace the Torah and the *Injīl* entirely as well, except for any parts that are corrected, changed, or added to in the Qur'an. The Qur'an, which contains God's perfect law (Sharīʿa), is to be endorsed and applied entirely, with no compromise to any other law. Any deviation from this law represents a return to *Jāhiliyya*, which he defines not as a specific historical period that preceded Islam, but as any moral deviation from the teaching of the Qur'an. He invites Muslims not to confuse the Qur'an's tolerant (*samāḥa*) attitude toward the people of the book with its uncompromising command to embrace and apply God's Sharīʿa.

Jesus Is a Highly Venerated Prophet

The most straightforward qur'anic verses about Jesus simply affirm his righteousness, on par with all the others of God's prophets. Al-An'ām 6:84–87 is part of the Abraham narrative, which the sūrah begins to focus on from verse 74 onward. Abraham's role as the paradigm of righteousness in his willingness to proclaim the one God in the face of his polytheistic contemporaries comes into focus:

> We gave him [i.e., Abraham] Isaac and Jacob. We guided each just as we guided Noah before. Among his [Abraham's] descendants were David, Solomon, Job, Joseph, Moses, and Aaron. In this way we reward those who do good; Zachariah, John, Jesus, and Elijah—every one of them was righteous. Ishmael, Elisha, Jonah, and Lot—we favored every one of them above other people, and also some of their forefathers, their offspring, and their brothers. We chose them and guided them on a straight path.

In his commentary on al-An'ām 6:74, Muhammad b. Jarīr aṭ-Ṭabarī (died 922) points out that through this section, God is inviting Muhammad to take Abraham as his *imām* (leader and model) and to emulate his behavior in parting ways with his father's religious tradition.

Fakhr ad-Dīn ar-Rāzī (died 1209), in his commentary, points out that the purpose of enumerating seventeen prophets in al-An'ām 6:84–86 is for God to emphasize the wealth of his grace on Abraham. The greatest form of grace (*an-ni'am*) that God grants to anyone is for them to know that prophets and messengers will derive from their descendants. One interesting comment that ar-Rāzī makes with regard to the reference to Jesus in al-An'ām 6:85 is that, by referring to Jesus as a descendent of Abraham despite this descent being through his mother, the Qur'an affirms the legitimacy of al-Ḥasan and al-Ḥussayn as descendants of Muhammad, despite this descent being through their mother, Fāṭima. Muhammad had no surviving male descendants (he had three sons who all died in infancy), and this no doubt would have been cause for embarrassment and challenge in an Arab tribal culture. The Muslim tradition therefore traces Muhammad's direct descendants through his two grandsons, al-Ḥasan and al-Ḥussayn, sons of his daughter Fāṭima and his cousin 'Alī.

Another verse, āl-'Imrān 3:45, not only affirms Jesus's greatness, but ascribes to him a special status and place of distinction before God:

"[When] the angels said, 'Mary, God gives you good news of a word from him, whose name will be the Messiah, Jesus son of Mary. *He will be highly distinguished in this world and the Hereafter, and brought near to God*'" (emphasis added).

Aṭ-Ṭabarī, in his commentary, does not make much of the reference to Jesus as "a word from him" in his promise to Mary. Though he knows of some traditions—clearly originating from Christian circles—that connect this announcement with the Johannine reference to Christ as Logos, he himself understands the reference to the *kalima* simply in the sense of a message that God revealed to Mary, namely that he would bring forth a son from her, without the intervention of a man.

On the other hand, aṭ-Ṭabarī elaborates on the qur'anic description of Jesus as *wajīh* ("distinguished") and *muqarrab* ("brought near"). *Wajāha*, he notes, is a mark of "high status, honor and nobility before God." *Muqarrab* is a reference to proximity to God on the day of the resurrection: "He is one of those whom God will bring close to himself on the day of the resurrection. He will make him dwell close to him and will bring him close."

But even in the most flattering verses of the Qur'an, where the greatness of Jesus is affirmed, there is often an underlying agenda, countering not the Gospel narrative about Jesus, but what the Qur'an seems to perceive as the later Christian doctrinal excesses (*ghuluw*) concerning him. In Maryam 19:34–36, some readers of the Qur'an, both in the Ḥijāz and in 'Irāq according to aṭ-Ṭabarī, read the words *qawlu al-ḥaqq* ("the word of truth" with the nominative ending *u* in *qawlu*) as a reference to Jesus. Others, and that seems to be aṭ-Ṭabarī's own preference, read the words as *qawla al-ḥaqq* (with the accusative ending *a* in *qawla*) as a reference to God's testimony about Jesus in the preceding verses. Whatever the case might be, the positive affirmations about Jesus are immediately followed with an accusation that Christians have erred in their belief about him by calling him God's son: "Such is Jesus, the son of Mary—*the word of truth* about which they are in dispute. It does not befit God to have a son; may he be exalted in his glory! When he decides on something, he simply says to it, 'Be!' and it is. [Jesus continued]: 'God is my Lord and your Lord, so worship him. That is a straight path.'"

Despite its disagreement with the way that Jesus and his message were received by Christians, the Qur'an is not shy in its exaltation of Jesus. It testifies in multiple places about his miraculous birth and all the miracles he performed. All of the great things that Jesus did are viewed as signs that he came from God. But the Qur'an is quick to add that it was "with

God's permission" (*bi-idhn Allāh*) that he performed them all. Al-Mā'ida 5:110 is the most striking among such verses:

> God will say, "Jesus, son of Mary, remember the grace that I bestowed upon you and your mother? How I strengthened you with the Holy Spirit so you could speak from your cradle, and as a grown man? [Remember] when I taught you the book, the Wisdom, the Torah, and the Gospel? [Remember] when, with my permission, you fashioned the shape of a bird out of clay, breathed into it, and it became, with my permission, a bird? [Remember] when, with my permission, you healed the blind person and the leper; when, by my permission, you brought the dead back to life? [Remember] when I kept the children of Israel from harming you when you came to them with all the evidence of the truth, and when those of them who were bent on denying the truth said, 'This is clearly nothing but deception'?"

Aṭ-Ṭabarī considers this verse a continuation of the previous (Al-Mā'ida 5:109), where God gathers his messengers on the day of judgment and asks each of them about the way that their contemporaries received them and their message: "On the day when God assembles all the messengers and asks, 'What response did you receive?' They will answer, 'We have no knowledge. You alone know these things that cannot be seen.'"

The messengers will then reaffirm that they know nothing more than what God already knows and what he has given them to know. Aṭ-Ṭabarī reports certain exegetical traditions that understood the messengers' claim that they "have no knowledge" as their initial reaction to the fearful day of judgment. Other traditions read God's question to be a reference to the way that their message was received after they had completed their mission and died. They thus affirmed that God alone knew what happened after they had departed from the earth.

The final statement in al-Mā'ida 5:110, containing the polemic against the Jews, is a recurring theme in the qur'anic verses about Jesus. God's protection of Jesus from the Jews is the context of the polemic. Aṭ-Ṭabarī here points to the connection between this affirmation and God's polemical refutation of the Jews when they wanted to kill Jesus, namely in an-Nisā' 4:157, which I examined in the previous chapter, where he denies them the satisfaction of the claim that they had killed Jesus.

Muhammad Is Part of the Same Divine Prophetic Line as Jesus

Now we come to those verses in the Qur'an that refer to Jesus in order to affirm that the message God gave to Muhammad was in the same line as the message he gave to prophets who preceded him. The affirmation of the prophethood of Judeo-Christian personalities, including that of Jesus, is viewed as an affirmation of Muhammad's prophethood. Chapters 8–9 will be dedicated to a broader coverage of this process, but the following verses are brought up in this chapter in order to highlight this important function of Jesus in the qur'anic program. Consider, for example, an-Nisā' 4:163, where God confirms his prophet Muhammad: "We have sent a revelation to you [prophet], just as we inspired Noah and all the prophets after him—as we inspired Abraham and Ishmael and Isaac and Jacob and their descendants, including Jesus and Job and Jonah and Aaron and Solomon; and to David we gave the Psalms."

According to Muhammad aṭ-Ṭabarī, the occasion of this revelation was when the Jews challenged Muhammad to bring a book from God as proof of his prophethood. They claimed that God had not revealed anything new to humanity after he had sent the Torah to Moses. Through an-Nisā' 4:163, God proved them wrong by informing them that he had inspired many messengers after Moses, both those enumerated in this verse and others unnamed.

With ash-Shūra 42:13, God reaffirms that Muhammad's message is not a new message and that the faith to which Muhammad is calling people is not an innovation:

> He has ordained for you the same faith he commanded Noah, and what we have revealed to you, and what we commanded Abraham and Moses and Jesus: "You shall uphold the faith and do not break up into factions." Although what you are calling the idolaters to do is too hard for them. [However] God draws to himself everyone who is willing, and guides unto himself everyone who turns to him.

Aṭ-Ṭabarī, in line with the early qur'anic exegetical tradition, reads this verse as an affirmation that God has only one *dīn*—one religion—and that all messengers of God had only one command to their followers, namely to "uphold *the* faith," the *true religion* (*dīn al-ḥaqq*). It comes out quite clearly from the early exegesis of these verses that Islam upholds unity in religious pluralism. It is not that there are many ways to reach

God, but that only the true religion is the way to God. This true religion, however, in the qur'anic vision, is not so much Islam as a new religion, but rather it is the act and posture of Islam ("surrender") to God.

Al-Aḥzāb 33:7 affirms the same. It confirms that Muhammad was himself a prophet and that he received a covenant like that of his predecessors: "We took a pledge from the prophets: from you and from Noah and Abraham and Moses and Jesus, the son of Mary. We took a solemn pledge from them." Interestingly, in reference to this verse, aṭ-Ṭabarī transmits a Ḥadīth ascribed to Muhammad, where he is said to have affirmed: "I was the first prophet among [God's] creation, and the last one to be sent." The statement is inspired from the chronology of the listed prophets, where Muhammad is mentioned first, before Noah.

Some verses that refer to Jesus in the Qur'an reflect a defensive position on the part of the early followers of Muhammad. In times of opposition, they are to affirm, not their distinctiveness from previous revelations, but the continuity of Muhammad's message with that of his predecessors. Early followers were taught what to say to those who persecuted them:

> Say, "We believe in God and what was revealed to us and what was revealed to Abram, Ishmael, Isaac, Jacob, and the tribes, what was given to Moses and Jesus, and what was given to the prophets from their Lord. We do not distinguish between any of them, and we submit to him." (al-Baqara 2:136)

> Say, "We believe in God and what he revealed to us and to Abraham, Ishmael, Isaac, Jacob, the tribes, and in what was given to Moses, Jesus, and the prophets from their Lord. We do not distinguish between any of them, and we have submitted to him." (āl-'Imrān 3:84)

The occasion of the revelation of these verses, according to aṭ-Ṭabarī, was the call of the Jews and the Christians for Muhammad's early followers to embrace Judaism or Christianity (respectively) if they wanted to be on the right path, as stated in the preceding verse of al-Baqara 2:135. To them they are to affirm that they have already believed in God and in all of the preceding revelations. The great challenge of Islam, from the perspective of the history of religions, was the refusal of Jews and Christians to recognize God's revelation to Muhammad. Aṭ-Ṭabarī laments that whereas Muslims recognize all the preceding prophets, the Jews refuse to accept the prophethood of Jesus and Christians refuse to accept the prophethood of Muhammad.

No doubt the most persistent foundation of Islam's "establishment of the proofs of [Muhammad's] prophethood" (*tathbīt dalā'il an-nubuwwa*) is found in aṣ-Ṣaff 61:6: "And when Jesus son of Mary said, 'O children of Israel, I am God's messenger to you, confirming what is available of the Torah, and bringing good news of a messenger who will come after me, whose name is Ahmad.' But when he came to them with clear evidence, they said, 'This is obvious magic.'" Much more will be said about this verse in chapter 9.

The Muslim View of Jesus

Jesus the Human Servant

We now move beyond the starting point of the qur'anic message about Jesus to what became the starting point of the Muslim theologians—receivers of the qur'anic message. The function of Jesus as confirmer of Muhammad's prophethood would never disappear in the later Islamic theological discourse. On the contrary, the argument will grow well beyond the boundaries of the Qur'an's simple message. One other argument, however, that became central among Muslim theologians, particularly as Islam grew and spread among the Christians of the East, was the emphasis on the human and servant nature of Jesus. I compared in the previous chapter the Muslim approach to Jesus's humility with the Christian approach, based on an-Nisā' 4:172. Here I present the same verse in order to point out that the attributes of humanity and servanthood are never demeaning in the Muslim worldview. But they were certainly emphasized as a polemic against the christological developments within Christianity: "The Messiah was never too proud to be God's servant, nor were the angels who are near to him. He will gather before him the arrogant and all those who are too proud to worship him."

The affirmation of Jesus's human servanthood was an extensively used argument in the Muslim theological discourse about Jesus. On the one hand, it was thought to destroy the lofty Christian claims about Christ, and on the other it affirmed the primary qur'anic claim that Christ was a mere man and faithful servant of God.

This argument, as we saw in the previous chapter, was very easy to establish, since Christianity always maintained the full humanity of

Christ, precisely by affirming the Gospel verses that substantiated it. In their confrontation with Docetic ideas, which sought to play down the real humanity of Christ and the reality of his suffering on the cross, church fathers maintained Christ's full humanity as an essential point in Christian soteriology, without which the whole idea of the incarnation was devoid of meaning.

With emerging Islam, an ever-recurring theme in the Muslim discourse became the following: how can Christians acknowledge and uphold the obvious Gospel references to Christ's humanity, while at the same time affirming daily in their creeds that Jesus is "true God from true God, begotten not made"?[1] With this critique raised against them, Christians in the context of Islam found themselves again in the same situation as Christianity several centuries earlier, which went through the process of developing a coherent theological doctrine while making sense of the diversity of the biblical witness. Back then, Christianity went through the process of explaining itself to Judaism's absolute monotheism on the one hand and to abstract philosophical Greek paganism on the other. And it was in careful balance between both of these currents that it defined itself. In the new Islamic context, the process was, in a sense, repeating itself. Only this time, the more institutionalized Christianity did not have as much flexibility to redefine itself in relation to outside factors as it did at the time of its tender youth.

Not surprisingly, among Islam's favorite passages to demonstrate Christ's pure humanity and servanthood were the opening verses of the Gospels. These verses placed the person of Christ in a specific historical context. And since it is assumed that God does not belong within space and time, which contradict eternity, Muslim theologians alleged that the very existence of these verses alone should be sufficient to place Jesus in a different category than God. The question raised is philosophical in nature, but its treatment was often quite simplistic. The argument is that

1. See, for example, ʿAlī b. Sahl Rabbān aṭ-Ṭabarī, *Kitāb ar-Radd ʿala an-Naṣāra*, in I. A. Khalifé and W. Kutsch's "Ar-radd ʿala-n-nasārā," *Mélanges de l'Université Saint Joseph* 36.4 (1959): 115–48 at 121; Ibn Ayyūb, *Risāla ila Akhīhi ʿAlī* (Letter to His Brother ʿAlī, Explaining to Him Why He Converted to Islam), preserved in Taqī ad-Dīn Aḥmad b. Taymiyya, *Al-Jawāb aṣ-Ṣaḥīḥ li-man Baddala Dīn al-Masīḥ* (Cairo: Nile Press, 1905), 1.2.360; and the citation of the whole Nicene Creed in Shihāb ad-Dīn al-Qarāfī, *Al-Ajwiba al-Fākhira ʿan al-Asʾila al-Fājira*, ed. Bakr Zakī ʿAwaḍ (Cairo: Wehbeh Publishers, 1987), 308–9, followed by a discussion and refutation of the creedal statements on the basis of the biblical text.

if Jesus ever existed in time or space, then he could not have been the eternal God. And since the Gospels clearly testify that Jesus did come into existence, move and die within the limits of time and space, it follows that he was not God. One anonymous ninth-century treatise, often attributed to an eighth-century letter originating from Umayyad Caliph ʿUmar II (died 720), did not even bother to produce any exegetical demonstration with specific verse citations, so much was the argument taken for granted. The author simply affirms: "But ʿĪsa ate and drank, and he slept and was circumcised, and he was afraid and human beings saw him, and he was preserved alive for thirty-three years. So how do you make him a god when he did all these things and testified about it himself?"[2]

This sort of affirmation seems to build on al-Māʾida 5:75, which established the qurʾanic foundation of the straightforward logic of this central argument, particularly in its final exclamation: "See how clear we make these messages for them! The Messiah, son of Mary, was only a messenger. All [other] messengers had passed away before him, and his mother was one who never deviated from the truth. *They both ate food*. See how clear we make these messages for them and how deluded their minds are."

Among Muslim theologians who produced evidence from the Gospels to demonstrate this point, it is possible to classify their scriptural citations into two categories: external evidence and internal evidence. The first group consisted of the Gospel verses that simply make mention of the specific time and space elements pertaining to Jesus's life, displaying very little analytical sophistication. The opening chapters of Matthew's Gospel were considered a prime choice as external evidence. For example, that one reads in Matthew 2:1 that Jesus was born "in the days of Herod the king" was sufficient for ʿAlī b. Rabbān aṭ-Ṭabarī (circa 782–860) to observe that Jesus's birth was human.[3] Other passages in Luke's Gospel lent themselves perfectly to the argument of Christ's mere humanity, particularly in the two opening chapters. In Luke 2:40, for instance, the boy Jesus is said to be growing in body and wisdom. Both aṭ-Ṭabarī at the beginning of our period (ninth century), as well as Shihāb ad-Dīn al-Qarāfī near the end (1228–85), would use the verse with that purpose in mind. Al-Qarāfī

2. D. Sourdel, ed./trans., "Un pamphlet musulman anonyme d'époque ʿabbâside contre les chrétiens," *Revue des études islamiques* 34 (1966): 27. A similar argument and statement is also found in Abū Ḥāmid al-Ghazālī, *Ar-Radd al-Jamīl li-Ilāhiyyat ʿĪsa bi-Ṣarīḥ al-Injīl* (Une réfutation excellente de la divinité de Jésus-Christ d'après le texte même de l'évangile), ed./trans. Robert Chidiac (Paris: Librairie Ernest Leroux, 1939), 17–18.

3. Aṭ-Ṭabarī, *Radd*, 126.

adds to 2:40 a large number of other verses from this chapter: Luke 2:1, 5–7, 21–24, 39, 42, 46, 51. He concludes about all these natural stages in the growth of a child: "Each one of these is irrefutable evidence that he is a servant under lordship, and not a worshiped lord."[4]

Al-Qarāfī brings in additional external evidence of Christ's human servanthood from the temptation narrative in Matthew 4:3–10. In his view, that the devil dared to challenge Jesus and that he was able to drag him from place to place is evidence that Jesus was not God. Had he been God, al-Qarāfī adds, "the devil would have had no ambition concerning him."[5] Assuming that the true identity of Christ could not have been hidden from the devil, al-Qarāfī sees the argument as evidence of Christ's purely *human* identity.

The second group of scriptural evidence is more interesting and imaginative. Here, specific utterances about Jesus, as well as utterances made by Jesus himself, are collected. Through this second group of verses, Muslim theologians wanted to show that it was not only through external factors relating to Jesus's earthly life that his divinity could be disproved, but also through the witness of heaven, of his close companions, and of Jesus himself. In fact, an early-ninth-century Zaydī Shīʿī imām, al-Qāsim ar-Rassī (785–860), suggests that five witnesses commonly accepted by Muslims and Christians should be the criteria for the establishment of Christian doctrine: God, the angels, Christ, Mary, and the disciples. These "reliable witnesses," in his opinion, can provide both a firsthand testimony about Christ, as well as a standard by which to interpret all of the Scriptures. This, he argues, is the sound principle upon which Muslims and Christians should agree and build their beliefs.

His contemporary, ʿAlī aṭ-Ṭabarī, appeals as well to the testimony of common witnesses, this time four in number: (1) the proclamation of the angel Gabriel to Mary, (2) the testimony about Christ that was heard as a voice from heaven,[6] (3) the testimony of John the Baptist, and (4) Christ's testimony about himself.[7]

Having established the hermeneutical principle of examining commonly accepted reliable witnesses, al-Qāsim ar-Rassī then appeals to the

4. Aṭ-Ṭabarī, *Radd*, 124; and al-Qarāfī, *Al-Ajwiba al-Fākhira*, 220–21.

5. Al-Qarāfī, *Al-Ajwiba al-Fākhira*, 217.

6. This is a reference to God's testimony to Christ at his baptism, at his transfiguration, and in a Matthean prophetic reference in Matt 12:18, all of which are often clustered together as one account in aṭ-Ṭabarī's treatise.

7. Aṭ-Ṭabarī, *Radd*, 139.

testimony of Matthew—"one of the disciples [*min al-ḥawāriyyīn*]"—in Matthew 1:1, to assert Jesus's humanity as "the son of David."[8] Similarly, as he argues for the uniqueness and oneness of God, ʿAlī aṭ-Ṭabarī cites the same verse in his mid-ninth-century treatise as proof of Christ's mere humanity, pointing out that Jesus is called "son of Abraham."[9]

Another convert from Christianity, late-tenth-century writer al-Ḥasan b. Ayyūb, follows the same argument, endorsing the Matthean assertion that Jesus was the "son of David, son of Abraham," as proof that Islam is right in refuting the Christian claims about Christ's sonship and divinity.[10] Finally, in a direct refutation of the creedal statement that Christ was "the creator of all things," thirteenth-century polemicist al-Qarāfī observes that it must be concluded from such a statement that Jesus also created his own mother and that his mother had then given birth to her own creator! Considering this an absurdity, he advances Matthew's affirmation that Jesus was "the son of David" as sufficient refutation of Christian claims.[11]

Ar-Rassī then moves to the reliable witness of the angel Gabriel. He cites from the Matthean birth account the testimony of the angel to Joseph in Matthew 1:18–21, when the latter had decided to divorce Mary in secret. The angel announced to him that the child would be "from God's Spirit" (*min Rūḥ Allāh*) and would be called Jesus. That the angel did not announce to Joseph that the child would be called "Son of God" is seen by the author as evidence that the later Christian claims are heretical.[12]

Among ʿAlī aṭ-Ṭabarī's favorites was the baptismal account in Matthew 3:13–17. Based on this passage he brings in the testimony of his second witness: God. Aṭ-Ṭabarī draws two conclusions from this narrative. The first is based on Christ's answer to John the Baptist in 3:15 that "all righteousness" will be fulfilled through his baptism. He concludes: "The rank of him who is approached for the increase of righteousness is not less than the rank of him who approaches seeking him."[13]

Second, aṭ-Ṭabarī notes that the testimony of the voice from heaven (3:17) makes no claim of divinity concerning Christ, but calls him only

8. Ar-Rassī, Ar-*Radd ʿala an-Naṣāra*, in Ignazio Di Matteo's "Confutazione contro I cristiani dello zaydita al-Qâsim b. Ibrâhîm," *Rivista degli Studi Orientali* 9 (1922): 321.

9. Aṭ-Ṭabarī, *Radd*, 121.

10. Ibn Ayyūb, *Risāla*, in Ibn Taymiyya, *Al-Jawāb aṣ-Ṣaḥīḥ*, 1.2.360.

11. Al-Qarāfī, *Al-Ajwiba al-Fākhira*, 312.

12. Ar-Rassī, *Radd*, 322.

13. Aṭ-Ṭabarī, *Radd*, 141.

"son" and "chosen one" (*al-muṣṭafa*). He explains that this word, *al-muṣṭafa*, is a *maf'ūl bihi* (a grammatical term indicating the accusative case, but literally meaning that "something is done to him"), and it denotes a recipient of grace (*mun'am 'alayhi*). Hence, Christ cannot be thought of apart from a human being. Ibn Ayyūb later takes over aṭ-Ṭabarī's second argument and adds that "the *muṣṭafa* being a *maf'ūl*, and the *maf'ūl* being created (*makhlūq*)," the humanity and createdness of Christ are clearly emphasized in this passage.[14] As for al-Qarāfī, Matthew's claim that at Christ's baptism the Holy Spirit came down on him from heaven in the form of a dove is a clear critique of the Christian creedal statement that he was incarnate from the Holy Spirit and another proof of his mere humanity.[15]

Further, in addition to the external evidence of Christ's human servanthood that al-Qarāfī derived from the temptation account in Matthew 4:1–11,[16] the author draws several conclusions from Christ's own testimony as internal evidence that all contribute to restoring his human and servant image. The first is that when the devil asked him to worship him, Jesus asserted that he worshiped God only. Second, Jesus replied to the devil's invitation to throw himself off the edge of the temple that one should not tempt God. By this, al-Qarāfī claims, Jesus was making clear that he walked the path of worshiping servants and was subject to the same laws. Once again, as in several of the preceding Muslim writers, al-Qarāfī paints a picture of Christ as a righteous Muslim prophet who worships and submits to God alone.

Finally, Ibn Qayyim al-Jawziyya in the fourteenth century briefly refers to the temptation narrative based on Luke 4:10. Ironically, he uses the devil's citation of the Old Testament prophecy that God "will command his angels concerning you, to protect you" as further proof that Christ was not himself Lord of the angels, since he was in need of them for protection.[17]

At the beginning of chapter 4, I noted that the intention of Muslim theologians in refuting the classical Christian doctrine of Christ was not to discredit Jesus, or even the text of the Gospels. The critique was against

14. Ibn Ayyūb, *Risāla*, in Ibn Taymiyya, *Al-Jawāb aṣ-Ṣaḥīḥ*, 1.2.323.

15. Al-Qarāfī, *Al-Ajwiba al-Fākhira*, 314.

16. Al-Qarāfī, *Al-Ajwiba al-Fākhira*, 216–17. In addition, al-Qarāfī refers to Matt 4:9 a second time on p. 312.

17. Shams ad-Dīn Muhammad b. Abī Bakr Ibn Qayyim al-Jawziyya, *Hidāyat al-Ḥayāra fī Ajwibat al-Yahūd wa an-Naṣāra*, ed. Aḥmad Ḥijāzī as-Saqā (Cairo: al-Maktaba al-Qayyima, 1980), 290.

misinterpretation that led to heresy, rather than against the text itself. If the first group of textual evidence just surveyed served mainly to purge the Gospel narrative of all heresy, by means of the second group, it was Jesus and other honored figures that were vindicated.

Jesus the Prophet and Apostle

After stripping the icon of its corrupt layers of paint, it is time for restoration. Having recast the portrait of Jesus where they felt that it belonged, in the category of creature, the Muslim exegetes, both of the Qur'an and of the Bible, set out to restore to the picture its authentic qur'anic identity. Primarily and most importantly, Jesus belonged in the line of biblical prophets called by God to preach the true religion to people. Second, having been called, the prophet is sent by God with a specific message to the world. The apostle recognizes his calling and confesses his state of servanthood to God.

Gospels Aligned with Qur'an

Muslim theologians built further on the qur'anic affirmation of Jesus's prophethood, using such verses as a springboard in their critique of Christian doctrines, based on the text of the Gospels themselves. As with other arguments against Christian theology, their issue was not so much with the biblical text as it was with Christian exegesis of the Gospels.

The first section of ʿAlī b. Rabbān aṭ-Ṭabarī's *Radd ʿala an-Naṣāra* (circa 851) contains an enumeration of what he calls the "seven silencing arguments" (*al-masāʾil al-musakkitāt*), which he intends as irrevocable arguments against Christian doctrine, demonstrated on the basis of the Christian Scriptures. In the second argument, aṭ-Ṭabarī raises the question of Christ's description of himself in the Gospels. If Christians accept some of his statements and reject others, then, he claims, "they will be blaspheming against him and transforming his testimonies into lies." If, on the other hand, they accept all of his testimonies about himself, then they will confess his servanthood and apostleship, and thus will be denying the claims of their own religious creeds.

One such testimony proceeding from him is his statement in Matthew 10:40–41: "The one who receives you and shelters you has received me, and the one who receives me receives the one who sent me. And the one who receives a prophet in the name of a prophet will receive the reward of one who has received the prophet." Although the first verse served as proof that Jesus was sent, the second verse proved most useful to ʿAlī aṭ-Ṭabarī, since he assumes that Jesus is referring to himself as being a prophet. An alteration of the text occurred at the end of his citation, aiming at bringing it in line with Islamic thinking: he who receives a prophet gets the recompense of "one who has received the prophet," rather than getting the recompense of a prophet. This represents a subtle difference in worldview, since the status of prophet in Islam bears more prestigious connotations than it does in the New Testament witness and can therefore not be achieved by just any mortal.[18] I refer again to this verse in chapter 7 in order to show on the basis of Ibn Ḥazm's treatise how this verse in its canonical version was not acceptable to the Muslim mind.

The textual alteration performed by early Muslim theologians served to rescue the Bible from total rejection on the basis of textual corruption. The peculiar use made of the quotation here should also be noted. The verse was just as well used by Christian theologians as the basis for the opposite argument: "He who receives me receives the one who sent me" was understood as Christ's claim that he can be spoken of interchangeably with God. But by the method of prooftexting, just about any argument could be built on the basis of a verse in isolation from its larger context.

Ibn Ayyūb took over this same argument from aṭ-Ṭabarī, citing the passage in the same peculiar way in his *Risāla*, the letter he wrote to his brother sometime before 987, explaining to him why he had converted to Islam. He concluded with the following statement about Christ's prophetic identity: "And he made clear here as in other places that he was a prophet who was sent, and that his status before God [*anna sabīlahu maʿ Allāh*] was the same as their [the disciples'] status before them [God and Christ]."[19]

By the fourteenth century, on the other hand, Ibn Qayyim al-Jawziyya (died 1350) cited Matthew 10:40 on its own as proof of Christ's apostleship, since in it Jesus recognized that he was sent.[20]

Another great favorite of the Islamic exegetical discourse was a statement of Christ where he quoted a popular proverb that, when taken

18. Aṭ-Ṭabarī, *Radd*, 122.

19. Ibn Ayyūb, *Risāla*, in Ibn Taymiyya, *Al-Jawāb aṣ-Ṣaḥīḥ*, 1.2.336.

20. Ibn Qayyim al-Jawziyya, *Hidāyat al-Ḥayāra*, 290.

outside its context, could be readily understood as an emphatic self-confession of prophethood. The affirmation is found once in each of the four Gospels. In Matthew 13:57 and Mark 6:4, Jesus expressed the saying with a double negative: "A prophet is not without honor except in his own country." In Luke 4:24 and John 4:44, on the other hand, he makes the statement with a single negative: "A prophet is not honored in his own country." This clue is useful in helping us identify the source of the citation every time it occurs. This statement is quoted eight times in six Muslim theologians between the ninth and the fourteenth centuries.

Christian convert ʿAlī aṭ-Ṭabarī was the first to make use of it, plainly inferring that Christ thus "confessed that he was a prophet." By totally ignoring the Gospel context, where the rebuke follows Jesus's fellow countrymen's rejection of his message, the statement sounds like a positive affirmation, simply part of his larger preaching. Aṭ-Ṭabarī's version of the citation originates from the Matthew/Mark tradition: "Jesus departed from the town of Nazareth and declared to people: 'No shame is felt toward [*yustaḥa bihi*] a prophet except in his own town.'"[21]

Ibn Ayyūb's *Risāla* contains three occurrences of this statement in two different places. He derives from it the same argument as the one developed by aṭ-Ṭabarī. Interestingly, however, his version of the citation is not the same as his predecessor's. In fact, Ibn Ayyūb seems to be aware of the two different versions found in the Gospels, and he cites both traditions as two separate occurrences of the same statement. He also departs from the narrative context of his predecessor when introducing the statement, moving away from the canonical setting. Nevertheless, like aṭ-Ṭabarī, he makes it sound as if it were a positive affirmation to the disciples about his identity:

> And he said to his companions: "Let us get out of this town, for a prophet is not honored [*lā yujall*] in his town." (citing Luke/John)[22]
>
> And [there is] also his saying somewhere in the Gospel: "*Let us get out of this town*, for a prophet is not honored [*lā yujall*] in his town." (citing Luke/John)

21. I modified the edited text to what it must have read originally, substituting *yustaḥaq bihi* ("is deserved") with *yustaḥa bihi* ("shame is felt toward him"). The reading as it appears in the edition does not make sense (aṭ-Ṭabarī, *Radd*, 145).

22. Ibn Ayyūb, *Risāla*, in Ibn Taymiyya, *Al-Jawāb aṣ-Ṣaḥīḥ*, 1.2.336.

> And in another place he said: "No prophet is dishonored [*lā yuhān*], except in his town, and among his family [lit., house] and relatives." (citing Matthew/Mark)[23]

The extracanonical narrative context of Ibn Ayyūb recurs in al-Bāqillānī's *Kitāb at-Tamhīd* (died 1013). The latter claims that Christians argue that though Christ may not have performed any greater miracles than other prophets before him, the other prophets confessed their prophethood while Jesus did not, which sets him apart from them. However, al-Bāqillānī sets out to demonstrate that Jesus did confess his prophethood. One evidence he presents is this statement of Jesus in its Luke/John version. The argument is the same one already encountered in aṭ-Ṭabarī and Ibn Ayyūb; the original Gospel narrative context is dropped as in his predecessors, and the new narrative context is the same as the one found in Ibn Ayyūb: "And he said in the Gospel: 'Let us get out of this town, for a prophet is not honored [*lā yukarram*] in his town.'"[24]

Even Ibn Ḥazm (died 1064), who is not accustomed to using the biblical text to draw a positive argument against Christian doctrines, makes an exception here for the sake of using Christ's statement as proof of his prophethood. He cites the statement three times, once according to Matthew, once Mark, and finally Luke. But aware that this would be inconsistent with his general exegetical method, he does not do so before providing his reader with an excuse:

> And in these paragraphs are elements of truth which God did not allow [lit., release: *yuṭliq*] their [i.e., the Christians'] hands to alter [*tabdīl*].[25]

> And this is what escaped their alteration [*aflata min tabdīlihim*], and what God (May he be honored and exalted!) preserved as an argument against them.[26]

23. Ibn Ayyūb, *Risāla*, in Ibn Taymiyya, *Al-Jawāb aṣ-Ṣaḥīḥ*, 1.2.357.

24. Abū Bakr Muhammad b. aṭ-Ṭayyib al-Bāqillānī, *Kitāb Tamhīd al-Awā'il wa Talkhīṣ ad-Dalā'il* (The Book of Establishment of First Principles and Summary of Proofs), ed. R. J. McCarthy (Beirut: Bibliothèque Orientale, 1957), 100.

25. Abū Muhammad 'Alī b. Aḥmad Ibn Ḥazm, *Kitāb al-Fiṣal fī al-Milal wa al-Ahwā' wa an-Niḥal* (Cairo: Al-Qahira Publishers, 1900), 2.34–36 (esp. 36).

26. Ibn Ḥazm, *Kitāb al-Fiṣal fī al-Milal*, 2.59.

This is a further addition to the complexity of the *taḥrīf* argument. Namely, even though one may hold such a radical view of *taḥrīf* as Ibn Ḥazm, as we will observe in chapter 7, one may still use rare citations of the Bible on the basis that God had held back the hands of the authors from corrupting some essential sections of it.

By the fourteenth century, the argument had become once again quite static. Ibn Qayyim al-Jawziyya also takes over the argument of his predecessors, but this time his citation is clearly from the Gospel of John. He concludes on its basis: "He made nothing more than the claim to prophethood."[27]

Finally, both aṭ-Ṭabarī and Ibn Ayyūb made use also of Luke 7:18–23 as a further affirmation of Jesus's prophethood. This can be described as an argument from silence. When John the Baptist sent some of his disciples to Jesus to ask him about his identity, both writers note that Jesus did not reply that he was God, his creator, or even indwelled by God, or any of the things that Christians claim about him. On the contrary, he warned people not to be mistaken about him (7:23) and mentioned only his miracles as a sign of who he was. Aṭ-Ṭabarī and Ibn Ayyūb then conclude that since Jesus did not perform any miracles that other prophets did not perform, he must not be greater or different from prophets that preceded him.[28]

Disagreements among Jesus's Followers

The affirmation of Christ's prophethood in the Qur'an served further to establish the role of Islam, not just as a confirmer of preceding revelations, but also as a corrector of them. The third qur'anic sūrah, āl-'Imrān, plays an important role in affirming the continuity of God's revelation through his prophets. But there is also in the Qur'an an ongoing polemic against those who do not accept the message of God's prophets. The Qur'an claims to bring resolution to age-old disagreements that had arisen with regard to former prophets. Jesus was no exception. As we saw above, Maryam 19:34, while affirming that Jesus was "the word of truth," in the same breath added that he is the one "about which they are in dispute."

27. Ibn Qayyim al-Jawziyya, *Hidāyat al-Ḥayāra*, 274.

28. Aṭ-Ṭabarī, *Radd*, 141; and Ibn Ayyūb, *Risāla*, in Ibn Taymiyya, *Al-Jawāb aṣ-Ṣaḥīḥ*, 1.2.323.

In āl-ʿImrān 3:52, the rejection of his message by many of his contemporaries is reported: "When Jesus sensed their refusal to acknowledge the truth, he asked, 'Who are my supporters in God's cause?' The disciples [*al-ḥawāriyyūn*] said, 'We are God's supporters. We have believed in God, so bear witness that we have submitted [*bi-annā muslimūn*].'"

The rejection is reported right after the account of Jesus's birth and ministry are narrated (āl-ʿImrān 3:45–51), in wording similar to the one examined earlier from al-Mā'ida 5:110. The Qur'an often does not seem decided on whether Jesus's disciples got him right or not. It is quite clear that the Jews erred in their belief in him, but it seems to distinguish between his "true" *ḥawāriyyūn*, the disciples who understood his message correctly, and his more general followers from among the children of Israel, who did not get him correctly. The *ḥawāriyyūn* ask Jesus to testify before God on their behalf that they are *muslimūn*. Some commentaries understand the word here in its more verbal meaning, similarly to Kaskas who, in his translation, renders *muslimūn* as those who "submitted." Whereas others, such as aṭ-Ṭabarī, use the opportunity of such verses to affirm the nominal meaning of Islam as a religion—God's religion: "And this is an assertion from God—mighty and high is he—that Islam is his religion, with which ʿĪsa and the prophets before him were sent; not Christianity nor Judaism. And it is God's way of declaring ʿĪsa innocent from those who invented Christianity and endorsed it as a religion. He did the same with Abraham, declaring him innocent from introducing any religion apart from Islam."

Al-Ḥadīd 57:27 is clearly aimed at Muhammad's Christian contemporaries, given the reference to monasticism. Though their intentions are not questioned, there is a clear implication that they erred, not despite of, but precisely because of, their excessive zeal:

> Then we sent our messengers to follow in their footsteps and followed up with Jesus, the son of Mary, and gave him the Gospel. We placed compassion and mercy in the hearts of those who followed him. As for monasticism, which they invented to seek God's pleasure, we did not ordain for them, and they did not observe properly. So we gave those who believed among them their reward, but many of them are wicked.

In his commentary on Maryam 19:34, aṭ-Ṭabarī reports a more detailed description of the various Christian groups that erred in their beliefs about Jesus, and about the historical circumstances surrounding those disagreements. The tradition is traced back to Qatāda (b. Diʿāma as-Sadūsī), a Ḥadīth narrator of the early eighth century:

> The children of Israel gathered together and split into four groups, each of which produced its own scholar, and they fell into disagreement after Jesus was raised [to heaven]. One of them said: "He is God, who came down to earth, raised the dead, caused others to die, and then ascended to heaven"; and those are the Jacobites. The other three [scholars] said: "You have erred." Then two of them said to the third: "What do you say about him?" He said: "He is the Son of God"; and those are the Nestorians. The other two told him: "You have erred." Then one of the remaining two said to the other: "What do you say about him?" He answered: "He is the third of three. God is a god, and he is a god, and his mother is a god"; and those were the Israelites, the kings of the Christians [this is a curious reference to the Melkite position, represented by the Byzantines, who were viewed by Arab Muslims as the "kings of the Christians"]. The fourth [scholar] said: "You have erred. He is the servant of God, his messenger, his spirit, and his word"; and those are the Muslims. And he [Qatāda] narrates that each of these four scholars had followers who fought wars against each other.

This exegetical tradition reflects some of the stereotypes about Christian doctrinal variations that were widespread among early Muslim scholars. One curious aspect is the way it reflects the notion that Christianity as well as Islam derived from the Israelites. The eventual military victory of the ones who affirmed the position of the Qurʾan that Jesus was "the servant of God, his messenger, his spirit, and his word" was viewed as strong proof that they were in the right. That aṭ-Ṭabarī traces the tradition back to a narrator of the early eighth century is an interesting reflection of how the very early Muslim community perceived itself and told its own story.

The Qurʾan sometimes implies that these disagreements were all part of the will of God, as in al-Baqara 2:253:

> We preferred some of those messengers over others. God spoke to some, and he raised some in degree; we gave Jesus son of Mary clear signs, and strengthened him with the Holy Spirit. If God had willed, those after them would not have fought each other after clear evidence of the truth had come to them, but they fought. Some of them believed,

> and others denied the truth. If God had willed, they would not have fought. But God does whatever he wants.

Yet at the same time, the Qur'an also affirms that the disagreements among Jesus's followers reflected a sort of rebellion against him and against God. Jesus may have been tolerant and forgiving toward such excesses, affirms al-Mā'ida 5:112 and 114, indulging them even when they challenged him:

> And [mention] when the disciples said, "Jesus, son of Mary, can your Lord send us a feast from heaven?" [Jesus] answered, "Remain mindful of God, if you are [truly] believers." . . . Jesus, the son of Mary, said, "God, our Lord, send us a meal from heaven so that we can have a recurring celebration for the first and the last of us, and a sign from you. Provide for us because you are the best of providers."

Aṭ-Ṭabarī comments that a number of Muhammad's companions (*ṣaḥāba*) and followers (*tābiʿīn*)—that is the first two generations of Muslims—transmitted an alternative reading of this verse. The tradition is traced back, through two separate *isnāds* (lines of transmission), to ʿĀ'isha, one of Muhammad's wives, and to Saʿīd b. Jubayr (one of the *tābiʿīn* who died around 712). They affirmed that the *ḥawāriyyīn* were believers in God and that, therefore, they would not have asked Jesus whether God could send them "a feast from heaven." However, aṭ-Ṭabarī himself considers the end of al-Mā'ida 5:112 as Jesus's rebuke of his disciples, calling them to be true believers. He therefore reads the opening of the verse as a rebellious challenge by the *ḥawāriyyīn* of Jesus.

The nature of the "feast" (*al-mā'ida*) that gave this sūrah its name is discussed extensively by the Qur'an commentators. A Christian reading the narrative in these verses hears undertones of the Eucharist. But none of the exegetical traditions conveyed by aṭ-Ṭabarī suggest that the food that God sent consisted of wine and bread. Rather, they almost unanimously transmit that the *mā'ida* consisted of bread and fish—though some also speak of meat and other foods. The sum of the exegetical traditions ends up blending together narratives of Jesus's miracles of food multiplication (Matt 14–15 and parallels) and carries undertones of the manna that God sent to the children of Israel in the desert. Thus, the disciples are instructed to eat from the feast but not to save any food for later. Furthermore, the gift also comes with a threat that, if they should go astray from the true faith after God answers

Jesus's request, they shall suffer terrible punishment. This exegesis is inspired by the verse that follows: "God answered, 'I will send it down to you, but anyone who denies the truth after this will be punished with a punishment that I will not inflict on anyone else in the world'" (al-Mā'ida 5:115).

The theme is also found elsewhere in the Qur'an, where it is affirmed that the punishment of those who strayed from the truth, despite the clear evidence provided, will be terrible, as in az-Zukhruf 43:63–65: "When Jesus came with clear evidence, he said, 'I have brought you wisdom and to clarify for you some of what you differ about. Be always mindful of God and obey me. God is my Lord and your Lord, so worship him. This is a straight path.' But the factions differed among themselves. How terrible is the punishment of a painful day to the unjust."

Az-Zukhruf 43:64 is particularly interesting in that it echoes Jesus's statement in John 20:17, when he appeared to Mary Magdalene after the resurrection: "Jesus said to her, 'Do not hold on to me, because I have not yet ascended to the Father. But go to my brothers and say to them, "I am ascending to my Father and your Father, to my God and your God."'"

I wrote elsewhere about the high recurrence of this verse in the Muslim exegetical tradition on the Gospels between the eighth and the fourteenth centuries.[29] This qur'anic occurrence is no doubt the reason why the Johannine verse became the ultimate prooftext to demonstrate Jesus's mere humanity. It also explains why the Gospel verse is sometimes cited with the qur'anic wording, "my Lord and your Lord," rather than with the original wording "my Father and your Father" or "my God and your God," when it is used by Muslims. The statement, both in the writings of Muslim theologians who cited the Gospels extensively, as well as in the commentary of Muhammad b. Jarīr aṭ-Ṭabarī, is simply heard as Jesus's equating of himself with his disciples as a human person. It is an affirmation of the worship of the one God alone.

Jewish Rejection of Prophets, Including Jesus

Some qur'anic verses about Jesus fit in the category of polemic against the Jews, and it may be that these Jews were in the wider audience of Jesus,

29. Martin Accad, "The Interpretation of John 20.17 in Muslim-Christian Dialogue (8th–14th Cent.): The Ultimate Proof-Text," in *Christians at the Heart of Islamic Rule*, ed. David Thomas (Leiden: Brill, 2003), 199–214.

which the Qur'an describes as having erred. The accusations against the Jews and their treatment of Jesus and other prophets can be quite harsh in the Qur'an. They are accused of arrogance, lying, and murder, and are therefore cursed and rejected for their rebellion. Such accusations can be found in a number of sūrahs. Al-Baqara 2:87 accuses Jews of crimes against God's messengers, despite all of the evidence they had of God's support: "We gave Moses the book, and he was followed by other messengers, and [we] gave Jesus, the son of Mary, all evidence of the truth, and strengthened him with the Holy Spirit. Whenever a messenger comes to you with a message you do not like, you become arrogant, calling some of them liars and murdering some of them."

Aṭ-Ṭabarī conveys three possible meanings advanced in the Muslim tradition about the identity of *rūḥ al-quds* (rendered "Holy Spirit" in Kaskas's translation). One tradition affirms that this is a reference to the angel Gabriel; another tradition explains that the *rūḥ* is the Gospel that Jesus brought; whereas the third affirms that Jesus performed miracles in the name of *rūḥ al-quds*. Aṭ-Ṭabarī favors Gabriel. He closes his exegesis of the verse with a harsh criticism of the Jews who, every time God sent them a messenger with a message that did not suit them, became prideful in the footsteps of their leader (*imāmuhum*) the devil. In response, he says, they ever call God's messengers liars and even kill some of them. But the testimonies of Moses, David, and Jesus stand against them, as per al-Mā'ida 5:78: "Those of the children of Israel who defied God and denied the truth have been cursed and rejected by the words of David and Jesus, the son of Mary, because they rebelled and persistently overstepped the limits."

In a sense, one function of God's messengers that consistently comes across in the text of the Qur'an was to sift through the children of Israel, so that the true believers among them will stand out from the imposters. In aṣ-Ṣaff 61:14, Jesus is portrayed as setting up the ultimate test for the children of Israel: "Believers, be supporters of God, as Jesus, the son of Mary, said to the disciples, 'Who are my supporters to God?' The disciples said, 'We are God's supporters.' A faction of the children of Israel believed, and another faction disbelieved. So we supported those who believed against their enemy, and they became dominant."

In this last verse, it appears that the Qur'an makes little distinction between Jews and Christians at the time of Jesus, which is of course accurate historically. They are the common children of Israel. In the qur'anic narrative, some of them believed in Jesus and became known as Christians, while others did not, and these are now the Jews.

Similarly to his commentary on Maryam 19:34, aṭ-Ṭabarī reports another tradition here in connection with aṣ-Ṣaff 61:14, about the groups that derived from Jesus's disciples after disagreeing about his identity. This tradition provides more clarity about early Islam's understanding of these factions:

> They divided into three groups. One of the groups said: "God was among us as he willed, and then he ascended to heaven"; and these are the Jacobites. And another group said: "The Son of God was among us as God willed, and then he raised him up to himself"; and these are the Nestorians. And another group said: "The servant of God and his messenger was among us as God willed, and then God raised him up to himself"; and these are the Muslims. But the two unbelieving groups rose up against the Muslim group and crushed it. And Islam remained subverted until God sent Muhammad (May God bless him and keep him!), and then a group of the children of Israel believed while the other one remained in unbelief.

In the perspective of early Islam, then, the Muslims who emerged victorious after Muhammad actually derived from the seed of remnants that had already believed correctly at the time of Jesus but had been quashed. Thus, aṣ-Ṣaff 61:14 confirms that God "supported those who believed against their enemy, and they became dominant."

A Christian Evaluation of the Muslim Positive Approach to Christology

In light of the often vitriolic and self-absorbed Muslim discourse on Christian doctrine, it can be fascinating and refreshing when one comes across a more creative and innovative argument. In their desire for rapprochement, some Muslim writers advance reinterpretations of terminology that they knew to be precious to Christian theologians, attempting to invest them with new meaning that aligns with Muslim thinking, while at the same time preserving the core of the Christian concept.

Jesus May Be Called a God

In his citation of Matthew 1:23, al-Bāqillānī curiously uses the passage not to deny Christ's divinity but to reinterpret the possible meaning of that status. The Muslim theologian deconstructs Jesus's divine identity while stretching the traditional boundaries of the Muslim argument against Christology. He cites the verse in the context of his discussion of several Gospel passages that he claims Christians might use in order to demonstrate their doctrines. The Matthean reference to the prophecy of Isaiah 7:14 is a confirmation of the angel's announcement to Joseph of the kind of child that Mary will bear. The form of the citation in al-Bāqillānī is very intriguing: "The pure virgin will become pregnant and will give birth to a son, and his name will be called 'a god.'"[30]

Clearly, the author did not draw his quotation from an actual biblical text, but rather this reflects a phenomenon that began to emerge at the end of the first millennium, whereby Muslim theologians seem to have cited Bible verses from collections that Christians were assumed to use and that became widespread among Muslims as a basis for the development of polemical refutations. It is otherwise not possible to understand how "Emmanuel, God with us" comes to be replaced simply by "a god." However he ended up with this reading, al-Bāqillānī argues from Exodus 7:1 that God also told Moses that he was making him a god to Aaron and Pharaoh. He then explains that this is just a way of talking, meaning that Moses would provide for his brother and order him, and the latter's duty would be to obey him. Further, al-Bāqillānī argues, God did not say that *he* would call him "a god," but that "he would be called a god." He notes that one might understand this to mean that some people will exaggerate wrongly in their magnification of Jesus, and thus be blaspheming.

Be this as it may, what is striking is that al-Bāqillānī is not simply quick to reject the Christian claim of Christ's divinity. Rather, he seeks to accept the biblical text (though erroneous in the specific citation he uses) while reinterpreting it in light of other biblical passages. In comparison to the overall Muslim-Christian discourse, this is unique and worthy of attention.

30. Al-Bāqillānī, *Kitāb Tamhīd*, 101.

A Reinterpretation of Fatherhood and Sonship

Some Muslims seem willing to allow for the principle of *bilā kayf* ("without questioning") in the development of Christian doctrine based on the Bible. In this somewhat more creative and enlightened approach to Christian doctrine, a rare concession was to allow for the preservation of this most essential biblical title of "Son" for Christ. Rather than reiterating the pointless accusation that Christians were attributing human characteristics to God through the titles "Father" and "Son," I present two Muslim theologians who undertook to explore alternative implications for the term, reinterpreting sonship and fatherhood into concepts more acceptable to Islamic thinking. It has to be said, to their credit, that they did come close to theological solutions that preserved many important aspects of Christian Christology. But it is perhaps due to the effort being born primarily as a polemical strategy that it did not yield more fruit and did not become the basis of a more creative and mutually upbuilding dialogue.

One of our earliest surviving anti-Christian polemical works, the *Refutation of Christians* of Zaydī Shīʿī theologian al-Qāsim ar-Rassī (written around 820), begins with a long philosophical discussion of the concepts of fatherhood and sonship on the basis of the theory of cause and effect. He then discusses the titles Father, Son, and Holy Spirit, exploring whether these are essential (having to do with the essence of a thing), personal (different names of different persons), or accidental (an effect resulting from a cause). Father and Son, he concludes, are normally accidental titles, since they must refer to the particular event of begetting. Ar-Rassī's philosophical discourse is interspersed with qur'anic quotations that object to assigning any kind of partner to God. In the final section of his treatise we find a number of New Testament quotations, through which the author seeks to demonstrate his views through the Christian Scriptures.[31] Though ar-Rassī mostly seeks to demonstrate based on the Gospel text that Jesus was the son of David and not God's son, he does not stop at that argument. Rather he points out that the biblical understanding of sonship must be different from what (in his conception) Christians mean by it. He wants to read here a symbolic sonship implying love and faithfulness and servanthood. Furthermore, he points out that Jesus also called his disciples "sons of God" and his "brothers." Therefore, he affirms,

31. Ar-Rassī, *Radd*, 321, 331 (line 14 to the end).

God's favor enjoyed by the disciples must not be inferior to that of Jesus himself.[32]

A bit later, after enumerating several Gospel verses that testify to Jesus's sonship, ar-Rassī begins to build on his preliminary philosophical remarks, attempting to invest the concept with new meaning. He explains that people in all places call "son" someone that they have adopted and loved. In fact, he explains, it is not at all rare to find that a wise man calls his disciple "son," and a disciple calls his teacher "father." Ar-Rassī here cites a verse of poetry that states that the teacher is greater than the natural father, for he is a "spiritual father" (*abū ar-rūḥ*) to his disciples, and not a "spermatic father" (*abū an-naṭf*). Ar-Rassī then sets out to demonstrate that this dimension of God's fatherhood is pervasive in the Gospels. To this purpose, building a very different argument from what we have already overviewed, he quotes the same beginning of the Lord's Prayer, where Jesus teaches his disciples to address God as Father (Matt 6:9–10): "Say: 'O our Father, may your name be sanctified. Let your kingdom and your prescriptions [*ḥikamuka*] descend upon the earth.'"

This fatherhood, he explains, has to do with God's creative activity. The love of the creator for humanity is of the nature of compassion and mercy, as that of an earthly father: "For he is more merciful toward us, more kind and gentle to us, and more compassionate than all the fathers and mothers."[33]

Another cluster of verses that ar-Rassī uses in his *Radd* in his attempt to reinterpret the concept of Christ's sonship combines John 1:12–13 and 1:16. The wording of the citation weaves into the canonical text some concepts peculiar to classical physiognomy: "As for those who accepted his words and surrendered to him [*sallamū lahu*] according to what they heard from him, they were born neither of flesh and blood, nor of the mixing of the bile and the phlegm. But—he claims—they were born of God [John 1:12–13]. And they were given, out of God's bounty, whatever was pleasing and satisfactory to them [1:16]."[34]

In addition to the adaptation to classical physiognomy, two other interesting translation strategies are worth noting in this quotation.

32. Ar-Rassī, *Radd*, 321.

33. Ar-Rassī, *Radd*, 323.

34. The rich theological content of the original version is transformed into a statement adapting classical physiognomy. Instead of the words "blood," "will of the flesh," and "will of man," the author uses the four humors of the body: "bile" (*al-murra*), presumably including yellow bile and black bile, "phlegm" (*al-balgham*), and "blood" (*ad-damm*).

First, ar-Rassī interprets "those who have *received him*" as "those who have *received his words*." The author thus plays down the importance of Christ as a person to the benefit of his teaching that he received from God. Second, instead of the Christian concept of "believing in Christ's name," ar-Rassī introduces the very Islamic concept of "surrender" (*wa sallamū lahu*).

Moving to the exegesis of this passage, ar-Rassī then explains that the interpretation of such a passage "should correspond with what is possible for it to mean, and not with what is impossible." This is an interesting and revealing hermeneutical principle to which we will return. Jesus's sonship, ar-Rassī goes on, is about love, servanthood, and worship, just as "all those who have accepted his words and surrendered to him are considered to be born . . . of God."[35]

Interestingly, Ibn Ḥazm would later manage to extract from John 1:12–13 the reverse of the argument used by ar-Rassī. He cites the passage twice, but instead of using it to reinterpret Christ's sonship, he infers sarcastically from it that since all Christians will be called children of God, they should all claim to be eternal and of the same nature as the Father. If this is not possible, then the only conclusion that can be drawn is that the "accursed John, who uttered this apostasy, has lied."[36]

In *ar-Radd al-Jamīl*, attributed to al-Ghazālī (died 1111), on the other hand, the author reverts to the reinterpretation of sonship and fatherhood by means of John 1:12. After elaborating on the symbolic meaning of sonship as a reference to obedience and submission, he cites several verses from the Old and the New Testaments to illustrate his point. He then quotes John 1:12 with the following interpretation: "'And he gave them the authority to become sons of God,' that is, he gave them the ability to attain the meanings inferred from fatherhood in the way that we have interpreted them."[37] The author of the work is in fact claiming that the title of sonship promised in John 1:12 belongs to those who, like him, are able to understand its symbolic meaning.

35. Ar-Rassī, *Radd*, 322.

36. Ibn Ḥazm, *Kitāb al-Fiṣal fī al-Milal*, 1.57; 2.62.

37. Al-Ghazālī, *Ar-Radd al-Jamīl*, 43.

The Soteriological Implications of the Muslim Approach to Christ

We can conclude from these two chapters on Christ that the Christian doctrine most negatively affected by the Islamic attack against Christ's divine nature is soteriology. It is the central concern for the salvific benefits of Christ's incarnation that always united the different Christian factions precisely in their very disagreements. Fourth- and fifth-century theologians in Alexandria emphasized Christ's divinity, leading to the affirmation of the one divine nature in the person of Christ (miaphysite or so-called Jacobite Christology). Only God himself, it was affirmed, could carry out human salvation. In Antioch, on the other hand, theologians emphasized Christ's full and very real humanity, in the belief that whatever part of the human person was not crucified with Jesus on the cross would have failed to be redeemed (diaphysite or so-called Nestorian Christology). In the end, the Council of Chalcedon in 451 emphasized both natures equally, albeit somewhat artificially, in recognition of the importance of both of these elements for human salvation to be complete.

To the Muslim mind, the very idea that God would go to such lengths in order to achieve a salvation that was in any case entirely up to his omnipotent will represented the height of absurdity. He could simply have said *kun* ("let it be"), *fa-yakun* (and it would have happened). Muslim theologians therefore launched a most virulent attack against this doctrine. The most popular Gospel passage that they used to build their attack was the account of Jesus's temptation. They derived both external and internal evidence from Matthew 4:1–11. Externally, they believed that the very occurrence of the temptation testified against Christ's divinity. Internally, the replies that Jesus made to the devil reflected his state of submission.

Besides pointing to Christ's hunger as an argument for his real humanity (Matt 4:3–4), aṭ-Ṭabarī also concluded on the basis of the whole episode (4:1–11) that if the Christian view about Christ were applied to this passage, this would imply that the eternal creator would have walked alongside the devil, followed him, and been tempted by him. Otherwise, assuming that even Christians would shrink before such an implication, then it is clear that this person tempted by the devil was not God himself, and hence the Christian faith falls apart. He concludes: "And if the one who walked and was led alongside him [the devil] was not the eternal creator, then he is a servant, son of his mother."

Aṭ-Ṭabarī's narration of the account does not represent the devil approaching Christ *after* he had fasted forty days, but rather *throughout* the forty days. His citation of Matthew 4:2 reads as follows: "And he kept on walking alongside the devil [*ẓalla yataraddadu maʿ ash-shayṭān*] in the desert, fasting forty days and forty nights."[38]

This rendering would play a crucial role in the future development of the exegesis of this passage in Muslim treatises, especially in connection with soteriology. Already in connection with his narration of Christ's temptation, ʿAlī aṭ-Ṭabarī raises a criticism against the Christian view of soteriology. Some Christians, he claims, pretend that, by coming down into the world in human form and challenging the devil and overcoming him, God was thereby rescuing humanity from sin and death and from the devil himself. But how could this have happened, he charges, since, according to Christians, Christ was subsequently taken hold of and beaten and eventually crucified and conquered?[39] As would be expected, the soteriological failure here is connected with the final outcome of the incarnation at the crucifixion, and it is somewhat surprising to find this statement in the context of aṭ-Ṭabarī's exegesis of the temptation account. Nevertheless, this begins to make more sense as evidence emerges of a similar use of the temptation narratives by Christian theologians of the period.

In his homily on the incarnation (written probably a few decades before aṭ-Ṭabarī's *Radd*), Orthodox theologian Abū Qurrah developed this very argument in connection with Matthew 4:3–4. He argued: "And so, God the wise hid his divinity in Adam, and with it he encountered Satan who had been Adam's conqueror, so that he [Satan] fled and victory was restored to Adam."[40] Abū Qurrah then wonders whether the devil really believed his own words that Christ was able to turn stones into bread with a single command. For wouldn't he then have trusted that the one who is able to do such things could not possibly go hungry? The answer is that it was Christ himself who blinded the devil's knowledge, in order that he might overcome him through his overcoming of food, the very means by which the devil had conquered the first Adam in paradise. This

38. Aṭ-Ṭabarī, *Radd*, 132–33.

39. Aṭ-Ṭabarī, *Radd*, 132, and again on 133.

40. Abū Qurrah, "al-Qawl fī Ta'annus Allāh al-Kalima," in *Vingt traités théologiques d'auteurs arabes chrétiens (ix–xiii siècles)*, ed. Louis Cheikho (Beirut: Imprimerie Catholique, 1920), 117.

soteriological view of Christ the Victor, which represents God as duping the devil in the manner of the Greeks using the Trojan horse to destroy the city of Troy, is one of the oldest models in the Christian tradition.[41]

A century later, in Ibn Ayyūb's letter to his brother, the main returning theme in his exegesis of the passage is the soteriological one. The author does not even mention the forty-day fast, and even less that it was the Holy Spirit who led Christ into the wilderness. Before reproducing a more-or-less accurate account of the three temptations in Matthew 4:3–10, he exclaims in a strong critique against his Christian brother:

> And you believe that the reason for his coming down from heaven is that he intended to save you and to bear sin and bind the devil. But we have found that salvation did not occur, that sin is still standing, and that the devil has become more arrogant than ever. He was not bound, but rather God gave him authority over himself—according to what you say—and he surrounded him in the mountain for forty days testing him.[42]

This account of Christ being "surrounded" by the devil in connection with the temptation account is quite intriguing. The verb used (*ḥāṣarahu*) has connotations of a fortress under siege. As already noted, aṭ-Ṭabarī's version tied the soteriological imagery ultimately with the crucifixion account, although it did so in the context of his exegesis of the temptation account. Here Ibn Ayyūb's version ties the soteriological critique exclusively to the temptation account and, moreover, represents the devil as testing Christ throughout the forty days. These are all features added by Ibn Ayyūb to the simpler version of the argument taken over from aṭ-Ṭabarī. His predecessor prepared the stage for him by using the expression *ẓalla yataraddadu*, implying that Christ stayed in the devil's company, being tempted, throughout the forty-day period.

Ibn Ayyūb's exegesis reflects an advanced stage in the development of the argument initiated by aṭ-Ṭabarī a century earlier. The temptation account, initially used by Christians to demonstrate God's work of salva-

41. For an excellent treatment of the idea of atonement in the early church, which emphasizes the prominence of this particular view, see Gustaf Aulén, *Christus Victor: An Historical Study of the Three Main Types of the Idea of the Atonement*, trans. A. G. Herbert (London: SPCK, 1950).

42. Ibn Ayyūb, *Risāla*, in Ibn Taymiyya, *Al-Jawāb aṣ-Ṣaḥīḥ*, 1.2.324.

tion in Christ, had now become a favorite passage to prove the failure of the soteriological mission, which Christians claimed had been initiated by God. By the time of Ibn Ayyūb, the Gospel story had become thoroughly detached from its original context, having acquired an independent status in the Muslim polemical discourse. In addition to the verb *yataraddadu*, another reason for this development may be found in the mistransmission of another verb in the course of just over a century: *ḥāṣarahu*. In his text, ʿAlī aṭ-Ṭabarī had "and that one who would test him appeared before him [*ḥaḍarahu*] and said to him."[43]

The falling off of a single diacritical point from *ḥaḍarahu* (the letter *ḍād*) in aṭ-Ṭabarī's version becomes *ḥāṣarahu* (the letter *ṣād*) in Ibn Ayyūb. All the remaining features in Ibn Ayyūb's analysis, such as the continuous forty-day temptation and the critique of the Christian soteriological view on the basis of this account, derive from this idea that Christ was "besieged" by the devil in the desert for forty days, resulting from the error in transmission. As a further consequence of this view, when Ibn Ayyūb arrives at the end of the account (Matt 4:11), "then the devil left him, and suddenly angels came and waited on him," his version of the text reads: "Then God (May he be glorified and exalted!) sent an angel who uprooted the enemy from his place and cast him into the sea, and set Christ free."

This clearly has no basis in the Gospel text. It is essentially an addition to the text, original to Ibn Ayyūb. On the one hand, this serves as the basis for his affirmation of the clear difference between God's mighty dealing with the devil and Christ's human inadequacy to face the power of his foe. On the other hand, this feature seems to indicate that, contrary to ʿAlī aṭ-Ṭabarī, Ibn Ayyūb was not making direct use of the Gospel text, but rather drew his polemical arguments from the common stock that, by his time, had become available to Muslim polemicists. The Gospel account of Christ's temptation as a whole stands as a clear testimony for Ibn Ayyūb that the person concerned in the passage could not have been God. If Christ had been divine, Ibn Ayyūb figures that he would have gotten rid of the devil before God sent an angel to set him free—a conclusion deriving from his rendering of Matthew 4:11. Furthermore, he claims, Christ would not have replied that one should not put God to the test (4:7) and that God alone should be worshiped (4:10). Ibn Ayyūb concludes, against the Christian soteriological view, that Christ should have set himself free

43. Aṭ-Ṭabarī, *Radd*, 132.

from the devil first, before undertaking to deliver others from his grip,[44] an accusation that brings to mind the sneering mockery of many of the passersby when Jesus hung on the cross.

Summarizing the Positive Metadialogue on Christ

The Muslim-Christian metadialogue affirms that Jesus is part of a continuous divine prophetic line (al-An'ām 6:84–87), and possibly the most highly venerated prophet—"Highly distinguished in this world and the hereafter and brought near to God" (āl-'īmrān 3:45)—even though in al-Mā'ida 5:110, the Qur'an insists on the idea that he performed his miracles *bi-idhn Allāh* ("by God's permission"). The Qur'an affirms that Muhammad is part of the same prophetic line as Jesus (an-Nisā' 4:163; ash-Shūra 42:13; al-Aḥzāb 33:7). And it teaches that al-Baqara 2:136 and āl-'Imrān 3:84 are to be affirmed to reassert continuity in the face of criticism.

Jesus as "servant of God" is affirmed as an honorable title, which is not demeaning of Jesus, as in an-Nisā' 4:172, which affirms that Jesus was not too proud to admit his human servanthood. The Qur'an claims that the *Injīl* contains the clearest affirmations, on Jesus's own testimony, that he was sent as a *rasūl* ("apostle/messenger") and a *nabī* ("prophet"), as he himself testifies in the Gospels. But it also observes that the early disciples were split in their understanding of who Jesus was (āl-'Imrān 3:52; al-Ḥadīd 57:27; al-Baqara 2:253) and that their views were heavily impacted by Jewish error and conspiracy (al-Baqara 2:87; al-Mā'ida 5:78; aṣ-Ṣaff 61:14). These divisions continued and are now reflected in the various Christian sects. It affirms that one of the functions of the biblical prophets was to sift through the children of Israel and separate the righteous ones from the imposters. Islam had to come in order to correct these misunderstandings and restore the right belief about Jesus.

More creative arguments come in, finally, to allow that Jesus may be called "a god," so long as it is understood in the sense of responsibility and obedience, such as Moses's relationship to Aaron (Exod 7:1), as maintained by al-Bāqillānī. A precious few others allowed for the integration of the title "Son" for Jesus, provided that a reinterpretation of sonship in a symbolic sense is introduced, in the sense of love, faithfulness, and servanthood (ar-Rassī and aṭ-Ṭabarī) and of obedience and submission

44. Ibn Ayyūb, *Risāla*, in Ibn Taymiyya, *Al-Jawāb aṣ-Ṣaḥīḥ*, 1.2.325.

(al-Ghazālī). Fatherhood too may be maintained, according to ar-Rassī, but in the sense of "spiritual fatherhood" (*abū ar-rūḥ*), reflecting compassion and mercy.

Hermeneutical Keys in Building Bridges beyond Conflict

I am convinced, after my extensive survey of the qur'anic *tafsīr* tradition on Jesus that the primary purpose of the Qur'an was to affirm the positive portrait of Jesus and that the negative portrait exists accidentally only to reaffirm the positive. Unfortunately, the political tensions that characterized most Christian-Muslim history led to the primacy of the negative portrayal. But we need not get stuck with this historical reality in our conversations today. Rather than focusing on the negative witness of the Qur'an with regard to Christ, we must now focus on the positive witness and find more common ground.

Using Deadlocks as Assets

As Christians in dialogue with Muslims, we need to affirm the Qur'an's high veneration of Jesus as "highly distinguished and brought near to God" as our starting point in finding common ground in our views about Jesus. Christians may not feel comfortable embracing Muhammad's prophethood, given the New Testament affirmation that Jesus fulfilled all things and given that the Qur'an, from the perspective of biblical salvation history, does not add anything to Christian soteriology. However, that Muhammad is affirmed by the Qur'an as a prophet who comes in the same line as the Judeo-Christian prophets should be celebrated. There is absolutely no reason for Christians to denigrate Islam's prophet. If he himself considered that he was confirming preceding revelations, why would we want to dismiss him as an imposter rather than believing in his genuine intention? We may disagree with the final outcome and implication of his message, and discussing whether his message really brought anything new to the biblical revelation can represent good ground for dialogue. But it would be a waste of an opportunity simply to dismiss the relentless qur'anic affirmation of continuity.

Furthermore, the Qur'an's affirmation that servanthood is not demeaning to Jesus is in line with the Gospel witness, and so is the affirmation that he was sent by God. Though Christians will continue to affirm that Jesus was more than a servant, and more than a prophet or messenger, the concept of Jesus's servanthood and the idea that he lived his life doing the work of his Father represent in the New Testament's witness an important model for his followers in providing for the nature of their relationship of submission to God and of mutual submission to one another.

The qur'anic chastisement of Jesus's followers for being divided in their understanding of the identity of Jesus is a healthy reminder that should lead us to seek more unity in our churches and to refuse the spirit of division. Jesus's admonishing that our unity and love for one another would be the clearest testimony for him, and his warning that our divisions would drive people away from him, are in a sense fulfilled in the qur'anic observations. The church's response to the qur'anic message should not be pride, self-defense, and further division, but confession, repentance, and reconciliation.

Finally, the shy attempts by some Muslim scholars in history to maintain the titles "sonship," "fatherhood," and "god" for Jesus are worth being aware of. Christians engaged in honest and genuine dialogue with Muslims may be able to revive such early attempts. The symbolic nature, but more especially the relational nature, of sonship and fatherhood is certainly not far from the Christian understanding of the relationship of the Father and the Son. Christians will want to maintain the further understanding of the church through history of a more ontological and eternal relationship of the Father and the Son within the Godhead, but they need not necessarily continue to use a more esoteric term like *uqnūm* ("hypostasis") in conversation with Muslims, since it has all but completely fallen out of everyday use in contemporary conversations among Christians as well. There is need to develop a theological discourse about the triune God that uses new and creative language beyond the traditional one, and it is this generation's responsibility to engage in this endeavor.

Concluding Thoughts

Just as arguing for the reality and fullness of Christ's humanity based on the Gospel witness was not difficult to substantiate, arguing for his apostleship was just as easy. The Gospels were written by Christ's followers as testimonies of their experience of him, whereas the later systematization of the diversity of this experience is what led to theologizing by early church fathers. It is from this theological venture that official creeds began to emerge, such as we find in the early ecumenical councils beginning with Nicea in 325. But it is important to remember that these conciliar statements were not innovations. They were summative statements deriving from several decades of sophisticated and complex theological debates within the Christian tradition. But they also represented the starting point of further theological elaboration.

For early church fathers, the affirmation that Jesus was sent by God, as later Muslim theologians vigorously asserted, represented no insult to Christ's identity in the Christian theological system. On the contrary, the Gospel of John in particular is replete with Christ's own affirmations that he was sent from God. Christ's apostleship (lit., "sent-ness") is foundational to what he revealed about God's structuring of power and authority. His apostleship is the healthy foundation of our own apostleship, and hence the theological foundation of the church's mission. Nowhere is this more clearly affirmed than in John 15, where he uses the analogy of a vine and its branches to describe both his connectedness with the Father and what ought to be our connectedness with him: "If you abide in me, and my words abide in you, ask for whatever you wish, and it will be done for you" (15:7).

In the divine-human structure revealed by Jesus, this is not an invitation to whimsical discipleship and reckless use of power. Rather, by being rooted in Christ, just as he was rooted in his Father, our unitedness to the divine will and love is the foundation of our behaving and acting on behalf of God in the world. This concept is central in Jesus's important prayer for his disciples in John 17. There Jesus affirms that the Father has "given [the Son] authority over all people, to give eternal life to all whom you have given him" (17:2). So important is the notion of being sent in the divine economy of mutual accountability and interdependency that Jesus asserts, "And this is eternal life, that they may know you, the only true God, and Jesus Christ whom you have sent" (17:3).

These are among the final words of Jesus recorded by John in his Gospel. They represent, once more, a major challenge to the human understanding of power. Divine power is not self-serving, and it is not about demonstrating independence and self-sufficiency. On the contrary, it is about mutual submission and interdependency, which is the essence of love. The Arabic word "Islam," of course, means "submission," and Islam affirms that total human submission to God as servants is the foundation of human salvation.

In the Christian understanding, however, based on the model and teaching of Jesus, humans know true submission, and they are able to practice it in mutual love, only *because* of its eternal existence within the triune life of God. Just as the disciples came to the knowledge of God as they understood that Jesus was sent and was acting on behalf of God, the world will come to this same knowledge of God only when they see in his church both mutual submission and the recognition that we do not speak for ourselves, but that we have been sent by Christ. Thus, near the end of his prayer, Jesus affirms once more: "The glory that you have given me I have given them, so that they may be one, as we are one, I in them and you in me, that they may become completely one, so that the world may know that you have sent me and have loved them even as you have loved me" (17:22–23).

As with our understanding of the cross as power in weakness, and of the incarnation as God's self-emptying to be fully present in Christ, early Christian theologians did not understand Christ's affirmations about being sent as a basis for abstract theologizing about his identity, but rather as powerful affirmations about the nature of the church's mission in the world. Christ was sent from God, and this is the foundation of our own mission to the world, without which the world cannot recognize God's glory. But at the same time, the world will come to glorify God when they recognize Christ's "glory, which you have given me because you loved me before the foundation of the world" (John 17:24). An affirmation by the early church that Christ was sent *from* God did not cancel out their conviction that he lived a glorious life *in* God before the foundation of the world. That too was a crucial element in the Christian understanding of the church's mission. Church fathers did not derive their mission praxis from their philosophical discourse about God. Rather, the philosophical discourse—theology that is—was born out of necessity, to make sense of the praxis and discipleship to which Christ's followers were called.

An approach to dialogue about Jesus that dilutes the full message of the Bible about Christ, both preexistent as eternal Logos, who lived among us in Jesus of Nazareth, and who continues to live in and with us in the Holy Spirit, will not yield much fruit in the long run. On the other hand, Christians should be prepared to review their understanding of Muhammad and of the Qur'an in a way that shows respect and appreciation. But Muslims also are invited to be open to new understandings of who Jesus was and his role in God's history of salvation in a way that does justice to the biblical witness.

Further Reading and Research

Beaumont, M. *Christology in Dialogue with Muslims: A Critical Analysis of Christian Presentations of Christ for Muslims from the Ninth and Twentieth Centuries.* Eugene OR: Wipf & Stock, 2011. Analyzing Christian approaches to presenting Christ to Muslims from the ninth and twentieth centuries, Beaumont explores creative prospects—ancient and modern—for dialogue in the present around some of the most contentious christological issues between Christians and Muslims.

Cragg, K. *The Call of the Minaret.* 3rd ed. Oxford: Oneworld, 2008 (originally 1956). Cragg offers an exploration of christological issues in the context of Islam that does not shy away from key differences. While his work was criticized for not engaging with contemporary New Testament scholarship on Jesus, it received wide praise from both Christians and Muslims for its sensitivity and integrity in representing both Christian and Muslim beliefs about Christ.

Cragg, K. *Jesus and the Muslim: An Exploration.* Oxford: Oneworld, 1999 (originally 1985). Cragg provides a highly nuanced, comprehensive exploration of the points of tension between Muslims and Christians about Jesus that engages with the best perspectives from within both. Rather than polemicizing this comparison, however, Cragg aims for this encounter to benefit both Christians and Muslims through engagement with what divides and unites them.

Kärkkäinen, V.-M. *A Constructive Christian Theology for the Pluralistic World,* vol. 1: *Christ and Reconciliation.* Grand Rapids: Eerdmans, 2013. Taking contextual theology seriously as an equal and essential dialogue partner with mainstream (white European and American male perspective), Kärkkäinen constructs a Christology that seeks to maintain, rather than neutralize, the traditional perspectives of the dialogue partners.

Parsons, M. *Unveiling God: Contextualising Christology for Islamic Culture.* Pasadena CA: William Carey Library, 2005. Parsons's somewhat obscure text, written for popular consumption, attempts a contextualized Christology for Islamic contexts, based on a Sunnī, orthodox framework.

Robinson, N. *Christ in Islam and Christianity,* New York: SUNY Press, 1991. Robinson offers an analysis of different Christian approaches to Jesus found in the Qur'an and classical Muslim commentaries, seeking to establish a context for the typical understanding of Christ by Muhammad and his companions.

6 Muslim Strategies in Approaching the Bible

My grandfather, Fouad Accad, grew up in the Arab Orthodox tradition in Beirut, Lebanon. I heard the story of his conversion to Protestantism many times while growing up. When he was young, the Orthodox church did not encourage its faithful to read the Bible. The story of the European reformation had demonstrated plentifully the dangers associated with the vulgarization and popularization of the holy text. Placing the Bible in the hands of the untrained populace easily led to the emergence of new interpretations and practices that were not sanctioned by the church institution. There are popular stories in the Arab world about the mushrooming of new churches, even denominations, on every street corner of some US cities. When you place a text into the hands of amateurs, every two people will come up with a different interpretation. So why open the door up to such heresy and discord?

As a young man, Fouad was a school teacher who loved literature and the Arabic language. He tells of a day when he came across a book in his father's bookshelf, whose cover had been torn away. He pulled it out and began to read, quickly getting gripped by the narratives and teaching. He later discovered that he had been reading the Bible, but had he known it from the start, he would have never dared indulge in such illicit activity. Around that time he also came upon some Protestant missionaries. As he took part in Bible studies, he grew more and more attached to his new teachers and eventually converted to the Protestant tradition. He was soon sent to Bible school in Switzerland to prepare for pastoral ministry. It was there that he met Suzanne Steudler, my grandmother, whom he eventually married. They returned to Lebanon, and having been transformed by the power of the biblical word, Fouad joined the Bible Society, which he eventually served until his death. For a number of years, he also lived in the Gulf, contributing to the development of Bible Society offices in Bahrain and elsewhere. He built rich and fruitful relationships with Christians and Muslims of all streams. He never became a fanatic about one Christian denomination over another. He was simply transformed by the word of God, and having dedicated his life to its service, all he desired now was to share that life-giving word with others.

During the late seventies and early eighties, I remember spending weekends at my grandparents' home in the charming village of Kafarshima in the eastern suburbs of Beirut, where they pastored a small congregation of the evangelical Church of God denomination. At some point in his life my grandfather had felt a strong calling to share the word of God with Muslims. For as long as I remember while growing up, every time my siblings and I spent the weekend in Kafarshima, my grandfather was mostly immersed in a sea of commentaries on the Qur'an. He wrote a number of booklets and courses on comparative scriptural study for Christians and Muslims, and his most significant lifetime achievement was published posthumously in 1997, *Building Bridges: Christianity and Islam* (NavPress). He was convinced that Christians and Muslims could journey together through their Scriptures and derive common spiritual principles that would lead them to Jesus and to salvation. His book contains a study series deriving seven principles from the Torah, the *Zabūr* (the qur'anic name for the Psalms), the *Injīl*, and the Qur'an, leading readers from creation to the cross and salvation in Christ. Many Christians that I meet still share with me how transformative Fouad's book was for them, helping them understand and practice a friendly and loving relationship with their Muslim neighbors in a way that many recent Christian books on Islam do not.

In the mid-eighties, my grandparents retired in Neuchâtel, Switzerland, and I had many opportunities to spend the summer with them there as a teenager. I remember one such occasion, when my grandfather was expecting some visitors from the Gulf. He needed to have a private conversation with them, but he allowed me to sit in the next room and listen in on the conversation. The visit naturally began with all the niceties and linguistic embellishments of Arab hospitality, but to my surprise the tone quickly intensified, as my grandfather became frustrated with his visitors. My grandfather was talking about Jesus in the Qur'an, but one of his guests kept taking the conversation away into the Ḥadīth. Every time my grandfather came back to the Bible, his guest would dismiss it as corrupted. *Muḥarraf! Muḥarraf!* ("corrupted") is what I could mostly hear the guest shout. *ʿAnīd!* ("stubborn") and *dmāghak maghsūl!* ("you're brainwashed!") is most of what I heard my grandfather repeat, to my astonishment. My grandfather was out of character that afternoon. I had never heard him use that tone of voice with the Muslims he loved. But I have, since then, experienced many a time this same frustration in conversation with Muslims, particularly in day-to-day talk rather than in official dialogue contexts.

The frustration comes from the Muslim accusation of *taḥrīf* becoming so entrenched in the Muslim discourse with Christians that it can all but kill any possibility of constructive theological conversation. As positive as the Qur'an can be in its references to the Bible, so can views of Muslims toward the same text be negative and destructive. As a young man, I had many conversations about Jesus with Muslim friends. Nearly every time, the conversation ended with their claim that the Bible was corrupted. The accusation left no common ground to build on. The integrity of the very source of my Christian faith and beliefs was being challenged and dismissed as worthless. It was with great surprise and delight that I discovered, while researching and reading ancient Muslim texts for my PhD at the University of Oxford, that the accusation of *taḥrīf* was by no means the only way that Muslims had viewed the Bible through the history of Muslim-Christian encounter.

Historically, Muslim approaches to the Bible have been much more diverse than is usually assumed today. Whereas the Muslim accusation of *taḥrīf* has all but driven Muslim-Christian dialogue to a deadlock today, the history of development of that concept indicates that this was not always the case. As a matter of fact, the Muslim approach to the Bible has two principal thrusts: one positive and the other negative. A return to the history of the Islamic approach to the Bible will indicate that the original intention of Muslims was mostly positive, namely an attempt at rescuing the text of the Bible from the perceived Jewish and Christian misinterpretation of it. This chapter focuses its attention on the positive Islamic approaches to the Bible. I leave the study of the argument of *taḥrīf* to the next chapter.

Muslim Attitudes to the Bible Historically

The Islamic view of the Bible has historically been more complex than it is sometimes made to appear. Contrary to what is often assumed, Muslim authors did not jump at the first opportunity to accuse Christians and Jews of corrupting the text of their Scriptures, that is, to the accusation of *taḥrīf*. In fact, historically the opinion of Muslim theologians with regard to biblical authority ranged from deep respect to outright disdain, with a strong bias in favor of the former before the eleventh century and of the latter beyond that. I classify the Muslim positions by organizing them under four themes, which represent most of the attitudes found in the texts I studied.

The first two themes, the *Injīl* used as an authoritative document, historical or other, and the *Injīl* as an authoritative key for the evaluation of Ḥadīth, represent the apex of Muslim theologians' respect for the biblical text. Not only did most authors cite extensively from the Bible in order to demonstrate their anti-Christian arguments, which is in itself revealing of a positive attitude toward the text, but authors such as Ibn Qutayba (828–89) and al-Yaʿqūbī (circa 825–905) went so far as to use the biblical text in works of history (*tārīkh*), literature (*adab*), jurisprudence (*fiqh*), and Ḥadīth (Muslim traditions), which were primarily written for a Muslim readership.

The third theme, on the other hand, is more neutral in nature, though it can be interpreted both positively and negatively. That authors such as al-Qāsim ar-Rassī (785–860) or al-Yaʿqūbī, for example, incorporated whole chapters from the Gospels into their treatises while altering specific key terms may indicate that they cherished the text too much to do away with it completely and preferred to preserve it by presenting a more acceptable version of it to their Muslim readers. On the other hand, this process can also be seen as already reflecting a suspicious attitude with regard to the text that they were reproducing.

Finally, the fourth theme—*taḥrīf*—represents an outright accusation against the Christians and the Jews of having corrupted their own Scriptures. But even this accusation is not as simple and straightforward as it is sometimes imagined. As will be discussed in more detail in the next chapter, there was a clear historical development in the understanding and use of the original qur'anic term, and the uncompromising attitude of Ibn Ḥazm in the eleventh century (994–1064) was not to be found elsewhere, either before or after him.

The Qur'anic Foundations of the Muslim Attitude to the Bible

As with every theological position of Muslim scholars toward Christian doctrine, the Muslim attitude to the Bible is rooted deeply in the qur'anic text. In the previous chapter, we saw how the Qur'an uses Jesus and all preceding messengers in order to advance the perspective of the continuity of prophethood. One of the primary functions of Jesus in the Qur'an was to provide continuity between the old (Israelite prophets) and the new (Muhammad). The same logic is maintained with regard to the Qur'an's attitude toward the Torah and the Gospel (the latter is always used in the singular in the Qur'an). The *Injīl* is viewed as a bridge between the Torah and the Qur'an, as well as providing continuity by confirming the Torah and being confirmed by the Qur'an.

In his commentary on āl-'Imrān 3:3–4, Muhammad b. Jarīr aṭ-Ṭabarī (died 922) asserts that the common source of all revelations guarantees that there are no contradictions between the various Scriptures and that all the preaching of former messengers is fulfilled in the final revelation: "He has sent down the book to you with the truth to confirm what is available of other revelations, as it is he who sent down the Torah and the Gospel beforehand as guidance to people, and he revealed the standard [*furqān*] by which we judge right from wrong. Those who do not believe God's signs will have severe punishment. God is almighty and capable of revenge."

Aṭ-Ṭabarī interprets the description of the Torah and the Gospel as "guidance to people" (āl-'Imrān 3:4) in the sense that they contained sufficient proof about God's unicity and about the coming of Muhammad. The Arabic word that Kaskas translates "standard" is the word *furqān*, which was traditionally understood as a synonym for "Qur'an." Literally it is a reference to what separates or distinguishes, and hence with reference to the Qur'an, aṭ-Ṭabarī provides the explanation that it means "separation between truth and falsehood, either by strength of argument, or through coercion and victory by force of arm." It is worth noting as well, however, that the Syriac verbal root FRQ means "to save," and that the Syriac word *furqānā* was a title for Christ, the Savior, since before the emergence of Islam, though no qur'anic commentary that I explored makes note of this.

Aṭ-Ṭabarī remarks that some commentators understood this to be a reference to separation between truth and falsehood with regard to the nature of Jesus, and others with reference to Islamic legal prescriptions. He himself prefers the first interpretation, namely that the Qur'an was revealed to affirm the truth regarding Jesus. Hence, he affirms that the latter part of the verse, which speaks judgment and punishment against "those who do not believe God's signs," is a statement against Christians who claim that Jesus was the Son of God and who have taken him as Lord and God.

That the Qur'an expresses neither knowledge of four Gospels nor even polemics against the matter leads us once again seriously to doubt that Muhammad had ever come into contact with the New Testament as we know it and that the early church knew, used, and transmitted. The Qur'an merely transmits the assumption that there is one *Injīl*, which came down upon Jesus, mirroring the belief in the coming down of the Qur'an upon Muhammad. Āl-ʿImrān 3:48 reflects well this understanding. The *Injīl* is God's portion to Jesus, which he would give to him after teaching him the Torah of Moses: "She said, 'Lord, how can I have a boy when no man has ever touched me?' He said, 'God creates what he wills, when he decides a matter, he simply says to it: "Be!," and then it is.' And he will teach him the Book, the Wisdom, the Torah, and the Gospel."

Many English translations of the Qur'an translate *al-kitāb*—the first of the four items listed in āl-ʿImrān 3:48—as "the Book" with capital B. This seems to insinuate that it is a qur'anic self-reference, as this is usually the word found in the text. However, the classical commentary tradition understands this differently. They believe that if it were a reference to the Qur'an, it would not be listed before the Torah and the Gospel. Aṭ-Ṭabarī and Fakhr ad-Dīn ar-Rāzī (died 1209) understand this as meaning that God "will teach him reading and writing." Second, after teaching Jesus how to read and write, God will teach him knowledge and ethics, which is what they believe "wisdom" is referring to in the verse. Only after he has learned these basic skills and disciplines is Jesus ready to study the Torah; and building on this foundation, God will then reveal the Gospel to him.

Although the Qur'an maintains a clear chronology of God's revelations, from Torah, to Gospel, to Qur'an (as in āl-ʿImrān 3:65, see below), there is also an underlying presumption that the qur'anic revelation precedes all others. Given the belief that the originator of all three is God and the view that all three represent God's progressive revelation, with the Qur'an as the fullest manifestation, the notion that the last one encompasses and somewhat precedes the former ones is not entirely surprising. This idea is further intimated in the Qur'an through the affirmation that Islam in its verbal sense of *submission* represented Abraham's religion, an idea expressed through the somewhat enigmatic concept of *ḥanīf* in āl-ʿImrān 3:67:

> People of the book: "Why do you argue about Abraham, when the Torah and the Gospel were not revealed until after him? Do you not understand? Here you are arguing about some things you know, so why

> do you argue about things which you do not know? God knows and you do not." Abraham was neither a Jew nor a Christian, but he was [one who turned away from all that is false][1] a monotheist [*ḥanīfan*] who submitted to God [*musliman*]; never an idolater.

This balance between continuity and discontinuity reflects the Qur'an's reformist tendencies. The Qur'an reaches back to the proto-religion of Abraham in an expression of discontent toward the inability of the Jews and the Christians to hold on faithfully to the Scriptures revealed to them through Moses and Jesus. This condemning accusation is clearly expressed in al-Mā'ida 5:66 and 68:

> And if they would truly observe the Torah and the Gospel and all that has been revealed to them by their Lord, they would have been given an abundance of grace from heaven and earth. Some of them are on the right course, but most of them do what is evil. . . . Say, "People of the book: You have no valid ground for your beliefs, unless you [truly] observe the Torah and the Gospel, and all that has been sent down to you from your Lord." Yet all that has been sent down to you [prophet] by your Lord is bound to make many of them more stubborn in their arrogance and in their denial of the truth. Do not worry about unbelievers.

Christians often cite these verses in order to appeal to the Qur'an's affirmation of the Torah and the Gospels. But classical qur'anic exegesis disagrees with this interpretation. According to aṭ-Ṭabarī, Jews and Christians should have held correctly to the teaching of their Scriptures, but they also should have accepted the revelation of the Qur'an. He notes in his commentary that the words "all that has been revealed to them by their Lord" (al-Mā'ida 5:66) and "all that has been sent down to you from your Lord" (5:67) are references to the Qur'an. Thus, these verses say that people of the book need to believe in all three revelations in order to be on the right path. And this logic is sustained by the claim that the Qur'an brought nothing new, since it was already the religion of Abraham. The problem, according to these interpreters, is that Jews and Christians changed, omitted, and added elements to their Scriptures, even though

1. These words are absent from the Arabic text of the Qur'an and were introduced by Kaskas in his translation.

the principal message of monotheism and of Muhammad's prophethood was preserved in them.

It is not surprising that Muslims have always been convinced of the finality and comprehensiveness of their religion, since the Qur'an in many places affirms that the Torah and the Gospels preannounced the coming of Muhammad, as in al-Aʿrāf 7:157. As we will see in the next chapter, it was at the intersection of the Muslim claim that the Bible prophesied about Muhammad and of the Judeo-Christian rejection of that very claim that the Muslim accusation of scriptural falsification (*taḥrīf*) was born.

The Qur'an wants to leave no confusion about the finality of Muhammad and the necessity of believing in him. In the immediately preceding verse (al-Aʿrāf 7:156), God is having a conversation with Moses, who is interceding for his people for mercy. Aṭ-Ṭabarī reads into it a strong polemic against all those who believe they can be in the truth without believing in Muhammad. When the devil heard God's affirmation that his mercy "encompasses everything," aṭ-Ṭabarī explains, God then added, in order to avoid any confusion, that mercy will be granted to "those who are mindful" of God, "who give *zakah* [alms] and who believe in our [God's] messages." But upon hearing this, the Jews jumped in and claimed that they did all these things. God adds that his mercy will be extended to "those who will follow the messenger." The measure of God's mercy then becomes unequivocal: believers in preceding religions will have to believe in Muhammad in order to benefit from God's mercy:

> [God] answered, "I punish whomever I will, but my mercy encompasses everything. I grant it to those who are mindful of me, give *zakah* and who believe in our messages; those who will follow the messenger, *the gentile prophet they find described in the Torah and in the Gospel*, the prophet who will command them to do what is obviously right and forbid what is obviously wrong and allow them the good things in life and forbid them the bad things. He will release them from their *burdens* [*iṣr*] and *shackles* [*aghlāl*] that bound them before. [It is][2] those who will believe in him and honor him and support him and follow the enlightenment that has been sent down with him who will succeed." (al-Aʿrāf 7:156–57)

The description of Muhammad found in al-Aʿrāf 7:157 will be taken up again in latter chapters of the present book, including the

2. Words missing in Kaskas's translation.

meaning of *an-nabī al-ummī*, rendered by Kaskas as "the gentile prophet," contrary to all previous translations that followed classical exegesis in rendering the expression as "the illiterate prophet." With respect to the Qur'an's view of the Torah and the Gospels, however, it is important to emphasize that though belief in Muhammad is presented as a nonnegotiable for Jews and Christians, he is presented not as an additional burden, but as the abolisher of previous constraints in those religions.

The qur'anic verse does not offer further clarification as to what it means by those "burdens [*iṣr*] and shackles [*aghlāl*]." Concerning Christians, this may refer to some of the more austere practices of ascetical expressions of Christian communities in Arabia at the time of Muhammad. What is not clear here is the extent to which the actual teaching of Jesus in the canonical Gospels is at stake.

As for the Jews, this may be a reference to stringent dietary laws and regulations on keeping the Sabbath. Āl-ʿImrān 3:50 argues, similarly, that Islam would relax some of the legal requirements of the Judaic law: "I will confirm what is available of the Torah, and I will make permissible for you some of the things that were forbidden to you. I have brought you a sign from your Lord, so be mindful of God and obey me."

Āl-ʿImrān 3:93 refers specifically to dietary regulations, which may be a hint to what the Qur'an has in mind: "Before the Torah was revealed, all food was lawful for the children of Israel except what Israel [Jacob] made unlawful for himself. If you are telling the truth, bring the Torah and read it."

Similarly in al-Aʿrāf 7:157, the lack of awareness about the actual teaching of the New Testament also seems to be reflected regarding matters of war and political engagement in at-Tawba 9:111: "God has purchased the souls and possessions of the believers, promising them paradise in return. They fight in God's cause, and they kill and are killed. *It is a true promise given by him in the Torah, the Gospel, and the* Qur'an. Who could be more faithful to his promise than God? Rejoice in this good news! This is the bargain you have made with him. This is the ultimate victory" (emphasis added).

The attribution to the *Injīl* of some sort of teaching on taking up arms for the sake of the Gospel may be reflective of contemporary practices in Byzantine political Christianity, for it is certainly not found in the actual teaching of Jesus of Nazareth. Neither the tenth-century cumulative commentary of aṭ-Ṭabarī nor the expansive twelfth-/thirteenth-century commentary of ar-Rāzī offers any insight into this qur'anic insinuation, perhaps reflecting as well that all they knew was the militant expression of Christianity.

Ar-Rāzī is himself not satisfied with an exclusively militaristic interpretation of at-Tawba 9:111. His exegesis leads him to a discussion of *jihād*. He conveys a number of exegetical traditions that promote the centrality of the *jihād* of war, but then adduces other traditions that emphasize the centrality of the verbal, argumentative *jihād*. The meaning of the affirmation that "God has purchased the souls and possessions of the believers, promising them paradise in return," he explains, is that the value of human life is so high that it can be exchanged for eternity only in paradise. He interprets the statement symbolically, for it cannot be predicated upon God that he would have to purchase anything, since he is the creator of all, whether "souls" or "possessions of the believers." Therefore, he concludes on the basis of this qur'anic understanding of the sanctity of human life that argumentative *jihād* should always precede any recourse to a *jihād* of war. For if the verbal "fight in God's cause" is won, then human lives are saved both in this life and the next.

Al-Mā'ida 5:43–45 reflects a more compassionate stream than we find often in the Qur'an. A more lenient judgment than that of the Torah is recommended with regard to questions of retribution:

> Why do they come to you for judgment, seeing that they have the Torah with God's law? Even then they will turn away from your judgment. These are not true believers. We revealed the Torah with guidance and enlightenment. The prophets, who had submitted themselves to God, as well as the rabbis and the scholars, all judged according to that part of God's book they were entrusted to preserve and to which they were witnesses. So do not fear people. Only fear me. Do not barter my verses for a small profit. Those who do not judge according to what God has revealed are unbelievers. In the Torah we prescribed for them a life for a life, an eye for an eye, a nose for a nose, an ear for an ear, a tooth for a tooth, and a similar retribution for wounds. However, *If anyone forgoes this out of charity, it will serve as atonement for them*. Those who do not judge in accordance with what God has revealed are unjust. (emphasis added)

With such a rich and positive qur'anic foundation with regard to the Bible we come to a survey of Muslim attitudes in later centuries.

A Survey of Positive Islamic Approaches to the Bible

The qur'anic invitation to people of the book, including Muslims, to acknowledge the common heritage and source of the Torah, the *Injīl*, and the Qur'an was not left unheeded. The default position toward the Bible, which we find among Muslim scholars until the tenth century, is overwhelmingly positive. It was only the rising political and military tensions brought on by the Crusades and the *Reconquista* that would change the tone of the conversation permanently.

The Injīl as a Reliable Historical Document

The two main representatives of this first attitude to the Bible are abū Muhammad ʿAbdallah b. Muslim Ibn Qutayba, respected Sunnī Qādī of Dīnawar, whose most important works date mainly from the latter half of the ninth century, and his contemporary, Shīʿī historian at the Ṭāhirid court in Khurāsān—Aḥmad b. Abī Yaʿqūb, known as al-Yaʿqūbī. These two ninth-century Muslim theologians were happy to glean authoritative knowledge outside the boundaries of Muslim texts and traditions. Both writers were scholars of history, among other sciences and literary genres, and like most classical historians, their interest was chiefly in sacred history. Muslim historians would often begin their account from Adam and come all the way to their own time, using primarily Muslim traditions as their source materials.[3]

Their attitude is nicely illustrated in the following statement of Ibn Qutayba in his *Kitāb ʿUyūn al-Akhbār*, a large compendium of traditions and stories written in the 850s, in which he deals with all sorts of subjects organized into ten large sections, or books: "Knowledge is a quarry for the believer, and it will benefit him, whencesoever he takes it, and it will not detract from the truth to hear it from an unbeliever . . . , nor is pure gold harmed by [the fact of] its extraction from the soil. He who fails to take a beautiful thing from its place lets an opportunity slip, and opportunities pass by like the clouds."[4]

3. Perhaps most famous among such works is *Tārīkh ar-Rusul wa al-Mulūk* (A History of Prophets and Kings), by Abū Jaʿfar Muhammad b. Jarīr b. Yazīd aṭ-Ṭabarī (see the 1960 Cairo edition of Muhammad Abū al-Faḍl Ibrāhīm).

4. Abū Muhammad ʿAbdallāh b. Muslim Ibn Qutayba, *Kitāb ʿUyūn al-Akhbār*

In his *Kitāb al-Maʿārif*, an encyclopedic work with entries on topics from all branches of knowledge, Ibn Qutayba quotes several times from the Gospels after he has cited other traditions from the *quṣṣāṣ* (storytellers of the Islamic tradition). The famous narrator of traditions, Wahb Ibn al-Munabbih, is generally his principal source of information on sacred history. But when he is transmitting information from the historical period of Jesus, he quotes from the Gospels. Unlike al-Qāsim ar-Rassī and ʿAlī aṭ-Ṭabarī who, as we saw in previous chapters, used the genealogy of Jesus in order to demonstrate his human descent and counter the Christian view of Christology, Ibn Qutayba has no polemical agenda. He examines the genealogy of Matthew's Gospel as he attempts to establish the chronology of the world and to set the life of the Prophet of Islam, Muhammad, in that larger context. After noting some discrepancies between the year counts of *Wahb*, *ʿAkrama*, the Gospel of Matthew, and others, he simply concludes: *wa Allāhu aʿlam* ("God knows better"), the classic closing statement of a Muslim scholar when he is before irreconcilable traditions especially in Ḥadīth scholarship.[5]

Ibn Qutayba uses the expression *qaraʾtu* ("I have read") with regard to Gospel traditions, whereas he uses *qāla Wahb b. al-Munabbih* ("Wahb b. al-Munabbih said"), *qāla ʿAkrama* ("ʿAkrama said"), and so on, when bringing in other traditions. This leaves no doubt that Ibn Qutayba actually had in his possession an Arabic version of the Gospels by the time he wrote his *Kitāb al-Maʿārif* about 870. And so with regard to the genealogies in Matthew, Ibn Qutayba affirms: "And I have read in the Gospel [*Injīl*] that the number of generations [*qurūn*] between Abraham and David were fourteen, and between David and the exile to Babylon fourteen generations, and between the exile to Babylon and Christ fourteen generations."

A few pages before, as Ibn Qutayba enumerated the prophets until Muhammad, he used Matthew 1:18–21 as the basis for his entry about Jesus and John the Baptist.[6] He repeats from Wahb b. al-Munabbih the erroneous identification of Herod and Herodias with Ahab (*Aḥb*) and Jezebel (*Azbīl*), whom he had already mentioned with reference to the life of Eli-

(Cairo: Dār al-Kutub al-Misriyya, 1925–30), 1.15. The English translation is by Joseph Horovitz, "Ibn Quteiba's 'Uyun al-Akhbar' (Translated into English)," *Islamic Culture* 4 (1930): 171–84, here taken from Camilla Adang, *Muslim Writers on Judaism and the Hebrew Bible: From Ibn Rabban to Ibn Ḥazm* (Leiden: Brill, 1996), 33.

5. Abū Muhammad Ibn Qutayba, *Kitāb al-Maʿārif*, ed. Saroite Okacha (Cairo: Dār al-Maʿārif, 1960), 57–58.

6. Ibn Qutayba, *Kitāb al-Maʿārif*, 53.

jah.[7] The same *Azbīl*, it is claimed there, lived very long, married seven of the kings of Israel, and killed John son of Zachariah. But beyond this serious anachronism, he continues his account, summarizing Mary's virginal conception of Jesus, the angel's annunciation to Joseph, and their escape to Egypt (Matt 2:14). He notes that the *Injīl* represents Herod (*Harādas*) as the king that Mary and Joseph had to flee from, clearly indicating that he was aware of the alternative tradition of Wahb who ascribes this role to *Aḥb*. But he does not pronounce himself about the correct identification. He recounts the return from Egypt after the death of Herod, and the family's settling down in Nazareth, adding that it is in this connection that Christ's followers were called *Naṣāra* (the qur'anic appellation for Christians).[8] Despite the discrepancies between the traditional account of the Muslim *quṣṣāṣ* and that of the Bible, Ibn Qutayba takes over the Gospel account without qualification, as a reliable source of information. He even preserves the idea present in the text that Mary's son will "save his people from their sins."

In his *'Uyūn al-Akhbār*, Ibn Qutayba argues at one point that historical records indicate that numerous prophets were rejected by their own people, in the same way as Muhammad was rejected initially in his own hometown. In that connection, he narrates the passage from Matthew 13:55–57 (parallel in Mark 6:3–4), where Jesus rebuked his fellow countrymen for rejecting him. The purpose of Ibn Qutayba's reference to this passage is markedly different from the one we saw in chapter 5 in aṭ-Ṭabarī, followed by Ibn Ayyūb. He simply quotes the episode as a *khabar* ("anecdotal evidence") to confirm his argument that a great man is least appreciated by his own relatives. The statement used to introduce the tradition is matter of fact: "And [it is found] in the Injīl that when 'Īsa (May God bless him!) showed them miracles, spoke to them with parables and wisdom, and performed these signs for them, they said: 'Is this not the son of the carpenter?' So 'Īsa said to them: 'A prophet is neither insulted [*lā yusabb*] nor belittled [*lā yuḥaqqar*] except in his town and environment.'"[9] There is no polemical intention behind the citation. Unlike aṭ-Ṭabarī who, in his *Radd*, used the passage to demonstrate Christ's mere prophethood, Ibn Qutayba is interested in the Bible per se, and not just as a tool for polemics.

7. Ibn Qutayba, *Kitāb al-Ma'ārif*, 51.
8. Ibn Qutayba, *Kitāb al-Ma'ārif*, 53.
9. Ibn Qutayba, *Kitāb 'Uyūn al-Akhbār*, 2.118.

If Ibn Qutayba had no polemical purpose when he used the Gospel text, our second historian, Shīʿī al-Yaʿqūbī, had even less of an axe to grind. He quotes extensively from the Gospels as a reliable historical authority in his *Tārīkh*. His work is in two parts. The first begins with the history of the patriarchs of Israel down to the time of Muhammad. The second part is double the size of the first, beginning with Muhammad and the early history of Islam until his own day in 872. The first part contains quite a long section on the life of Jesus and the apostles.[10] His account of the life of Jesus is based on quotations drawn from all four Gospels, and in each case he spells out the verse reference he is citing. This in itself is quite significant, since the writers referred to so far mainly drew from Matthew's Gospel. He also reports briefly on the early church on the basis of passages from the book of Acts.

On the whole, the New Testament documents are used as objective sources. For instance, when he gives the account about the birth of Mary and then her pregnancy with Jesus and her giving birth, he mentions, in agreement with the Qur'an, that Jesus spoke in the cradle. But a little further, he adds: "But as for the people of the Gospel, they do not say that he spoke in the cradle, and they say that Mary was betrothed to a man called Joseph, a son of David, and that she became pregnant."[11]

His exposition of both versions could not be any more objective. Not only does he freely give the Gospel account, but he does not make any attempt at evaluation or harmonization. When he comes to the Matthean genealogy (Matt 1:1–16) he differs from other Muslim theologians who distrusted the genealogies because of the discrepancies they found between the Matthean and Lukan versions. Al-Yaʿqūbī refers to it in summary form: "As for Matthew, he said in the Gospel with regard to the genealogy of Christ: 'Jesus [*īsūʿ*][12] son of David, son of Abraham,' all the way down to where he gets to 'Joseph, son of Jacob, son of Matthan,' after [enumerating] forty-two fathers. Then he said: 'And Joseph was the husband [*baʿl*][13] of Mary.'"[14]

10. Al-Yaʿqūbī (Aḥmad b. Abī Yaʿqūb), *Tārīkh*, ed. M. T. Houtsma (Leiden: Brill, 1883), 1.74–89.

11. Al-Yaʿqūbī, *Tārīkh*, 1.74.

12. This spelling of the name for Jesus is basically a direct transliteration of the Syriac form *īshūʿ*.

13. This is another Syriacism, though the Peshitta Syriac version uses *gabrā* instead of *baʿlā* in Matt 1:16. But a little further (1:19) *baʿlā* is used with reference to Joseph.

14. Al-Yaʿqūbī, *Tārīkh*, 1.75.

Further, al-Yaʿqūbī records the episode of the Magi (Matt 2:1, 10–11), again without expressing any doubt about the authenticity of the account. As we will see later, aṭ-Ṭabarī expressed some skepticism about the account in his *Radd*. And seeing that al-Yaʿqūbī was often selective in his choice of narrative, it is surprising that he did not omit the account as trivial or unacceptable,[15] as the story is entirely absent from the Qur'an.

The Bible as Corrective of Islamic Traditions

The interpretation of Ḥadīth (prophetic traditions) was one of the most important disciplines in Islam, and for some schools, only material originating from within Islam was considered a legitimate source, for both the interpretation and authentication of such materials. That such an important religious figure as Ibn Qutayba should make extensive use of the Bible as an additional tool for the authentication of Muslim traditions is significant.

The work on which the present section is based is Ibn Qutayba's *Kitāb Ta'wīl Mukhtalif al-Ḥadīth* (Interpretation of Divergences in the Ḥadīth). In it, Ibn Qutayba deals with a large number of *aḥādīth* (plural of Ḥadīth) whose authenticity has been questioned by various Muslim scholars. After discussing diverse opinions on a particular tradition and compiling evidence from multiple sources, Ibn Qutayba states his own preference and concludes whether he considers a certain Ḥadīth authentic or spurious. On several occasions, he cites a passage from the Gospels after citing other Islamic traditions, and every time he does that, it is in order to support his own conclusion.

The first example pertains to a particular Ḥadīth where Muhammad affirmed that we will see God in the afterlife. Some Muslim scholars repudiated its authenticity because of the anthropomorphism (i.e., usage of human bodily language with reference to God) or simply said that it should be understood allegorically. Ibn Qutayba, however, argues that when the prophet Muhammad said that believers would see God on the day of the resurrection, he did not mean it in a figurative sense as many people claim—in the sense of "understanding God" (this was the argument of the *Muʿtazilī* rationalists). If it were so, Ibn Qutayba advances, then there would be no difference between the way we see God in the

15. Al-Yaʿqūbī, *Tārīkh*, 1.75–76.

present life and the way that we will see him in the life to come, and that is not possible. His assertion is that all statements that speak of not being able to see God, whether in the Qur'an, the Ḥadīth, or the Bible, are said with reference to the present age. At the resurrection, however, God will be seen, but how and in what form no one knows.

In what was becoming typical Sunnī traditionist fashion, Ibn Qutayba does not necessarily try to resolve the tension of such wording rationally, but he is instead satisfied with adducing examples that indicate the existence of precedent for such language. To that end, he brings in the testimony of Matthew 5:7–8, a verse from the Sermon on the Mount where Jesus says that the pure in heart will see God. His appreciation of the Gospel tradition is clear from the words that he uses in introducing the citation: "And I have read in the *Injīl* that Christ (Peace be upon him!), when he opened his mouth through inspiration [*bi al-waḥyi*], said. . . ."[16]

Ibn Qutayba's method in dealing with the Islamic tradition was in line with what was becoming the standard Orthodox Islamic way, challenging the more rationalist method of the *Muʿtazilī*. When a statement in the received tradition was difficult to understand from a human perspective, it would be accepted without further qualification rather than dismissed or played down intellectually.[17] In other words, the interpreter has to adopt an agnostic attitude of submission to the authority of the tradition and should not try to resolve the difficulty by doing away with it or reducing it to the limits of what is possible according to the human intellect. It is significant that Ibn Qutayba placed the text of the Gospels at such a level of authority.

It is enlightening, in contrast with this unqualified acceptance of the Gospel verse, to observe that even al-Qāsim ar-Rassī, who otherwise cited the biblical text extensively, had problems accepting the anthropomorphism implied by Matthew 5:8. Clearly uncomfortable with the idea of seeing God, he uses in his version of the text the expression *naẓara ila*, rather than *ra'a* or some other similar verb. His rendering, though somewhat ambiguous, is more readily understood in context as: "to be in expectancy of" God.[18]

16. Ibn Qutayba, *Kitāb Ta'wīl Mukhtalif al-Ḥadīth* (Cairo: n.p., 1908), 262.

17. The technical term that became current was *bilā kayf* ("without asking how").

18. Ar-Rassī, *Ar-Radd ʿala an-Naṣāra*, in Ignazio Di Matteo's "Confutazione contro I cristiani dello zaydita al-Qâsim b. Ibrâhîm," *Rivista degli Studi Orientali* 9 (1922): 326.

Another Ḥadīth discussed by Ibn Qutayba mentions the geographical location of *Wajj* as being "God's last footstool on earth," once more speaking anthropomorphically about God. Different interpretations of this saying tried to eliminate the anthropomorphism, and Ibn Qutayba is especially in favor of the one that interprets the footstool as representing God's treading of a nation. Hence, the saying would be telling about the prophet's final victory over polytheists in *Wajj*. But after asserting his appreciation that this interpretation is "far from dislike and close to the hearts," Ibn Qutayba stops short of endorsing it and affirms that this could not have been the original intention of Muhammad. His reason for doing so is revealing:

> Because I have read in the true Gospel that Christ (Peace be upon him!) said to the disciples: "Did you not hear that it was said to the ancients: 'Do not lie if you have sworn by God (May he be exalted!), but say the truth'? And I say to you: Do not swear by anything. Neither by the heaven for it is God's throne (May he be exalted!), nor by the earth for it is his footstool, nor by Jerusalem—*Bayt al-Maqdis*—for it is the city of the Great King [*al-malik al-akbar*]. And do not swear by your own head, for you are unable to add a single black or white hair to it. But let your word be yes [for] yes, and no [for] no. And whatever else besides this is from the devil."[19]

Here again, Ibn Qutayba prefers to avoid resolving the tension created by the anthropomorphism and simply endorses the legitimacy of such language based on the testimony of the Gospel (Matt 5:33–37). It is clear that our jurist takes the words of Jesus at face value and as fully authoritative, even against other Islamic interpretations of this tradition. Ibn Qutayba also appeals to what he calls the "true Gospel" (*al-Injīl aṣ-ṣaḥīḥ*), which in his case is no other than the text used by his Christian contemporaries.

In contrast, al-Qāsim ar-Rassī, who again preserves the same passage, omits any mention of the earth being God's footstool. Instead, he recasts Matthew 5:35 in totally new language: "Neither by the earth, for it is the dwelling of God's mercy and signs."[20] In the same way, al-Yaʿqūbī also omits any anthropomorphism by transforming Matthew 5:34–35: "And

19. Ibn Qutayba, *Kitāb Ta'wīl Mukhtalif al-Ḥadīth*, 269.
20. Ar-Rassī, *Radd*, 327.

do not swear by God, either saying the truth or lying, nor by his heaven or by his earth."[21]

Further, Ibn Qutayba discusses passages in the Ḥadīth and the Qur'an that assign to God a geographical location. He notes that the most natural human intuition is that God is in heaven and that it is alright to express oneself in this way. However, he points out that this is not to be taken literally, just as when God is said to go from one place to another. In the latter case, this reflects more a movement in the intention and the will. However, he argues for the authenticity of this sort of Ḥadīth by showing once again the legitimacy of such language. To that end, he cites three verses from the Gospel of Matthew: 5:34 (cited above), which describes heaven as being "God's throne"; 6:14, which refers to the "heavenly Father" forgiving those who forgive others; and 6:26, which speaks about the "heavenly Father" who feeds the birds of the air.[22]

It is astounding that Ibn Qutayba unapologetically uses the expression "heavenly Father" twice, even though the reference to God as Father would have been offensive to many of his readers. As far as he was concerned, the citations represented a precedent for referring to God as being "in heaven." In contrast, as noted earlier, al-Yaʿqūbī omitted the reference to God's throne altogether, and in citing Matthew 6:14, ar-Rassī replaces "heavenly Father" simply with "God" (*Allāh*). Though both ar-Rassī and al-Yaʿqūbī use Matthew 6:26, ar-Rassī replaces "heavenly Father" with "God, your Lord who is in heaven," and al-Yaʿqūbī's text simply reads "God."[23]

Finally, one more interesting passage indicates that Ibn Qutayba possessed even a supraliterary knowledge of the Gospels. While still introducing his *Kitāb Ta'wīl Mukhtalif al-Ḥadīth* at the beginning of the book, he weaves Jesus's words in Matthew 7:3 into his sentence, possibly without conscious awareness. He is not yet dealing with the authenticity of any Ḥadīth, but simply making a rhetorical statement against *ahl al-kalām* (clearly a reference to the *Muʿtazilī*, whom he repeatedly argues against in

21. Al-Yaʿqūbī, *Tārīkh*, 1.77.

22. With regard to the last quotation, although the edited text of the *Mukhtalif al-Ḥadīth* I use contains the reading "your Lord in heaven," the editor signals two other manuscripts where "your Father in heaven" is retained. It is likely that Ibn Qutayba originally used "Father in heaven," as in the biblical text, and that the reading was altered by a later copyist in reaction to the use of the title "Father" for God. Indeed the opposite would be hard to substantiate; see Ibn Qutayba, *Kitāb Ta'wīl Mukhtalif al-Ḥadīth*, 347nn1–2.

23. Ar-Rassī, *Radd*, 328–29; and al-Yaʿqūbī, *Tārīkh*, 1.77–78.

his work): "They make claims about God which they do not understand and lead people astray with what they say. They judge the claims of others with suspicion, without any clue about the absurdity of their own claims, *looking for the straw in the eyes of people, while their own eyes are shutting over trunks.*"[24] The reference to Jesus's statement in the Sermon on the Mount is a free citation, suggesting that the saying had become part of the author's natural speech.

Islamization of the Gospel Text

The final section of this chapter presents a less optimistic approach that does not unconditionally receive the text as Christians preserved it. It may be seen as an attempt by Muslim writers to rescue the Bible from what they viewed as an abuse of the text by Christian theologians. That process reflects an inherent attachment of those authors to the Bible. While Muslim theologians in the last two sections made virtually unconditional and unqualified use of the Gospels, under this third heading a more critical outlook is displayed. The archetypical example of this process of Islamization of the Gospel text is the treatise of one of our earliest theologians, the Zaydī Shī'ī imām al-Qāsim ar-Rassī. In his *Radd 'ala an-Naṣāra*, the first eight chapters of Matthew's Gospel are retranslated almost in full, but with additions, subtractions, and alterations that made them more compatible with the Islamic worldview.

In a sense, one can say that the philosophy behind ar-Rassī's attitude toward the Christian Scriptures is not very different from the early Christian attitude toward the Hebrew Scriptures. He viewed Islam as an extension and culmination of God's revelation to humanity, and he sought the appropriation of former revealed Scriptures for the new religion. His approach, however, differed from that of the early orthodox Christian fathers in that alterations are brought into the received text and doubts are expressed as to the reliability and honesty of the transmitters. A striking parallel attitude among early Christians can be found in someone like Marcion, who charged that the Gospels were full of Judaizing influences and felt it was his duty to purge these received texts from any passages reflecting unfaithful transmission. In the following survey, I mention the most interesting Gospel passages rendered by ar-Rassī and others and will point out textual

24. Ibn Qutayba, *Kitāb Ta'wīl Mukhtalif al-Ḥadīth*, 15–16 (emphasis added).

alterations they made that have polemical and exegetical significance. Only attention to detail will uncover some of their deeper intentions.

As part of the testimony that angels gave about Christ and that, as we have already seen, ar-Rassī tries to use as a common denominator for Muslim-Christian agreement, the quotation of Matthew 1:20–21 is quite significant. The writer had already used the passage to demonstrate Christ's mere humanity and servanthood, but closer attention to the wording should be given here: "O Joseph son of David! Do not dismiss your wife, for the one who is in her is from the Spirit of God. And he will be called Jesus, and through him God will save [lit., will give life (*yuḥyī*), as in the Peshitta: *naḥēw*[*h*]*y*][25] his people from their sins, by God's permission."[26] Ar-Rassī's text is substantially altered to suit his exegetical need. The first minor adaptation is the replacement of "Holy Spirit" with "Spirit of God," which reflects better the qur'anic verse where Jesus is called "a spirit from God" (an-Nisā' 4:171) and which is generally more in line with the Islamic tradition. But the most radical adaptation is made to the last part of the verse, where God himself is the one to "save his people from their sins," whereas the canonical Gospel text ascribes this role to Jesus. This reconstruction leaves us with a rather awkward text, since the verse makes the illogical assertion that "God will save his people . . . by God's permission."

Ibn Qutayba does away altogether with the idea of the Holy Spirit's participation in the virginal conception. In his *Kitāb al-Maʿārif* he cited Matthew 1:18–21 as an authoritative source regarding Christ's birth, but he avoids mention of the Holy Spirit in both 1:18 and 1:20.[27] The same may be observed in al-Yaʿqūbī's citation of 1:18.[28] Thus, even those authors who, on the surface, seem to use the Gospel text unconditionally turn out to be carefully selective of the wording of their citations.

Another adaptation may be observed in ar-Rassī's narration of the holy family's flight to Egypt in Matthew 2:13–15. His version more or less faithfully reflects the canonical text until we reach the end of 2:15, where the author uses the word *ṣafī* ("chosen") instead of *Ibn* ("son"): "Out of

25. This may be a useful hint to conjecture that ar-Rassī was using an Arabic version of the Gospel text influenced by the Syriac Peshitta translation of the Gospels, rather than by the Harklean or the Greek, since the Harklean uses the root FRQ (a more accurate rendering of the Greek *sōzō*) rather than the root ḤYA.

26. Ar-Rassī, *Radd*, 322.

27. Ibn Qutayba, *Kitāb al-Maʿārif*, 53.

28. Al-Yaʿqūbī, *Tārīkh*, 1.74–75.

Egypt I have called my *chosen one*."[29] This is, in fact, a key term that ar-Rassī uses quite often as a substitute for "son" when it refers to Christ. Ar-Rassī also omits a detail in 2:13, 19, 22. God is said to "inspire" (*awḥa*) Joseph's escape to Egypt, his return to Palestine, and his settling down in Nazareth of Galilee. The canonical text reads in the first two instances that "an angel of the Lord" appeared to Joseph "in a dream," and in the third that he was "warned in a dream." At first glance, this seems to be quite trivial. However, as I note in the next chapter, aṭ-Ṭabarī dislikes the idea that an angel appeared to Joseph, as that would make him into a prophet who received revelations from God in the same way as Islam's prophet Muhammad. He makes no mention that it happened "in a dream," and there is no indication that he was aware of this. The same point of view is perhaps reflected in al-Yaʿqūbī's version of the text, since he makes no mention of a supernatural revelation at all, in either Matthew 2:13–14 or 2:22–23. His citations simply read as follows: "And Herod, the king of Palestine, wanted to kill Christ. And Joseph took him and his mother away to the land of Egypt. And when Herod died, he returned him and established him in Nazareth of the Galilee Mountain."[30]

Another significant set of alterations enters ar-Rassī's narration of John the Baptist's announcement and baptism of Jesus in the Jordan River in Matthew 3:11–15. His text displays six departures from the canonical version, which all are part of his effort at Islamizing the text of the Gospel:

1. In 3:11, instead of the canonical reading "one who is more powerful than I is coming after me," ar-Rassī's text reads: "the one who is coming after me is more favored by God than I am." The emphasis is shifted from a power inherent to Jesus to a divine favor bestowed on him.
2. At the end of 3:11 ar-Rassī avoids altogether mentioning the Baptist's assertion that Christ would baptize people with the Holy Spirit and fire. He may have wanted to avoid the difficult implication that this would have on the usual Islamic designation of the angel Gabriel by the name *rūḥ al-quds* ("holy spirit") and possibly also the undesirable association with the Paraclete of John's Gospel.
3. In 3:12, instead of "his winnowing fork is in his hand," ar-Rassī's text reads "he is the one in whose hand God will place the winnow-

29. Ar-Rassī, *Radd*, 324–25.
30. Al-Yaʿqūbī, *Tārīkh*, 1.76.

ing fork." Again, Christ's full reliance on God for his ministry is emphasized.

4. In 3:13, instead of preserving the canonical reading that Christ came to John "to be baptized by him," ar-Rassī's text reads "so that he would baptize him with water and purify him." The addition of "purify" (*yuṭahhirahu*) consigns Christ to a purely human status, since he needed "purification from sins" in the same way as the rest of the crowds that came to John.[31]
5. In 3:15, instead of Christ's baptism taking place in order "to fulfill all righteousness," ar-Rassī's version reads: "Thus we ought to be fulfilled/perfected [*nastatimm*] through [the practice of] all righteousness."
6. At the end of 3:15 ar-Rassī adds "or whatever of it [i.e., righteousness] is accessible to us."

All of the above alterations are clearly introduced in order to reduce Christ to a more purely human status.[32]

More alterations are introduced by both ar-Rassī and al-Yaʿqūbī in their narration of the account of Christ's temptation (Matt 4:1–11 and Luke 4:1–12). Two alterations occur in the first two verses in ar-Rassī's citation (Matt 4:1–2): "Christ left the villages and withdrew and fasted in the wilderness for forty mornings, not eating or drinking anything." Rather than repeating the canonical attribution to the Holy Spirit of the role of leading Jesus into the desert, ar-Rassī makes it Jesus's own initiative. On the one hand he may have wanted to avoid mention of the third person of the Trinity, and on the other he may have wanted to avoid the association of God's initiative with the devil's temptation scheme. Al-Yaʿqūbī, for his part, asserts that Christ left for the wilderness "with the confirmation of God's Spirit [*bi ta'yīdi Rūḥ Allāh*]." Again, it is primarily Christ's own initiative, and rather than using the usual Christian term "Holy Spirit," the author favors the more neutral "God's Spirit." Second, ar-Rassī uses the statement that Christ fasted "forty mornings" rather than "forty days and forty nights." This is probably to make it more in line with the Islamic fast of *Ramaḍān*, which is kept only during daytime, and thus emphasize Christ's identity as a faithful Muslim prophet. Again, al-Yaʿqūbī adopts a more neutral stance here, asserting that Jesus fasted "forty days."

31. Ar-Rassī introduced John's baptism in this section as one that served "purification from sins for those who repented and believed."

32. Ar-Rassī, *Radd*, 325.

When it comes to the actual temptations, one notable addition in ar-Rassī's account of the first temptation (Matt 4:3–4)[33] is that the devil challenges Jesus to ask *God* for the transformation of the stones (*fa-dʿu Allāh*), rather than to command it himself as we find in the Gospel. The important Gospel connotation that the devil was aware of the identity of his foe as "God's son" is thus lost to the reader. Furthermore, in his attempt to use this verse as a means of reinterpreting Christ's sonship, the author replaces the wording of the devil's challenge "if you are the Son of God" with "if you are the beloved of God [*in kunta lahu ḥabīban*]." In the immediately preceding context, ar-Rassī asserted that one was the son of whom one obeyed. And here he illustrates Christ's faithfulness by mentioning this passage where he did not obey the request of the devil. The alteration in the wording of the text is the author's further exegetical effort to reinterpret Christ's sonship in terms of being the "beloved" of God, an honorific form of sonship that, as we saw in chapter 4, was favored by several Muslim theologians as the solution to the Gospel appellation.

Finally, ar-Rassī's conclusion to this first temptation reads as follows: "So he said to him: 'Did you not know, you accursed one, that the word of God suffices to the one who is satisfied with it—to the one who loves God—over all food and drink?'" This reveals a further effort on the part of the writer to Islamize his Gospel text, replacing "word from the mouth of God" with "word of God." Although there is no doubt that this alteration helps ar-Rassī to maintain the rhythm and balance of his poetic text (his treatise is written entirely in *sajaʿ* form), it is clearly an attempt also to attenuate the anthropomorphic nature of the original Gospel quotation. It also helps him to draw his final conclusion: "And the word of God which he mentioned (May God bless him!), is what he brought down [or revealed: *nazzala'*], which is without equal in any other book."[34]

Al-Yaʿqūbī's only alteration in this first temptation is again the elimination of the anthropomorphism in Matthew 4:4. Christ's reply to the devil reads as follows: "It is not only with bread that people live, but [also] with the word of God."[35]

33. In ar-Rassī's text, the order of the first and third temptations is inverted, and the second one is omitted altogether.

34. Although this seems to be a reference to Christ's words, "May God bless him" (*ṣalla Allāh ʿalayhi*) may also be a reference to Muhammad, and hence the "word of God" would be a reference to the Qur'an. For all of the above, see ar-Rassī, *Radd*, 324.

35. Al-Yaʿqūbī, *Tārīkh*, 1.76.

About a century later, Ibn Ayyūb's text would repeat the same alteration: "It is written that a person's life is not by bread, but with every word that comes from God."[36]

There is little evidence of a direct textual connection between the treatises of ar-Rassī, al-Yaʿqūbī, and Ibn Ayyūb, either on the argumentative level or on the level of the Gospel version employed. All three independent witnesses to this alteration of the anthropomorphism underline the conscious effort of Muslim theologians to render the Gospel text more acceptable to their coreligionists. This serves to strengthen the legitimacy of their own usage of the biblical text, in fact countering any suspicions of textual *taḥrīf* among their readers and strengthening their main allegation that the principal dispute between them and the Christians was the latter's misinterpretation, rather than textual corruption, of their sacred texts.

Ibn Ḥazm's version of the temptation accounts also fits under the present theme. First, in his Matthean account, he has the devil addressing Christ as *walad Allāh* both times (Matt 4:3, 6), rather than *Ibn Allāh*, both words meaning "son." *Walad* in Arabic contains, however, an explicit physical and even sexual connotation that is not present in the word *Ibn*, since it derives from the verb *walada* ("to engender"). His Lukan account (Luke 4:3, 9) nevertheless preserves the more usual *Ibn Allāh* in the first temptation and reverts to *walad Allāh* in the third. For Ibn Ḥazm's highly polemical work, this wording supports his case for the Bible's corruption. Second, in response to the second Matthean temptation (Matt 4:6–7), where the devil challenges Jesus to throw himself from the edge of the temple, Ibn Ḥazm has Jesus reply: "It is written also: 'No servant/slave [*aḥad al-ʿabīd*] shall tempt/measure [*yaqīs*] his God.'" This addition to the Gospel text, not found elsewhere even in the other Muslim writers, contains a clear confession from Jesus himself that he was God's servant rather than his Son, or even less God himself.

Our last author to introduce alterations into the text of the temptation accounts in order to suit his polemical purpose is thirteenth-century theologian Shihāb ad-Dīn al-Qarāfī. Though he claims explicitly that his quotation comes from Matthew's Gospel, his text is in fact clearly a combination of both Matthean and Lukan readings. Everything, from actual errors in his Gospel text to the confusion of different accounts, points

36. Ibn Ayyūb, *Risāla ila Akhīhi ʿAlī* (Letter to His Brother ʿAlī, Explaining to Him Why He Converted to Islam), preserved in Taqī ad-Dīn Aḥmad b. Taymiyya, *Al-Jawāb aṣ-Ṣaḥīḥ li-man Baddala Dīn al-Masīḥ* (Cairo: Nile Press, 1905), 1.2.324.

to, by the thirteenth century, Muslim writers not citing the biblical text directly any longer, but dogmatically drawing from collections that had been put together within Muslim circles for the specific use of Muslim polemicists. The following is the evidence:

1. Though the author begins by claiming that his reading originates from Matthew's Gospel, he ends up offering the order of the temptations as they are found in Luke, reversing the second and the third one.
2. Instead of reading that the Holy Spirit led Jesus into the desert, al-Qarāfī's text has the devil himself taking him there. This is even more extreme than Ibn Ayyūb's omission of the context altogether. Furthermore, like in Ibn Ayyūb, there is at first no mention of fasting. The sojourn in the desert is represented entirely as the devil's initiative, aimed at testing Jesus. Only at the end of the passage is there mention of fasting.
3. We observe the same feature already found in several of our earlier Muslim writers, whereby the anthropomorphic expression "mouth of God" in Matthew 4:4 is replaced simply with "from God."
4. Instead of having the angels come and "serve him" at the end of the episode (Matt 4:11), al-Qarāfī's text reads that they came to "protect him." This feature is very close to the idea already encountered in Ibn Ayyūb, where the devil was described as being totally in control of Jesus, and hence the angels are seen as his deliverers at the end of the account. That this was his understanding of the temptation account becomes even clearer when al-Qarāfī refers to Matthew 4:9 a second time in his polemical treatise. This time, in the context of his refutation of the creedal statement that Christ was "the perfecter of all creatures and the maker of all things," al-Qarāfī concludes that surely this would imply that he was also the creator of the devil. "How then," the author asks, "is the maker and sustainer of all creatures besieged [*yanḥaṣir*] at the hand of one [of these] creatures in such a way?" Not only is the idea inherited from Ibn Ayyūb, but even the verb *ḥāṣara* ("besieged"), which was introduced by Ibn Ayyūb, is taken over by al-Qarāfī, indicating a textual correspondence between the two authors, whether direct or indirect.[37]

37. Shihāb ad-Dīn al-Qarāfī, *Al-Ajwiba al-Fākhira ʿan al-Asʾila al-Fājira*, ed. Bakr Zakī ʿAwaḍ (Cairo: Wehbeh Publishers, 1987), 312.

5. Going back to al-Qarāfī's principal reference to the temptation account, we find that he mentions only at the end that "at that point, Christ (Peace be upon him!) fasted thirty days and thirty nights." This is the reverse of the Gospel version, where the temptations came at Christ's most vulnerable point, after he had fasted forty days and nights. Here, it appears almost as a process of purification, after the devil had moved him about, testing him for ten days. Therefore, presumably the forty days are reduced to thirty in order to allow some time for the occurrence of the temptations.[38]

Summarizing the Metadialogue on Scripture

The metadialogue on the doctrine of Scripture and revelation reveals that the Muslim attitude to the Bible was more diverse historically than is usually assumed today, primarily as a result of a largely positive portrayal of the Judeo-Christian Scriptures in the Qur'an. The Qur'an presents itself in a relationship of delicate balance between continuity and discontinuity vis-à-vis the Torah and the Gospel. This stems from the belief that all three revelations came from a common source (āl-ʿImrān 3:3–4). The qur'anic understanding of previous revelations is, at its simplest, a book (the Torah) revealed to Moses and another to Jesus (the Gospel), in the same way it presents itself as the book revealed to Muhammad (āl-ʿImrān 3:48). The idea is also conveyed, however, that the Qur'an supersedes previous revelations because it also preceded them (āl-ʿImrān 3:65–67). And the need for the Qur'an to precede and supersede results from Jews and Christians having not held faithfully on to their own Scriptures (al-Mā'ida 5:66, 68).

The Qur'an affirms that the Judeo-Christian Scriptures preannounced Muhammad (al-Aʿrāf 7:157) and that therefore believing in his message is a nonnegotiable in order to become recipients of his mercy (al-Aʿrāf 7:156). The Qur'an, furthermore, presents itself as an easier message to follow than the preceding revelations (āl-ʿImrān 3:50, 93).

There is no doubt that in the Muslim view, the Qur'an will always take priority over any of the preceding revelations, and the qur'anic affirmation of the importance of believing in the Judeo-Christian Scriptures, hand in hand with the Qur'an, does not preclude the necessity of believing in the

38. Al-Qarāfī, *Al-Ajwiba al-Fākhira*, 217.

divine origin of Muhammad's calling. Yet the Qur'an's veneration of the Judeo-Christian revelation was not left unheeded in the early Muslim theological tradition. This was reflected in early Muslim texts' consideration of the *Injīl* as a reliable historical document, the Bible often as a corrective of Islamic traditions (specifically Ḥadīth), and in the emergence of a process of Islamization of the Gospel text, in an effort to maintain its authority both within the Muslim-Christian conversation and within Islam itself.

Hermeneutical Keys in Building Bridges beyond Conflict

The survey of the Islamic exegetical discourse on God and Christ in the previous three chapters demonstrated the centrality of the biblical text in the Muslim-Christian encounter. The Christian doctrines are so fundamentally connected with the Holy Scriptures that it is impossible to discuss the Islamic challenge to Christian theology without approaching it exegetically. Judaism, Christianity, and Islam all claim to be revealed religions. In other words, they claim to have come into the world as a manifestation of God's decision and initiative to reveal himself, rather than having emerged through a human effort to reach out and understand the divine. In addition, however, Christianity can be described as a religion of personal encounter par excellence. Whereas in Islam, God revealed his will to the world in a book through the intermediary of a prophet, the fundamental premise of the Christian faith is that God revealed himself in the person of Christ. Judaism is somewhat closer to Islam in that it understands that God revealed his will in the Torah through Moses. But short of stopping there, God continued to reveal his will and to address his people through a line of prophetic recipients.

Christians believe that this encounter experience is reflected upon and narrated in the Scriptures and that theological doctrines are then derived from this record. As such, Christians through the ages have not attempted to come up with theological doctrines primarily in line with plain logic. Rather, while using the philosophical language of their time and striving toward a reasonable theological discourse, they usually attempted to construct their theology and derive it from the received Scriptures that reflected the divine encounter with them. Having established the importance of the biblical text in the development of Christian doctrines in chapter 2, and having observed in chapters 3–5 the centrality of the Bible in the Muslim discourse with Christians, we examined in the present chapter the underlying attitude of Muslim theologians toward the Bible. How can these attitudes now be harnessed in our efforts to unlock some of the most persistent obstacles in the Christian-Muslim theological dialogue?

Using Deadlocks as Assets

That the Muslim position toward the Bible historically has not been limited to the accusation of *taḥrīf* is great news for Christian-Muslim dialogue today. It allows well-intentioned Christians and Muslims to reopen channels of theological dialogue by giving central place to the biblical text. From a Christian perspective, a theological conversation cannot take place without this starting point, as Christian theological discourse has always been rooted in biblical hermeneutics.

Even if most Christians may not be comfortable admitting the divine origin of a third revelation beyond the New Testament, due to their understanding of the finality of God's self-revelation in Christ, the qur'anic affirmation of its continuity with the Judeo-Christian Scriptures should at least lead us to affirming the intimate connection that exists between the Qur'an and the Bible. Muslims will not be satisfied with such a position, but they may at least appreciate it in light of the other common option within Christianity—that the Qur'an is an antiscripture. Even though at this point, it may remain impossible for either of the three traditions to embrace fully the other's perspective on divine revelation, a conversation between Jews, Christians, and Muslims about their respective Scriptures should at least offer new opportunities for each to express more genuinely their understanding.

The inability of Christians to allow for a third revelation is paralleled by Islam's supersessionist view of their own Scripture and the Qur'an's insistence that belief in the prophethood of Muhammad is a prerequisite to becoming recipients of God's mercy. Neither Christian nor Muslim should get frustrated by these positions. They derive naturally from religious systems that tend to be by nature exclusivist of others. But it remains the responsibility of all of us to seek ways continually to practice an open type of exclusivism. In the kerygmatic model expressed in chapter 1, which holds to the centrality and primacy of Christ within a suprareligious understanding of Jesus's message, I demonstrated the possibility for followers of Jesus to practice a form of Christ-centered inclusivity as a biblically faithful alternative to exclusivistic religiosity.

The Muslim notion that Judaism and Christianity are austere religions, as opposed to the easy path of Islam, may lead us to fruitful conversations about the centrality of love in the message of Jesus. The message of the New Testament is that religion is by nature legalistic and that legalism is both safe because of its clarity yet also impossible to practice due to the inability of human beings to please God through their own strength and efforts. The New Testament answer is that salvation is not achieved through good works but through God's self-giving grace. Works become a natural outcome of a loving relationship between humans and God, as they are drawn into a filial relationship with him as Father through Christ the Son. Abiding in God's love as a way of life surpasses any achievements that could be reached through the most stringent obedience to a legal system. And a proper understanding of the centrality of grace need not lead us to an austere ascetical life. Through the practice of self-giving love, followers of Jesus are invited to become peacemakers, embracing gentleness and kindness, as they respond to his invitation in Matthew 11:28–30: "Come to me, all you who are weary and burdened, and I will give you rest. Take my yoke upon you and learn from me, for I am gentle and humble in heart, and you will find rest for your souls. For my yoke is easy and my burden is light."

Finally, the three-pronged approach of the Muslim tradition before the eleventh century, which held on to the authority of the Bible, should be promoted in Christian-Muslim theological dialogue, for it is the best safeguard against the deadlock of the *taḥrīf* accusation.

Concluding Thoughts

In the context of dialogue with Islam about the question of the nature of biblical revelation and of the reliability of the biblical witness, it is no doubt most important for Christians to remember the biblical affirmation that in Christ, God revealed himself to us as a person, rather than sending us another book or another set of rules or laws. Though the written word is crucial for our understanding of God's nature and of his relationship with humanity, followers of Christ may never forget that they are not primarily a people of the book. They are first a community birthed by the eternal Logos, and only second a community guided by the written word.

Further Reading and Research

See bibliography at end of chapter 7.

7 Taḥrīf and the Corruption of Scripture

A few years ago, I was invited to give a talk in California about current attitudes and approaches to Islam. I gave my talk on the eve of another talk, which a famous anti-Muslim polemicist would give. As I listened to his polemical presentation about Islam the next morning, I realized that I could have refuted every one of his arguments, despite my standing outside a position of faith vis-à-vis the religion that was being debunked. Granted, he may not have been offering his best arguments on that morning, since he was speaking to a Christian audience only. But still, this left me pondering on how much better a committed Muslim scholar would have been able to dismiss his arguments, had one been in the room.

Having anticipated what my audience would be hearing the next morning, I had concluded my talk the previous evening with the following words: "I respect the approach of those who choose polemics in their engagement with Islam and Muslims, because they often speak out of hurt and frustration. But as for those of us who have a heart to live in the Muslim world and to love Muslims as our neighbors, these approaches will not do. Give us tools that will permit us to survive in the pursuit of our calling in the Muslim world."

Current Christian Perspectives

In the approaches toward Muslim accusations against the Christian Scriptures that are current these days in the church, attempts are often made to defend the reliability of the Bible apologetically. Important as these may be, I find that such approaches are mostly useful with well-meaning and genuinely inquisitive Muslims. They are less helpful in sustaining the reliability of the biblical text when Christians and Muslims are engaged in debates to prove the superiority of their religion over the other.

On the other hand, attempts to hit back polemically by discrediting the Qur'an—such as those of Zakaria Botros[1] or Jay Smith[2]—should also perhaps not be dismissed too quickly. Some of their findings and arguments may be useful in forcing Islam to deal with some real problematic issues in their tradition. But in my opinion, the aggressive attitude needs to be abandoned. Aggressiveness leads only to further conflict and is useless for those who desire to live a life of Christlike witness among Muslims. Attacking another religious tradition is too easy from the comfortable and secure position of geographical distance or when waged from behind pseudonyms on the internet or published books.

Those who use the polemical approach often argue that they do so in response to Islam's aggressive methods. It is true that many scholars of the Muslim tradition use polemical approaches to Christianity. (We have looked at examples from history, and these approaches still exist today, not just in books and television programs, but also in the Friday preaching of many imams, particularly in the Muslim world—as Arab Christians, for example, know all too well.) But if followers of Jesus are to imitate his example, more balanced approaches that seek to do justice to the biblical witness without giving in to the polemical tools and attitudes that Muslim scholars and imams sometimes display are direly needed these days.

Taḥrīf in the Muslim Polemical Tradition

Having examined in the previous chapter the mostly positive approaches that Muslims adopted toward the Judeo-Christian Scriptures up until the

1. Zakaria Botros is a Coptic priest who became well known across the Arab world over the first decade of this millennium for his polemical programs about Islam on the *al-Hayat* satellite television channel. His stated goal is "to attack Islam," though he affirms that his goal is "not to attack Muslims, but to save them because they are deceived. I love Muslims, I hate Islam" (cited from David Garrison, *A Wind in the House of Islam: How God Is Drawing Muslims around the World to Faith in Jesus Christ* [Monument, CO: WIGTake, 2014], Kindle location 3198).

2. Jay Smith also specializes in polemical attack of Islam. He works primarily in London, heading up the Hyde Park Christian Fellowship, and became famous for standing regularly on Speakers' Corner at Hyde Park, where he publicly challenges Muslim beliefs; see his Wikipedia page at en.wikipedia.org/wiki/Jay_Smith_(Christian_apologist).

eleventh century, we now come to the fourth Muslim attitude toward the Bible found in the discursive literature. Sadly, this attitude is currently the most widespread in conversations between Muslims and Christians. It was important, before coming to the accusation of *taḥrīf*, to come to terms fully in the previous chapter with how positively Muslims viewed the Scriptures of Jews and Christians before the eleventh century.

The most rewarding approach to the Islamic *taḥrīf* accusation is historical. Beginning with the concept's qur'anic origins, examining the Muslim exegesis of the relevant qur'anic verses, followed by an examination of the concept's development in dialogue history, reveals that the deadlock assumed today was historically far from static. A turning point in that development will be identified in the eleventh century, with origins both in political and textual history. The chapter closes with practical suggestions to move us beyond the deadlock, since the Bible is such a fundamental element of all Christian ministry, from dialogue to mission to discipleship and leadership development.

The Qur'anic Origins of Ḥarrafa

The Arabic verb *ḥarrafa* and its substantive *taḥrīf* have become such common currency wherever Muslims and Christians come into contact with one another that there seems to be little room left, or indeed little demand, for further examination of the concept. If you are a Muslim living in the twenty-first century, you take for granted that the Scriptures of Jews and Christians have been *corrupted* (*ḥurrifat*). If you are a Christian, particularly an Arab Christian, on the other hand, you view these accusations as empty words, transmitted among Muslims through generations, and you likely learned from your ancestors what appropriate responses to offer against such claims.

Beyond polemics on the one hand and apologetics on the other, therefore, not much has been done to examine the origins of the accusation, the rationale behind it, or a way together to move beyond it in dialogue. In the present chapter, rather than try to defend the reliability of the biblical text in the face of the accusation—as Christians have naturally been inclined to do—I will examine the trajectory of the concept within the Islamic tradition, in light of the general attitude of Muslim theologians of the early period toward the Judeo-Christian Scriptures.

My conclusion is that the accusation was born in struggle, in the heat of the encounter rather than in a climate of dispassionate objectivity. The accusation of *taḥrīf* was born in the context of an interfaith encounter, and it hardened as an outcome of struggle rather than as its rational starting point. In that sense, it is primarily a hermeneutical rather than a dogmatic issue, and therefore there may be some lessons to be learned by both Christians and Muslims from their common history of encounter that might move them beyond the deadlock reached today with regard to that question. The Islamic attitude toward the Bible in the first few centuries of encounter was always quite diverse rather than homogenous, creative rather than hardheaded (see previous chapter). As we discover that story, it may be possible to use it as a resource to help us move forward with dialogue on that issue of the Bible's reliability, which is such an important starting point for any Christian who desires to engage in dialogue. Perhaps fellow Muslims with a similar desire to engage will more willingly embrace a line of tradition from within their own literature.

Many terms in the Qur'an have been cited in support of the accusation of *taḥrīf*. Most of them originate from the second sūrah, *al-Baqara*, which is largely concerned with the rebellious disobedience of the children of Israel. One that is commonly referenced and that occurs in various contexts of the Qur'an is the verb *baddala*, which means "to exchange or change." This verb, found a number of times in Sūrat al-Baqara 2, seems connected primarily with Jews who received certain commands and then ignored them and acted contrary to what they were told (al-Baqara 2:59, 181). Al-Baqara 2:79 implies that some who write (*yaktubūna*) Scripture with their own hands claim that it is from God. Further, the verb *katama* ("to hide or conceal evidence") is another accusation found in al-Baqara 2:159 and 174, implying that some who received Scriptures conceal some of their contents from those who ask them. But the Muslim accusation of scriptural corruption derives primarily from occurrences of the verb *ḥarrafa*, found in four verses of the Qur'an.

Almost as words of comfort for early adherents to the qur'anic message, al-Baqara 2:75 exhorts: "Do you really hope that they will be true to you, when some of them heard God's word, comprehended it and then knowingly alter it?"

From that early point already, it is clear that the term emerged in a context of struggle, namely the struggle of the Prophet of Islam, Muhammad, as he sought for his message to pierce through and affirm itself amid the preceding revelations. There is a connection between understanding the meaning of the word of God and then consciously rejecting it. The focus here is on a perversion of *meaning* rather than *text*. The next three verses from Sūrat an-Nisā' and Sūrat al-Mā'ida all contain the same construction: *yuḥarrifūna al-kalima ʿan mawāḍiʿihi*, implying an extraction of words out of their proper context, which should most accurately be understood as "misinterpretation." Hence again the accusation is one of misinterpretation rather than textual corruption:

> Among those of the Jewish faith, some distort [*yuḥarrifūna*] the meaning of the [revealed] words, taking them out of their context and saying, "We have heard, but we disobey," and, "Listen," [adding the insult] "May you not hear"—thus speaking abusively and implying that the [true] faith is false. If they had said, "We have heard, and we obey," and "Hear us, and have patience with us," it would have been better and more appropriate for them. God has rejected them because of their refusal to acknowledge the truth. They have little faith. (an-Nisā' 4:46)

> But, because they broke their pledge, we rejected them and hardened their hearts. They distorted [*yuḥarrifūna*] the meaning of the revealed words, and they have forgotten a lot of what they have been told to remember. You will always find deceit in all but a few of them. Forgive them and forget. God loves those who honor him by forgiving. (al-Mā'ida 5:13)

> Messenger, do not be saddened by those who hurry to deny the truth; such as those who say, "We believe," and do not have any faith in their hearts and the Jews who eagerly listen to any lies and to those who have never met you. They distort [*yuḥarrifūna*] the meaning of the words, taking them out of their context, saying, "If you have already been given this (in your Scriptures), accept it, but if you have not, then be on your guard!" (al-Mā'ida 5:41)

Some essential questions that come to mind concern the actual place that the argument occupies in the overall Islamic discourse. Is it the starting point of that discourse, or a conclusion reached as a result of extensive study and reflection? Is it really a polemical argument, or is it more apologetic in nature? And when does the accusation actually enter the discourse?

The general scholarly opinion leans toward the impression that the accusation of *taḥrīf* is the starting point of the Muslim polemical discourse. Thomas Michel, in his extensive introduction to Ibn Taymiyya, asserts that "the question of *taḥrīf* was a central issue in all polemical debates between Christians and Muslims." Michel discerns two types of accusations on the part of Muslims, which started early in the polemical tradition: (1) *taḥrīf al-lafẓ*, which refers to an actual textual corruption of a revealed book by its receivers, and (2) *taḥrīf al-maʿna*, which refers to the misinterpretation of a text. While Michel considers the second accusation as the more widespread in the earlier polemical period of ʿAlī aṭ-Ṭabarī, al-Qāsim b. Ibrāhīm ar-Rassī, and al-Ḥasan b. Ayyūb as well as among the later *Ashʿarī* polemicists, such as al-Bāqillānī, al-Ghazālī, and Fakhr ad-Dīn ar-Rāzī, he discerns a principal alteration to this mood in the writings of Ibn Ḥazm, during the first part of the eleventh century. According to this last writer, the Bible was "an antiscripture, 'an accursed book,' the product of satanic inspiration." Although subsequent writers did not generally adopt his extreme position, Ibn Ḥazm's writings marked a definite shift in the more optimistic mood of the earlier period.[3]

Although I agree with most of Michel's accurate picture of the *taḥrīf* accusation, I nevertheless question the assumption that the accusation was central to the debate from the beginning. It is true that *taḥrīf* became *eventually* a central point of debate between Muslim and Christian polemicists, but it might be useful to attempt to trace its entry into the Islamic discourse, in order to determine the exact nature of the argument. In the qur'anic context, *taḥrīf* is principally an ambiguous accusation raised against the Jews. Moreover, all four verses more readily lend themselves to being understood as accusations of misinterpretation, *taḥrīf al-maʿna*, rather than textual corruption, *taḥrīf al-lafẓ*. One should not therefore too quickly conclude, as many—both Christians and Muslims—do today, that these verses were automatically understood in the sense of textual corruption of the whole Bible, for this would represent an anachronism.

What most are unaware of today, both among Muslims and Christians, is the lack of uniformity in the view of early Muslim scholars with regard to the Bible. The previous chapter dealt with just that phenomenon. As Michel points out, the hardline accusation of textual corruption of the Bible (*taḥrīf al-lafẓ*) did not actually enter the debate until the eleventh century. Before that, the main understanding of the concept among Muslim scholars was in the sense of misinterpretation (*taḥrīf al-maʿna*). It is no surprise, therefore, that the Bible is cited so extensively by Muslims of

3. Thomas F. Michel, *A Muslim Theologian's Response to Christianity: Ibn Taymiyya's Al-Jawāb al-Ṣaḥīḥ* (New York: Caravan Books, 1985), 89–90.

the early period. Beginning from the assumption that the unacceptable doctrines of Christians and Jews were the result of an erroneous scriptural interpretation, Muslim scholars set out to reinterpret these same texts in line with Islamic doctrinal thinking and essentially to safeguard rather than discredit the sacred texts.

The Muslim Exegetical Tradition on Taḥrīf

The comprehensive and influential Sunnī commentary of Muhammad b. Jarīr aṭ-Ṭabarī (died 923) confirms my previous observation by understanding the references to *taḥrīf* in the Qur'an in the sense of misinterpretation. Two of his comments on al-Baqara 2:75 explain this clearly. In a first note he discusses the group to which the Qur'an refers as those who "heard God's word, comprehended it, and then knowingly alter it." He begins by affirming that this is a reference to the Jews. But he explains that the verse is not speaking about the Jews who hear the Torah in general, but specifically about those who lived at the time of Moses and who requested to hear God's voice directly as he did at Mount Sinai. Having heard God's voice, they went back to the rest of the Israelites, and when Moses conveyed to them God's instructions they knowingly contradicted him.

Near the end of his exegesis of the verse, aṭ-Ṭabarī explains: "What he means by 'and then they alter it' is that they change its meaning [*maʿnāhu*] and alter its interpretation [*ta'wīlahu*]. The etymology of the word is when an object is diverted from its intended course and is drawn into a different direction."

Over three hundred years later, commenting on that same verse, Fakhr ad-Dīn ar-Rāzī (died 1210) largely agrees with aṭ-Ṭabarī. He proposes four possible ways to understand the qur'anic accusation. The first one consists in verbal *taḥrīf*, and though ar-Rāzī does not consider this impossible if one makes the assumption that both the Jewish people and Jewish scholars were very few in number and would therefore have succeeded in doing so, he does not favor this interpretation. His second proposed interpretation is that *taḥrīf* consisted in corrupt interpretations of the text and the derivation of false interpretations instead of the correct ones, just as—he observes—Muslim heretics in his own days were doing with the Qur'an. The third possibility is that the Jews were in the habit of going to Muhammad for insight into their text, and when he gave them the correct interpretation, they just went out and immediately twisted his words. In his fourth suggestion, he aligns the accusation in Sūrat al-Baqara with the one found in al-Māʾida 5:41 and suggests that the Jews assigned false interpretations to their texts. He concludes: "And there is no proof in this [accusation] that they introduced new words into their Scripture."

Al-Bayḍāwī (died 1286?) in his widely popular commentary on the Qur'an does not state his position clearly. His commentary is generally abridged, and he presents both interpretations of the verse as equally possible: the Jews corrupted both their scriptural text (*taḥrīf al-lafẓ*) as well as its interpretation (*taḥrīf al-maʿna*). Al-Bayḍāwī's lack of interest in discussing the difference between the two types of *taḥrīf* or in discerning which type the Jews had practiced on their Scriptures reflects the common trend found among post-eleventh-century Muslim scholars. In this he is preceded by al-Qurṭubī (died 1272) and succeeded by al-Gharnāṭī (died 1344), and al-Jalālayn (died 1459 [al-Maḥallī] and 1505 [as-Suyūṭī]), who do not even present the two options anymore. The first two simply affirm that the verse is a reference to seventy Jewish men who accompanied Moses on Mount Sinai, and after receiving God's revelation through Moses simply corrupted it and falsely retransmitted the divine instructions to their people. And the two Jalāls join them in implying that the corruption performed was textual, in the sense of a change introduced into the text itself. These later commentaries were abridged in size, and therefore less interested in exegetical details. Sadly, these abridged commentaries are also the most popular. The brevity of the commentary of al-Jalālayn makes it readily available in the margins of certain contemporary qur'anic editions and thus easy to find on the market. The harsh accusation of textual *taḥrīf* continues thus to be perpetrated among Muslims.

Short commentaries are primarily interested in the main point of the verse, which was that neither Muhammad nor his later followers should expect the Jews to accept the message of Islam, since they did not even accept God's very words transmitted to them through Moses. Most commentaries connect al-Baqara 2:75 with 2:76 to emphasize the hypocrisy of the Jews, who claimed before the early Muslims that they believed in the truth of Muhammad's message, yet denied it as soon as they went away: "When they meet believers, they say, 'We believe,' and when they are alone by themselves, they say, 'Do you tell them what God has disclosed to you so they dispute with you about it before your Lord?' Have you no sense?"

Commentaries further explain the meaning of the second statement: "Do you tell them what God has disclosed to you so they dispute with you about it before your Lord?" "What God has disclosed," they affirm, are all the preannouncements of Muhammad found in the Torah. Yet the Jews intentionally concealed these passages from Muslims and did not confess that they were found in their Scriptures. The reason why this connection between al-Baqara 2:75 and 76 is important is that it reveals the hermeneutical place of the *taḥrīf* accusation as a reaction to the Jews' and the Christians' refusal to admit the preannouncement of Muhammad in the Torah. The accusation is not the result of a careful examination of the Jewish text by Muslim scholars, but rather a polemical accusation resulting from the desire to prove that their leader belonged in the Judeo-Christian prophetic line.

Shīʿī commentaries largely agree with the Sunnī ones in understanding the qur'anic accusation of *taḥrīf* as a corruption of meaning rather than a corruption of text. The overarching theme here is the stubbornness of the Jews. Aṭ-Ṭabarsī (died 1153), in his commentary *Majmaʿ al-Bayān*, is very straightforward about his understanding of the meaning of the word *taḥrīf* as "the alteration of a word's meaning." The question of whom the Qur'an is talking about, and whether the accusation should be leveraged against all Jews or just a section of them, also preoccupies the Shīʿī commentators. Aṭ-Ṭabarsī transmits three traditions in this regard. The first is that the Jews who committed *taḥrīf* are the Jewish scholars who twist certain prescriptions of the Torah in exchange for a bribe, legalizing certain things that are forbidden and forbidding certain things that are permitted. The second tradition suggests that the accusation concerns the seventy Jews who ascended Mount Sinai with Moses, heard God's commands to him, yet twisted what they had heard when they reported back to the people. In this tradition, the twisting (*taḥrīf*), says the commentator, was not of the entire Torah, but specifically about the instructions received by Moses and heard by the seventy. The third tradition reported by aṭ-Ṭabarsī is related to the "proofs of prophethood." In this accusation, Jews committed *taḥrīf* by withholding their knowledge of the occurrences in the Torah of clear evidence concerning the prophethood of Muhammad. All three of these traditions refer to Jews who, affirms aṭ-Ṭabarsī, receive God's instructions, are convinced of its meaning and truth, yet out of stubbornness "corrupt it [*yuḥarrifūnahu*] and interpret it [*yata'awwalūnahu*] against its [true] interpretation."

As we move closer to the contemporary period, commentators' main focus with regard to the *taḥrīf* verses becomes the proof of prophethood. Shīʿī commentator aṭ-Ṭaba'ṭabā'ī (died 1982) paints a gloomy picture of

Jews in Medina, who knew full well that their Scriptures contained pre-announcements of Muhammad as prophet, yet whose rabbis prohibited them from revealing these truths so that they would not be held to them. The commentator draws a parallel between Jewish denials of Muhammad's prophethood and their denial of Jesus of Nazareth as the awaited Messiah.

Rashīd Riḍa (died 1935), in his *Tafsīr al-Manār*, also focuses his critique on the Jews by discussing their geopolitical ambitions that he observed in his own time. In his exegesis of an-Nisā' 4:46, Riḍa argues that the Jews were quite happy with the Muslim conquests, given that the Arab victory over the Byzantines rid them of their archenemies under whose oppression they had been living. This is why, in his view, the Jews of Medina used trickery to pretend that they recognized Muhammad as prophet when they were with Muslims, but then denied his prophethood when they were among themselves. Riḍa warns that the Jews of his time also played this role to subvert Christianity in France and Spain and that they now had ambitions against the Ottomans in order to reestablish their kingdom in Jerusalem. He warns that if the Ottomans were not careful, the Jews would succeed in lighting the fires of chaos and conflict throughout the Middle East. He died before the establishment of the State of Israel in 1948, but described accurately the advance that Zionism was making in the region during his time.

In his exegesis of the *taḥrīf* verses of Sūrat an-Nisā' 4 and Sūrat al-Mā'ida 5, Riḍa refers to contemporary text-critical Jewish and Christian biblical scholarship, in particular source criticism. He moves beyond the traditional Muslim exegesis of the concept of *taḥrīf*, implying that his predecessors were not versed in the history of the biblical text and therefore were primarily aware of *taḥrīf al-ma'na* in the sense of misinterpretation. But now, he argues, it has become clear that Moses could not be the author of the present form of the Torah, since portions of it were clearly written after his death. He refers the reader back to his exegesis of āl-'Imrān 3:2, where he discussed more specifically a few points related to the history both of the Torah and of the Gospels. In addition to his questioning of the authorship of the Torah, based on Moses's death being mentioned in Deuteronomy, as well as on the affirmation that no prophet comparable to Moses would ever emerge again among the Israelites, Rashīd Riḍa mentions that there are numerous Babylonian words in the Torah and that this is evidence that it was written during or after the time of the exile. He refers to al-Mā'ida 5:14, "but they have forgotten part of what they were told to keep in mind," as qur'anic evidence that the Torah was lost early on and that only parts of it were recovered at the time of Ezra at the end of the Babylonian exile. He cites the writings of "some Europeans," to the effect that the language of the Pentateuch reflects multiple authors, as further evidence that Moses was not its author and that the books we currently have are not the same as the ones that the Qur'an refers to.

Riḍa then moves to a critique of the Gospels, arguing that their transmission was unreliable and that there is no agreement among Christians about the year in which each Gospel was written or about John's authorship of the fourth Gospel. He argues as well that, although the Torah was widespread among a great multitude of Jews when it was revealed, the Gospels were kept among only a few until the fourth century because Christians were a persecuted minority until the time of Emperor Constantine. The four Gospels as we know them, he claims, suddenly appeared only in the fourth century. He argues, furthermore, that the four books that Christians refer to as Gospels are not the same as the one referred to in the Qur'an, since Muhammad would have referred to the Gospels in the plural to please the Christians if he had believed that they were authentic. And since he was "illiterate" (*ummī*), he could have learned that Christians had forgotten parts of the Gospel ("they have forgotten part of what they were told to keep in mind") only through God's inspiration. Riḍa's logic is quite insular and circular here. From a critical historical perspective, it would make more sense, for instance, to argue that the Qur'an's reference to the Gospel always in the singular is a reflection of Muhammad never having met an orthodox form of Christianity and therefore having no idea that Christians had four Gospels. For Riḍa's argument to stand, on the other hand, one would have to presuppose the faith-based trust in the reliability of the Qur'an.

With Sayyid Quṭb (died 1966), the discussion of the *taḥrīf* verses takes a peculiarly anti-Jewish turn. Previous commentators had pointed out that the *taḥrīf* rhetoric of the Qur'an was primarily directed at the Jews, but now the qur'anic rhetoric is framed in a polemical tone inspired by twentieth-century Middle Eastern geopolitics. In his commentary on al-Baqara 2:75, he laments, "And the Muslim *umma* continues to struggle with the machinations and cunningness of the Jews, just as its ancestors did." He has strong words for Muslims in his days, particularly their leaders who assist the Jewish agenda knowingly or unknowingly, warning that the *umma* has failed to learn from the successes of its ancestors in Medina and will continue to suffer until it realizes that it needs to access again the tools offered by the Qur'an against the Jews. Quṭb's interest in the concept of *taḥrīf* has ceased to be primarily exegetical. The text of the Qur'an for him contains revolutionary guidance for today rather than pietistic reflections on the past. Al-Baqara 2:75 is less about how Jews treated their Scriptures during the time of Muhammad and more about their machinations against Muslims today. Just as they cunningly rejected Muhammad's prophethood by concealing the clear preannouncements about him found in their Torah, with the purpose of harming Muslims in Medina, they continue to act cunningly today as they seek the destruction of the Muslim *umma*.

In his comments on an-Nisā' 4:46, Sayyid Quṭb continues to be mostly obsessed with the Jews. As with other commentaries before, he is primarily disturbed with the latter half of the verse, where the Jews are represented as interacting insolently (*sū' adabihim*; lit., "their rudeness of manners") with Muhammad, "saying, 'We have heard, but we disobey,' and, 'Listen,' (adding the insult) 'May you not hear'—thus speaking abusively and implying that the [true] faith is false." Quṭb, based on the way that this verse reflects the Jews' address of Islam's prophet, argues against the traditional occasion of the revelation of Sūrat an-Nisā' cited by preceding commentators as being on the occasion of the visit of the Christian delegation from Najrān in the eighth year of the *hijra*. He argues that the Jews would never have dared to address him so insolently at such a late time, after he had demonstrated his might on the military stage. For such reasons, he prefers to consider this sūrah as having been revealed for the larger part in the early years of the *hijra* to Medina. Quṭb has a passing comment related to *taḥrīf* in the first part of the verse: "And it is likely that what is meant by this ['some distort the meaning of the (revealed) words'] is that they interpreted the words of the Torah differently from their original intent."

As we come to Sayyid Quṭb's exegesis of *taḥrīf* in al-Mā'ida 5:13, 41, we find an interesting paragraph on his view of previous Scriptures in his introductory section to the sūrah. He relates his comments first to verse 3: "Today I have perfected your faith for you and have shed my grace upon you and have chosen submission [Islam] to be your faith." And then he also cites in this connection verse 48 of the sūrah: "We sent you the book, setting forth the truth, confirming what is available of earlier revelations and with final authority over them. Judge between them in accordance with what God has sent down. Do not follow their whims, which deviate from the truth revealed to you." These two verses represent the hermeneutical key through which Quṭb understands the relationship of the Qur'an to previous revelations:

> The Scripture of this community [*umma*] is God's final Scripture to humanity; for it confirms what Scripture it had already received previously about true belief and understanding. However, given that it is the final Scripture, it has final authority over all that preceded it, and it is the final reference for the legislation that God commanded for his followers until the day of judgment. Therefore, what it confirms from previous legislation of the people of the book belongs to God's law. But what it abrogates has lost its status as divine legislation, even if it occurs in one of the previously revealed [*munazzala*] Scriptures.

It is clear from this passage that Sayyid Quṭb, largely in alignment with general consensus among Muslim scholars, does not ascribe inherent authority to the Bible. As positive a view of the Judeo-Christian Scriptures as some Muslim scholars may have, in the final analysis the Bible is authoritative only insofar as it agrees with the final revelation in the Qur'an.

In his exegesis of al-Mā'ida 5:13, Quṭb continues his virulent attack against the Jews, calling them all sorts of names and describing them with the vilest of attributes. He does the same, though to a lesser extent, in his description of the Christians. Both communities had received covenants from God, which they broke intentionally and for which reason they are now rejected until the day of judgment. But Quṭb also reads these qur'anic verses as a warning for the Muslim community and as a sort of threat that if they continue to break God's covenant—as he considers is the situation in his own days—they too will be rejected and cursed by God. That of course is the primary agenda that Quṭb set out to address in his commentary, as he invites Muslims everywhere to walk "in the shadow of the Qur'an" (the title of his commentary) in order to be renewed and brought back to the right path.

As he moves through the exegesis of Sūrat al-Mā'ida 5, Sayyid Quṭb moves to the heart of his commentary's purpose and to his entire life's mission as he reaches the pericope that begins with verse 41. Quṭb wants to see the emergence of a community that establishes God's law (Sharīʿa) as the law of the land. He has scathing criticism for Muslims in his days who have accepted international and European legal systems as the law of his country. In his comprehensive system, there are only two ways: either the way of faith for a community ruled by Islamic Sharīʿa or the way of *kufr* ("disbelief") and paganism, where a community lives in *jāhiliyya* ("ignorance") under laws made by human beings. Quṭb does not comment on the *taḥrīf* issue in reference to verse 41. What he cares about is for his Muslim contemporaries to recognize that Jews and Christians have broken their covenants, rejected the correct interpretation of their Scriptures, and then to realize that these two communities stand for them as a warning concerning the divine judgment that they will incur if they (continue to) do the same within Muslim societies.

A Survey of Taḥrīf in the Seventh to Fourteenth Centuries

Having surveyed the qur'anic commentary tradition, which represented primarily the internal instructions of the Qur'an for the Muslim community, we now come to the dialogical literature. These works were destined to be read both by Muslims for their instruction on how to address the people of the book as well as by non-Muslims as an apologetic and polemical narrative.

Seventh Century

The earliest recorded polemical/apologetic encounter between officials of Christianity and Islam after the time of Muhammad took place between Patriarch John of Sedreh and a Muslim official (probably ʿUmayr b. Saʿad al-Anṣārī), less than three decades after the *hijra* (around 644).[4] Although the discussion no doubt must have taken place in Arabic, the report of it through a letter written by a Christian was made in Syriac. Because of its early date, the letter is very important for our attempt to trace the origins of the accusation of *taḥrīf*. That it does not even make mention of the accusation should be noted. The Muslim prince's first question to the pa-

4. The exact date and personalities involved in this dialogue are the subject of controversy among scholars. Having examined the evidence, I align with the conclusions of Abdul Massih Saadi, "The Letter of John of Sedreh: A New Perspective on Nascent Islam," *Journal of the Assyrian Academic Society* 11.1 (1997): 68–84; P. Crone and M. Cook, *Hagarism: The Making of the Islamic World* (Cambridge: Cambridge University Press, 1977); and Sidney H. Griffith, "Disputes with Muslims in Syriac Christian Texts: From Patriarch John (d. 648) to Bar Hebraeus (d. 1286)," in *Religionsgespräche im Mittelalter*, ed. Bernard Lewis and Friedrich Niewöhner (Wiesbaden: Otto Harrassowitz, 1992), 251–73.

triarch on whether all Christians have and use the same Gospel is clearly intended merely as a steppingstone for his second question on the reason why Christians are divided, seeing that their Gospel is one. It contains no implication of *taḥrīf*.[5] After the patriarch explained that the problem lies not in the document itself but rather in the interpretation of it, the prince quickly moves on to theological issues that obviously seem to be of greater concern to him. In this context, the patriarch demonstrates that the detailed events of the life and ministry of Jesus had been announced by Moses and the prophets in the Old Testament. After the doctrinal issues, the prince leads the patriarch to territory that is more familiar to Islam: that of religious law.[6]

No precise quotations from the New Testament are given in this work. It is only implied that Christian doctrines are demonstrated by means of Old Testament passages, but even these are not quoted specifically. I draw three conclusions from the Muslim prince's threefold argument in the treatise. First, the prince's question about the uniqueness of the Gospel version implies that little knowledge exists at that point about the nature of the Gospels. And when further questions are asked, Greek and Syriac documents are used to reply, implying that no Arabic version of the Scriptures was yet in existence. It follows as well, therefore, that to assume the existence of doubt about the authenticity of the Bible and the presupposition of *taḥrīf* in the mind of the Muslim interlocutor at that point in time is an anachronism.

The second issue raised by the prince shows that the main tenets of Christology and the incarnation, with their implications for Islamic *Tawḥīd*, were in fact at the heart of the Muslim polemical concern of that early period. However, due to the complications resulting from the very scarce knowledge of the Bible and their inability to access the text in Greek and Syriac languages, even these doctrinal issues could not be discussed thoroughly as yet.

This leads our prince to his third argument in the discussion, where he tries to draw his Christian interlocutors onto more familiar ground: the law. This would have been a losing ground for Christians, and it is reflected in the dialogue, where the patriarch tries to show as much as possible that the laws that the Christian community follows are in line

5. F. Nau, "Un colloque du patriarche Jean avec l'émir des Agaréens et faits divers des années 712 à 716," *Journal asiatique* 11.5 (1915): 225–79 at 257.

6. Nau, "Un colloque," 260–62.

with the teaching of the Bible. In other words, Patriarch John is trying to escape the argument. This leads to an interesting observation. In both Muslim and Christian polemical/apologetic works surveyed between the eighth and the fourteenth centuries, the first seven chapters of Matthew's Gospel, containing the Sermon on the Mount (Matt 5–7) and the bulk of Jesus's teaching, represent more than a third of the Gospel citations that I collected from this literature. This is most strikingly represented in the retranslation and Islamization of these seven chapters by al-Qāsim ar-Rassī in his *Radd ʿala an-Naṣāra* surveyed in the previous chapter. Perhaps Christians highlighted these Gospel portions in an attempt to show that they had their own equivalent to Islamic Sharīʿa.

Eighth Century

The next literary record comes to us from the latter half of the eighth century, namely from the report written by Patriarch Timothy I about encounters he had at the court of Caliph al-Mahdī.[7] This work deals primarily with theological issues, and it is after the patriarch's long demonstration of the inapplicability of the Paraclete title to Muhammad (see chapter 9) that he reports the caliph's resort to the *taḥrīf* accusation, almost as a kind of refuge, for lack—it seems—of any further argumentative means.[8] Although the patriarch may have taken some liberties in organizing the caliph's questions and his elaborate answers in order to suit the didactic nature of his treatise, there is no reason to question this logical sequence. As already observed in the qur'anic commentary tradition, it seems to be in the matrix of this very sequence of arguments, where Christians rejected the preannouncement—and hence the legitimacy—of the Prophet of Islam, that the most robust and longstanding stalemate in the Muslim-Christian polemical discourse was born. The emergence of the argument at this point constitutes one of the earliest testimonies of Muslim-Christian encounter. But apart from a reference to the accusation here, and a second time near the end of the conversation,[9] Timothy

7. The Arabic version was edited by Hans Putman, *L'église et l'Islam sous Timothée I (780–823)* (Beirut: Librairie Orientale, 1975). The edition of the original Syriac version of the letter reporting the encounter can be found in Alphonse Mingana, "The Apology of Timothy the Patriarch before the Caliph Mahdi," *Woodbrooke Studies* 11 (1928): 1–162.

8. Putman, *L'église et l'Islam*, 24–25, stanzas 111–20.

9. Putman, *L'église et l'Islam*, 47, stanza 248.

does not report any extensive *taḥrīf* accusation on the caliph's part. The patriarch manages to dismiss the accusation essentially (but not solely) with a general methodological reply: "Where is that book that is free of corruption [*taḥrīf*] from which you have learned that we have corrupted our book? Bring it forth that we might see it and apply ourselves to it and abandon the corrupted book!"[10]

This reply of Timothy is important, because it indicates that he understood the accusation in its hardline sense of textual corruption, and thus that the term was being used also in this sense at that early stage. From this perspective, it is all the more intriguing that most of the subsequent authors until Ibn Ḥazm did not use the term in this sense, but in the sense of misinterpretation and misunderstanding. It would remain the task of Ibn Ḥazm and a few later authors to develop the argument and bring biblical testimonies to justify and strengthen it.

Ninth Century

The extent to which the Gospels were quoted in many of the Muslim writers of the ninth century, such as al-Qāsim b. Ibrāhīm ar-Rassī, 'Alī aṭ-Ṭabarī, Ibn Qutayba, al-Ya'qūbī, and the anonymous text attributed to 'Umar II, has already become quite clear from the preceding chapters. The positive perspective that these writers must have held on the Gospels is reflected quite clearly in the extent and in the kind of usage that they made of them.

The attitude reflected in ar-Rassī's *Radd*, for instance, tends toward respect for the text of the Gospels with, however, a reception of it on Islamic terms. It is important to point this out, since the treatise is one of the earliest polemical anti-Christian works recorded by a Muslim. This work is therefore also a good representative of the earliest Muslim attitude toward the Gospels. The problem, as ar-Rassī saw it, was not so much in the text itself as in its misguided interpretation by Christians. Ar-Rassī's approach to the biblical text was nevertheless ambiguous, and his attitude toward its integrity was dictated by his primary purpose of drawing Christians to Islam. This ambiguity begins to articulate itself when attention is paid to some of the premises underlying his exegetical method. David Thomas discerns three of these principal premises, two of which are of interest to us here.[11]

10. Putman, *L'église et l'Islam*, 26, stanza 125.

11. These are described in David R. Thomas, "The Bible in Early Muslim Anti-

First, ar-Rassī reproaches Christians for having an unsound theory of Gospel transmission. Christians, he claims, accuse Jews of having crucified Jesus and are suspicious of them in all things, yet they must regard them as trustworthy when it comes to recording the Gospels that are in their possession, since the Gospel writers were Jewish.[12] If the Gospels thus do not meet the criterion of sound transmission, how can Christians accept them? Though it is clearly biblical *isnād* ("line of transmission") that is under fire here, ar-Rassī nevertheless does not draw the conclusion of textual *taḥrīf*. We should therefore not be too swift in drawing it ourselves from his argument, since the treatise as a whole does not sanction such an interpretation. Second, ar-Rassī explains that the Gospel texts have been used for philosophically unsound purposes. Christians, he maintains, have used their texts to support doctrines acceptable to no other religion, or even to any heresy. He thus reclaims the right for other scholars—in this case Muslims—to recover for those texts their true meaning. And he invites Christians to review their understanding of their books in order to be led back to the right track.[13] In this latter premise, it is clearly *ta'wīl* ("interpretation") that is considered the problem with Christianity.

The accusation of *taḥrīf* in the treatise of al-Jāḥiẓ, which comes to us from the middle of the ninth century, should also be read with specific qualification. He measures the reliability and authenticity of the Bible by comparing it with the Qur'an. If something in it does not correspond with the qur'anic text, it follows that it is an error of transmission or translation. He jeers that the confusion of the Christians and the Jews comes from their inadequacy in making proper use of language, symbols, and translation techniques and their ignorance of matters pertaining to God: those things that can legitimately be said about God and those that are improper.[14] An error of transmission does in fact imply some notion of corruption, coming closer to the harder view of *taḥrīf*, except that the alteration is not intentional. Nevertheless, al-Jāḥiẓ was primarily a satirist. He made virtually no use of the Bible to sustain his accusation, and his voice therefore seems to have been virtually forgotten.

Christian Polemics," *Islam and Christian-Muslim Relations* 7 (1996): 33–34, as ar-Rassī's three "stages of exegesis."

12. Ar-Rassī, *Ar-Radd ʿala an-Naṣāra*, in Ignazio Di Matteo's "Confutazione contro I cristiani dello zaydita al-Qâsim b. Ibrâhîm," *Rivista degli Studi Orientali* 9 (1922): 319.

13. Ar-Rassī, *Radd*, 319–20.

14. Abū ʿUthmān ʿAmr b. Baḥr al-Jāḥiẓ, *Al-Mukhtār fī ar-Radd ʿala an-Naṣāra*, ed. Muhammad ʿAbdallāh Sharqāwī (Beirut: Dar al-Jil, 1991), 25–33.

ʿAlī aṭ-Ṭabarī's attitude toward *taḥrīf* did not lack in ambiguity either. In the introduction to his *Radd*, he mentions "contradictions" (*tanāquḍ*), "abominations" (*kabāʾir*), *taḥrīf*, and "corruption" (*fasād*). The Arabic text of the passage is not free from difficulties. However, by examining carefully both the context of his statements and the later development of these points in the treatise, it becomes clear that the author is talking about Christian *misinterpretation* of the biblical text, rather than about actual *textual* corruption. What his first sentence seems to be saying is not that these contradictions and abominations are found in the Gospel text, but in the interpretations made of the text in Christian creeds (*sharīʿat īmānihim*). As seen earlier, comparing the Christian creeds with the text of the Gospels was one of the favorite demonstrative tools of the Muslim theologians. The development of this argument can be found in the actual body of aṭ-Ṭabarī's *Radd* (pp. 136–38). It is clear there that aṭ-Ṭabarī's disagreement is with the content of the Nicene Creed (which he fully cites in the middle of p. 136), and he brings in testimonies against it from the Gospels in order to demonstrate its "corruption" (*fasāduhā*) and "the deceit of those who composed it" (*ghishsh man allafahā*).

In the final sentence of the introduction cited above, aṭ-Ṭabarī says that he will "explain, with God's help, the words that they have interpreted [*taʾawwalūhā*] against their [true] meanings, and the *taḥrīf* and corruption found in it." Again, what aṭ-Ṭabarī seems to be saying is not that the *taḥrīf* and corruption are found in the Gospel text, but rather he objects to the inadequate interpretation of the words found in it.[15] This representation of t*aḥrīf* does not yet carry in it the more developed accusation of textual corruption of later Muslim polemicists. Maurice Bouyges, who discovered the manuscript in 1931, did not seem to be aware of this point. He based his article on very sporadic extracts, which he had copied hastily from the Istanbul manuscript some time earlier. Thus, he was led to place the work's arguments among "the great mass of accusations that the most famous polemicists would develop, the accusation of *taḥrīf* being no exception: see folio 3r."[16] However, the clusters that he had of folio 3r

15. The difficulty in this sentence is the masculine relative suffix in *fīhi*. We cannot connect it with *al-Injīl*, for the two words are too far apart. The remaining option would be to understand *fīhi* as referring to an implied *taʾwīl*; that is, the *taḥrīf* and corruption are found in the "interpretation" of terms against their true meaning.

16. Maurice Bouyges, "Nos informations sur Aliy . . . at-Tabariy," *Mélanges de l'Université Saint Joseph* 28 (1949–50): 71 (my translation).

misrepresented the picture for him by reading *at-tanāquḍ wa al-kabā'ir al-latī fī al-Injīl . . . wa adhkur at-taḥrīf wa al-fasād.*

His inaccurate understanding of these incomplete statements is probably also the reason why, in an earlier article, Bouyges had thought that the copy of the manuscript was missing important sections at the end. He claims that "the reading stops abruptly, folio 45r, 9, before the program indicated in the opening pages was fulfilled."[17] Contrary to that assumption, however, a closer study of the full work yields evidence that aṭ-Ṭabarī did come almost to the end of the program he had set for himself in his introduction. He discusses the contradictions between the Christian creeds and the Scripture testimony in seven main points.[18] He discusses the main Christian sects and refutes their major arguments.[19] And he discusses and reinterprets the meanings of sonship, fatherhood, and incarnation, ending with a refutation of the Christian interpretation of such terms.[20] For the history of Muslim-Christian polemics, it is very important to come to terms with this issue of completeness of the manuscript or the lack of it. Otherwise, it might easily be supposed (as Bouyges and the text's editors do) that a fully developed *taḥrīf* argument actually was contained in the final missing section of the manuscript. We will examine further some more specific examples where aṭ-Ṭabarī hints at textual inconsistencies, without however pronouncing himself on *taḥrīf.*

In a second work bearing his name, entitled *Kitāb ad-Dīn wa ad-Dawla* (The Book of Religion and State), aṭ-Ṭabarī is also hesitant about accusing the Bible of *taḥrīf.* One can cite as an example of the author's attitude to the Judeo-Christian Scriptures the following passage, in which he argues for the authenticity of the qur'anic text:

> What can a man say against these miracles, while the Kur'ān mentions them and the Muslim community bears witness to their veracity, and all its members subscribe to their authenticity, and men and women converse about them? If, while they are contained in the Kur'ān, it is allowed to consider them as false and revile them, we will not believe

17. Maurice Bouyges, "Aliy Ibn Rabban at-Tabariy," *Der Islam* 22 (1935): 120 (my translation).

18. Roughly pp. 136–38 in his *Radd.*

19. Roughly pp. 138–39 in his *Radd.* Aṭ-Ṭabarī also discusses and refutes different theological positions of the Jacobites (*al-Ya'qūbiyya*) and the Nestorians and Melkites (*man qāla bi al-musākana wa al-ḥulūl wa al-ittiḥād*) in other parts of the work, such as pp. 128, 130, 131.

20. Roughly p. 139 until the end of his *Radd.*

> the adversaries who say that the Torah and the Gospel do not contain falsehood to which the eyewitnesses of events had deliberately shut their eyes. *If then this cannot be said about the Torah and the Gospel and their contemporaries, it is not allowed with regard to the Kur'ān and its holders.*[21]

Interestingly at this stage, the author argues only for the authenticity of the Scriptures of the people of the book as a safeguard for the Qur'an's authenticity. He takes for granted that it "cannot be said about the Torah and the Gospel" that they "contain falsehood," which may reflect the general understanding of his time. But it is obvious that aṭ-Ṭabarī would be willing to waive this understanding if it did not meet with a reciprocal attitude toward the Qur'an among the opponents of Islam.

Ibn Qutayba's and al-Ya'qūbī's approaches to the Gospels were furthermore in the same line as ar-Rassī's. They were happy to use the text as an authoritative source in their works of *tārīkh* and *fiqh*, as long as they could alter some of its Arabic wording that they found inappropriate from their Islamic perspective. But this was by no means always the case. Ibn Qutayba was quite clear about the high level of authority that he attributed to the Bible in his *Kitāb Ta'wīl Mukhtalif al-Ḥadīth*. Subscribing to the standard *Sunnī* attitude toward difficult issues within the authoritative texts of Islam, he addressed the following rebuke to those who intellectualized difficult traditions:

> We reply: "We do not conclude about his [God's) attributes anything other than what God's prophet concluded. And we do not reject what is right about him [simply] because it does not conform to our understandings and does not make sense in our opinion. But we believe in it without qualification or limitation, not applying that which has not been revealed to that which has been revealed. And we hope that this thinking and agreement will safeguard us and eliminate all speculation in the near future, God willing."[22]

This is an extremely important statement, especially since it comes right after he used a verse from Christ's Sermon on the Mount as a tes-

21. 'Alī aṭ-Ṭabarī, *The Book of Religion and Empire*, trans. Alphonse Mingana (Manchester: Manchester University Press, 1922), 38 (emphasis added).

22. Ibn Qutayba, *Kitāb Ta'wīl Mukhtalif al-Ḥadīth* (Cairo: n.p., 1908), 262–63.

timony to the reliability of a *ḥadīth* (see previous chapter). Ibn Qutayba plainly recognizes the divine inspiration of the Bible by stating that only what "has been revealed" can be used to interpret other parts of the revelation.

Tenth Century

From the tenth century come two influential figures: Abū al-Ḥasan Muhammad al-ʿĀmirī, a philosopher from central Asia, and the respected Basran jurist and theologian Abū Bakr Muhammad al-Bāqillānī. Neither entertains any suspicion of textual *taḥrīf* of the Bible.

Al-ʿĀmirī does, however, consider that Jews and Christians have failed to understand and interpret their Scriptures correctly. He attributes their inability to accept their books' prophecies on Muhammad to their priests' fear of losing their ecclesiastical positions. He mentions that there occurred a "corruption" (*taḥrīf*) of symbolic terms by means of "corrupt interpretations."[23] His accusation is therefore against the religious leaders of the Jews and the Christians who preferred to keep their positions of power rather than submit to the truth that would have been clear through a correct interpretation of their books. That is the same understanding of *taḥrīf* held by most of his contemporaries. Al-ʿĀmirī then proceeds to provide the *correct* interpretation of those verses.

Al-Bāqillānī is not concerned with the *taḥrīf* issue either. He does not mention it at all in the whole section of his *Kitāb at-Tamhīd* that deals with Christian doctrines. The only place where he mentions the word is in a section against the Jews.[24] But even there, *taḥrīf* is mentioned in connection with the transmission and translation of the words of Moses. It is not an intentional *taḥrīf* as will be implied in the typical later conspiracy theory. The accusation is part of al-Bāqillānī's rejection of the legitimacy of any scriptural translation, which is merely a typically Islamic concept. As a result, al-Bāqillānī freely uses biblical verses without doubting their authenticity.

23. Abū al-Ḥasan Muhammad al-ʿĀmirī, *Kitāb al-Iʿlām bi-Manāqib al-Islam* (On the Merits of Islam), ed. A. Ghorab (Cairo: Dār al-Kitāb al-ʿArabī, 1967), 202.

24. Abū Bakr Muhammad b. aṭ-Ṭayyib al-Bāqillānī, *Kitāb Tamhīd al-Awāʾil wa Talkhīṣ ad-Dalāʾil* (The Book of Establishment of First Principles and Summary of Proofs), ed. R. J. McCarthy (Beirut: Bibliothèque Orientale, 1957), 181 §307 line 4.

Eleventh Century

It is beginning only with the time of Ibn Ḥazm in the eleventh century that the *taḥrīf* argument became something of a starting point in the Islamic polemical discourse, however to varying degrees between one Muslim author and the other. Jewish-Arab philosopher and theologian Maimonides, in the twelfth century, prohibited the Jews from teaching the tenets of Judaism to Muslims, explaining his prohibition by Muslims not accepting the text of the Torah as divine. This may reflect the influence that Ibn Ḥazm's hardened views already began to play further east. It also must be as a consequence of such warnings that hardly any recorded Jewish apologetics in response to Islamic polemics have come down to us.[25] Presumably, the sociopolitical situation of the Christians of the time did not allow them to adopt such an attitude. My examination of the new era inaugurated by Ibn Ḥazm will focus on one specific issue in the Gospels—the genealogies of Jesus in Matthew 1:1–17 and Luke 3:23–38—in order to study the influence of Ibn Ḥazm's exegesis over Muslim scholars of ensuing centuries. His influence was phenomenal, and pursuing it through only two Bible portions does not do it justice, but this will have to do within the limitations of the present book.

Ibn Ḥazm

Ibn Ḥazm was an Andalusian poet, historian, jurist, philosopher, and theologian. He adopted the *Ẓāhirī* approach to all Islamic sciences, an extreme form of literalism that attempted to interpret the Qur'an, develop jurisprudence, and hold a theological discourse that relied exclusively on the qur'anic text with as little use as possible of the Ḥadīth. Born at Cordova in 994, he lived through the most tragic times of the history of Islam in Andalusia until his death in 1064. He witnessed the downfall of the last caliphs of Cordova, which resulted in the splitting up of al-Andalus into a multitude of smaller states under minor kings known as *mulūk aṭ-Ṭawā'if*, in the midst of great power struggles between Andalusians, Berbers, and Slavs. This situation of great instability was inviting for Christian monarchs in the north, who initiated the *Reconquista*, which eventually

25. On this issue, see Hava Lazarus-Yafeh, *Intertwined Worlds: Medieval Islam and Bible Criticism* (Princeton: Princeton University Press, 1992), esp. 7–8 and n8.

brought the downfall of Andalusian Muslim Spain.[26] In the East, the eleventh century marked also the beginning of the Crusades, which would eventually lead to the tragic degradation of Christian-Muslim relations, whose negative impact we are still reaping today.

Ibn Ḥazm's principal work that is of interest to us belongs to the genre of heresiography. With very narrow margins in his understanding of truth, which was a characteristic of the *Ẓāhirī* school, Ibn Ḥazm was as severe toward his non-*Ẓāhirī* coreligionists as he was toward non-Muslims. His *Kitāb al-Fiṣal fī al-Milal wa al-Ahwā' wa an-Niḥal* (Book of Sects) contains the most extensive treatment of biblical inconsistencies that we find in the whole of Muslim-Arabic literature, as well as the severest.[27] Hava Lazarus-Yafeh affirms about him:

> Given that in the West, in Muslim Spain, and especially in Cordova, literary contacts and translations, as well as disputes between members of different religions and sects, may have been even more common than in the Muslim East, it is not unlikely that Ibn Ḥazm of Cordova [died 1064] was the true founder of Muslim polemics against the Bible. He has been described by scholars as "the first scholarly critic of the Bible," or the one "who anticipated much of modern Bible criticism."[28]

Though the impressive extent to which the Bible was put to use by Muslim writers before Ibn Ḥazm shows how central the Judeo-Christian Scriptures already were in the Muslim-Christian discourse, it is certainly true that Ibn Ḥazm was the first to launch such an extensive attack against the Bible's internal consistency, based on the most extreme understanding of the *taḥrīf* concept. His polemical language is the most offensive and insulting that we can find in that genre. His attack is launched not only against the early church or some particular interpretation of the Scriptures, but is carried out against the whole Bible, the early as well as later disciples, the early creeds, and any issue related to Christianity that is not sanctioned by the Qur'an. A good example is what he has to say about Jesus's disciples. Unable to reconcile the New Testament twelve with the

26. For historical background, see E. Levi-Provençal, "Andalus," in *Encyclopaedia of Islam*, ed. P. Bearman et al., 2nd ed. (Leiden: Brill, 1954–2005), 1.486–96, esp. 494–95.

27. Abū Muhammad ʿAlī b. Aḥmad Ibn Ḥazm, *Kitāb al-Fiṣal fī al-Milal wa al-Ahwā' wa an-Niḥal* (Cairo: Al-Qahira Publishers, 1900).

28. Lazarus-Yafeh, *Intertwined Worlds*, 135.

ḥawāriyyīn of the Qur'an, he postulates a new theory not found elsewhere in the Islamic polemical tradition:

> And as for the *ḥawāriyyūn* [the qur'anic disciples of Christ] whom God has commended, these are the ones who are truly God's faithful, God's supporters (May he be honored and glorified!) through their love. And we do not know their names, for God (May he be exalted!) did not name them for us. Nevertheless, we affirm and confirm and reassure categorically that Peter the liar [*al-kadhdhāb*], Matthew the vile [*ash-sharṭī*], John who leads people to ignorance [*al-mustakhiff*], Judah and James the despised [*an-nadhīlayn*], Mark the transgressor [*al-fāsiq*], Luke the devious [*al-fājir*], and Paul the ignorant [*al-jāhil*] were certainly not of the *ḥawāriyyīn*. Rather, they were of the sect about whom God said: "and one sect blasphemed [*wa kafarat ṭā'ifatun*]."[29]

Strangely enough, though there is clear evidence that Ibn Ḥazm's work became known further East (in Egypt and Syria), his approach was never followed with the same intensity in the Islamic polemics that followed his time. Even though some authors adopted his aggressiveness, it is with him that the accusation of *taḥrīf* attained and stopped at its most extreme form. But even if most of the later writers did not subscribe fully to his views, it is clear that Islam was going to become from that point onward much more suspicious of the Judeo-Christian Scriptures and of these religious traditions in general. Roger Arnaldez describes Ibn Ḥazm's approach to the thinking of his opponents in the following words:

> Starting from the qur'anic principle that one may not question God, he regards philosophical and theological speculation as no more than the expression of the vain curiosity of a disobedient human spirit. Thus, from the beginning he has no sympathy with the basic steps which form the various points at issue. This is why his sole aim is to trap his interlocutors by means of his dialectic, to make them contradict themselves by processes which are merely splitting hairs over verbal expressions or disproving the validity of their ideas by confronting them with facts of experience which are striking rather than convincing.[30]

29. Ibn Ḥazm, *Kitāb al-Fiṣal fī al-Milal*, 2.38–39.

30. Roger Arnaldez, "Ibn Ḥazm," in *Encyclopaedia of Islam*, ed. P. Bearman et al., 2nd ed. (Leiden: Brill, 1954–2005), 3.790–99 esp. 796.

Ibn Ḥazm starts to deal with the issue of *taḥrīf* at the beginning of a section entitled "Reference to the Contradictions in the Four Gospels, and the Clear Lies Present in Them."[31] He obviously had a complete biblical text in his possession and did careful textual work on it, citing from it extensively in order to demonstrate its unreliability. Thus, he begins by citing the whole of Matthew 1:1–17, preserving the full Matthean genealogy name by name. The critic's first claim is that the Matthean genealogy is not consistent with its equivalents in the *Tawrāt* ("Torah") and "the other books of the Jews that they regard as highly as the *Tawrāt*, which are the book of *Malākhīm* [1–2 Kings] and the book of *Dabrāhayāmīm*[32] [1–2 Chronicles]." The inconsistencies that he draws are of two types, either corruptions in the form of the names or omissions of names in the chain. Three examples are given of the first type:[33]

> Matthew [1:3] reads *Tārikh* son of *Yahūdhā*, while the Torah [Gen 46:12 and 1 Chr 2:4] has *Zāriḥ* son of *Yahūdhā*.
>
> Matthew [1:8] reads *Aḥazyāhū* son of *Hūrām*, while in the books of the Jews [1 Chr 3:11], we read *Aḥazyā* son of *Yūrām*.
>
> Matthew [1:9] reads *Aḥazyāhū* son of *Aḥāz* son of *Yūthām*, while in the books of the Jews [1 Chr 3:12–13] *Ḥezeqyā* son of *Aḥāz* son of *Yūthām*.

One further example of inconsistency of the omission type is given, while a last one containing both, omission and corruption, is given:

> Matthew [1:9] reads *Yūthām* son of *Aḥazyāhū*, while the books of the Jews [1 Chr 3:11–12] have *Yūthām* son of *ʿAzaryā* son of *Amaṣyā* son of *Ash* son of *Aḥazyā*. Thus, Ibn Ḥazm claims, Matthew has omitted three fathers in between the ones he mentions.
>
> Matthew [1:10–11] reads *Naḥalyā* son of *Yūshyāhū* son of *Amūn*, while in the book of the Jews [1 Chr 3:14–16], we read: *Naḥanyā* son of *Elyāqīm* son of *Mūshyā* son of *Amūz*. Here, the author claims, Matthew has omitted one father and given a corrupt form of some of the names.

31. Ibn Ḥazm, *Kitāb al-Fiṣal fī al-Milal*, 2.10.

32. The edition reads *wabrāhayāmīm*, but this must be either a copyist's or the editor's mistake, as Ibn Ḥazm simply uses an Arabic transliteration of the Hebrew name.

33. These are found in Ibn Ḥazm, *Kitāb al-Fiṣal fī al-Milal*, 2.11–12.

Though Ibn Ḥazm is outraged enough by these inconsistencies and wonders how such flagrant lies can all be attributed to supposedly inerrant prophets (*maʿṣūmīn*), there is a further point that he finds even more impossible to bear—that Matthew claims he is presenting Jesus's genealogy and ends up giving Joseph's, who was only the caretaker of Jesus son of Mary. This earns the evangelist the insults "urinating goat" and "dirty liar."[34] Ibn Ḥazm points out that while Muslims, most Christians, and even some Jews hold that Jesus was the son of Mary without the intervention of Joseph, one section of the Jews claims that Jesus was Joseph's son. Thus, Matthew was serving a Jewish purpose by recording this genealogy.

Ibn Ḥazm dwells further on Matthew 1:17, which claims that there were fourteen generations from Abraham to David, fourteen from David to the Babylonian exile, and fourteen from the exile to Jesus. He points out that Matthew's calculations do not add up. Furthermore, in his own version of the quotation, Ibn Ḥazm adds at the end of 1:17: "Thus, the total generations [*mawālīd*] from Abraham to Christ are forty-two generations."[35]

In a final section on the genealogies, Ibn Ḥazm brings in Luke's version (3:23–38) and compares it with Matthew's. He notes the differences between the two Gospels in the section from Joseph back to David: where Matthew traces Joseph back to Solomon, Luke traces him back to another of David's sons, Nathan. Apparently, Ibn Ḥazm heard of two Christian responses to this challenge. The first explained that one of the genealogies was the natural physical one, while the other was an adoptive genealogy, meaning that it referred Joseph back to the deceased husband of his natural mother who had left her without children. This was according to Jewish custom, where the firstborn of the stepfather was considered to be the son of the deceased. But Ibn Ḥazm rejects this interpretation, saying that no evidence can be brought to support it. Indeed, it cannot even be said which of the two genealogies was the natural one and which was the adoptive one, he affirms. The second Christian argument that Ibn Ḥazm heard is that Luke referred to his genealogy as that which "was thought" (cf. Luke 3:23), but was not Joseph's actual descent. But, Ibn Ḥazm argues, if this is accepted as the explanation to the inconsistencies from Joseph to David, then it should also apply to David's descent from Abraham and to Abraham's descent from Adam. But it would be absurd to pretend that

34. Ibn Ḥazm, *Kitāb al-Fiṣal fī al-Milal*, 2.12.

35. Ibn Ḥazm, *Kitāb al-Fiṣal fī al-Milal*, 2.11.

Luke was putting in doubt all of this genealogy. To Ibn Ḥazm, the conclusion is clear; one of the two Gospel writers is lying. But he prefers yet another conclusion: "Both genealogies are lies, and hence both accursed men [Matthew and Luke] are lying."[36]

Abū al-Maʿālī al-Juwaynī

Another central figure of the eleventh century was Abū al-Maʿālī al-Juwaynī, a man educated in the *kalām* method of famous theologian Abū al-Ḥasan al-Asʿarī. For four years beginning in 1058, he taught at Mecca and Medina, where he acquired the honorific title *Imām al-Ḥaramayn* ("imām of the two great mosques"). His work was mainly in the areas of jurisprudence (*fiqh*) and dialectic theology (*kalām*). In his polemical work entitled *Shifāʾ al-Ghalīl fī Bayān mā Waqaʿa fī at-Tawrāt wa al-Injīl min at-Tabdīl* (Healing the Exaggerations by Revealing the Alterations That Have Made Their Way into the Torah and the Gospel),[37] al-Juwaynī approaches the Gospel genealogies with a mark of skepticism similar to Ibn Ḥazm. He begins by spelling out the complete Matthean genealogy, pointing out that Matthew's counting error of thrice fourteen generations in 1:17 does not properly reflect the actual enumeration that precedes it. To this remark already encountered in Ibn Ḥazm, al-Juwaynī brings one Christian defensive argument, which differs from the two found in his predecessor. Al-Juwaynī heard some Christians claim that Matthew omitted mentioning the names of certain fathers because of their sinfulness. A further absurdity that al-Juwaynī points out is that Matthew should include in his count of Joseph's fathers Joseph and Jesus themselves, for he says "from the exile to Jesus, fourteen generations."[38]

After this, al-Juwaynī cites the whole Lukan genealogy and points out the inconsistencies between the two. Al-Juwaynī cites both genealogies from Joseph backward, while Matthew began his genealogy with

36. Ibn Ḥazm, *Kitāb al-Fiṣal fī al-Milal*, 2.14–15 (misspelled names are due either to Ibn Ḥazm himself or to the Arabic translation he was using).

37. Michel Allard, the editor of the work, thinks it may have been written in Baghdād when al-Juwaynī took refuge there before 1058. See the introduction to his edition of Abū al-Maʿālī ʿAbd al-Malik b. ʿAbdallāh al-Juwaynī, *Textes apologétiques de Ǧuwainī (m. 478/1085): Shifāʾ al-Ġalīl fī l-Tabdīl; Lumaʿ fī Qawāʿid Ahl al-Sunna*, ed./trans. M. Allard (Beirut: Dar El-Machreq, 1968), 11.

38. Al-Juwaynī, *Shifāʾ al-Ghalīl*, 59–63.

Abraham down to the time of Jesus. This suggests that al-Juwaynī drew up a list of the two genealogies side by side in order to compare the names in detail. Here again, the author heard of a Christian reply that argues that each of the forefathers had two synonymous names, one of which each of the evangelists made use of. Al-Juwaynī complains that this argument is so ridiculous that he refuses to refute it, for there is no evidence of such a thing in any of the books of the ancients or in any other history.[39]

Despite al-Juwaynī's approach to the genealogies being similar to the one that we encountered in Ibn Ḥazm, it seems certain, on the basis of the different Gospel version used and on the basis of the differences in the detail of the arguments, that his is an independent tradition from that of his predecessor. This is reinforced by both authors being close contemporaries but living in different parts of the world. It is quite possible that they were influenced by some more general trend of argumentation that was occupying an increasingly important place in Muslim polemics, or that they had an earlier common source that has not yet come to light. Alternatively, we could assume that the influence of Ibn Ḥazm's new approach to biblical criticism had already traveled to Baghdād via North Africa by the end of the first half of the eleventh century and that al-Juwaynī came under its influence during his stay there in the decade of the 1050s.

Thirteenth Century

Shihāb ad-Dīn al-Qarāfī grew up in al-Qarāfa in Old Cairo. He acquired a solid reputation as the greatest Mālikī legal theoretician of the thirteenth century in Egypt, attracting students of all legal schools to study jurisprudence with him. Theologically, he adhered to the doctrine of al-Ashʿarī. His polemical work against Christianity, *al-Ajwiba al-Fākhira ʿan al-Asʾila al-Fājira* (Glorious Answers to Brazen Questions), is one of the most verbose in the genre.[40] After drawing a derogatory caricature of the Christianity of his day, he begins to refute a polemical letter written by a Christian against Islam, which had come to his attention.

39. Al-Juwaynī, *Shifāʾ al-Ghalīl*, 63–67.

40. Shihāb ad-Dīn al-Qarāfī, *Al-Ajwiba al-Fākhira ʿan al-Asʾila al-Fājira*, ed. Bakr Zakī ʿAwaḍ (Cairo: Wehbeh Publishers, 1987).

In his refutation of the sixth argument, al-Qarāfī enumerates fifteen contradictions that he finds in the Gospels.[41] The Christian *su'āl* ("question or claim") was that according to several qur'anic verses, Muslims were obliged to accept the honesty of the *Ḥawāriyyīn* ("Christ's disciples") and the authority of the Gospels. Accepting the authority of both the early disciples and the original *Injīl*, al-Qarāfī sets out to demonstrate that the guilt of *taḥrīf* falls on the later transmitters and that the Gospels in existence in his own days are not the same as the Gospel (*Injīl* singular) vouchsafed by the Qur'an. As a result of this perspective, there is a difference between his conclusion and that of Ibn Ḥazm. Essentially, whereas Ibn Ḥazm concluded from textual inconsistencies that the evangelists were liars and had written corrupt and altered Gospels, al-Qarāfī concludes that the disciples were "innocent of them" (*tabarra'a*). He demonstrates this by pointing out the contradictions in existence in the Gospels of his day.

The first contradiction that al-Qarāfī points out is the difference in the number of ancestors given by Matthew and by Luke. While Matthew[42] states that there were forty-two generations between Joseph and Abraham, al-Qarāfī claims that Luke counts fifty-four.[43] Since the genealogy given in Matthew actually gives thirty-nine generations between Joseph and Abraham, it is obvious that rather than counting the actual names, al-Qarāfī ends up with forty-two by relying on Matthew 1:17, which summarizes the genealogy as thrice fourteen. Al-Qarāfī never enumerates the full genealogy, either in Matthew or in Luke. Earlier on though, after enumerating all the names, Ibn Ḥazm quotes Matthew 1:17 as though the total of forty-two was part of the verse: "Thus from Abraham to David, there were fourteen fathers, and from David to the time of the exile, fourteen fathers, and from the time of the exile to Christ, fourteen fathers. Hence the total of generations from Abraham to Christ was forty-two generations."[44]

The notion of the forty-two in total was also known to the historian al-Ya'qūbī, who summarized Matthew 1:1–17 with the following words: "Jesus son of David son of Abraham, all the way down until he reaches Joseph son of *Ya'qūb* son of *Māthan*, after forty-two fathers."[45]

41. This whole section (the sixth argument) is found in al-Qarāfī, *Al-Ajwiba al-Fākhira*, 98–123.

42. Al-Qarāfī wrongly attributes this to John.

43. Al-Qarāfī, *Al-Ajwiba al-Fākhira*, 110.

44. Ibn Ḥazm, *Kitāb al-Fiṣal fī al-Milal*, 2.11.

45. Al-Ya'qūbī (Aḥmad b. Abī Ya'qūb), *Tārīkh*, ed. M. T. Houtsma (Leiden: Brill, 1883), 1.75.

It does not seem impossible that al-Qarāfī knew of Ibn Ḥazm's *Kitāb al-Fiṣal fī al-Milal* and was using it for his treatment of these passages. In this passage both men also use derivatives of the verb root WLD for "generations": Ibn Ḥazm uses forty-two *mawlūdan* (lit., "born ones") while al-Qarāfī uses *wilādatan* ("births"). On the other hand, Ibn Qutayba used *qarnan* ("centuries"), al-Yaʿqūbī used *aban* ("fathers"), and al-Juwaynī used *jīlan* ("generations") in Matthew 1:17. But it is also possible that they were simply using a similar version of the Gospel text.

Al-Qarāfī makes a second reference to the Gospel genealogies in his exposition of the eighth contradiction in the Gospels.[46] Here he raises two objections. First, while Matthew asserts that the name of Joseph's father was *Yaʿqūb* (1:16), Luke refers to him as *Hāl* (3:23). Second, al-Qarāfī wonders how Jesus could have thought for thirty years that he was the son of Joseph, while everyone, including the Jews, knew that Jesus was born without a father. Al-Qarāfī is reading the verb *ẓanna* ("thought") in the active voice (*yaẓunnu*) rather than the passive as it should be read (*yuẓannu*: "it was thought"). He is the first to introduce this confusion, which of course is possible only in Arabic. And the reason why he believes that the virgin birth was well known and widespread must be because of the qur'anic claim that the Jews accused Mary of adultery (see an-Nisā' 4:156 and Maryam 19:37), rather than from any evidence within the Gospel text. Here again in Matthew 1:16 there is a special correspondence between Ibn Ḥazm's version and that of al-Qarāfī. They are the only two authors that mention that Joseph was Mary's "fiancé" (*khaṭīb*). Otherwise, al-Yaʿqūbī mentions that he was her husband (*baʿl*), while al-Juwaynī did not mention anything.

The paradox of al-Qarāfī's approach to the Gospels is that while imitating the usage of the genealogies by early Muslim polemicists, such as ar-Rassī and aṭ-Ṭabarī, in order to demonstrate the purely human descent of Christ, al-Qarāfī nevertheless upholds the accusation of textual *taḥrīf* of the later polemicists since the time of Ibn Ḥazm. The earlier trend necessarily invested the Gospels with some degree of authority and authenticity, while the later one divested it totally of any usefulness. Possibly due to the long polemical tradition before him of which he was aware, and the sheer length of his own treatise, al-Qarāfī fell into this inconsistency. He simply applied to his bow every possible arrow at hand, so long as it discredited Christianity to the advantage of Islam.

46. Al-Qarāfī, *Al-Ajwiba al-Fākhira*, 114.

Fourteenth Century

In the same line as the post-eleventh-century authors, our last author, Ḥanbalī jurist of Damascus, Shams ad-Dīn Muhammad b. Abī Bakr Ibn Qayyim al-Jawziyya, also deals with the Gospel genealogies as part of his treatment of the contradictions that he finds in the Gospels. Although he begins by drawing attention to the inconsistency between the accounts of Matthew and Luke, his principal argument is one already encountered in Ibn Ḥazm—namely that Jesus was attributed a human father, while everyone knows that he was born of Mary without the intervention of a human father. Ibn Qayyim al-Jawziyya concludes somewhat cynically: "Having [claimed] that he was a perfect God, they made him into the Son of God, and then they made him into the son of Joseph the carpenter."[47] Ibn Qayyim al-Jawziyya's final conclusion on the matter is that there necessarily occurred a corruption in the text and that such an error could not possibly have originated from God.

Additional Muslim Accusations of Textual Corruption

To supplement this historical survey focusing exclusively on the genealogical passages, I present a few other favorites used by Muslim theologians in order to discredit the biblical text. The reader will thus get a sense of the sort of passages that lent themselves to the *taḥrīf* argument. First, we return to the earlier period, before the accusation of textual *taḥrīf* (*taḥrīf al-lafẓ*) had become widespread, in order to examine some of the forerunners of this hardened position.

The Angel's Annunciation to Joseph

In his *Radd ʿala an-Naṣāra*, aṭ-Ṭabarī collated some Gospel verses together and noticed a few elements that did not correspond, without however pronouncing himself as yet about textual corruption. One example is his comparison of Matthew 1:20, where the angel announces to Joseph

47. Shams ad-Dīn Muhammad b. Abī Bakr Ibn Qayyim al-Jawziyya, *Hidāyat al-Ḥayāra fī Ajwibat al-Yahūd wa an-Naṣāra*, ed. Aḥmad Ḥijāzī as-Saqā (Cairo: al-Maktaba al-Qayyima, 1980), 215.

that the child who will be born from Mary is from the Holy Spirit, with the Holy Spirit's descent at Jesus's baptism. He wonders: "If Christ himself was [born of the Holy Spirit] as the angel said, what is the meaning of the Holy Spirit's descent upon him for a second time?" Aṭ-Ṭabarī makes a further comment about the angel's annunciation to Joseph, noting that since Joseph received the visitation of an angel, he should have been called a prophet in the Gospels, which is not the case. All of these, he sees as suspicious.[48]

Jesus's Brothers and Sisters

Another suspicious element from the Gospels is brought up in a work edited by Dutch scholar Floris Sepmeijer, who compiled Ibn Ayyūb's *Letter to His Brother ʿAlī* by collating portions of the letter preserved in Ibn Taymiyya with others preserved in the work of a certain Naṣr b. Yaḥya (who lived sometime between the end of the eleventh and the beginning of the thirteenth century). The author of this material, however, is more likely to have been Naṣr b. Yaḥya himself rather than the genuine Ibn Ayyūb. That he advances the theory that Christians cannot agree on whether Mary had any biological children after Jesus raises some questions about the integrity of the biblical text. He introduces the section with the following statement containing the word *taḥrīf*, together with several of its synonyms: "And then you say that the Gospels that are in your hand were neither transformed [*lam tubaddal*] nor altered [*lam tuḥarraf*], nor was anything in them changed [*ghuyyira*], nor was anything added [*zīda*] or subtracted [*nuqqiṣa*]."

The commentary on the Gospels (*tafsīr al-Anājīl*), he notes, ascribes four brothers and three sisters to Jesus. Hence, based on the Matthean statement that Joseph did not have marital relations with Mary "until she gave birth to her first son" (Matt 1:24–25), some Christians declared that she did bear other children after Jesus. Further, the text reads, others attribute the children to Joseph's marriage to another wife, who was also called Mary. So far, it is difficult to see how our critic could draw implications of *taḥrīf* from these elements. However, he then recounts the story of a

48. ʿAlī b. Sahl Rabbān aṭ-Ṭabarī, *Kitāb ar-Radd ʿala an-Naṣāra*, in I. A. Khalifé and W. Kutsch's "Ar-radd ʿala-n-nasārā," *Mélanges de l'Université Saint Joseph* 36.4 (1959): 115–48 at 142.

boy called *yawānīs* (who turns out to be the famous church father John Chrysostom). This man, he narrates, asserted that it was impossible for the body that bore the Savior to have borne any other body. At that point, an icon of Mary hanging on a wall before the assembly spoke and affirmed: "You have spoken rightly, O golden mouthed!" People then stopped arguing about the issue and accepted the icon's statement.[49]

What seems to be bothering Ibn Yaḥya here is, that instead of reading and accepting the plain meaning of the Gospels, Christians accept the interpretation made of it by a child and confirmed by an image—in itself repulsive to Muslims. The accusation here again may be understood as that of erroneous *ta'wīl* ("interpretation"). This also means that such things as *tabdīl*, *taḥrīf*, *taghyīr*, *ziyāda*, and *tanqīṣ*—which he used in his introductory statement—may perhaps sometimes be understood by Muslim theologians to occur as a result of misinterpretation rather than of textual corruption. This is an important observation, with the consequence that it should not immediately be assumed that every occurrence of the word *taḥrīf*, or one of its synonyms, implies textual corruption.

The Episode of the Magi

Another element that ʿAlī aṭ-Ṭabarī sees as inappropriate in Matthew's birth narrative is the episode with the Magi (Matt 2:1–12), which he roughly paraphrases. In fact, the author seems to doubt the historicity of the event altogether, both from a plain historical perspective and from a theological point of view. Historically, he affirms that nothing confirms the event in the records of the Magi. Theologically, if the narrative were true, then the Magi would need to be considered prophets as well, but aṭ-Ṭabarī's view is that they receive their inspiration from the devil. Furthermore, prophecy would have to be inspired by the stars, and that is not acceptable either. Aṭ-Ṭabarī concludes: "If none of these options is a possibility, then the account is false [*al-khabar idhan bāṭilun*]."[50]

49. Floris Sepmeijer, "Een weerlegging van het Christendom uit de 10e eeuw: De brief van al-Hasan b. Ayyub aan zijn broer ʿAli," PhD thesis, Vrije Universiteit Amsterdam (Kampen: van den Berg, 1985), 162. This citation comes, not from Ibn Taymiyya, but from reconstituted segments that Sepmeijer says are part of Ibn Ayyūb's *Risāla* preserved in the work of Naṣr b. Yaḥya al-Mutaṭabbib, *An-Naṣīḥa al-īmāniyya fī Faḍīḥat al-Milla an-Naṣrāniyya.*

50. Aṭ-Ṭabarī, *Radd*, 142.

Revelations to Joseph

In the same way, aṭ-Ṭabarī is suspicious of Matthew 2:13–14, where it is said that an angel appeared to Joseph. If Joseph had received a revelation (*waḥiy*), aṭ-Ṭabarī notes, then the Gospels should have called him a prophet, which they don't. I note that the author's citation reads that an angel "appeared" (*tarā'a*) to Joseph and "commanded" him, with no mention of dream. Had he known that the canonical text mentioned "in a dream," this would probably have resolved the problem for him.[51]

John the Baptist's Testimony about Jesus

Further, in a passage attributed to John's Gospel, Naṣr b. Yaḥya quotes John the Baptist's announcement of Jesus in a version somewhat closer to the Synoptic text. After the opening Johannine statement, the Baptist's words are in fact closest to Luke 3:16–17, where he declares that he is "unworthy to untie the thong of his [Christ's] sandals." In Matthew, John declares that he is "unworthy to *carry* his sandals." The final statement, however, is again Johannine. The reading is as follows:

> Here is the Lamb of God who has borne the sins of the world [John 1:29]. And he is the one of whom I said that he comes after me, and that he is more powerful than I, and that *I am not worthy to untie the thong of his sandals* [Luke 3:16]. He is the one in whose hand is the winnowing fork, and he clears his threshing floor, gathering the wheat into his granary and burning the chaff with unquenchable fire. *And he is the one of whom I said that he comes before me* [*mutaqaddim lī*; Syriac Peshitta reads *qadmāy men*[*i*]] [John 1:30].

Based on his assumption that the passage is Johannine, the author alleges that Matthew and Luke contradicted (*khālafa*) these words and that Mark omitted them altogether. In fact, Mark 1:7–8 also preserves the account with wording very close to that of Luke. Also, on the basis that the passage is Johannine, the author again charges that the Gospel text

51. Aṭ-Ṭabarī, *Radd*, 141–42. Compare aṭ-Ṭabarī's interpretation of these verses with those of ar-Rassī and al-Ya'qūbī by referring to the previous chapter in the section on the Islamization of the Gospel text.

was altered, since he alleges that Matthew records different claims from John the Baptist. Here he cites Matthew 3:14, which is indeed found only in Matthew. To top it all, the author cannot understand how, after John the Baptist gave all of these testimonies, he later sent some of his disciples to ask Jesus about his identity (Matt 11:2–3). What the confused accusations indicate is that, unlike the authentic Ibn Ayyūb, Naṣr b. Yaḥya was not in fact working on an actual text of the Gospels, but was instead repeating the elements of an argument of *taḥrīf* that he had in front of him.

Al-Qarāfī seems to take over all of this argumentation directly from Naṣr b. Yaḥya, but reorganizing his confused citations. In his "seventh contradiction" (*tanāquḍ*), al-Qarāfī begins by citing John 1:29–30 (the Baptist's testimony about Jesus as the Lamb of God), followed by Matthew 3:14 (the Baptist's initial refusal to baptize Jesus), and ending with Matthew 11:2–3 (the Baptist's inquiry from prison about Jesus's identity). He concludes, like his source, that all these accounts are contradictory. Furthermore, he repeats his predecessor's allegation that Mark remained silent about the whole issue.[52] This clear connection between both authors, as well as the developed argument of *taḥrīf* in the text that Sepmeijer reports, is a further indication that the earlier Ibn Ayyūb is unlikely to be the author of those passages of the *Risāla* preserved in Ibn Yaḥya, but that these must rather originate from later, probably from Naṣr's own hand sometime between the end of the eleventh and the thirteenth centuries. In addition, the Baptist's inquiry about Christ's identity was cited in the genuine aṭ-Ṭabarī's *Radd* without any mention of *taḥrīf*, but only to demonstrate Christ's apostleship through the answer that he sent back to the inquirer (see chapter 5). There, the citation was attributed to Luke 7:19, and the argument taken over exactly as is in a passage of Ibn Ayyūb's *Risāla* preserved in Ibn Taymiyya, without any mention of *taḥrīf*.

Temptation of Jesus

Ibn Ḥazm is the first of our Muslim authors who raises the accusation of *taḥrīf* on the basis of the Gospel accounts of Christ's temptation (Matt 4:1–11 and Luke 4:1–12). In accordance with his usual method, he sets the accounts of Matthew and Luke in parallel, so that he might compare them and point out any discrepancies and differences between them. The first

52. Al-Qarāfī, *Al-Ajwiba al-Fākhira*, 113–14.

objection that Ibn Ḥazm raises against the legitimacy of the account is Christ being repeatedly led by the devil from place to place (a high mountain, the edge of the temple, etc.). The author postulates two possibilities: "Either he [the devil] was leading him, and he [Christ] was being led to him in submission and obedience . . . or he was leading him by force."

Ibn Ḥazm finds both options absolutely unacceptable with reference to prophets: "So how much more [with reference to] a god or the son of a god?!" he exclaims. The first possibility—that Christ obeyed the devil—would place Jesus "in a very vile position" (*manzilatin radhīlatin jiddan*), and the second—that Christ was being led by force—is the position of those who are demon possessed.

Second, Ibn Ḥazm claims that even the devil himself would not have such arrogance as to request of "his creator," "his Lord," or "he who possesses the Spirit of the divine," to bow, worship, and submit to him.

The third objection raised by Ibn Ḥazm is how the devil should offer the riches of the world to "him who is Lord, creator, and master of the world, and [even] his own master and our God and his God." This, Ibn Ḥazm claims, calls to mind the popular proverb that states: "He offered him a morsel from his own bread!"

Then Ibn Ḥazm anticipates an objection that some Christians might make to his attacks, on the basis of their dual-nature doctrine. They may claim that, in this episode, the devil was actually addressing the humanity of Christ. Nevertheless, Ibn Ḥazm objects that Christians still claim divinity for Christ because of the union of both natures in him. This would imply that the devil was addressing only half of Christ, offering him riches and taking him here and there, which in itself is impossible. But furthermore, Ibn Ḥazm's claim that the devil addressed Jesus with the words, "If you are the Son of God," proves—on the Christians' own terms—that he was actually addressing the divine in him.[53]

It is interesting that Ibn Ḥazm should make use here of an idea of Christian diaphysite provenance, where the two titles "Son of God" and "son of man" found in the Gospels were sometimes seen as references to the divine Son (Christ's divinity) and the son of Mary (Christ's humanity) respectively. However, even the Church of the East, which inherited the thinking of Theodore of Mopsuestia, refused to speak of "two Sons" in the one Christ. Rather, the insistence on "one Son" was an important expression that this church used as a "guarantee of the union" between

53. Ibn Ḥazm, *Kitāb al-Fiṣal fī al-Milal*, 2.16–17.

God and man in Christ. Nevertheless, that this statement should be found in Ibn Ḥazm is a further indication of the man's thorough knowledge of Christianity, Christians, and their Scriptures.

To conclude, in his exegesis of this passage, it is clear that Ibn Ḥazm continues to launch against Christianity a double and circular attack. On the one hand, he demonstrates that their Scriptures are totally worthless because of textual contradictions and inconsistencies within them, and on the other he also refutes any arguments and objections that Christians might raise, assuming that their Scriptures had not been corrupted.

A Prophet's Reward

Matthew 10:41 ("the one who receives a prophet in the name of a prophet will be rewarded with the same reward as the prophet") was used by aṭ-Ṭabarī and Ibn Ayyūb in order to demonstrate Christ's prophetic identity as opposed to a divine one. To make the verse acceptable to the Islamic mind, they used a modified text, which stated that "the one who receives a prophet in the name of a prophet" would "receive the reward of *one who has received the prophet*." This is somewhat different from the canonical reading, which seems to imply that both the prophet and his receiver will be rewarded in the same way. It is according to this canonical version that Ibn Ḥazm cites the passage. And that he derives from it an additional argument of *taḥrīf* shows how incompatible with mainstream Islamic thinking the verse is. He argues as follows: "If everyone who followed a prophet received the reward of a prophet, believers [*ahl al-īmān*] would all be equal in the afterlife [*al-ākhira*], none favored by God (May he be exalted!) above any other. And it is known that this is necessarily a lie [*kadhib*] and an impossibility [*muḥāl*]."[54]

No Prophet Is Honored in His Own Town

As noted in chapter 5, Ibn Ḥazm made something of an exception when he cited three times the statement of Jesus that no prophet is honored in his own town, since he had used the passage positively to demonstrate Christ's prophetic nature, whereas he would usually have refrained from

54. Ibn Ḥazm, *Kitāb al-Fiṣal fī al-Milal*, 2.29–30.

using the Gospels for anything else than a demonstration of *taḥrīf*. Nevertheless, he did so only after drawing some other elements of *taḥrīf* from the same passages.

From the first two occurrences, in Matthew (13:54–58) and Mark (6:2–4), Ibn Ḥazm notes, first, that the evangelists attribute a human father as well as brothers and sisters to Jesus, while both Christians and Muslims agree that Jesus was born of Mary without the intervention of a male. Second, after hearing these errors, that Jesus does not appear in the Gospels to have corrected them is further proof for Ibn Ḥazm that the Gospels are corrupt.[55] The author then repeats this second element in relation to his Lukan citation, pointing out in addition the error of the claim that Christ did not perform any miracles in his hometown, while according to Luke 4:23 he had performed some in Capernaum.[56]

Jesus's Cry from the Cross

While five earlier authors used Jesus's cry on the cross, "My God, my God, why have you abandoned me" (Matt 27:46 and Mark 15:34), as proof that he was not God, since he addressed God in supplication, our last author, Ibn Qayyim al-Jawziyya, uses it as further proof of textual *taḥrīf*. How, he points out, could the Gospels claim on the one hand that Jesus would lay down his life by his own will, and on the other that he protested his death with such words? And second, if he really uttered such words, how come his Father did not save him by sending down thunder from heaven?[57]

Concluding Considerations

I do not claim, based on the preceding study, that Muslim authors considered the Gospels to be at the same level of authority and reliability as the Qur'an. That was of course out of the question. Nevertheless, what I hope to have demonstrated is that until the time of Ibn Ḥazm in the eleventh century, the accusation of *taḥrīf* in the sense of "intentional corruption

55. Ibn Ḥazm, *Kitāb al-Fiṣal fī al-Milal*, 2.34–36.

56. Ibn Ḥazm, *Kitāb al-Fiṣal fī al-Milal*, 2.59. This is obviously an unfounded accusation, since Capernaum was not his hometown. It is unclear what Ibn Ḥazm means by this.

57. Ibn Qayyim al-Jawziyya, *Hidāyat al-Ḥayāra*, 213.

of the Holy Scriptures" was virtually nonexistent. Even where some grave and serious suspicions were raised against the integrity of the text, the accusation can certainly not be considered to have been a central or foundational element of the Muslim discourse against Christianity.

The two different understandings that Muslims have of the concept of *taḥrīf* (corruption of meaning [*al-maʿna*] and corruption of text [*al-lafẓ*]) gave rise to two different approaches to biblical exegesis. In the traditional, pre–Ibn Ḥazm period, the Bible was used positively to build pro-Islamic arguments against Christian doctrines. In the new approach of Ibn Ḥazm and his heirs, the Bible is used negatively to demonstrate its textual corruption. In the traditional approach, some biblical passages appear unacceptable to the author, and the problem is pointed out in passing as something intriguing, but hardly ever in connection with the term *taḥrīf*. But with the new approach, the argument of *taḥrīf* is developed intentionally, mainly by comparing passages that appear to be contradictory. This comparative approach to exegesis is the chief basis of Ibn Ḥazm's work and was hardly ever found before him.

Even after him, among those who adopted a similar line, the attack was usually not as virulent and certainly not as comprehensive. For instance, al-Juwaynī's opinion about the integrity of the evangelists is not as harsh and hardline as that of Ibn Ḥazm. Whereas the attributes liar, vile, ignorant, despised, transgressor, and devious are only a few of the insults that Ibn Ḥazm hurls at Christ's apostles, al-Juwaynī still gives the evangelists the benefit of the doubt. For example, in connection with the differences in the details of the crucifixion, he concludes: "And there is no doubt about the contradictions [*takādhub*] in these events, and that those who have recounted them have suffered from the length of time [since the time of their occurrence], so that they said things about which they were not perfectly sure."[58]

If the accusation of *taḥrīf* has often become the starting point of Muslim-Christian encounter today, it is certainly worth knowing, both for Christians and Muslims, that it was not always the case, and that it is therefore possible to think otherwise. Even after Ibn Ḥazm, as late as the fourteenth century, the great Muslim scholar Ibn Taymiyya recognized that the Islamic position toward *taḥrīf al-lafẓ* ("textual corruption") was still diverse and ambiguous: "If . . . they [Christians] mean that the Qur'an confirms the textual veracity [*alfaẓ*] of the scriptural books which

58. Al-Juwaynī, *Shifāʾ al-Ghalīl*, 77.

they now possess—that is, the Torah and the Gospels—this is something that some Muslims will grant them and what many Muslims will dispute. However, most Muslims will grant them most of that."

On the other hand, from Ibn Taymiyya's perspective, the Islamic position toward *taḥrīf al-maʿna* ("misinterpretation") was unambiguous: "Concerning the corruption of the meaning of the sacred books by their explanation and interpretation and their replacing its legal judgments with their own, all Muslims, Jews, and Christians witness to this corruption and substitution of theirs."[59]

It may be pointed out in conclusion that Ibn Ḥazm's outrage about the biblical text, which was to affect Muslim-Christian dialogue ever after, was the result of his reading of the Gospels as histories through chiefly Islamic eyes, armed with the qur'anic notion of *ʿiṣma* ("inerrancy"). Like Ibn Ḥazm, al-Juwaynī approached the Bible and the evangelists from the typically Islamic understanding of divine inspiration—the same notion of divine dictation applied by Muslims to the Qur'an, which is meant to guarantee its infallibility. He thus considers the disagreements between Matthew and Luke and wonders: "How can lies proceed from those who are considered [to have been made] infallible [*maʿṣūmān*] by the Holy Spirit after it dwelt on them?"[60] The Gospels are henceforth considered to be unreliable as a result of a literalist approach to the text.

Summarizing the Metadialogue on Taḥrīf

The accusation of *taḥrīf* originates in the Qur'an, but it is not as straightforward as it is often understood in today's conversations between Muslims and Christians. The primary corrupters in the qur'anic context were the Jews, and a number of qur'anic commentators use this as a platform to develop what sometimes becomes a vicious attack against Jews. Twentieth-century commentators, such as Rashīd Riḍa and Sayyid Quṭb, adopt this platform as a starting point for a violent political discourse against the Jews and the Zionist agenda in the context of twentieth-century realities.

59. This and the previous citation are from Ibn Taymiyya's *al-Jawāb aṣ-Ṣaḥīḥ* as translated by Thomas Michel, *A Muslim Theologian's Response to Christianity* (Tehran: Caravan, 1985), 213. For the Arabic original, see 1.1.373–74.

60. Al-Juwaynī, *Shifāʾ al-Ghalīl*, 67.

The eleventh-century turning point, whose occurrence we find first in the writings of Ibn Ḥazm, reflected both the political tensions and conflicts generated by the beginnings of the Crusades in the East and the *Reconquista* in the West. But Ibn Ḥazm's attitude was also reflective of his intransigent position toward all religious groups, Muslim or non-Muslim, who did not adhere to his literalist *Ẓāhirī* sect.

Hermeneutical Keys in Building Bridges beyond Conflict

Christians desiring to engage in constructive dialogue with Muslims are invited to resist being drawn to thinking about their Scriptures as though they were another descended Qur'an. To be fair to their tradition, they need to affirm that it is Christ, the culmination of the Judeo-Christian revelation, who is the eternal and living Word of God, whereas all human frailty that might appear in God's other means of revelation are subservient to God's salvific act in Christ.

Muslims who are committed to fair dialogue are invited to draw their inspiration not from the tedious and repetitive accusations of *taḥrīf* that force the biblical text into an Islamic paradigm, but from the gracious and creative diversity that existed for a long time in their own tradition and emerged from some of their finest thinkers.

On the one side as on the other, there is a risk to be taken: that of meeting the other on their own terms, resisting the temptation to force them into our own mold. For it is only at this juncture that true encounter can occur, an encounter that is truly incarnational. The good news is that it is at such a juncture, and precisely such alone, that redemption occurred once before.

Using Deadlocks as Assets

The starting point of the conversation that can help us move beyond the deadlocks of history in the Muslim accusation of Judeo-Christian *taḥrīf* is in distinguishing between *taḥrīf al-maʿna* and *taḥrīf al-lafḍh*, a distinction that was always maintained in the Muslim tradition. The development of the *taḥrīf* accusation into a strong polemic against the Jews historically and until today helps us see the impact of politics on interfaith discourse. The accusation within the Qur'an was itself born in Medina, as a result of growing conflict between Muhammad's community and the Jewish tribes who allegedly controlled the city before Muhammad's arrival. Christians and Muslims today should avoid continuing this unhindered line of rhetoric against the Jews and separate the religious and theological conversation from contemporary political realities. Christians, Muslims, and Jews need to find ways to use their faith traditions to transform current political conflict rather than using interfaith debates to exacerbate the conflict as they further express their disagreements.

The circumstances of the shift in the discourse on *taḥrīf*, from an accusation of misinterpretation (*taḥrīf al-maʿna*) to an accusation of textual corruption (*taḥrīf al-lafḍh*), should stand as a warning for Christians, Muslims, and Jews today. It is clear that political conflict can have a protracted negative implication on interfaith and intercommunal relations. All three traditions need to find ways to put their faiths to the service of political peace rather than allowing political conflict to poison the relationships between their communities. Ibn Ḥazm's sectarian intransigence is also a good reminder for all of us that we are ultimately not called to be God's defenders, for his truth in the end will surely prevail. And it is my conviction that it will not prevail through one particular religious tradition, but through suprareligious criteria that transcend all of our human understandings.

Concluding Thoughts

It is easy to get drawn into a defensive, or even offensive, position in reaction to the Muslim accusation of *taḥrīf*. But followers of Jesus have to resist this temptation and take the time patiently to explain to Muslims the history of the New Testament text, particularly of the text of the Gospels. The perspective that the Qur'an teaches Muslims about the Torah and the *Injīl* leaves them with the impression that they are to expect books that are in the same format as the Qur'an. The complex, cumulative nature of the Bible is largely absent from the Qur'an's perspective on these Scriptures, conveying a sense that Muhammad never encountered these texts in Arabic, but learned about them only through oral tradition. As far as the New Testament is concerned, this is reflected in the Gospels being always referred to in the Qur'an in the singular (*al-Injīl*) and that some of the teaching of this *Injīl* conveyed in the Qur'an is alien to the canonical Gospels, or in certain cases even conflicts with them, such as the claim in at-Tawba 9:111 that the Gospel teaches to fight *jihad* in God's name (see chapter 6).

Though we have come to take it for granted, it is rather fascinating that the Qur'an refers to the Gospel only in the singular—*Injīl*. The Muslim tradition easily causes us to forget this peculiarity, as it projects the notion of a book that was revealed to Jesus on par with the Qur'an that was revealed to Muhammad. From that rationale, there can be only one book, and later Muslim theologians who had to explain why Christians had four Gospels rather than one were quick to resort to the argument of *taḥrīf*. Although Jesus gave his disciples the Gospel, it is argued, the original was lost and what we are left with are four attempts at a reconstruction.

This, of course, does not reflect the actual history of the Christian text. Ample early manuscript data shows that the church never thought of the Gospels as a single book revealed by God to Jesus. The Christian tradition never claimed about the Gospels what the Muslim tradition maintains about the nature of the Qur'an. The four Gospels are four testimonies about Jesus, written by four of his early followers, reflecting the *euangelion* (Greek for "good news") that Jesus's teaching and ministry represented to the early disciples. Jesus taught in Aramaic/Syriac, and soon after his ascension, his disciples transmitted the content of this message as the *euangelion* proclamation in that same language to the people in the Palestine region, but very soon afterward also in Greek within the remaining Greco-Roman culture of the Roman empire of the time.

Our earliest extant Greek manuscript segments of the Gospels date from less than a hundred years after the ascension of Jesus and are considered to reflect texts written in Greek between thirty-five and seventy years after Christ's ascension. They were never understood to contain solely God's direct discourse to the world, nor even simply to be a repository of Jesus's conversations with God and people, which are the primary genres found in the Qur'an. They do of course contain a record of his words and actions, but in the way that they are organized and the narrative choices they make, they provide us primarily with rich theological perspectives on the Christ event. If such had not been the understanding of the function of the Gospels from the beginning, the early church would not have bothered to preserve four different testimonies or interpretations of the same event and person.

Further Reading and Research

Arkoun, Mohammed. *Lectures du Coran*. Paris: Maisonneuve & Larose, 1982. Arkoun was a leading figure in his critique of Islam's intellectual history. In this book, he uses modern literary critical methods to deconstruct the classical Islamic discourse about the Qur'an. He argues, against much of the classical Muslim tradition, that any reading of the Qur'an is necessarily a human construct, challenging traditional views of the Qur'an's status as the word of God, by revisiting hot issues such as Sharīʿa, *jihad*, Islam's relationship with politics, and the status of women.

Lodahl, Michael. *Claiming Abraham: Reading the Bible and the Qur'an Side by Side*. Grand Rapids: Brazos, 2010. Lodahl employs a comparative theological approach to the reading of the Bible and the Qur'an side by side, attempting to reflect theologically upon what the text claims about God and his relation to the world. While the main focus of the book is on the character of Abraham, it discusses other theological themes, and one of them is the nature of the revealing word of God (chap. 4). This chapter addresses the debate over whether the Qur'an was created or uncreated. While recognizing the Muslim view of a heavenly Qur'an, Lodahl emphasizes its human elements, concluding that the heavenly Qur'an became an earthly text. In this regard, Lodahl draws parallels between the Word—Jesus Christ who "became flesh"—and the Qur'an. The latter, thus, becomes the incarnated Muslim revelation, while the former is characterized as the incarnated Christian revelation. This comparative theological approach sees the Word Jesus Christ, not the Bible, as "the functional equivalent to the Qur'an."

Raheb, Mitri. "Contextualizing the Scripture: Towards a New Understanding of the Qur'an: An Arab-Christian Perspective." *World Christianity* 3 (1997): 180–201. Raheb develops a contextual Arab Christian approach to the Qur'an as the basis for Christian-Muslim relationship. In this view, the Qur'an is seen as an attempt to contextualize and to Arabize the biblical message, since it is shaped by Arab culture, the Judeo-Christian heritage, and the experience of Islam's prophet, Muhammad. This approach to the Qur'an is based on two methodological principles. First, it considers the historical life of Muhammad, the *Sunna*, as the matrix for meaning. Second, it attempts to be a truly local Arab theology, particularly when the two religious traditions share a common cultural and religious heritage. In this sense, Raheb considers the

Qur'an as a contextualized Arabic version of the Christian heritage. This approach, thus, aims to encourage a deeper engagement and understanding of the Qur'an.

Smith, W. C. *What Is Scripture? A Comparative Approach*. Minneapolis: Fortress, 2005 (originally 1993). Smith addresses the concept of Scripture, moving the conversation from a Western, Bible-centered understanding to a more comprehensive conception of a text that *becomes* Scripture within a believing community as a result of its reception and interpretation within that community. This book is relevant both for my chapter 2, comparing biblical and qur'anic interpretation, as well as for chapters 6–7, which explore the Muslim understanding and interpretation of the Bible. When we understand the relationship of a Scripture with its receiving community, then we are able to approach all and any Scripture respectfully, without abandoning the more academic and critical approach.

8 Islam's Muhammado-Centric Reading of the Bible

One summer in the mid-nineties, I was involved in Bible distribution efforts to North Africans, out of the southern ports of Spain. Many cars crossing over the strait of Gibraltar into Morocco received our literature respectfully and gratefully, though finding biblical portions in the neighboring trash cans was not a rare occurrence either. But one of the most striking memories I keep from that experience was the wildly popular argument with which a number of bearded men faced us in an expression of severe discontent with our activities. It was the popular accusation that we had failed to see throughout the pages of our Scriptures the plain description of Muhammad.

I remember, in particular, being drawn on a number of occasions into polemical debates regarding Muhammad as the fulfilment of Jesus's promises of the Paraclete. The debate turned polemical, not so much because of our failure to see these clear proofs, but rather as a result of the accusation that Christians had corrupted their text and substituted the original *periklytos* of the Johannine text into the suspicious *paraklētos*, which was now found in the Gospel. The argument always puzzled me, until I was able, a few years later, to explore this argument in greater detail in the context of my PhD research at the University of Oxford.

In the present chapter and the next, the reader will be presented with the essence of my own discoveries about this question of Muhammad's preannouncement in the Judeo-Christian Scriptures. My particular focus will be on the text of the Gospels, and I will dedicate the entirety of chapter 9 to the question of Muhammad the Paraclete. As such, both the present chapter and the next need to be viewed as two parts of the same issue. I present some introductory thoughts here and will leave my concluding reflections for the end of the next chapter.

Current Perspectives

Muhammad is perhaps the most misunderstood figure in history. His depiction has triggered death threats and assassinations, mob violence, and the burning down of embassies. From more covert novels such as Salman Rushdie's *The Satanic Verses* (1988) to openly insulting caricatures that have made the news headlines in recent years, we are left in a quandary about who Islam's prophet really was.

The majority of depictions of Muhammad followed uncritically the official narrative of the *Sīra*. We have the epic Muslim depictions of his life, such as the highly acclaimed Hollywood film *The Message* by Moustapha Akkad (1976), also released in an Arabic version the same year largely with an Arab Egyptian cast as *Muhammad: Messenger of God*. More recently, an animated production was made by Badr International, *Muhammad: The Last Prophet* (2004), and an Iranian film, *Muhammad: The Messenger of God*, by Majid Majidi (2015). From a more secular perspective, a number of television documentaries were produced on the life of Muhammad, such as the PBS productions *Islam: Empire of Faith* (2000) and *Muhammad: Legacy of the Prophet* (2002), or the three-episode BBC production, *The Life of Muhammad* (2011).

At the other end of the spectrum stand the caricatured and offensive representations of Muhammad, such as the infamous and frankly ridiculous *Innocence of Muslims*, produced by Sam Bacile in 2011 and released on the tenth anniversary of 9/11, or the more generally devastating representation of global Islamism as standard Islam by Geert Wilders in his seventeen-minute short film, *Fitna* (2008). We have, as well, hundreds of websites representing both the most negative perspectives as well as the most eulogizing ones about Islam's prophet.

The irony is that, on both sides, the major source of data for these representations has been the same official biography transmitted down through the ages by Muslim scholars: *As-Sīra an-Nabawiyya* by Ibn Isḥāq and preserved by Ibn Hishām. But the problem is that the *Sīra* is based on a collation of traditions (*aḥādīth*), most of which originate from the eighth and ninth centuries—in other words from over a hundred to two hundred years after the event of the historical Muhammad. Ḥadīth has been shown, by a number of respected scholars in recent decades, to be of questionable reliability from a historian's perspective.[1] My purpose in saying this is by no means polemical. I am not demeaning who Muhammad was historically, but rather simply pointing out that the usual narrative that we accept about him is questionable from a critical historian's perspective. And this applies not only to the positive portrayals of him, but also to the vast majority of offensive representations, such as the ones referred to above. Where does this leave us? This leaves us with the Qur'an as the surest reflection of how Muhammad thought and of how he perceived himself, various frames of which have been interspersed throughout this book and a topic to which I return briefly in the final chapter, as it pertains particularly to a Christian understanding in its engagement with Islam.

The present chapter looks at some of the classical Christian polemics against Islam and how Islam accommodated itself to these criticisms by adopting the original strategy that Christians had used, already in the New Testament, in their rereading of the Hebrew Bible christocentrically. This creative Muslim strategy will be examined in several Muslim classical texts, after we have established the rhetorical context of the discourse, by exploring the challenging questions that Eastern Christians of the time were asking about Islam and Muhammad. The qur'anic origins of the Muslim Muhammado-centric approach to the Bible have been amply laid out in previous chapters, where we looked at the insistence on continuity that Islam has always affirmed with regard to the preceding Judeo-Christian revelation.

Who Do People Say That Muhammad Son of ʿAbdallah Is?

When a movement or event is recognized as significant in history, people turn to the founder or originator and become interested in learning more about them. This is, to some extent, the origin of biography. We are interested in a person's life, the factors that shaped them, their teaching and behavior, the legacy they have left, insofar as they are recognized as somehow impacting and influencing our present reality. When it comes

1. For an account of the historical problems inherent to the traditional Muslim narrative on Islam's and Muhammad's origins, see Gabriel S. Reynolds, *The Emergence of Islam* (Minneapolis: Fortress, 2012).

to religious movements, the founders are all the more paramount. Followers are interested in their religious founder's life because, presumably, it is a reflection and outcome of their teaching legacy. And it is often in the Scriptures associated with a particular religious founder that the core of that leader's self-perception, as well as the way that their community wished to remember them, can be found.

In the case of Jesus, an account found in all three Synoptic Gospels preserves this phenomenon. We learn as much about the identity of Jesus from the direct conversation he has on the topic with his disciples as from the literary setting provided by the Gospel writers. In all three Gospels, the core narrative follows Jesus's question to his disciples: "Who do people say I am?" (Mark 8:27 and parallels in Matt 16:13 and Luke 9:18). After a report about the false perceptions among the people, the correct answer, as we know, is provided by the disciple Peter. Jesus is the Messiah (Hebrew and Aramaic), the Christ (Greek), the "son of the living God," adds Matthew in what may be his interpretation of the messianic title from the perspective of the Hebrew Scriptures. But even that famous confession is precisely shown to trigger a whole lot of misguided assumptions in the minds of the disciples, as becomes clear after Jesus rebukes Peter for not understanding that the Messiah must suffer. Jesus's identity as the expected Messiah is now invested with the specific meaning that he wants it to carry.

In all three Synoptic Gospels, the core confession of Peter is preceded by miracles that demonstrate Jesus's healing power and his authority over the spirit world and the natural world. It is also immediately followed by a direct discourse where Jesus announces to his followers that the mission of the Messiah will not be crowned by outstanding political success, but rather by his personal suffering and death and the apparent failure of his mission. This unappealing paradox represents Jesus's signature style, which challenges our notions of marketing ourselves always as strong and victorious. Jesus then proceeds to invite those who wish to follow him to embrace as well that same way of suffering and death. This new (though Old Testament–inspired) meaning invested in the Messiah title is further reinforced by Peter's opposition to that plan and Jesus's swift rebuttal of his objection.

Crucially perhaps, all three Gospels follow this important narrative with the account of what became known as the transfiguration (Mark 9:2–13; Matt 17:1–13; Luke 9:28–36). In the sight of his three closest disciples, Peter, James, and John, Jesus's appearance goes through a metamorphosis (Greek *metemorphōthē*). His face and clothes shine brightly, he suddenly appears in the company of two key Israelite figures, Moses and Elijah, and he receives the endorsement of God himself, who shelters him with a bright cloud, declares his love for him, and reveals him as his Son. Through the whole narrative, Jesus stands out as a miracle worker, a man of astounding authority, whose self-giving life leads him to suffering and death, and is finally followed by God's personal endorsement and raising up into glory. The answer to the important question, "Who do people say I am?," is provided through this schema, which is the same as the one encapsulated in the early Christian hymn found in Philippians 2:6–11.

Turning to Islam, it seems clear that it was initially less centered on the person of Muhammad than Christianity was on the person of Jesus. The Qur'an presents itself as the vehicle of God's message, rather than the words or biography of Muhammad. But even though the Qur'an plays down the role and identity of Muhammad, the early Muslim tradition quickly made him into the central paradigm of Muslim life. So much so that, as seen in chapter 2, the biography (*Sīra*) of Islam's prophet became the hermeneutical key to the classical exegetical approach to the Qur'an, particularly in the step consisting in establishing the "occasions of the revelation" of qur'anic verses: *asbāb an-nuzūl*. As mentioned in chapter 2 as well, some recent scholars of Islam question this traditional order of priority. Gabriel Said Reynolds in particular recently demonstrated that the primacy of the Qur'an as a repository of history is convincingly demonstrable.[2] From that perspective, the centrality of Muhammad is historically secondary to the centrality of the Qur'an. The Qur'an's playing down of the identity of Muhammad as receiver of the revelation may have contributed to this shift of focus. It was also that factor that exposed Islam to harsh criticism by Christians from early on.

One factor that quickly became something of an embarrassment for Islam was that its prophet had performed no miracles. From the witness of the Qur'an itself, it would appear that this criticism was already being raised during Muhammad's lifetime, as evidenced in the following verses from al-Isrā' 17:90–93:

> And so they say, "We will not believe you [prophet] until you cause a spring to gush up from the earth; or, unless you have a garden of dates and grapes and cause rivers to pour through it abundantly. Or, until the skies fall down upon us—crushing us, as you have threatened to

2. Reynolds, *Emergence of Islam*, 2012.

> do. Or [until] you bring God and the angels face to face before us, or, you have a house of gold or you go to heaven—but we would not even believe in your ascension unless you return with a book that we can read!" Say, "May my Lord be exalted in his glory, am I other than a man appointed as a messenger?"

The final demand that he should send down "a book that we can read" represents the beginning of what, especially in the ninth century, would develop into the elaborate argument of the "inimitability of the Qur'an" (*i'jāz al-Qur'an*).[3] Short of the conventional miracles as signs of his prophethood, Muhammad's answer to the demand is reflected a few verses later. The Qur'an itself is his miracle, the sign given to him by God: "We sent down the Qur'an with the truth and with truth it has come down. We only sent you [prophet] to bring good news and to give a warning" (al-Isrā' 17:105).

Christian Accusations against Islam

Evidently, the issue was not settled through the exchange on the problem of a lack of miracles, as reported in the Qur'an. In the early encounter between Christians and Muslims, Christian theologians discussed the different grounds upon which one accepts or rejects a particular religion, and these texts reflect the same skepticism as is evidenced in the Qur'an with regard to Muhammad's prophethood, on the basis of the same argument from miracles. I will survey this phenomenon in a number of Christian texts, and then examine the creative and elaborate Muslim response in defense of their prophet.

Miracles in the Authentication of a Prophet and His Religion

The subject of the authentication of prophecy and prophethood based on the performance of miracles is already treated extensively by one of the

3. In this argument, the Qur'an is represented as Muhammad's greatest and only miracle, mainly through the claims of the book's inimitability and of the messenger's illiteracy. For a full discussion of the argument, see G. E. von Grunebaum, "I'djāz," in *Encyclopaedia of Islam*, ed. P. Bearman et al., 2nd ed. (Leiden: Brill, 1954–2005), 3.1018.

earliest Eastern Christian fathers writing in Arabic, namely Abū Qurrah, who was bishop of Harran from the late eighth to the early ninth centuries. The treatise in question is entitled *Mīmar* ["treatise"] *on the verification* [*taḥqīq*] *of the law of Moses and the prophets who prophesied concerning Christ and the pure Gospel, which the disciples of Christ—who was born of Mary the Virgin—transmitted to the world; and the verification of Orthodoxy, which people attribute to Chalcedonianism, and the refutation of every sect that claims to be Christian, except that sect.*[4] As transpires from the lengthy title, Abū Qurrah's primary purpose is to demonstrate the veracity of Christianity, in its specific Chalcedonian (or Melkite) interpretation, on the basis of the Bible. Although the title does not claim to be a refutation of the authenticity of Islam, presenting itself instead as an inter-Christian treatise, judging from the nature of its arguments, there is little doubt that the author had in mind to cast doubts over the divine origin of the young and budding religion. After illustrating how Moses argued his way with God in order to obtain the ability to perform miracles, he concludes: "From this, those who have discernment learn that it is not right for those who look into the veracity of a religion to accept it from its founder except through miracles."[5]

On the basis of this reasoning, Abū Qurrah argues for the authenticity both of Judaism and Christianity. He affirms his own faith to be true, thanks to all the miracles performed by Jesus that accompanied and confirmed his teaching. He argues that Christ's testimony was even stronger than that of Moses, because the former empowered his disciples to perform miracles as well. Furthermore, while Moses performed miracles by God's power, Jesus performed them by his own.[6] In this last statement, again, the underlying axe to grind seems to be the recurring qur'anic assertion that Jesus (ʿĪsa) and other prophets performed miracles only "with God's permission" (*bi-idhni Allāh*) (e.g., āl-ʿImrān 3:49; ar-Raʿd 13:38; Ghāfir 40:78). After Abū Qurrah, the same theme is again taken up by practically every other early Arab Christian writer that I have looked into, including Patriarch Timothy I, Ibrāhīm aṭ-Ṭabarānī, Abū Rā'iṭa at-Takrītī, ʿAmmār al-Baṣrī, ʿAbd al-Masīḥ al-Kindī, and Ḥunayn b. Isḥāq.

4. Abū Qurrah, *Les oeuvres arabes de Théodore Aboucara évêque d'Haran*, ed. C. Bacha (Beirut: Alfawaïd, 1904), 140–79.

5. Abū Qurrah, *Les oeuvres arabes*, 141.

6. Abū Qurrah, *Les oeuvres arabes*, 142–43.

Ibrāhīm aṭ-Ṭabarānī, a Melkite monk of Palestine, uses the same argument in a debate before Prince ʿAbd ar-Raḥmān al-Hāshimī in Jerusalem around 820. This time it is an unequivocal challenge to Islam. He concludes:

> Rather, know with your mind that kings and people did not accept this religion and the Gospel from John and his companions out of a desire for their riches, nor out of precaution against their armies, nor out of fear from their swords, nor out of the easiness of their commandments. But instead they demonstrated to the kings and the common people, and they received this book, thanks to the signs and miracles that they performed.[7]

He picks up Abū Qurrah's second argument as well:

> But what a great difference there is between the signs performed by the prophets and those performed by Christ! For when a prophet wanted to perform an act, he fasted and prayed and implored and petitioned and intensified his prayer, after which he interceded. As for Christ, he was not in this position. Rather, he walked in public places and among people, and performed signs and miracles through a command issuing from his own person.[8]

Still some time later, a third author, this time a West Syriac,[9] ʿAbd al-Masīḥ al-Kindī (ninth century) also argues in the same way for the uniqueness of Christ's miracle performance, since while all prophets petitioned and implored God before they performed their mighty works, he claimed, "he, on the other hand, did things with an irresistible power,

7. Ibrāhīm aṭ-Ṭabarānī, *Le dialogue d'Abraham de Tibériade avec ʿAbd al-Raḥmān al-Hāshimī à Jérusalem vers 820*, ed. Giacinto Būlus Marcuzzo (Rome: Institut Oriental et Université Pontificale du Latran, 1986), 399 (my translation).

8. Aṭ-Ṭabarānī, *Le dialogue*, 387.

9. Throughout this book, I avoid the appellations *Jacobite* and *Nestorian* with reference to the two Syriac traditions that rejected the statement of the Council of Chalcedon due to their pejorative connotations. I instead use *West Syriac* for the Jacobites and *East Syriac* for the Nestorians, also known as Syrian Orthodox and Syriac Church of the East, respectively. Even though the authors were writing in Arabic, they belonged to these Syriac Christian traditions. On the other hand, *Melkite* is a reference to the initially Greek-speaking, and eventually mainly Arabic-speaking, Chalcedonian tradition, otherwise referred to as Greek Orthodox, or even better, *Rūm* Orthodox.

which is the Logos [*al-kalima*] that created the heavens and the earth, and which was united to him."[10]

Elsewhere and around the same period on the West Syriac side, the same argument from miracles was adopted by Abū Rā'iṭa at-Takrītī (died around 825). He had a very well worked out argument to demonstrate that miracles did actually take place at the hand of the early church. He advances that intelligent people would accept a nonrational worldview only by force, and that force was either achieved with the sword or by God's medium through the performance of miracles. Since history testifies that no intelligent person was converted to Christianity by means of the sword, since the church did not possess political and military power until the fourth century, clearly they must have been convinced by miracles that they saw. On the other hand, foolish people, who would normally blindly follow their passions, also must have come to the Christian faith because they witnessed many miracles, otherwise they would not have received such a passionless religion as Christianity. Hence all early Christian converts were won through the performance of miracles that came from God, and not through the use of force as was the case in Islam. Abū Rā'iṭa concludes: "And miracles are the strongest proof that the religion of which you would be a follower is the true religion from God's perspective."[11]

ʿAmmār al-Baṣrī, another ninth-century Arab Christian, this time belonging to the East Syriac church, also struggles to set the right criteria for the legitimization of true religion. He observes that there exist so many religions, and each one claims to be the true one. His own position differs somewhat from Abū Rā'iṭa's conclusion, as he rejects the appeal to miracles alone as proof of the veracity of a religion. He indeed points out that many religions claim that miracles were performed at the hand of their founder. At the same time, however, al-Baṣrī also rejects the claim of the "stubborn" (*al-mutaʿannit*) who pretends that the true religion can be discovered only through rational thinking. This, our author remarks, would

10. ʿAbd al-Masīḥ b. Isḥāq al-Kindī, *Risālat ʿAbd Allāh b. Ismāʿīl al-Hāshimī ila ʿAbd al-Masīḥ b. Isḥāq al-Kindī Yadʿūhu bihā ila al-Islam, wa Risālat ʿAbd al-Masīḥ ila al-Hāshimī Yaruddu bihā ʿAlayhi wa Yadʿūhu ila an-Naṣrāniyya* (The Letter of ʿAbd Allāh b. Ismāʿīl al-Hāshimī to ʿAbd al-Masīḥ b. Isḥāq al-Kindī, Inviting Him to Embrace Islam, and the Letter of ʿAbd al-Masīḥ to al-Hāshimī in Response to Him, Inviting Him to Embrace Christianity), ed. W. Muir (London: W.H. Allen, 1885), 253.

11. Abū Rā'iṭa at-Takrītī, *Min Qawl Abī Rā'iṭa at-Takrītī* (From the Sayings of Abī Rā'iṭa at-Takrītī), in *Vingt traités théologiques d'auteurs arabes chrétiens (ix–xiii siècles)*, ed. Louis Cheikho (Beirut: Imprimerie Catholique, 1920), 146.

be unfair on the part of God, since not all human beings are endowed with the mental abilities to engage in an objective intellectual investigation. Moreover, he remarks, there exist so many wise people who adhere each to a different religion, for religion is of such sacred and profound nature that it is not possible to discover its truth by means of human reason alone. ʿAmmār al-Baṣrī therefore appeals to the necessity of both miracles and the intellect. The intellect is needed in order to discover the importance and place of miracles for the early development and spread of the true religion. For when all humanly conceivable causes fail to explain the success of the true religion, the mind then is forced to conclude that it achieved its sweeping spread by the powerful performance of unquestionable miracles.[12]

Another variant on this theme is found in the already-mentioned work of ʿAbd al-Masīḥ al-Kindī. Al-Kindī is the most polemical Christian author of the period, so much so that his exchange of letters with al-Hāshimī is generally viewed as a literary artifact rather than a historical exchange, as the arguments it contains do not naturally fit in the literary corpus of the time. The anti-Muhammad sentiments expressed in his letter are the most flagrant among his fellow Christian writers. While Timothy I, Ibrāhīm aṭ-Ṭabarānī, and later Paul of Antioch conceded to a certain measure the prophethood and apostleship for Muhammad, al-Kindī conceded to none. In reply to an alleged claim by his interlocutor that Muhammad did not differ from Moses or Joshua in the killings and wars that he waged against people, al-Kindī affirms that while the miracles performed by Moses and Joshua sanctioned their use of force, the Prophet of Islam had no such works to testify to his integrity. He concludes: "God did not send your master, neither as an apostle nor as a prophet, nor did he command him to wage war against anyone or to make peace with anyone. Rather, he [Muhammad] is an aggressor [*mutaghallib*], who claimed what he claimed about himself, and a group of people from his own tribe and family and country supported him in his endeavor."[13]

Finally, in the same way as ʿAmmār al-Baṣrī did, ninth-century Ḥunayn b. Isḥāq makes use of this very argument from miracles. He too prefers to rely on an intellectual argument to verify the authenticity of

12. ʿAmmār al-Baṣrī, *Kitāb al-Burhān* (The Book of Proof), 24–29, in *Kitāb al-Burhān; wa Kitāb al-Masāʾil wa al-Ajwiba* (Apologie et Controverses), ed. Michel Hayek (Beirut: Dar el-Machreq, 1977).

13. Al-Kindī, *Risālat ʿAbd al-Masīḥ ila al-Hāshimī*, 114–17.

Christ's miracles, which in turn will serve as a demonstration of the true religion. Like al-Baṣrī, Ḥunayn b. Isḥāq sets six criteria to demonstrate the error of a religion,[14] although it is not always the same criteria: (1) the use of force (al-Baṣrī summarized it with *as-sayf* ["the sword"]); (2) taking refuge in ease of life, in flight of difficulties (*at-tarkhīṣ* ["licentiousness"] in al-Baṣrī); (3) attraction to nobility, power, and riches (*ar-rashā wa al-muṣāna'a* ["bribery and favors"] in al-Baṣrī); (4) the deception of a person by a wicked propagator of the new message (al-Baṣrī used *at-tawāṭu'* ["conspiracy"]); (5) taking advantage of the ignorance and lack of education of people; and (6) natural kinship between the adherents of a religion (al-Baṣrī refers to this as *al-'aṣabiyya*). One final criterion peculiar to 'Ammār al-Baṣrī and not found in Ḥunayn b. Isḥāq is *al-istiḥsān*. This refers to a kind of worldview that comes naturally to the mind and intellect, a sort of natural revelation that need not come from an external, supernatural origin. Its opposite, which 'Ammār al-Baṣrī claims for Christianity, could be translated as the "criterion of nonconformity." In his view, that a religion finds wide acceptance despite its clashing with natural human expectations and logic guarantees its suprahuman origins.[15] Since, as Ḥunayn b. Isḥāq argues, it can be demonstrated that Christianity was not established by any of these six means, then it naturally follows that only one criterion insured the success of the religion, namely: miracles.[16]

Along with the argument from miracles, Abū Qurrah also advances the argument from prophecy, whereby Christ's religion is verified thanks to all the Old Testament prophecies that predicted his life, ministry, death, and resurrection.[17] He then reproaches the Jews for not accepting Christianity and Christ, in spite of all this, especially since Moses never commanded them not to believe in prophets that would come after him, whereas Jesus had done just that.[18] It is difficult to imagine that this last

14. In *Kitāb al-Burhān* (32–41), al-Baṣrī mentions five criteria. But later he enumerates six criteria in his *Kitāb al-Masā'il wa al-Ajwiba* (The Book of Questions and Answers), 135–37.

15. 'Ammār al-Baṣrī refers to this criterion in both *Kitāb al-Burhān* (31 and 36) and *Kitāb al-Masā'il wa al-Ajwiba* (136).

16. Ḥunayn b. Isḥāq, *Kayfiyyat Idrāk Ḥaqīqat ad-Diyāna* (How to Discern the Truth of a Religion), in *Vingt traités théologiques d'auteurs arabes chrétiens (ix–xiii siècles)*, ed. Louis Cheikho (Beirut: Imprimerie Catholique, 1920), 143–46.

17. Abū Qurrah, *Les oeuvres arabes*, 144–45.

18. Abū Qurrah, *Les oeuvres arabes*, 146.

argument was not addressed primarily against Islam, as a way of justifying the Christian rejection of Islam.

Further, Abū Qurrah also rejects the possibility that Christians might have received Christ favorably because of some kinship with him that would have guaranteed them prestigious positions in his new religion. Rather, the author turns this accusation back against the Jews, arguing that they themselves may have had such incentives to follow Moses because of their kinship to him, while Christians were converts from all the nations, with no relationship whatsoever to Jesus, and being called to a religion without any sort of prestige.[19] Here again, it is difficult to imagine that this was not intended as a covert blow against Islam.

As we will see in the next section, a whole portion of ʿAlī aṭ-Ṭabarī's *Kitāb ad-Dīn wa ad-Dawla* is dedicated to pointing out the biblical prophetic passages that are seen as containing predictions of Muhammad's prophethood. It is clearly designed as a direct refutation of the arguments just surveyed. In fact, the similarities between Abū Qurrah's argumentation and that which aṭ-Ṭabarī is refuting are so striking that one would almost be tempted to think that Abū Qurrah was in fact ʿAlī aṭ-Ṭabarī's Christian uncle, Abū Zakkār, whose arguments he is purportedly refuting. He mentions him on several occasions as "famous in debate and skill."[20] But Patriarch Timothy I also raises similar points in his dialogue with Caliph al-Mahdī, arguing that while Jews should have believed in Christ because of all the Old Testament prophecies about him, Christians had no reason to believe in Muhammad, because there were no previous announcements of his advent.[21]

We have to conclude, having examined this overwhelming evidence, that ʿAlī aṭ-Ṭabarī's claim that his uncle Abū Zakkār was *the only one he knew of* who had raised this argument from miracles against Islam and its prophet was essentially a rhetorical device.[22] It is clear that the argument was extremely widespread and popular among Christians at the time of ʿAlī aṭ-Ṭabarī in the ninth century. It is likely that aṭ-Ṭabarī, who could

19. Abū Qurrah, *Les oeuvres arabes*, 149.

20. Among other places, aṭ-Ṭabarī mentions this uncle of his, who was so skilled in debate and whose discourse he found so convincing until he finally saw the light of Islam, in his *Kitāb ad-Dīn wa ad-Dawla*, ed. Alphonse Mingana (Cairo: Maṭbaʿat al-Muqtaṭaf, 1923), 124.

21. Hans Putman, *L'église et l'Islam sous Timothée I (780–823)* (Beirut: Librairie Orientale, 1975), 25.

22. This claim of aṭ-Ṭabarī is found in *Kitāb ad-Dīn wa ad-Dawla*, 129.

hardly have been unaware of the popularity of the argument he was refuting, used the rhetorical device in order to lend greater weight to his own argumentation.

Gospel-Based Proof of Muhammad's Prophethood

Having surveyed the pervasiveness of the argument against Muhammad's prophethood among Christian theologians of the time, writing in Arabic, we now have a firm rhetorical context to understand the Muslim theologians' arguments. Indeed, in such a climate as described above, it is not surprising that Muslims spared no effort to defend the prophethood of Muhammad by all means available to them. One popular approach was based on the actual text of the Gospels.

In order to support his argument in favor of Muhammad's prophethood, ʿAlī aṭ-Ṭabarī seeks to justify Muhammad's performing no miracles. In his *Kitāb ad-Dīn wa ad-Dawla*, he cites three occasions in the Gospel of Matthew where Jesus was challenged to prove that he was the Son of God, yet where he refused to perform any miracles. He was first challenged by the devil in the temptation account (Matt 4:3–4), then by the high priest at his trial (Matt 26:63–64),[23] and finally by the Jews while he was hanging on the cross (Matt 27:40). These citations are found in a section where aṭ-Ṭabarī addresses the accusation that Muhammad's early supporters adopted Islam without witnessing any miracles on his part.[24] The implication of the critics, of course, is that they did so for some personal gains or under pressure or threat rather than out of genuine personal conviction.

Aṭ-Ṭabarī's argument in favor of the Prophet of Islam is that there are numerous other cases in the Scriptures where prophets did not act upon the request and desire of those who asked them to. After citing an example where Ezekiel failed to respond positively to his people's requests under the pretext that God was preventing him, aṭ-Ṭabarī moves on to the examples in the Gospels where Jesus was requested for a sign but gave none. His conclusion is that no human has the right to require of a prophet

23. Aṭ-Ṭabarī attributes this statement to Pilate, but in fact the wording of his quotation corresponds to Jesus's interrogation by the high priest.

24. The section's Arabic title is *Fī ar-radd ala man dhakara anna al-Muhājirīn wa al-Anṣār dakhalū fī ad-dīn min ghayri āyatin* (Answering Those Who Have Claimed That the Muhājirūn and the Anṣār Entered Islam without Seeing Any Miracle), in aṭ-Ṭabarī, *Kitāb ad-Dīn wa ad-Dawla*, 124–29.

anything, since he stands accountable to God alone. In the same way, Jesus did not succumb to the request of those who pressed him to change stones into bread, or come down from the cross because, he adds, as was often the case for all prophets, "God had not allowed them to perform them [the miraculous acts], and had not given them his approval [lit., had not opened that miracle's door for them: *lam yaftaḥ lahum bābahā*] at those specific moments." With this exegesis, aṭ-Ṭabarī not only argues in defense of the founder of his newfound faith, but he is also implying that Jesus was simply a prophet and apostle, subject to God's omnipotent will, in exactly the same way as other prophets and apostles had been before him and would remain after him.[25]

Aṭ-Ṭabarī's next step is to prove that it is not necessary for a prophet to do miracles for people to follow him and that he is no less of a real prophet for it. To that end he cites Matthew 4:18–22 and 9:9, where Peter, Andrew, James, John, and Matthew are all called to follow Christ before seeing any miracle from him or hearing any of his words, and they do so without any hesitation. This is again in defense of the early followers of Muhammad converting to Islam without seeing any miracles on his part, meaning that they did not necessarily do so with some ulterior motive.[26]

Another passage that aṭ-Ṭabarī uses for the same purpose is Matthew 24:36: "And the disciples asked Christ (Peace be upon him!) about the hour; and he said: 'This is a secret and a hidden thing from me, which God alone knows.'" Rather than use this passage to show Jesus's inferiority to God, as several other Muslims did at his time, he moves beyond this argument and argues that a prophet cannot be reprobated for anything he does or does not do, because God has not permitted him to act otherwise at that particular time. Rather than arguing against Christ's divinity, aṭ-Ṭabarī here assumes Jesus's *prophetic* identity and constructs an argument in Muhammad's favor.[27]

Islam and Muhammad as the Fulfillment of Christianity

Beyond dispelling the Christian rejection of their prophet's authenticity, Muslim writers were busy demonstrating that Muhammad fulfilled

25. Aṭ-Ṭabarī, *Kitāb ad-Dīn wa ad-Dawla*, 128–29.
26. Aṭ-Ṭabarī, *Kitāb ad-Dīn wa ad-Dawla*, 125–26.
27. Aṭ-Ṭabarī, *Kitāb ad-Dīn wa ad-Dawla*, 129.

the prophetic expectations of the New Testament. I call this process "the Muhammado-centric reading of the Bible." The epitome of this strategy is summarized in the fourteenth-century text of Syrian Muslim scholar Ibn Qayyim al-Jawziyya:

> For when the Torah announced him [Jesus] and his prophethood, his very coming was a confirmation of it [the Torah]. Then he announced a prophet that would come after him, and the coming of [Muhammad] the previously announced prophet became a confirmation of him [Christ], just as his [Jesus's] own coming was a confirmation of the Torah. For God's habit with regard to his prophets is that the former would announce the one to come, and that the latter would confirm the one who preceded him. *It follows that if Muhammad son of ʿAbdallah had not appeared and had not been sent, the prophethood of all former prophets would have been reduced to nothing.*[28]

Through this approach, the validity and authenticity of the Bible stands or falls based on the extent of its agreement with perspectives upheld in the Qur'an. Muslims will acknowledge the reliability of the Bible only if Christians will accept that their Scriptures foreannounced the coming of Islam's prophet. Otherwise, the accusation of textual *taḥrīf* will be leveled against Christians and Jews, rendering interfaith engagement sterile.

The key passages that are well known today as a foundation for this argument are those in the Gospel of John where Jesus promises the coming of the Paraclete, the Holy Spirit, to his disciples. These references to the Paraclete, as we will see in the next chapter, were and continue to be used by Muslims in an attempt to prove the New Testament's expectation of Muhammad.

The root of this Muhammado-centric rereading of the Bible derives from the idea of continuity between the three Scriptures, which is found in the Qur'an itself. For example, the opening verses of āl-ʿImrān 3:2–4

28. Shams ad-Dīn Muhammad b. Abī Bakr Ibn Qayyim al-Jawziyya, *Hidāyat al-Ḥayāra fī Ajwibat al-Yahūd wa an-Naṣāra*, ed. Aḥmad Ḥijāzī as-Saqā (Cairo: al-Maktaba al-Qayyima, 1980), 300–301, cited from my own translation in Martin Accad, "Muhammad's Advent as the Final Criterion for the Authenticity of the Judeo-Christian Tradition: Ibn Qayyim al-Jawziyya's *Hidāyat al-Ḥayāra fī Ajwibat al-Yahūd wa an-Naṣāra*," in *The Three Rings: Textual Studies in the Historical Trialogue of Judaism, Christianity and Islam*, ed. Barbara Roggema, Marcel Poorthuis, and Pim Valkenberg (Leuven: Peeters, 2005), 233 (emphasis added).

provided a solid starting point: "God! There is no God but him. The eternal, the self-sustainer. He has sent down the book to you with the truth to confirm what is available of other revelations, as it is he who sent down the Torah and the Gospel beforehand as guidance to people, and he revealed the standard by which we judge right from wrong."

Historically, many more Gospel passages, beyond those referring to the Paraclete, were used to support this argument. Christian polemicists from the beginning attacked some of Islam's ethical stances and practices to dislodge its claim to authenticity.[29] Two favorite Achilles heels were Islam's embrace of the use of war and violence to fulfill its mission and Islam's view of paradise. In response, Muslim theologians found ways to use precisely these two themes in order to affirm the necessity and finality of Islam.

Islamic Violence

Following a citation from John the Baptist's statement, "the one who comes after me is more powerful [*aqwa*] than I" (Matt 3:11–12 and parallel in Mark 1:7), Naṣr b. Yaḥya (circa twelfth century), followed by al-Qarāfī (thirteenth century), remarks: "Now Christ did not come after him but with him. Therefore, the one whom he meant by this is other than Christ. In fact, the one indicated here is the prophet [*an-Nabī*] (May God bless him and keep him!)."[30] Furthermore, the author explains that the chaff Christ will burn (Matt 3:12) represents the evildoers (*al-fujjār*). This, he affirms, is contrary to what Christians claim about Jesus, who is supposed to have removed sin by his coming, whereas Islam fought evildoers with the sword. The implication is that Islam represents the true heir of Christ's mission as well as of all the rest of the divine revelation.

29. See in particular the letter of 'Abd al-Masīḥ al-Kindī referred to above. But also John of Damascus's treatise *On Heresies*, in D. J. Sahas, *John of Damascus on Islam: The "Heresy of the Ishmaelites"* (Leiden: Brill, 1972); and Nicetas of Byzantium's *Refutation of the Qur'an* (excerpts in Jean-Marie Gaudeul, *Encounters and Clashes: Islam and Christianity in History*, vol. 2: *Texts* [Rome: Pontificio istituto di studi arabi e d'islamistica, 2000]).

30. Ibn Yaḥya, *An-Naṣīḥa al-īmāniyya*, in Floris Sepmeijer, "Een weerlegging van het Christendom uit de 10e eeuw: De brief van al-Hasan b. Ayyub aan zijn broer 'Ali," PhD thesis, Vrije Universiteit Amsterdam (Kampen: van den Berg, 1985), 134. Same argument in Shihāb ad-Dīn al-Qarāfī, *Al-Ajwiba al-Fākhira 'an al-As'ila al-Fājira*, ed. Bakr Zakī 'Awaḍ (Cairo: Wehbeh Publishers, 1987), 432.

Not surprisingly perhaps, the author who tried hardest to establish Islam as the fulfillment of Christianity was himself a convert from Christianity. The idea of placing Islam at the receiving end of a progressive revelation would have been a sort of justification for ʿAlī aṭ-Ṭabarī's personal conversion. His second work, *Kitāb ad-Dīn wa ad-Dawla* (The Book of Religion and Empire), is almost fully consecrated to this argument and is by nature more apologetic than polemical, unlike the author's former work: *Kitāb ar-Radd ʿala an-Naṣāra* (The Book of the Refutation of Christians). After demonstrating, in the first part of his book, the authenticity of Islam from within the Muslim tradition,[31] aṭ-Ṭabarī begins to demonstrate its veracity through the previous revealed books.[32] The final sections are more apologetic, defending Islam against specific criticism of opponents.

Aṭ-Ṭabarī argues that violence, though legitimate in Islam, was not sanctioned for Christians. He explains that judgment, sword, and violence were announced in several New Testament verses, while on the other hand Jesus's followers were called to peace and to reward evil with good. Interestingly, instead of deriving an accusation of *taḥrīf* from such apparently contradictory commands, as some of his coreligionists would do, aṭ-Ṭabarī discerns through this ambiguity two clearly distinct dispensations: Christianity and Islam. One passage from the Gospels where he discerns a clear foreshadowing of this shift in dispensation is Luke 22:35–36: "Christ said to his disciples: 'I had sent you without a purse, or provision bag[33] or sandals. And has that harmed you or deprived you in any way?' They said: 'No.' He said: 'As from now on, let the one who had no purse buy a purse, and the one who had no provision bag, a provision bag. And let the one who had no sword sell his clothes and buy himself a sword.'"

The second command, in aṭ-Ṭabarī's understanding, does not suit the Christian religion, which is built on principles of peace and whose adepts

31. Aṭ-Ṭabarī, *Kitāb ad-Dīn wa ad-Dawla*, 21–66.

32. Aṭ-Ṭabarī, *Kitāb ad-Dīn wa ad-Dawla*, 66–124.

33. The text reads *wa lā tirmāl*, adding the explanation *yaʿnī bihi al-mizwad*. This is an interesting reading, for aṭ-Ṭabarī seems to be using an Arabic version of the Gospel containing a Syriacism that he has to explain to an Arab Muslim reader. If aṭ-Ṭabarī had translated from Syriac, whether mentally or textually, it is likely that he would have rendered the Arabic word directly, rather than mentioning the Arabic transliteration of Syriac *tarmālā* first. This suggests that the author was using an already existing version of the Gospels in Arabic. This also indicates that he was using a Bible version in the tradition of the Peshitta, since the Harklean uses *marsūpā*, a transliteration of the Greek *marsyppion*.

are not allowed to carry the sword. This was made clear by Jesus himself when he reproved Peter for striking the ear of one of the soldiers during his arrest (Luke 22:50–51 and parallels in Matt 26:51–52 and John 18:10–11): "Put up the sword into the sheath. He who draws the sword shall be killed with the sword." Aṭ-Ṭabarī explains that this warning was addressed to Jesus's followers only. But "swords are not bought except for the sake of unsheathing them and striking with them." This, then, according to him, refers to another nation, Islam, whose advent was necessary for Jesus's words to be fulfilled.[34]

Not only does aṭ-Ṭabarī use this text to demonstrate that Islam has supplanted Christianity, but he applies it very specifically to defend the legitimacy of Islam's use of violence. In defense of Islam, aṭ-Ṭabarī begins by surveying numerous Old Testament passages where violence is not only permitted but is even ordered by God. After mentioning that Jesus recommended peace and good in exchange for evil (Matt 5:39–40 and parallel in Luke 6:29), he argues that no religion can stand with such obligations, for its adherents will quickly be in search of a safer situation. He then notes that this is what happened to the Christians, whom he describes as surviving only in small minorities. Therefore, since violence and killing was not to be the business of Christianity, Islam had to appear, by which God would fulfill such expectations of war and sword as are announced in the aforementioned Luke 22:36 and Matthew 10:34: "Do not think that I have come to sow peace, but war."

This latter command, aṭ-Ṭabarī states, abrogates (*nasakha*) the earlier one.[35] It is fascinating that the author should defend the authenticity of both passages by means of the Islamic principle of abrogation (*naskh*), rather than using the apparent contradiction as the basis of an accusation of *taḥrīf*. Ibn Ḥazm and Ibn Qayyim al-Jawziyya use the verse precisely to draw that latter accusation.[36] As a linguistic side note, one might wonder about the reason why aṭ-Ṭabarī's citation of Matthew 10:34 contains the word "war" rather than "sword." Most translations render the Greek *machairan* simply as sword. This further indicates that the Arabic translation that aṭ-Ṭabarī was using was based on the Syriac Peshitta, which renders

34. Aṭ-Ṭabarī, *Kitāb ad-Dīn wa ad-Dawla*, 121.

35. Aṭ-Ṭabarī, *Kitāb ad-Dīn wa ad-Dawla*, 133.

36. See Abū Muhammad ʿAlī b. Aḥmad Ibn Ḥazm, *Kitāb al-Fiṣal fī al-Milal wa al-Ahwāʾ wa an-Niḥal* (Cairo: Al-Qahira Publishers, 1900), 2.22; and Ibn Qayyim al-Jawziyya, *Hidāyat al-Ḥayāra*, 214.

machairan as *ḥarbā*. *Ḥarbā's* primary meaning in Syriac is "sword, blade, or dagger." Only metaphorically can it mean war or slaughter.[37] Without this specific Syriac reading, which the Arabic Gospel that aṭ-Ṭabarī was using translated idiomatically as *ḥarb* (primary Arabic meaning: "war"), it would have been difficult for our polemicist to construct this particular argument on the basis of the verse.[38]

While aṭ-Ṭabarī used the previous citations mainly for apologetic purposes, later polemicists—al-Qarāfī (thirteenth century), Ibn Taymiyya (thirteenth century), and Ibn Qayyim al-Jawziyya (fourteenth century)—would use another passage from the Gospel of Matthew (21:42–44) rather positively. Here the "rejected stone" that became the "cornerstone" is read as a reference to Muhammad, confirming his role as fulfiller of biblical prophecy. And the "other nation" in 21:43 is read as a reference to Islam, to whom the kingdom of God would be given. Finally, 21:44 is used as a confirmation of the legitimate use of force in Islam: "The one who falls on this stone will be broken into pieces."[39]

Islamic Paradise

The other major problem that Muslims had to deal with in the face of Christian polemics, particularly issuing from the rather austere form of Syriac monastic Christianity, was the very different notion that they held about paradise. However, Muslim theologians managed to find several verses in the Gospels from which they drew a depiction of the Christian paradise that conformed with its qur'anic counterpart, equally equipped with food, drink, and pleasure.

Christian convert to Islam ʿAlī aṭ-Ṭabarī goes about defending his newly adopted faith by arguing on the basis of three Gospel passages that its view of paradise does not clash with Jesus's representation of it. He begins by citing Matthew 26:29 (parallel in Mark 14:25) to this effect: "I will not drink of the fruit [lit., daughter] of this vine, until I drink it another

37. See R. Payne Smith and J. Payne Smith, *A Compendious Syriac Dictionary* (Oxford: Clarendon Press, 1903).

38. The Old Syriac Gospels and the Harklean translated Greek *machairan* with Syriac *sayphā* ("sword"). Only the Peshitta has *ḥarbā*.

39. Al-Qarāfī, *Al-Ajwiba al-Fākhira*, 432; Taqī ad-Dīn Aḥmad b. Taymiyya, *Al-Jawāb aṣ-Ṣaḥīḥ li-man Baddala Dīn al-Masīḥ* (Cairo: Nile Press, 1905), 4.6; Ibn Qayyim al-Jawziyya, *Hidāyat al-Ḥayāra*, 118, 132, 172.

time with you in the kingdom of heaven."[40] The author argues on this basis that where there is drink, there must also be food and pleasures. Second, he also cites Luke 22:30, which speaks of food: "You will eat and drink at my Father's table."[41] And third he cites John 14:2, his version mentioning both rooms and dwellings, thus intimating sensual pleasures: "How numerous are the rooms and the dwellings at my Father's."

These three passages, which are traditionally given a sacramental and symbolic interpretation by Christians, are here removed from their literary context and given a more materialistic interpretation, making them perfectly suitable for the Muslim argument.

The anonymous treatise attributed to ʿUmar II was a direct retaliation against a Christian critique of Islamic ethical and ritualistic behavior. After counterattacking by pointing out Christian behavioral shortcomings through an exegetical critique based on the teaching of Jesus, the author moves on to defend the specific teachings in Islam that had apparently come under Christian fire. By doing this he is at the same time reclaiming the biblical text for the Islamic tradition in his attempt to show that his religion is more faithful to the Bible than its original receptors. In the same line as aṭ-Ṭabarī, he cites again Matthew 26:29 in order to confirm the legitimacy of the sensual nature of the Muslim paradise: "Amen I say to you: None of us will drink from this tree after the present day until we drink from it in the kingdom of heaven."

Christ having said these words, and Adam having eaten, drunk, dressed up, and married in paradise, "how can you accuse us of lies and blame us for [such teaching]?" exclaims the author.[42] He further reinforces his conviction by referring to another verse in the same line: "And you have claimed that ʿĪsa said: 'There is in paradise of God's lavishness [*karāma*] what no eye has seen nor ear heard, or any human heart imagined.'" Though this last citation is quite close to 1 Corinthians 2:9, the author attributes this saying to Christ himself, and he is generally not in the habit of quoting from anywhere but the Gospel of Matthew. As Sourdel points out in his edition of the work, it is in fact possible to trace

40. Aṭ-Ṭabarī, *Kitāb ad-Dīn wa ad-Dawla*, 133–34. In this quotation aṭ-Ṭabarī replaces "the kingdom of my Father" in the Gospel with "the kingdom of heaven."

41. The author replaces "at the table of my kingdom" (Peshitta) or "at my table in my kingdom" (Harklean and Greek) with "at my Father's table," removing Christ's prominence from the picture.

42. D. Sourdel, ed./trans., "Un pamphlet musulman anonyme d'époque ʿabbâside contre les chrétiens," *Revue des études islamiques* 34 (1966): 31.

back the saying to a logion from the Gospel of Thomas. The original reads as follows: "Jesus said: I will give you what eye has not seen and what ear has not heard and what hand has not touched and [what] has not arisen in the heart of man."[43]

A similar argument is later found in Ibn Ayyūb's *Risāla*, although the argumentative context is somewhat different. The author cites aṭ-Ṭabarī's second passage (Luke 22:28–30) in his attempt to prove Christ's mere humanity. He is mainly interested in Jesus's saying: "I promise you [*aʿidukum*] as my Father has promised me," which he sees as evidence that Christ is other than God. But he does also draw the other argument as follows: "And this is contrary to what you say about his destiny, and about eating and drinking and pleasure [*an-naʿīm*] there [i.e., in the kingdom]."[44]

By the eleventh century, a polemicist like Ibn Ḥazm is somewhat torn, on the basis of these passages, between deriving his usual accusation of *taḥrīf* and arguing, like the three authors before him, that Christ's description of paradise conforms with the Islamic view. Beginning with a citation of Matthew 22:30, where Jesus teaches that people would neither marry nor have any sexual relations at the resurrection, but would be *like the angels* of heaven, he places it in parallel with Matthew 26:29 and Luke 22:28–30. But instead of deriving his usual accusation of *taḥrīf*, he finds it more useful to reinterpret Matthew 22:30 differently, arguing that since in the Old Testament angels are depicted as eating and drinking food (for instance, when it was offered to them by Lot and Abraham), Jesus's statement does not need to be understood in contradiction to his other statements. Even if we will be "like the angels of heaven," he argues, this will not preclude eating and drinking in paradise.[45]

In the period after Ibn Ḥazm, one of the "shameful questions" (*al-As'ila al-Fājira*) that al-Qarāfī has to answer in his thirteenth-century treatise is precisely the one to which aṭ-Ṭabarī had to reply several centuries earlier. In his version, he reports that both Jews and Christians shamed Muslims for what they saw as a hedonistic view of paradise. But al-Qarāfī

43. A. Guillaumont et al., *The Gospel according to Thomas: Coptic Text Established and Translated* (Leiden/London: Brill/Collins, 1959), 13 logion 17. I owe the reference to Sourdel, "Un pamphlet musulman anonyme," 23n1.

44. Ibn Ayyūb, *Risāla ila Akhīhi ʿAlī* (Letter to His Brother ʿAlī, Explaining to Him Why He Converted to Islam), preserved in Taqī ad-Dīn Aḥmad b. Taymiyya, *Al-Jawāb aṣ-Ṣaḥīḥ li-man Baddala Dīn al-Masīḥ* (Cairo: Nile Press, 1905), 1.2.358–59.

45. Ibn Ḥazm, *Kitāb al-Fiṣal fī al-Milal*, 2.44–45.

refutes their accusations with a long string of passages from both the Old and the New Testaments, where he reads a similar description of the afterlife. Among these are Matthew 26:29 and Luke 22:30. The argument he derives is the same as in his predecessors.[46]

The Qur'anic Account of the Crucifixion

A final issue that somewhat fits under the present theme is that of Christ's crucifixion. The famous verse of the Qur'an in an-Nisā' 4:157, denying that the Jews crucified Jesus, has always been central to the Muslim-Christian debate. One Muslim position, which would enter the debate after the eleventh century, was to accuse the Gospels of corruption because of their affirmation of the crucifixion. However, the usual interpretation found in the qur'anic *tafāsīr* ("commentaries") was that God replaced Jesus with another at the point of the crucifixion, without the knowledge of those present (see chap. 4). In light of this classical interpretation, the argument of several Muslim polemicists was that the divine subterfuge remained hidden from all people until it was revealed for the first time to Muhammad in the Qur'an. Since this great mystery would have remained hidden from humankind if the last prophet had not appeared, they argued that the advent of Islam was an absolute necessity in fulfillment of biblical revelation.

In order to demonstrate the subterfuge, many Gospel verses are used. For example, al-Qarāfī argues that the man who was arrested and crucified was not Jesus since, in spite of Jesus's being very well known (Matt 13:54–55), the Jews had to pay one of his disciples to point him out to them (26:14–15) and Judas had to use the sign of a kiss for them to recognize him (26:47–50). Furthermore, still in doubt about his identity, the high priest had to ask him whether he was the Messiah,[47] and his reply in an unclear manner is a further indication that there was confusion about the identity of the man being crucified (26:63–64). Moreover, the Gospels testify that the disciples in any case would be unreliable witnesses about

46. Al-Qarāfī, *Al-Ajwiba al-Fākhira*, 227–33 (esp. 232).

47. Al-Qarāfī omits from the high priest's question "are you the Son of God?" By having him ask simply "are you the *Masīḥ*?" the interlocutor appears to be asking Jesus the banal question: "What is your name?" since for Islam *al-Masīḥ* ("the Christ") is simply the name of Jesus.

the matter, since Jesus predicted to them that they would abandon him and that Peter, their "leader," would deny him (26:31–34). After offering all this demonstration, al-Qarāfī concludes: "Either Judas [knowingly] did not betray [the right man, and hence ended up committing suicide out of remorse], or Christ (Peace be upon him!) did not speak the truth [when he previously declared the good will of his disciples including Judas], or your book is corrupt [*muḥarraf*]."

These three choices that al-Qarāfī offers his Christian readers show clearly that what matters to him is to demonstrate the veracity of the qur'anic verse above all else. Since the latter two choices are excluded from the Christian perspective, they are left with only the option of accepting the Muslim claim, confirming the qur'anic verse that the Jews were tricked by God and, in this case, also by Judas.[48]

Summarizing the Metadialogue on Muhammad

According to the qur'anic witness, Muhammad performed no miracles, created something of a dilemma for Muslims from the start (al-Isrā' 17:90–93, 105). It put Muslims on the defensive, especially when Christians argued that miracles were the surest sign of prophethood.

Though some Muslims, historically and still today, try to ascribe miracles to Muhammad, Muslims traditionally derived much of their "proofs of Muhammad's prophethood" (*dalā'il an-nubuwwa*) from the Bible. They argued that Islam and Muhammad represented the best fulfillment of Christian expectations, and hence that the authenticity of the Bible could not be maintained without the affirmation of Muhammad's prophethood.

Muslims came to represent Islam as a second dispensation, without which Christianity as the first dispensation would not have come to its fulfillment. Christianity, for example, was to be a religion of peace, whereas Islam came to fulfill supposed New Testament expectations that there should come after it a time when war would be legitimate in God's name. And Christianity was a religion of austerity and asceticism, whereas Islam came to fulfill the legitimacy of more hedonistic practices, such as are portrayed in the Qur'an's depictions of paradise.

Finally, the nebulous circumstances that Islam saw in the Gospel narratives about the crucifixion, resurrection, and ascension of Jesus would

48. Al-Qarāfī, *Al-Ajwiba al-Fākhira*, 190–97.

have never come into light were it not for the Qur'an's accounts about Jesus's last days, as these were richly developed in the exegetical tradition.

Hermeneutical Keys in Building Bridges beyond Conflict

The starting point for unlocking the burden of historical conflict and debate between Jews, Christians, and Muslims about Muhammad will need to question the sufficiency of the traditional narrative of the classical Muslim sources about their prophet. Too many questions and doubts about the historical reliability of this material have been raised by Western scholars to permit us to make use of them without a serious critical lens. On the other hand, the Qur'an will prove to be a far better starting point in such conversations, and the sooner the dialogue partners are willing to accept this starting point, the more fruitful our conversations will be.

Using Deadlocks as Assets

The history of debates between Christians and Muslims about the primacy of miracles in the demonstration of prophethood may need to be put to rest today. Though miracles were an important feature in the earthly ministry of Jesus, the Gospel itself indicates that these did not necessarily bring people to faith (John 12:37). Jesus had these ominous words for those who did not believe as a result of his miracles: "Woe to you, Chorazin! Woe to you, Bethsaida! For if the miracles that were performed in you had been performed in Tyre and Sidon, they would have repented long ago in sackcloth and ashes" (Matt 11:21). Jesus also warned that "false messiahs and false prophets will appear and perform signs and wonders to deceive, if possible, even the elect" (Mark 13:22), indicating therefore that signs are not necessarily an indication of true prophethood. The uniqueness of Jesus should focus not so much on his miraculous signs, but rather on his radical teaching about love, forgiveness, and peace and reconciliation.

Though Christian hermeneutics may not allow for a derivation of Muhammad's prophethood based on the Bible without a significant stretch of biblical exegesis, the popular use of biblical passages for the demonstration of Muhammad's legitimacy has the merit and potential of bringing Christians and Muslims together to a reading of the Bible. Conversations about peace and violence and about understandings of paradise can lead to fruitful discussions on the loving and peaceful teaching of Jesus on sin, salvation, and God's judgment.

Finally, the frankly often outlandish Muslim interpretations of the cross and ascension of Jesus could nevertheless be harnessed to bring people of faith back to a more fruitful conversation about the place of the cross in an overall understanding of God as a self-giving God through divine love as sacrificial love. These conversations will be most useful when they are not kept in the realm of theoretical debate, but when the practical ethical implications of self-giving love are discussed in the context of the role of our faith traditions in bringing peace and reconciliation between our communities.

Further Reading and Research

See bibliography at end of chapter 9.

9 Muhammad as Paraclete

The present chapter continues to survey the Muslim strategy of integrating Islam within the Judeo-Christian tradition by focusing on the most widespread and persistent element of that strategy, which represents the Prophet of Islam as the fulfillment of Christ's promise of the Comforter, the Paraclete of John's Gospel. After surveying the Muslim use of this argument in history, I will look at the most common expression of it in modern times and take a critical look at some of the more recent contributions to this argument and their origins. The chapter ends with a focus on the Paraclete passages proper and how they have been understood by Christians through history and today.

One particular Muslim exegetical strategy used for the affirmation of Islam, as we saw repeatedly in previous chapters, was to represent the emerging religion as the final fulfillment of God's revelation. What we witnessed in the previous chapter, and what we continue to explore in the present one, is an adaptation to the Christian-Muslim context of the technique used by early Christians to establish continuity with Judaism. From that perspective, the whole Bible is reread through the Muhammado-centric perspective, just as early Christians (already in the New Testament itself) had reread the Old Testament from a Christocentric perspective. aṣ-Ṣaff 61:6 sanctioned that effort: "And when Jesus son of Mary said, 'O children of Israel, I am God's messenger to you, confirming what is available of the Torah, and bringing good news of a messenger who will come after me, whose name is Ahmad.' But when he came to them with clear evidence, they said, 'This is obvious magic.'" From the moment that Muslim theologians read in their holy book the claim of a preannouncement of their prophet in the words of ʿĪsa, they set out to probe the Christian Gospels in search for the hard evidence.

From very early on, already in the *Prophetic Biography* (*as-Sīra an-Nabawiyya*), the Johannine passages of a promised Paraclete became the focus of attention of Muslim scholars, who saw in the Paraclete title the most appropriate recipient of the qur'anic prophetic expectation. As we will see in the final section of the present chapter, this mysterious *Fāraqlīṭ* (as he became known among Arab Muslims) quickly became the subject of numerous speculations. Many scholars have since tried to find some rationale to explain the emergence of this firmly established link between the Paraclete concept and aṣ-Ṣaff 61:6. In retrospect, it appears that some Orientalists may have been too quick in postulating a philological link between the two, when perhaps the connection was more intuitive. It is to this story that we now turn.

Muhammad as Paraclete

After it failed to secure the support of Christians and Jews, Islam adopted a new tactic from early on, namely the demonstration of their founder's authentic prophetic calling through the testimony of the venerable religious books of the religions they were seeking to convince. There was ample praise in the Qur'an for the *Tawrāt* (Torah), the *Zabūr* (Psalms), and the *Injīl* (Gospel) to legitimize such an endeavor as soon as someone would appear with enough knowledge of the Judeo-Christian Scriptures to provide the necessary evidence. Although early traces of such a usage of the Christian Gospels can already be found in the words of Patriarch Timothy I's interlocutor, Caliph al-Mahdī in the late eighth century, this undertaking would not become fully fledged until the contribution of the Christian convert to Islam, ʿAlī aṭ-Ṭabarī, in the middle of the ninth century. From this writer onward, the Paraclete passages would acquire such a prominent position in the Muslim discourse addressing Christianity that they quickly came to receive a life of their own. So much so that it is extremely difficult to distinguish the various verses in the sources. When speaking of Paraclete passages, we are therefore dealing with citations of Johannine verses in various combinations: John 14:15–18, 23, 25–30; 15:7, 26–27; 16:7–8, 12–14, 25.[1]

1. Though the present chapter will not expand on what the qur'anic *tafsīr* tradition

Caliph al-Mahdī and Patriarch Timothy I

There is already a shy attempt at using the Paraclete argument by Caliph al-Mahdī in the middle of the eighth century, as reported by Patriarch Timothy I. After the patriarch extensively supported his exposition of Christ's supernatural character by means of testimonies from the Old Testament, al-Mahdī indignantly and repeatedly asks him: "Did you not find a [single] testimony about Muhammad (Peace be upon him) [in your books]?" After Timothy's answer in the negative, the caliph then asks: "And who is the Paraclete?"[2]

Clearly al-Mahdī was not improvising this intervention, but rather was raising an issue already familiar, at least to some extent, to adherents of both religions. As an answer to his question, the patriarch explains that the Paraclete is the Holy Spirit, who is divine in nature (*ṭabīʿa*), but possessing the property (*khāṣṣa*) of emanation. He then cites a combination of several verses from John's Gospel and one from the apostle Paul's first letter to the Corinthians that make mention of the Paraclete Spirit. The quotation reads as follows:

> Christ told his disciples: "When I ascend to heaven, I will send you the Paraclete Spirit that proceeds from the Father [John 15:26], whom the world was unable to receive, and he is with you and among you [14:17]; he who knows everything, and searches everything, even the depths of God [1 Cor 2:10]. And he will remind you of all the truth that I have said to you [14:26b]. He will glorify me, for he will take from what is mine and declare it to you [16:14]."[3]

The patriarch is obviously quoting portions of the Scriptures from memory here, given the intricate nature of the citation. The Pauline citation is particularly surprising, as I have not found it in use by other authors in this context. With this passage, Timothy assumes that he has appealed to enough of the Holy Spirit's characteristics to be able to prove

---

had to say on the issue, as it does not present any material that is different from the one found in the dialogue texts, it is worth mentioning that Rashīd Riḍa has a whole section on the Paraclete in his commentary on an-Nisā' 4:172, thus showing the continued popularity of the argument into the twentieth century.

2. Hans Putman, *L'église et l'Islam sous Timothée I (780–823)* (Beirut: Librairie Orientale, 1975), 23.

3. Putman, *L'église et l'Islam*, 23.

that this promised Paraclete was other than the prophet Muhammad. But after quoting the caliph's claim that "all of these [words] indicate the coming of Muhammad," the patriarch elaborates over the next two pages. Timothy explains that since the Paraclete is God's Spirit then, like God, he is "unlimited" (*ghayr maḥdūd*), "invisible" (*lā yudrak bi an-naẓar*), "incorporeal" (*ghayr mujassam*), and "pure essence" (*ghayr murakkab*). It follows that since no Muslim would claim such characteristics for Muhammad he cannot be the Holy Spirit and consequently cannot be the promised Paraclete.

The patriarch then follows this syllogism with a few additional comparisons between the Holy Spirit Paraclete as described in the New Testament on the one hand and the prophet Muhammad as Muslims recognize him to be on the other. First, while the Paraclete is from heaven and of the same nature as the Father (based on the first clause of his quotation: John 15:26), Muhammad is from earth and of Adam's nature. Second, while the Paraclete "knows the depths of God" (according to 1 Cor 2:10), Timothy points out that Muhammad himself acknowledged that he ignored what would become of him and of his followers. Third, while the Paraclete was with the twelve disciples (*al-ḥawāriyyīn*) and dwelt among them (according to John 14:17), Muhammad was never with the disciples, nor did he ever dwell among them. Fourth, while the Paraclete revealed himself to the disciples ten days after Christ's ascension to heaven, Muhammad did not appear until more than six hundred years later. Fifth, while the Paraclete taught the disciples about God's three hypostases (*aqānīm*), Muhammad did not uphold this belief. Sixth, while the Paraclete performed many miracles at the hands of the disciples, Muhammad did not perform a single miracle at the hands of his followers. Seventh and finally, while the Bible indicates that the Paraclete is equal in nature to the Father and the Son in that he partook in the process of creation,[4] Muhammad clearly did not take part in creation.[5]

The argument that the patriarch develops over these two pages gives justification to the form of the quotation itself, which combines several New Testament passages on the Paraclete rather than conforming to any one citation. It obviously serves the purpose intended by Timothy,

4. Timothy cites here the latter part of Ps 33:6 to substantiate his argument, rendering "by the breath/spirit of his mouth" simply as "by his Spirit" (*bi rūḥihi*), in Putman, *L'église et l'Islam*, 25.

5. All this demonstration found in Putman, *L'église et l'Islam*, 24–25.

namely the construction of an argument against the Muslim claims about the Paraclete. Thus, our author can conclude victoriously that since no statement exists, in either the Old or New Testament, which predicts the coming of Muhammad, Christians cannot be blamed for rejecting the Prophet of Islam. The wording of especially the beginning of the quotation is quite interesting, as it is certainly not free from interpretive concerns. It immediately connects the coming of the Paraclete with Christ's ascent to heaven and explicitly makes it dependent on it. This interpretation is sanctioned by the canonical text, which reads: "When the Advocate comes, whom I will send to you from the Father" (New Revised Standard Version). The understanding is that if Christ sends the Paraclete *from* the Father, then he must be *with* the Father when he does it. Making this more explicit, as he does, helps Timothy to distance the *then imminent* advent of the Paraclete from Muhammad's advent, which would occur only several centuries later. With this opening statement, Timothy presents in a nutshell the three persons of the Trinity with a clear Eastern Christian understanding of their relationship to one another within the Godhead: it is Christ who sends the Holy Spirit, and the Spirit proceeds from the Father through the agency of the Son. This was the Eastern Christian position on the so-called *filioque* controversy.

ʿAlī aṭ-Ṭabarī

While in his earlier *Kitāb ar-Radd ʿala an-Naṣāra*, ʿAlī aṭ-Ṭabarī mainly set out to demonstrate the error of Christian doctrines, his *Kitāb ad-Dīn wa ad-Dawla* is better described as an apologetic work. In fact, the greater part of it is an attempt to demonstrate the legitimacy of Islam and Muhammad on the basis of the Judeo-Christian Scriptures. His favorite New Testament passages, as would be expected, are those that mention the Paraclete, and he has three different quotations to that effect, each combining one or more Johannine verses.[6]

Taken together, both works of the author complement each other quite nicely when his Paraclete citations are examined. In his first work, as seen in chapter 4, his only interest in John 14:16 was in the words "I will ask my Father" as a means of demonstrating that Jesus was therefore

6. These three citations are found in aṭ-Ṭabarī, *Kitāb ad-Dīn wa ad-Dawla*, ed. Alphonse Mingana (Cairo: Maṭbaʿat al-Muqtaṭaf, 1923), 118–19.

different from God. But in his second work aṭ-Ṭabarī pays no attention to this detail, simply taking at face value what he now considers to be Jesus's testimony about the founder of his newly adopted religion. Aṭ-Ṭabarī is guided by his purpose of demonstrating Muhammad's authentic divine calling and is not concerned here with attacking Christian doctrines about Christ.

In a seemingly disinterested manner, he quotes a combination of verses 7, 8, 13 without further comment: "And John said about him in the sixteenth chapter: 'The Paraclete will not come to you if I do not go away. And when he comes, he will reprove the world of sin. And he will not speak anything of himself, but will direct you in all truth, and will announce to you events and hidden things.'" Though the passage seems disinterested, I note that aṭ-Ṭabarī omits the last part of 16:7, which mentions that Christ will send the Paraclete to his disciples.

The Paraclete verse that seems to be of greatest interest to aṭ-Ṭabarī, however, is John 14:26, which he quotes first: "The Paraclete, the spirit of truth that my father will send in my name, will teach you everything."[7] Jesus is promising here to send someone who would teach the disciples everything that they did not know before. According to aṭ-Ṭabarī, since down to his time no one had appeared who taught anything that Christ had not already taught, the Paraclete must therefore be the prophet Muhammad, and the Qur'an is that knowledge that Christ had promised would be given to the disciples. Furthermore, the reason why Jesus said "in my name," aṭ-Ṭabarī points out, is that Jesus himself was also called Paraclete and Muhammad's name always appears in parallel with Christ's name in the Old Testament prophecies. In a somewhat circular way, this becomes for aṭ-Ṭabarī a confirmation of the correctness of his way of reading Muhammad's name all over the Hebrew Scriptures.

None of these quotations about the Paraclete make any mention of the Holy Spirit. The closest we get to this identification in the present quotation is "spirit of truth." In contrast, the canonical version of John 14:26 does mention Holy Spirit, whether in the Syriac or in the Greek. This reinforces the probability that the omission is purposeful, since it becomes easier totally to ignore the traditional Christian attribution of such passages to the Holy Spirit's descent at Pentecost.

Finally, aṭ-Ṭabarī puts forward a more esoteric interpretation of the name Muhammad based on numerology. He explains that the numer-

7. Aṭ-Ṭabarī, *Kitāb ad-Dīn wa ad-Dawla*, 118.

ical value of the Arabic word *Fāraqlīṭ* matches that of *Muhammad b. ʿAbd Allāh, an-Nabī al-Hādī* (Muhammad son of ʿAbdallāh, the guiding prophet). Aṭ-Ṭabarī challenges anybody who objects to his calculation and who claims that the same can be applied to other persons to find a person both whose name count matches Paraclete, as well as whose personality matches the description of the Paraclete given by Christ in these verses.[8]

On the basis of the documents presently known, ʿAlī aṭ-Ṭabarī's *Kitāb ad-Dīn wa ad-Dawla* was historically the first extensive treatment of prophecies announcing the prophet Muhammad on the basis of the Bible. Although we had already found an awareness of the argument in Patriarch Timothy's report of his conversation with Caliph al-Mahdī, there had been no systematic treatment of the question, and in many ways it comes as no surprise that such treatment should originate from the hand of a former Christian possessing a good familiarity with the Bible. In doing this, he was setting a trend for many Muslim theologians after him. We now turn to the remaining story of that *Fāraqlīṭ* in the Muslim tradition.

Al-Yaʿqūbī

The Shīʿī historian al-Yaʿqūbī cites three passages from the Gospel of John that deal with the concept of Paraclete. These are adequately placed in the context of Christ's final speeches to his disciples before he was betrayed. Even though, in his usual manner, al-Yaʿqūbī simply quotes Gospel passages without any exegetical comments, it is quite easy to infer what his intention is by the actual wording of his text. His first citation reads as follows: "Keep my command then [John 14:15], and the Paraclete will come to you [14:16b], and he will be with you as a prophet."[9]

Two points should be noted. First, Christ is deprived of any role in the coming of the Paraclete, whether direct or indirect. The Paraclete is represented as coming through no generative or mediative agency, while in the biblical text it was Jesus who was going to ask the Father to send him. Second, the Paraclete is plainly personalized as a prophet, clearly a reference to Muhammad. It does not seem possible to justify al-Yaʿqūbī's

8. Aṭ-Ṭabarī, *Kitāb ad-Dīn wa ad-Dawla*, 119–20.

9. Al-Yaʿqūbī (Aḥmad b. Abī Yaʿqūb), *Tārīkh*, ed. M. T. Houtsma (Leiden: Brill, 1883), 1.84.

introduction here of the term "prophet" (*nabiyyan*) instead of "forever" on the grounds of a misreading or of a scribal error. Most likely, al-Yaʿqūbī changed the term deliberately in order to make his scriptural citations more acceptable to a Muslim audience. On the other hand, this factor demonstrates that by this writer's time the assimilation of Paraclete with the Prophet of Islam was definitively fixed in Islamic circles, needing no further justification.

Al-Yaʿqūbī continues with this intentional Islamization of the Gospel text in his next quotation of John 15:26: "And when the Paraclete comes to you in a spirit of truth and honesty, he is the one who will testify concerning me."[10] Even though the passage is clearly from John 15:26, important portions of the Gospel verse are removed. First, as in his previous quotation, al-Yaʿqūbī removes the idea that Christ either mediated or effected the coming of the Paraclete. The canonical reading represented Christ as sending the Paraclete from the Father, but in the *Tārīkh* it is once again the Paraclete himself who "comes to you." Second, after having made the leap from the Paraclete directly to Muhammad in his previous quotation, al-Yaʿqūbī now attempts to remove any connection between the Paraclete and the Holy Spirit. Instead, the Paraclete now comes "in a spirit of truth and honesty."

In his third and final quotation on the subject, however, al-Yaʿqūbī mentions the spirit of truth. But in the context of the previous two passages, it stands as a clear reference to Muhammad: "So when the spirit of truth comes, he will guide you into all the truth [16:13a]. And he will declare to you the things that are to come [16:13c], and he will praise me [16:14a]."[11] As a historian, al-Yaʿqūbī seems to have had an actual Christian version of the Gospels rather than adopting his biblical citations from within the Islamic tradition. This makes his alterations even more meaningful, since they most likely originated from him rather than having been taken over from the preceding apologetic tradition. Not only did al-Yaʿqūbī use the Bible as a historically reliable source, but he also presented it in such a way that it would become acceptable as a testimony to the authenticity of Muhammad's prophetic calling.

10. Al-Yaʿqūbī, *Tārīkh*, 1.84.
11. Al-Yaʿqūbī, *Tārīkh*, 1.85.

Naṣr b. Yaḥya

Naṣr b. Yaḥya's reliance on ʿAlī aṭ-Ṭabarī's *Kitāb ar-Radd ʿala an-Naṣāra* in much of his *an-Naṣīḥa al-īmāniyya* has been pointed out. He then makes use of much of the Paraclete treatment of aṭ-Ṭabarī's second treatise, *Kitāb ad-Dīn wa ad-Dawla*.[12] There are several *developmental* characteristics between the two works, which seem to imply that the passages preserved in Naṣr b. Yaḥya were dependent on *ad-Dīn wa ad-Dawla*.

There is close literary link between the three converts from Christianity. Naṣr b. Yaḥya himself, who preserved parts of Ibn Ayyūb's work, was also a convert. And that this strand of thinking should end up surviving in the work of such an important Muslim scholar as Ibn Taymiyya emphasizes the importance that converts played in the development of Muslim polemics and apologetics against Christianity. Naṣr b. Yaḥya broadened the popularity of the Paraclete argument, which was developed extensively for the first time by ʿAlī aṭ-Ṭabarī in his second work. After falling into oblivion for over two hundred years—I have found it briefly mentioned only by al-ʿĀmirī in the interim—it begins to resurface in developed form after Naṣr b. Yaḥya.

Four portions of Johannine Scriptures related to the Paraclete are preserved in Naṣr b. Yaḥya.[13] At the beginning of this section, the author charged: "You have claimed that Christ (Peace be upon him!) declared that no prophet would come after him. . . . And you have claimed that not a single prophet announced his [Muhammad's] coming, and this is an error on your part."[14]

Ibn Yaḥya explains that the announcement of a prophet by another one preceding him cannot be a condition for accepting the legitimacy of that prophet. For no one announced the coming of Moses, Isaiah, Jeremiah, and others. Then he addresses the Christian claim that no prophet would come after Jesus: "And how can you say this, when you

12. Floris Sepmeijer, who reconstructed Ibn Ayyūb's *Risāla*, was the first to point out this dependence and provides a table with exact references to parallel texts; "Een weerlegging van het Christendom uit de 10e eeuw: De brief van al-Hasan b. Ayyub aan zijn broer ʿAli," PhD thesis, Vrije Universiteit Amsterdam (Kampen: van den Berg, 1985), 8. David Thomas adopts Sepmeijer's findings and adds them to his defense of the authenticity and ancientness of aṭ-Ṭabarī's work; see "Tabarī's Book of Religion and Empire," *Bulletin of the John Rylands University Library* 49 (1986): 1–7.

13. Found in Sepmeijer, "Een weerlegging," 163.

14. Sepmeijer, "Een weerlegging," 162.

call the twelve disciples after Christ 'apostles' [*rusul*] and you call Paul 'the apostle'?"

Since the Qur'an refers to Muhammad as both *nabī* ("prophet") and *rasūl* ("apostle") interchangeably, Ibn Yaḥya evidently makes the assumption that this is the Christian definition of these terms as well. This would imply that Christians also consider the New Testament apostles to be prophets, hence the inconsistency of the Christian claim that there could be no prophets after Christ. To this the argument is also adduced that Christ himself, far from claiming that he was the last of the prophets, actually announced that another would come after he had left: the Paraclete. To emphasize this idea of continuity between Christ and Muhammad, our author places the Paraclete passages in the context of Christ's ascension to heaven, in the same statement where he announced that he was going up to the Father:

> *I am going to my Father and your Father, to my Lord and your Lord* [20:17], so that he might send you the Paraclete who will bring you the interpretation [*ta'wīl*] [16:25], which means that he will take from what I have received [*ya'khudhu fī al-ladhī akhadhtu*] [16:14]. And he is the spirit of truth who does not speak on his own behalf, but speaks whatever is spoken to him. And he will announce to you everything that was prepared for you [16:13].

This is the beginning of Naṣr b. Yaḥya's argument to counter the Christian claim, namely, after Christ another will come. The citation as it stands rephrases Gospel statements about the Paraclete in such a way that the connection to Muhammad rather than to the Holy Spirit would be easy to infer. The canonical version of John 16:25 reads as follows: "I have said these things to you in figures of speech. The hour is coming when I will no longer speak to you in figures, but will tell you plainly of the Father" (New Revised Standard Version). In aṭ-Ṭabarī's *Radd*, the verse was rendered as follows: "And I speak to you in parables [*unbi'ukum bi al-amthāl*], but he will bring you the interpretation [*ya'tīkum bi al-bayān*]."

The recognition of John 16:25 is easy enough here. The main alteration is that while the canonical version potentially identifies Christ with the coming Paraclete, the Islamic version of aṭ-Ṭabarī ascribes the parables to Christ and the interpretation to another (i.e., to Muhammad the Paraclete). The version of the quotation as found in Naṣr b. Yaḥya uses still a different wording: "So that he might send you the Paraclete who will bring you the interpretation [*ya'tīkum bi at-ta'wīl*]."

This more advanced form of the quotation explicitly spells out the word "Paraclete" even though it is not found in the canonical text. Since there is no mention of Christ speaking in parables in the later citation, and since it uses the word *ta'wīl* rather than *bayān*, it may seem like a long shot to consider it as a reference to John 16:25. However, let us remember that *ta'wīl* is the more usual word used for "interpretation" and would have come more readily to the mind of a Muslim author than *bayān*. Furthermore, a later quotation in still another author, Ibn Qayyim al-Jawziyya (fourteenth century), as well as in his predecessor Ibn Taymiyya (thirteenth century), seems to allow that leap. (These two writers will be examined later.)

The next three quotations in Naṣr b. Yaḥya, together with their interpretation, originate directly from aṭ-Ṭabarī's *Dīn wa Dawla*. They also contribute to the author's argument to demonstrate the fallacy of the Christian claim that Christ did not allow for another prophet after him. Like aṭ-Ṭabarī before him, he cites John 14:26, which announces that the Paraclete will be a teacher. Like him as well, he omits to mention that the Paraclete is the Holy Spirit, which is how the verse presents itself in the canonical text. Unlike aṭ-Ṭabarī, however, he does not even mention "the spirit of truth," moving even further away from the traditional Christian reference to the Holy Spirit and leaving no other option than to see in Muhammad the fulfillment of the Paraclete promise.

The next quotation is also the same as aṭ-Ṭabarī's next. It combines John 16:7b with 16:13. The wording and structure of the verse are quite different from the canonical version, but identical to aṭ-Ṭabarī's, except that the later author omits 16:8a, which aṭ-Ṭabarī had inserted after 16:7b. The idea that "he will reprove the world of sin" simply seems to have appeared to Ibn Yaḥya as unnecessary to mention about Muhammad. The author cites 16:13 twice in this paragraph, but each time with a different wording. This indicates not only that the writer is citing from secondary texts rather than from the Gospel itself, but also that he is combining citations from two different works, namely the two bearing the name of ʿAlī aṭ-Ṭabarī. Like aṭ-Ṭabarī's *Dīn wa Dawla*, Naṣr b. Yaḥya's final quotation on the Paraclete is John 14:16 with the exact identical wording: "And the meaning of his [Christ's] statement that 'he [the Father] will send him [the Paraclete] in my [Jesus's] name' is that the truth about the Paraclete is the apostle [*rasūl*, i.e., Muhammad], and the meaning of [the name] Christ is the 'apostle' as well."

To summarize, not only does Naṣr b. Yaḥya reiterate ʿAlī aṭ-Ṭabarī's affirmation that Christ's promise of the Paraclete found its fulfillment in Muhammad, but he further reinforces the conclusion by totally doing away with the Holy Spirit in connection with the Paraclete verses. Only once is the "spirit of truth" mentioned, and this is done in such a way that it can be understood only as an attribute of Muhammad the Paraclete.

Abū al-Ḥasan al-ʿĀmirī

In al-ʿĀmirī's treatise *Kitāb al-Iʿlām bi Manāqib al-Islam* (On the Merits of Islam), there is one main section containing biblical quotations, dealing exclusively with the question of Muhammad's foreannouncement in the Torah and the Gospel.[15] After quoting and interpreting several verses from the Old Testament, the only one he mentions from the Gospels is John 14:26a. The version that he quotes is exactly the same encountered in ʿAlī aṭ-Ṭabarī's *Dīn wa Dawla*, together with the minor addition of "spirit of truth" from 15:26b also found in aṭ-Ṭabarī. It is the same one also reproduced in Naṣr b. Yaḥya, which occurred without the "spirit of truth" addition. It reads as follows: "Paraclete, the spirit of truth that my Father will send in my name, will teach you everything."[16]

Al-ʿĀmirī's contribution to his predecessors' argument based on this citation is his removal of the definite article usually found on *al-Fāraqlīṭ*. He thus turns *Fāraqlīṭ* into a proper noun, inherently continuing the process of total identification of Muhammad with the Paraclete. Al-ʿĀmirī follows his quotation with a discussion of two elements in the verse that he considers as evidence that this Johannine reference points to the Prophet of Islam. The first is the statement "the spirit of truth that my Father will send in my name."[17] His argument is that, in the Qurʾan, Jesus is the only

15. Abū al-Ḥasan Muhammad al-ʿĀmirī, *Kitāb al-Iʿlām bi-Manāqib al-Islam* (On the Merits of Islam), ed. A. Ghorab (Cairo: Dār al-Kitāb al-ʿArabī, 1967), 201–8.

16. Al-ʿĀmirī, *Al-Islam*, 203.

17. When we come to this development, the edited text of al-ʿĀmirī's treatise actually reads "the Holy Spirit" rather than "spirit of truth." I have not been able to check the manuscript, but I suspect that the original read "spirit of truth," for the author previously cited the verse with "the spirit of truth" and there is no reason why he should suddenly revert to the better-known term, especially since the verse was known in that form in previous authors. Furthermore, if we accept the text as it stands in the Cairo edition of Abd al-Hamid Ghorab, the whole ensuing argument becomes circular and loses its logic.

prophet to be called "Spirit of God and Word of God" par excellence (*'ala al-iṭlāq*). That is, he was not only confirmed by and received God's Spirit, but *was* it.[18] Furthermore, he adds, no one benefited from the confirmation of the Holy Spirit after Jesus as Muhammad did.[19] Therefore, al-ʿĀmirī concludes, if anyone was expected to come "in my [Christ's] name, meaning that he would be sent together with that by which I was called—which is the Holy Spirit," then it can only be a reference to Muhammad who, according to the Qur'an's testimony, was confirmed by the Holy Spirit. The final implication being that this *Fāraqlīṭ*, who was also referred to as "the spirit of truth," is none but Muhammad himself.[20]

The second element indicating that John 14:26 points to Muhammad is the affirmation that "he will teach you everything." Al-ʿĀmirī explains that this can point only to Muhammad because at the time, "the people of the book [*al-kitābiyyūn*] were in desperate need for someone to set them upon the truth and the proclamation of God's unity, . . . and to open before them the advantages of both worlds [*maṣāliḥ ad-dārayn*]." Only a little bit of that was revealed in the previously revealed books, he argues. For example, while some laws were revealed in the Torah, the four Gospels are merely an account of Jesus's life and proclamation. The book of Acts (*brāxīs*), established by Simon Peter, is an account of the disciples' situation, and the epistles of Paul "contain what is contradictory to the Gospel in clear contradiction." Al-ʿĀmirī's conclusion is that, as a teacher, Muhammad came to complete the revelation of God to the people of the book, who so far had received only one or the other element of God's message to humanity.[21]

Shihāb ad-Dīn al-Qarāfī

In the fourth chapter of his treatise *Glorious Answers to Brazen Questions* (*al-Ajwiba al-Fākhira 'an al-As'ila al-Fājira*), al-Qarāfī presents fifty-one passages from the Bible announcing the coming of the prophet Muhammad. A large number of these are from the Old Testament, and some are from the New. Five of them are Johannine Paraclete passages.

18. Here the author cites al-Baqara 2:87, 253 and seems to hint to an-Nisā' 4:171 in order to demonstrate his point.

19. He quotes ash-Shūra 42:52 and an-Naḥl 16:102 as support.

20. Al-ʿĀmirī, *Al-Iʿlām*, 206–7.

21. Al-ʿĀmirī, *Al-Iʿlām*, 207–8.

The first passage is the most common one already encountered in the previous writers. It is John 14:26a, with the replacement of "Holy Spirit" with "spirit of truth" (*rūḥ al-ḥaqq*) found in 15:26b.[22] We encountered the same citation in practically the same format first in ʿAlī aṭ-Ṭabarī's *Dīn wa Dawla*, followed by Naṣr b. Yaḥya and al-ʿĀmirī. Al-Qarāfī's citation differs from aṭ-Ṭabarī's only in the omission of the expression "in my name." But at the same time, al-Qarāfī does not use any of his predecessors' arguments connected to those words. Rather, he undertakes to explain what is meant by the word *Fāraqlīṭ*. He gives two possible explanations: (1) *al-ḥammād* ("the one who intensifies his praise") or *al-ḥāmid* ("the one who praises") and (2) *al-mukhalliṣ* ("the savior"). It is not at all clear from where the first meaning originates. Indeed, *ḥāmid* or *ḥammād* can mean "the one who praises" but not "the one who is praised." The author's second suggestion that *Fāraqlīṭ* could mean "savior" must come from a popular belief that the word originated from the Syriac root FRQ ("to save"). It is merely a linguistic incident, however, that the transliteration of the Greek original into Arabic letters transforms it into a Syriac cognate. He infers, "And our prophet (May God bless him and keep him!) saves people from unbelief [*kufr*]."

Al-Qarāfī continues to explain that Jesus announced that the Paraclete would teach them everything because this is what Muhammad did. He cites a Ḥadīth to the effect that one of the early companions was mocked by a Jew who derided that Muhammad had even taught Muslims how to defecate! The companion answered in the affirmative, stating that the prophet had taught them to purify themselves before prayer. Al-Qarāfī takes this as a confirmation that Muhammad was the Paraclete because he indeed taught them all things about all aspects of life. Finally, al-Qarāfī points out that Jesus called Muhammad "the spirit of truth, which," he asserts, "is the greatest possible eulogy" (*ghāyat al-madḥ*).[23]

The second Paraclete passage found in al-Qarāfī is John 14:15–17. The author first discusses the significance of 14:16, where Jesus promises "another Paraclete who will be with you forever." He rejects the Christian claim that this is a reference to "tongues of fire" (*alsun nāriyya*) that came down from heaven over the disciples. Instead, he believes that it is a clear reference, not to Muhammad this time, but to his message (the Qur'an),

22. Shihāb ad-Dīn al-Qarāfī, *Al-Ajwiba al-Fākhira ʿan al-As'ila al-Fājira*, ed. Bakr Zakī ʿAwaḍ (Cairo: Wehbeh Publishers, 1987), 423.

23. Al-Qarāfī, *Al-Ajwiba al-Fākhira*, 424.

which on Christ's own testimony will survive until the end of time. As for the Christian claim that the early disciples performed signs and miracles after the tongues of fire descended on them, al-Qarāfī asserts that it cannot be upheld, because it is well known that the early disciples were persecuted and humiliated in all sorts of ways, which would not have happened if they had been assisted by tongues of fire from heaven. This idea that persecution and humiliation are not compatible with divine assistance is characteristically Islamic. It is on the same basis that Muslims historically rejected the historicity of Christ's death on the cross, since according to their thinking it would imply that God had let his servant down. Bearing the cross and suffering for the Gospel, on the other hand, are quite fundamental to a Christian understanding of Jesus's call to discipleship.

Al-Qarāfī appeals to John 14:17, which he sees as a confirmation that Jesus was speaking about Muhammad when he said that he is "the spirit of truth that the world could not bear to receive because they did not know him." He takes the verse as a reference to Muhammad's call to monotheism in a time of idol worship and ignorance. "In contrast," al-Qarāfī adds, "the disciples only addressed the Jews who were already monotheists, even though they had corrupted the law and some of them worshiped stars and idols." Furthermore, al-Qarāfī asserts that Jesus could not have been speaking about the disciples, since they were a whole group, while it is clear that Jesus was speaking about a single individual. This last argument is the first time that a Muslim author suggests that Christians understand the Paraclete promise as a reference to the early disciples. Al-Qarāfī is clearly misinformed about Christian pneumatology and has a superficial understanding of the tongues of fire account in the book of Acts.[24]

Al-Qarāfī continues his survey of Gospel preannouncements of Muhammad with a third passage consisting of John 14:23, 25, 26. The nature of the quotation suggests a new source for it, since he repeats 14:26 with a different wording. This citation contains the "Holy Spirit," not the "spirit of truth" as in his first one. Interestingly, al-Qarāfī seems unaware that the reference is to the same verse, since he marvels that Jesus called Muhammad not only "spirit of truth" but also "Holy Spirit"—"the epitome of praise and eulogy."[25]

Al-Qarāfī's fourth annunciation passage combines John 15:26 and 14:29. The emphasis is on the latter part of 15:26: "He will testify on my

24. Al-Qarāfī, *Al-Ajwiba al-Fākhira*, 424–25.

25. Al-Qarāfī, *Al-Ajwiba al-Fākhira*, 425–26.

behalf." Once again, he objects to the Christian claim—as he understands it—that the promise of the Paraclete was realized in the "tongues of fire." Al-Qarāfī points out that that event did not testify in any way on Christ's behalf against the Jews' accusations that he was possessed by a demon and was born of an adulterous relationship. In contrast, he argues that the Qur'an did so, speaking in defense of his mother's pregnancy by God's power and the authenticity of his miracles. Al-Qarāfī sees the summary of the Qur'an's testimony encapsulated in an-Nisā' 4:171: "The Messiah, Jesus son of Mary, is the messenger of God; his word conveyed to Mary and a spirit from him." Such testimony is, to al-Qarāfī, the clearest affirmation that Christ's promise of the Paraclete was fulfilled in Muhammad and his message, the Qur'an.[26]

Al-Qarāfī's final Paraclete passage combines five verses: John 16:7–8 and 16:12–14. The author wants to summarize his argument on the Paraclete here by drawing five conclusions from this last passage. First, al-Qarāfī concludes that Christ's promise announced one who would be "better" (*afḍal*) than him, since he said that it is better for him to leave so that the Paraclete can come (16:7). Second, the author wonders about the words "I will send him to you" (16:7b). This is the first time in any quotation that a Muslim author preserves this implication that Christ will send the Paraclete. The issue does not go unnoticed by him. Al-Qarāfī suggests two possible solutions. Either these words were just another way to say that Muhammad would not come until Christ had gone, thus the latter participating indirectly and symbolically in the sending of Muhammad, or the first-person singular pronominal suffix *tā'* has to be removed from the verb, thus *arsaltuhu* ("I will send him") becomes *arsalahu* ("he [the Father] will send him"). Third, al-Qarāfī notes, Christ announced that the one who was coming was going "to reprove the world about sin." And this, asserts the author, is what Muhammad did to Jews, Christians, Magi, and Arabs, for he found that they had all gone astray. Fourth, al-Qarāfī argues that only Muhammad led people into "all the truth" about earthly and heavenly things, which neither Christ himself nor the presumed "tongues of fire" did (16:13). Fifth and finally, al-Qarāfī advances that the Qur'an confirms that 16:13b says the Paraclete does not speak of his own accord. He cites an-Najm 53:3–4: "Nor does he speak from his own whims. It is a revealed revelation."

Al-Qarāfī's version of John 16:14 is significant, for although the five-verse citation was quite literal, this final cluster is very different from the

26. Al-Qarāfī, *Al-Ajwiba al-Fākhira*, 426–27.

canonical version, which reads: "And he will reveal to you everything that belongs to the Father." This verse of John's Gospel says that the Paraclete will take what is Christ's and will reveal it to the disciples. But this of course contradicts al-Qarāfī's first conclusion that the Paraclete would be better than Jesus. The present reading can actually be derived from the next verse, where Jesus says: "All that the Father has is mine." This implies that whatever the Paraclete reveals is from both the Father and the Christ, and from a Christian perspective this verse would be used to emphasize the identification of the Father and the Son.[27]

This is the first time that we had such an extensive and organized presentation of the biblical annunciations of Muhammad. Though al-Qarāfī seems to be the original author of this systematic collection, there is no doubt that he was also relying on earlier existing lists of similar passages such as we find in aṭ-Ṭabarī's *Dīn wa Dawla* and Naṣr b. Yaḥya. It was clear throughout that al-Qarāfī was engaged in a quasi-monologue, where the assimilation of the Paraclete with the prophet Muhammad was total. He seems convinced without the shadow of a doubt that Jesus was speaking about the Prophet of Islam whenever he spoke of the Paraclete and that all references to the "spirit of truth" and even to the "Holy Spirit" were references to him.

Taqī ad-Dīn b. Taymiyya

Much of what Ibn Taymiyya has to say against Christianity in his *Al-Jawāb aṣ-Ṣaḥīḥ* by means of a reinterpretation of the biblical passages is contained in his reproduction of Ibn Ayyūb's *Risāla* in this same work. And in this sense his opinion can also be found in all sections relating to Ibn Ayyūb's treatise. Nevertheless, Ibn Taymiyya has another section dealing specifically with biblical announcements of Muhammad. Many of these are from the Old Testament, but we will turn our attention only to the New Testament ones.

The section relating to this issue is the longest I have found so far, and it is somewhat unconventional. Instead of quoting passages one by one and dealing with them, as al-Qarāfī did, Ibn Taymiyya introduces the section with a long tirade of twenty-seven verses before beginning to deal with all sorts of issues related to them. Some of these are the usual

27. Al-Qarāfī, *Al-Ajwiba al-Fākhira*, 428–29.

Paraclete passages and those mentioning the "Holy Spirit" or "spirit of truth," already encountered in previous authors: John 14:26, 15–18, 23, 25–28; 15:7–8, 26; 14:29; 16:7–8, 12–14. Others are less known passages or ones used in other contexts but that Ibn Taymiyya chose to include here: John 14:30; Matthew 21:42–44; 1 John 4:1–3; and 1 Pet 4:17.[28] We will examine the more usual passages first, followed by John 14:30, before moving to the exegetical arguments. The Matthean passage will be dealt with later, together with its parallels in other authors, and the last two passages will be ignored since they are outside the Gospels, which I have established as the focus of the present investigation.

His first quotation, John 14:26, seems to be adopted directly from al-Qarāfī, or at least both authors were quoting from the same collection of biblical texts. It follows it word for word and adopts its two main features: it contains the expression *Rūḥ al-ḥaqq* ("the spirit of truth") and omits *bi-ismī* ("in my name"). This sets apart from all previous ones the last two authors' version of 14:26. The second portion, 14:15–18, is also directly drawn from al-Qarāfī, except that the latter does not have 14:18. John 14:17 in Ibn Taymiyya contains a corruption that can be reconstructed on the basis of al-Qarāfī's text. It reads as follows: "The spirit of truth that the world could not bear to *kill* for they did not know him." The verb *yaqtulūh* ("to kill him") is most definitely a corruption of *yaqbalūh* ("to receive him"), through a simple misplacement of the diacritical points on the third letter. But as a result of this alteration, the author is able to connect the verse easily to a person (Muhammad) rather than to the Holy Spirit.

The next three verses, John 14:23, 25–26, are again practically identical with the ones found in al-Qarāfī. Ibn Taymiyya's text omits, however, three corruptions from his predecessor's: it uses *yattakhidh* ("he will take" [a dwelling]) rather than *yattaḥid* ("it will be agreed upon") (14:23); it has *li'annī 'indakum muqīm* ("for I am [still] with you") in accordance with the canonical version, rather than al-Qarāfī's *ghayr muqīm* ("I am not with you") (14:25); and the end of 14:26 in Ibn Taymiyya is "he will remind you everything that [*kulla mā*] I have told you," which reads better than al-Qarāfī's *kamā qultu lakum* ("as I have told you"). It is quite possible that these corruptions entered in a later manuscript of al-Qarāfī's text, after the time of Ibn Taymiyya, and that the latter did not know them, for on other levels both treatises are remarkably similar, and the same combi-

28. Taqī ad-Dīn Aḥmad b. Taymiyya, *Al-Jawāb aṣ-Ṣaḥīḥ li-man Baddala Dīn al-Masīḥ* (Cairo: Nile Press, 1905), 2.4.5–6.

nation and order of biblical quotations is striking. The first combination of 15:26 and 14:29 and the second combination of 16:7–8 and 16:12–14 are good examples of this.

Having examined the Gospel quotations that Ibn Taymiyya cites in bulk, we now move to the second stage of his work where he begins to discuss the supposed etymology of the word "Paraclete." He mentions, first, two categories of suggestions that had already been put forward by al-Qarāfī. First, he suggests that it is the equivalent of *al-ḥammād*, *al-ḥāmid*, or *al-ḥamd*. Second, he advances that some people claim that it means "the savior" (*al-mukhalliṣ*) in Syriac. Here he adds the explanation given by those claimants, which confirms our earlier inference in the case of al-Qarāfī, namely, that *Fārūq* in Syriac means "savior" and that the final syllable *līṭ* adds emphasis to the word. He probably has in mind the Syriac *īth*. That Ibn Taymiyya's presentation of these meanings is more elaborate than al-Qarāfī's, while at the same time he attributes them to other people (he introduces his statements with *qīla* ["it is said"] and *qālū* ["they say"]), seems to indicate that these etymological explanations originate from a period earlier than both authors (i.e., pre-thirteenth century). Others, Ibn Taymiyya continues, interpret the term to mean "the comforter" in Greek. He concludes: "But we refute both of these claims by the fact that Christ's language was neither Syriac nor Greek, but Hebrew."[29]

After this treatment of popular etymology, Ibn Taymiyya examines who and what the Paraclete indicates for Christians. He points out that some explain the Paraclete to be the "Holy Spirit" or "tongues of fire" that descended upon the disciples and empowered them to perform miracles—a claim, he says, that was rejected by those who followed the accounts of the early Christians and did not witness any acts of power on their part. Others say that it indicates Christ's coming back after his death and resurrection. However, Ibn Taymiyya rejects both allegedly Christian claims. The first because all people of the book acknowledge that the Holy Spirit dwelt on God's prophets already before Christ and on other people after Christ as well. And that the promised Paraclete was Christ himself is excluded by his promise of another Paraclete.[30]

Therefore, Ibn Taymiyya sets out to build his own case on the appropriateness of applying the name "Paraclete" to Muhammad, based on a comparison between all that Jesus said about him and the Prophet of

29. Ibn Taymiyya, *Al-Jawāb aṣ-Ṣaḥīḥ*, 2.4.7.
30. Ibn Taymiyya, *Al-Jawāb aṣ-Ṣaḥīḥ*, 2.4.7–8.

Islam's actual achievements. First of all, since Christ promised that the Paraclete would be "with you forever," it is clear that he was not only pointing to another like him, but he was affirming that the teaching of this other would remain forever, while his own would die out. This is Ibn Taymiyya's way of inferring that Islam would supersede Christianity. Furthermore, that the Paraclete would "testify to Christ," "teach them everything," "remind them of all that Christ had told them," "reprove the world about sin," "lead people into all the truth," and "not speak anything from himself" is clear evidence for Ibn Taymiyya that it will not be some invisible angel, guidance, or knowledge hidden in the hearts of a few. Rather, Ibn Taymiyya asserts, this can be only the announcement of a great man like the prophet Muhammad.[31]

After these general remarks, Ibn Taymiyya further develops individual statements of Jesus in these Gospel passages. The first deals with John 16:12: "I have many words to say to you, but you cannot bear them." Ibn Taymiyya receives these words with enthusiasm, asserting that the Torah and the Gospels have very little to say about God's qualities and about his kingdom and the end days. In contrast, Muhammad came fulfilling Christ's promise that the Paraclete would tell them everything that was to come, since he said many words concerning final resurrection, last judgment, rewards and punishments for good and evil works, various forms of pleasure kept in heaven, and punishments of hell—all recorded in the Qur'an.[32]

He then uses a second verse to summarize what Christ said about the alleged preaching of Muhammad, John 16:14c: "He will make known to you everything concerning the Lord [*ar-Rabb*, sometimes rendered *al-Abb*: 'the Father']." This is taken by Ibn Taymiyya to mean that Muhammad would reveal to humanity the names of God and his qualities, their duty to believe in his angels, his books, and his prophets; in brief that he would summarize and fulfill all previous revelations in a way that was never accomplished by Christianity.[33]

The history of transmission of this verse is quite unfortunate, for it was never known to Muslim authors except amputated. We encounter it first in the ninth-century historian al-Yaʿqūbī, who preserves only the first cluster of it: "and he will glorify me [*yamdaḥunī*]." Its middle cluster is

31. Ibn Taymiyya, *Al-Jawāb aṣ-Ṣaḥīḥ*, 2.4.9–10.
32. Ibn Taymiyya, *Al-Jawāb aṣ-Ṣaḥīḥ*, 2.4.10–11.
33. Ibn Taymiyya, *Al-Jawāb aṣ-Ṣaḥīḥ*, 2.4.11.

then rendered on its own about a century later in Naṣr b. Yaḥya: "Which means that he will take from what I have received [*ya'khudh fī al-ladhī akhadhtu*]." Its last third is found in al-Qarāfī in the thirteenth century in the same form adopted by Ibn Taymiyya and later transmitted to Ibn Qayyim al-Jawziyya. This is not to say that the first three authors drew their quotation from the same source. But it represents clearly enough in what inadequate form John 16:14 was known in Muslim circles. The canonical version of 16:14–15 reads as follows: "He will glorify me, because he will take what is mine and declare it to you. All that the Father has is mine. For this reason I said that he will take what is mine and declare it to you" (New Revised Standard Version). This form of 16:14, which was totally Christ-centered in the canonical version, becomes God-centered in the Muslim treatises. Furthermore, 16:15 justifies the later Christian reading of the passage as a reflection of Trinitarian economy, as we see developed by Patriarch Timothy I (see above). This whole dimension is totally lost by the truncation of the verse throughout the Islamic tradition.

Further statements of Christ about the Paraclete are interpreted as clear references to Muhammad: "he will testify to me," "he will rebuke the world about sin," "he will not speak of his own but will speak everything that he hears." All this comes to the following conclusion that wraps up Ibn Taymiyya's whole argument: "Therefore, the meaning of 'the Paraclete,' whether it be 'the one who gives praise' [*al-ḥāmid*], who 'intensifies his praise' [*al-ḥammād*], who 'is praise' [*al-ḥamd*], or is [the comforter] [*al-mu'azzī*], this description is quite clear in Muhammad (May God bless him and keep him!)."[34]

In the context of this development, another verse used by Ibn Taymiyya seems to have played an important role in the Muslim reception of the Paraclete concept: John 16:25. When we encountered this verse in Naṣr b. Yaḥya, I discussed its transmission from aṭ-Ṭabarī's *Radd* to Ibn Yaḥya, Ibn Taymiyya, and Ibn Qayyim al-Jawziyya. Ibn Taymiyya presents it in the following form: "And it is told that Christ said: 'I have come to you with parables, but he will come to you with the interpretation.'" That he introduces the statement with "it is told" (*ruwiya*) confirms once more that Ibn Taymiyya was taking over his quotations from a previous similar collection, rather than from an actual Gospel text. And the author takes this as a further indication that Islam and Muhammad came as the final fulfillment of God's revelation, for after both Judaism and Christianity

34. Ibn Taymiyya, *Al-Jawāb aṣ-Ṣaḥīḥ*, 2.4.11–14.

were unable to bear what God had to reveal to them, the fine community of Muhammad was given the strength to bear it.[35]

Finally, one more verse mentioned by Ibn Taymiyya is of interest because it was not encountered in any previous author. This is John 14:30: "The ruler of this world is coming and I have nothing."[36] The word used for "ruler" is *arkūn*, the transliteration of the Greek term (*archōn*), which was also common to Syriac Gospel versions. Curiously, although Christians always understood this term in 14:30 as a reference to the devil, Ibn Taymiyya manages to take it as yet another of Christ's announcements of Muhammad's coming. He is aided in this by the wording of the latter part of the verse: "and I have nothing" instead of "he has nothing on me." Thus, the quotation appears as a further testimony that Islam would supersede Christianity and that Muhammad would be greater than Christ. A little later, Ibn Taymiyya even interprets this supposed claim of Christ, "I have nothing," as a distancing of himself from all the claims to "divinity" (*rubūbiyya*) that Christians have made about him.[37] This alteration in the wording is just one example of how much the Islamic reinterpretation of the Gospels relied not only on argumentation, but also on the very translations of the texts handed down in the Muslim milieu.

In conclusion, Ibn Taymiyya's treatment of Christ's Paraclete promises is the most orderly and thorough encountered so far. He analyzes every statement and manages to find its fulfillment in Islamic religion and history. But how does he turn to Islam's advantage passages that had so far been foundational pillars of the Christian theological system? The preceding survey shows that Ibn Taymiyya was the receiver of a long tradition of Islamic reinterpretation of these Paraclete passages. By his time, the key verses had become no more than collections, often repetitive, deprived of all theological and textual contexts and quite often containing erroneous readings that had been solidified through several centuries of transmission. By taking the quotations outside their Gospel context and placing them as it were outside a specific historical time, Ibn Taymiyya and his coreligionists were able to steer them to the advantage of Islam. Christ's statements became generalities that referred to God's dealings with humanity throughout history. Prepassion and resurrection statements that were traditionally understood by Christians as fulfilled in the post-Easter

35. Ibn Taymiyya, *Al-Jawāb aṣ-Ṣaḥīḥ*, 2.4.13.
36. Ibn Taymiyya, *Al-Jawāb aṣ-Ṣaḥīḥ*, 2.4.15.
37. Ibn Taymiyya, *Al-Jawāb aṣ-Ṣaḥīḥ*, 2.4.17.

events were now being read as predictions of things that were to take place six hundred years later. The radical events around Easter were the key to understanding much of Christ's ministry. But having lost this hermeneutical key by its denial of the event and centrality of the cross, Islam was bound to be dissatisfied with Christian exegesis and to search for a more relevant fulfillment for many of Christ's statements and promises.

Shams ad-Dīn b. Qayyim al-Jawziyya

If it became apparent that Ibn Taymiyya was taking over his Gospel quotations from al-Qarāfī, it is equally clear that Ibn Qayyim al-Jawziyya had Ibn Taymiyya's *Al-Jawāb aṣ-Ṣaḥīḥ* before him while writing his own work: *Hidāyat al-Ḥayāra*. This, of course, is not surprising, seeing that Ibn Taymiyya was the latter's master.

Like his two predecessors, Ibn Qayyim al-Jawziyya devotes about a hundred pages to the issue of biblical prophecies about Muhammad. Again, my focus will be on his Johannine Paraclete quotations.[38] With a few exceptions, these quotations have already been encountered in previous authors. But Ibn Qayyim al-Jawziyya brings together more traditions than any of his predecessors, which explains why many of these verses are repeated sometimes in up to three different versions of the Gospel text. Some of these quotations can be traced back to ʿAlī aṭ-Ṭabarī's *Dīn wa Dawla*, probably received through the transmission of Naṣr b. Yaḥya. This link between Ibn Qayyim and Ibn Yaḥya is independent from Ibn Taymiyya's mediation, since it represents traditions not found in Ibn Qayyim al-Jawziyya's master. Other traditions found in Ibn Qayyim al-Jawziyya originate from al-Qarāfī and have arrived to him through Ibn Taymiyya. And still a few other Gospel traditions are unique to the author himself and must have reached him either through another author or through some other Gospel version in his possession.

Ibn Qayyim al-Jawziyya adopts the same method as his master, beginning by enumerating a long list of Gospel quotations before under-

38. The full treatment can be found in Shams ad-Dīn Muhammad b. Abī Bakr Ibn Qayyim al-Jawziyya, *Hidāyat al-Ḥayāra fī Ajwibat al-Yahūd wa an-Naṣāra*, ed. Aḥmad Ḥijāzī as-Saqā (Cairo: al-Maktaba al-Qayyima, 1980), 109–210. The section dealing with the Johannine passages is found on 116–31, though some repetitions can be found spread out on other pages as well.

taking their analysis. The first part is a slightly modified version of passages found in Naṣr b. Yaḥya, originating partly from aṭ-Ṭabarī's *Radd* and partly from his *Dīn wa Dawla* and integrated freely with additional fragments of citations original to Ibn Yaḥya.[39] As has become a familiar feature, these citations are quite difficult to locate precisely in the canonical Gospel for having clearly spent many centuries in an Islamic mold. They comprise roughly portions from John 14:16, 26; 15:26–27; 16:7–8, 13, 25. Most notably, already in this first series of quotations, we have two different versions of 16:7 and 16:13, one originating from aṭ-Ṭabarī's *Radd* and the other from his *Dīn wa Dawla*, but both through the mediation of Naṣr b. Yaḥya. Ibn Qayyim al-Jawziyya himself seems to be surprised by the amount of repetitions of similar concepts found in these passages on the Paraclete. But he explains them away with a quotation from Abū Muhammad b. Qutayba, whom he mentions explicitly, to the effect that all these statements, though similar in meaning, are different "because those disciples who transmitted them in the Gospel on the part of Christ (May God bless him and keep him!) were numerous." He follows this statement with a first search for the etymology of the word *al-Fāraqlīṭ*, similar to, though at this point much briefer than that already found in al-Qarāfī and Ibn Taymiyya. He simply mentions that in the language of the Christians, *al-Fāraqlīṭ* is a term of praise (*min alfāẓ al-ḥamd*), either *aḥmad* or *Muhammad* or *maḥmūd* or *ḥāmid* "or something of the sort." He adds an additional comment, particularly significant because it is not found in his two predecessors: "And in the Ethiopic Gospel, it is *bar naʿṭīs*."[40]

It seems that Ibn Qayyim al-Jawziyya took over this first etymological tradition from Ibn Qutayba. Unfortunately, I have not succeeded in tracing this tradition in Ibn Qutayba's work. In the three works that I surveyed, I did not find any references to the Johannine Paraclete passages. It is possible that he treated the topic in a work that did not survive. Later authors attribute to him a *Kitāb Dalāʾil an-Nubuwwa* (The Book of Proofs of Prophethood). And notably, Ibn al-Anbārī retains the title of this treatise as *Kitāb Dalāʾil an-Nubuwwa min al-Kutub al-Munazzala ʿala al-Anbiyāʾ* (The Book of Proofs of Prophethood from the Scriptures Brought Down [or Revealed] upon the Prophets), clearly a work that demonstrated the prophethood of Muhammad on the basis of Old and New Testament quo-

39. Ibn Qayyim al-Jawziyya, *Hidāyat al-Ḥayāra*, 117.

40. Ibn Qayyim al-Jawziyya, *Hidāyat al-Ḥayāra*, 117–18. Intriguingly, the printed Geʿez text has a transcription of the Greek in all places.

tations.[41] The etymological connection between the Paraclete and the root ḤMD possibly originated in a work that did not survive. Furthermore, Gérard Lecomte notes that Ibn Qutayba owes a tremendous amount of his recorded traditions to scholars of the second and early third centuries of the Hijra.[42] His transmission of traditions may have come from historians like Wahb Ibn al-Munabbih (died 729) and Muhammad b. Isḥāq (died 768), who were the most reputed transmitters of biblical traditions, or *Isrāʾīliyyāt*. Though unfortunately only some of the work of these men survived, it is quite possible that many of the rather islamicized versions of the Gospel passages under study here originated in such circles.

In a second collection Ibn Qayyim al-Jawziyya is mostly indebted to al-Qarāfī, which he received through the intermediary of his master Ibn Taymiyya. The passages featured here are the following:

- John 14:15–18 (14:18 is Ibn Taymiyya's addition to the Qarāfite tradition) and 14:23, 25–28; 15:7 (these belong to Ibn Taymiyya traditions)
- the combination of John 15:26; 16:1; and 16:12–14 (all in the version of al-Qarāfī)
- John 14:30, which Ibn Taymiyya introduced to draw a parallel between the promised *Arkūn* ("ruler of this world") and Muhammad

Not much needs to be said here, since Ibn Qayyim al-Jawziyya mainly plays the role of passive transmitter of his master's exegetical teaching, repeating the three supposed etymologies of *al-Fāraqlīṭ*, this time in their full version: (1) *al-Ḥāmid, al-Ḥammād, al-Ḥamd*; (2) *al-Mukhalliṣ* from Syriac *Fārūq*; and (3) the Greek etymology meaning *al-Muʿazzī* ("the comforter"). He goes on for several pages repeating the teaching of his master on the issue, throughout which he repeats many of the already mentioned quotations, usually in the same version.[43] One point worth noting: Ibn Qayyim al-Jawziyya repeats twice the ḤMD etymology, once in the tradition he attributes to Ibn Qutayba and once in the one received from Ibn Taymiyya and originating from al-Qarāfī. Most likely, he is the recorder of two different versions of the same tradition, which as far as one can

41. The mention of this work, as well as the later Arab scholars who knew of it, is found in Gérard Lecomte, *Ibn Qutayba (mort en 276/889): L'homme, son oeuvre, ses idées* (Damascus: Presses de l'Ifpo, 1965), 154.

42. See Lecomte, *Ibn Qutayba*, esp. 75–80.

43. Ibn Qayyim al-Jawziyya, *Hidāyat al-Ḥayāra*, 119–28.

tell was authored by Ibn Qutayba. All of this to arrive to the conclusion that the qur'anic verse, "Announcing to you an apostle who will come after me whose name is Aḥmad" (aṣ-Ṣaff 61:6), is actually a confirmation of Christ's promise of the Paraclete since, Ibn Qayyim al-Jawziyya insists, *al-Fāraqlīṭ* means *al-Ḥamd*.[44]

As far as Ibn Qayyim al-Jawziyya's treatment of the Paraclete passages is concerned, one more section in his work deserves our attention. It exhibits yet another version of the citation of John 15:23–16:1. In the first group of quotations noted above, the following version of John 15:26c–27 was used: "And he will testify to me and you will testify, for you were with me before other people."[45] John 15:26c–27a is in exactly the same version as found in aṭ-Ṭabarī's *Radd*.[46]

In the second group of quotations, received from Ibn Taymiyya and originating with al-Qarāfī, the combination of John 15:26 and 16:1 was found in the following second version: "When the Paraclete comes, which my Father will send, the spirit of truth that is from my Father, he will testify to me. I have told you so that when it happens you will believe and not doubt him."[47]

This same quotation is found at least another two times in the following pages where the author develops his exegetical argument, and both times in slightly different wording. It is quite likely that Ibn Qayyim al-Jawziyya juggled these Gospel quotations mainly from memory, or possibly that much of his work was based on notes taken from lectures given by Ibn Taymiyya on the subject in the last years he spent in teaching at Damascus. This explains the frequent lack of literality. Also, John 16:1 contains an element from 14:29, namely the combination of "you will believe" and "you will not doubt," either of which is found in only one of the verses in the canonical text. The additional precision of "*so that when it happens*,

44. There is no question yet of the modern accusation that the original word found in the Gospel was *periklytos* ("renowned or glorious," and hence *Aḥmad* or *Muhammad*) rather than *paraklētos* ("comforter"). On the other hand, the editor of Ibn Qayyim al-Jawziyya's work, Aḥmad Ḥijāzī as-Saqā, has a footnote drawing this late inference (128n33).

45. Ibn Qayyim al-Jawziyya, *Hidāyat al-Ḥayāra*, 117.

46. ʿAlī b. Sahl Rabbān aṭ-Ṭabarī, *Kitāb ar-Radd ʿala an-Naṣāra*, in I. A. Khalifé and W. Kutsch's "Ar-radd ʿala-n-nasārā," *Mélanges de l'Université Saint Joseph* 36.4 (1959): 115–48 at 125.

47. Ibn Qayyim al-Jawziyya, *Hidāyat al-Ḥayāra*, 118. This combination is repeated again on 122 and 125.

you will believe," is characteristic of 14:29. This combination was introduced originally by al-Qarāfī and taken over exactly by Ibn Taymiyya.

Then we come to the third version of John 15:23–16:1, this time in full:

> The one who hates me hates the Lord. And had I not performed deeds for them, which no one [else] had performed, they would have no sin. But from now they have become ungrateful [*baṭirū*]. So the word of the law had to be fulfilled: "For they hated me gratuitously [*majjānan*]." And when the *mnaḥmānā* will come, that which God will send to you from the Lord, the spirit of truth, then he will be my witness. And you too, for you were with me from of old. This is my word to you, so that you will not doubt when he comes.[48]

This is at first a curious quotation, for it was not found in any of the previous authors. However, the same quotation—with very minor differences—is found in Ibn Isḥāq's biography of Muhammad (*As-Sīra an-Nubawiyya*).[49] Scholars of the *Sīra* point out that the Gospel used by Ibn Isḥāq was a Palestinian Aramaic version of John's Gospel.[50] Particularly the term *mnaḥmānā* betrays the Palestinian origin, whereas the Syriac always uses a transliteration of the Greek: *Fāraqlīṭā* (so in the Old Syriac, Peshitta, and Harklean).[51]

Ibn Qayyim al-Jawziyya brought several alterations to the text of John 15:23–16:1 found in the *Sīra*, mainly stylistic improvements. First, he shortens the end of 15:24. He stops at *baṭirū* ("they have become ungrateful"), whereas Ibn Isḥāq, as preserved in Ibn Hishām, continued: "and they thought that they overpowered me [*yaʿizzūnanī*], as well as the Lord." The biblical text reads: "But now they have seen and hated both me and my Father" (New Revised Standard Version). It is likely that at some point,

48. Ibn Qayyim al-Jawziyya, *Hidāyat al-Ḥayāra*, 168.

49. Ibn Isḥāq/Ibn Hishām, *As-Sīra an-Nabawiyya*, ed. M. as-Saqā, A. al-Abyārī, and A. Ḥ. Shalabī (Cairo: Muṣṭafa al-Babī al-Ḥalabī, 1936), 1.248. For an English equivalent, see Ibn Isḥāq/Ibn Hishām, *The Life of Muhammad: A Translation of Isḥāq's Sīrat Rasūl Allāh*, trans. A. Guillaume (Oxford: Oxford University Press, 1955), 104.

50. See L. Bevan Jones, "The Paraclete or Mohammed: The Verdict of an Ancient Manuscript," *Muslim World* 10 (1920): 112–25; and A. Guthrie and E. F. F. Bishop, "The Paraclete, Almunhamanna, and Aḥmad," *Muslim World* 41 (1951): 251–56.

51. Cf. A. S. Lewis and M. D. Gibson, *The Palestinian Syriac Lectionary of the Gospels: Re-edited from two Sinai Mss. and from P. de Lagarde's edition of the "Evangeliarium Hierosolymitanum"* (London: Paternoster House, 1899), 187.

possibly through a scribal confusion, an original *naẓarū* ("they saw") was transmitted as *baṭirū* by the displacement of two diacritical points. Ibn Qayyim al-Jawziyya does not see the necessity of extending the verse with a somewhat synonymous statement.

Second, while the Cairo edition of the *Sīra* reads *rūḥ al-quds* ("the Holy Spirit") in 15:26, the editors also inform us in a footnote that one manuscript contains the variant reading: *rūḥ al-qisṭ* ("justice or truth").[52] This must have been the original reading, which again was a transliteration of the Palestinian Aramaic: *rūḥā d-qūshṭā*. Ibn Qayyim al-Jawziyya came across that term and rendered it with the more usual term *rūḥ al-ḥaqq*, or possibly the alteration was introduced earlier in what became his source. It is quite possible that Ibn Qayyim al-Jawziyya also received this tradition via Ibn Qutayba whom, as seen above, he uses elsewhere. Lecomte shows that Ibn Qutayba never made use of Ibn Hishām, but knew the *Sīra* directly from its original author, Ibn Isḥāq.

The final short exegetical comment by Ibn Qayyim al-Jawziyya concerning this passage takes over the one found in the *Sīra* almost literally: "And *al-munḥamannā*[53] is in Syriac, and its explanation in Greek is *al-bāraqlīṭ*." But to this Ibn Qayyim al-Jawziyya adds the other tradition that probably originated from Ibn Qutayba: "And in Hebrew it is *al-ḥammād* and *al-maḥmūd* and *al-ḥamd*, as we have already said."[54]

On the basis of all the above evidence, I argue that Ibn Qayyim al-Jawziyya's *Sīra* quotation also arrived to him through Ibn Qutayba without the intermediary of Ibn Hishām.

Overall, Ibn Qayyim al-Jawziyya is found dealing with the Judeo-Christian Scriptures as well as with their interpretation as the typical Muslim transmitter of Ḥadīth material. He simply passes on material that he finds in the works of his predecessors with no great deal of critical or analytical sense. What we end up with is an unprecedented amalgam of different versions of the same biblical citations with many of their respective Muslim exegetical traditions. I reconstruct the textual history of many of these traditions within the limits of the texts I studied. And though this attempt proves quite helpful in revealing the relationships between the different authors, it is not excluded that the study of the relationship of other works to the same material may change some of the tentative

52. Ibn Hishām, *As-Sīra an-Nabawiyya*, 1.248.

53. I use the vocalization adopted by the editors of the *Sīra*.

54. Ibn Qayyim al-Jawziyya, *Hidāyat al-Ḥayāra*, 168.

conclusions arrived at above. What is certain, however, is that the history of transmission of the Paraclete traditions is extremely complex, and more importantly that it soon became primarily an exercise of polemics and apologetics in the genre of *tathbīt dalāʾil an-nubuwwa* ("establishing the proofs of prophethood"), bereft of any notion of dialogue with Christianity. This is another example of what emerges as a common feature in the Muslim-Christian dialogue.

Summary of the Paraclete Passages

The Paraclete verse most recurring among the different Muslim authors is John 14:26, which represents the Paraclete as a teacher. Not only is it the most frequent, but it is also cited in almost the exact same wording in several of the texts, whether originating from Egypt, Syria, Iraq, or Khurāsān. However, since there are not enough other such examples to postulate a common Arabic version of the Bible in use throughout the region, the best explanation for this evidence seems to be that there was a collection of verses on the Paraclete circulating among Muslim authors. Also comparing the Islamic version of the verses (14:26a is a good example) with their canonical counterparts, it is clear that they were separated from their biblical context from the start, since they never recover their original form. As far as I can trace these back in textual history, at least part of the collection seems to have originated from the hand of early Christian converts to Islam, in this case ʿAlī aṭ-Ṭabarī and Naṣr b. Yaḥya. Though a number of them have also entered independently through al-Qarāfī (again, as far as I can tell from the authors I studied).

Apart from the arguments used by the various authors, the actual version of the verses used was important in shaping their understanding of the Gospel passages. Because so many of these verses became cut off from their original Christian Gospel context early on, they quickly got stuck in specific new islamicized forms that imposed new meaning on Christ's words.

One very clear link is between our last three authors: al-Qarāfī, Ibn Taymiyya, and Ibn Qayyim al-Jawziyya. This link was historically viable. Al-Qarāfī was an influential teacher in Cairo until his death in 1285. At the end of the thirteenth century, Ibn Taymiyya visited that city, first on diplomatic missions and later as a result of theological controversies. On and off, he was detained in Egypt until 1313, after which he returned to

Damascus, where his influence as a teacher became widespread for the last fifteen years of his life.[55] It is easy to imagine that during that extensive Egyptian period Ibn Taymiyya became familiar with the writings of al-Qarāfī, even though he arrived a couple of decades too late to have known him personally. Later on, he passed on this knowledge to Ibn Qayyim al-Jawziyya, who became his main pupil in Damascus until his death.

Finally, neither Ibn Ḥazm nor al-Juwaynī dealt with a single verse mentioning the Paraclete throughout their treatises *Kitāb al-Fiṣal fī al-Milal* and *Shifā' al-Ghalīl* respectively. Their distrust in the book of the Christians was such that they were willing altogether to abandon the argument that legitimized the prophetic calling of their prophet on the basis of the Gospels, and this despite its long and complex history within the Islamic tradition.

The Modern Travesty of the Paraclete Argument

As seen from personal experience in the opening section of the previous chapter, those who engage in a conversation with a Muslim today quickly run into the explanation that the original Johannine texts on the Paraclete contained the promise of the *periklytos* (Greek for "famous or glorious," which can be translated into the Arabic near-equivalent *Muhammad* or *ahḥmad*), which supposedly was later intentionally corrupted by Christians into *paraklētos* (Greek for "advocate or comforter"), in order to erase from their texts any reference to the Prophet of Islam. The impression today is that this accusation always existed in the Muslim polemical tradition. This was not the case, since it is not so much as hinted at in any of the texts covered in the present study from the seventh to the fourteenth centuries. One example of how the argument was used anachronistically can be found in Si Boubakeur Ḥamza's French translation of the Qur'an (1972), where he claims on Ibn Isḥāq's (eighth-century) authority that *paraklētos* came into use later, while earlier *periklytos* appeared in the Gospel text.[56] Tartar thinks that Ḥamza may have taken over this idea from Ḥamidullah who, already in 1959, had given the same explanation in his own French translation of the Qur'an, where he claimed that Ibn

55. H. Laoust, "Ibn Taymiyya," in *Encyclopaedia of Islam*, ed. P. Bearman et al., 2nd ed. (Leiden: Brill, 1954–2005), 3.951–55.

56. Si Boubakeur Ḥamza, trans., *Le Coran* (Paris: Fayard, 1972), 1100.

Isḥāq explained that *biriklutos* meant Muhammad in the language of the Greeks.[57] He concludes: "Who knows . . . whether, in the Gospels of his day, he did not read *periklytos* instead of *paraklētos*?"[58]

This misguided conclusion is based on a grossly inaccurate claim. Ibn Hishām's reproduction of Ibn Isḥāq's *Sīra* contains no mention of *periklytos* (or *bīrīqlūṭas*), but only of *al-baraqlīṭas* (with the long vowel *ī* after *lām* and not after *bā'*, making Ibn Hishām's text unambiguous). Putman remarks that, in her version of the Qur'an, D. Masson relied for similar explanation of aṣ-Ṣaff 61:6 on an earlier conjecture made by Cheikho, where the latter explained how the Greek word *paraklētos* became *bīriqlūṭas* in its Arabic transcription.[59] In fact, Masson makes no mention of Cheikho. Rather, she attributes this inference to the same Ḥamidullah in his translation of the Qur'an.[60] It seems, therefore, that Ḥamidullah is the source of the confusion for both Ḥamza and Masson though, to be sure, he is not the original source of this confusion, which has been going around in the East long before the middle of the twentieth century. Another explanation, put forth by Duncan Macdonald, suggests that the tracing back of the qur'anic verse to John's Paraclete passages, based on the confusion between *paraklētos* and *periklytos*, goes back to a conjecture made by Italian Orientalist Lodovico Marracci (1612–1700), which then made its way into the Islamic literature through the work of Orientalist Georges Sale (1697–1756).[61] This is a much more plausible explanation, and in this case Ḥamidullah's contribution was merely to refer the interpretation back to a medieval scholar of Islam in order to lend the claim more authority.[62]

57. Georges Tartar, "Jésus a-t-il annoncé la venue de Muhammad? Exégèse du verset coranique 61/6," *Parole de l'orient* 16 (1990): 317.

58. M. Ḥamidullah, trans., *Le Coran* (Paris: Le Club Français du Livre, 1959), 545 (my translation).

59. Putman, *L'église et l'Islam*, 196.

60. The following is her claim: "Ishac, selon M. Hamidullah (Traduction du Coran : LXI,6, note) rend ce même terme par *biriklutus*," in *Le Coran*, trans. D. Masson (Paris: Gallimard, 1967), 951n6.

61. This information was communicated by Macdonald in a letter to Percy Smith. See P. Smith, "Did Jesus Foretell Ahmed?" *Moslem World* 12 (1922): 74n*. This explanation is repeated in Tartar, "Jésus a-t-il annoncé la venue de Muhammad?" 319.

62. Guthrie and Bishop, though affirming the philological impossibility that *al-munḥamanna* be read in the sense of Muhammad, are surprised by the *Sīra* not making any mention of aṣ-Ṣaff 61:6 in that context. They conclude: "The implication is that neither Ibn Hishām nor his predecessor (i.e., Ibn Isḥāq) knew anything about the surmised

All of the above, although it may explain the infiltration of the conspiracy theory into modern times, does not however resolve the problem of the presence of aṣ-Ṣaff 61:6. If one does not adhere to the belief that the verse was inspired from God, then it becomes necessary to understand, for example, why the verse does not simply provide a preannouncement of Muhammad rather than Aḥmad. In early times, that the Gospels did not contain such a clear preannouncement of Muhammad's prophetic mission as the Qur'an claimed in this verse surely would have represented a problem for Muslims with regard to the reliability of its message.

Percy Smith provides the most plausible explanation for this puzzle. In his 1922 article "Did Jesus Foretell Ahmed?" he argues that the origin of the qur'anic verse may actually be found in the Gospel passages where John the Baptist announces a messenger who will come after him and will be greater than him. During the time of Muhammad, in Christian Arabic-speaking circles, the Bible was likely still being read out in Syriac during the celebration of the Eucharist and interpreted afterward into Arabic, in the manner of the Targumim's earliest stage. In the same way, Europeans before Vatican II still read the Scriptures in Latin, and the Maronites in Syriac, before paraphrasing them and preaching a sermon in a vernacular language (Arabic in the case of the Maronites).

On an occasion when Muhammad would have been present in an Arabic-speaking congregation of Arabia, it is quite possible that the Arabic word *aḥmad* (the comparative or superlative of the root ḤMD) was used to render the Syriac word "greater" in John the Baptist's preaching.[63] It would then have made its way into the Qur'an. In conjunction with this thesis, one must assume that Muhammad's notion of *Injīl* was the same that he held about his own message, which would be logical, especially given the occurrence of the word "Gospel" exclusively in the singular in the Qur'an. In other words, the *Injīl* would have been expected to contain the statements of God himself, and be transmitted entirely through the mouth of the one man who is the bearer of the revelation. From such a perspective, words of John the Baptist could easily have been attributed

---

reading of *periklytos* for *paraklētos*, and its possible rendering as *Aḥmad*"; see Guthrie and Bishop, "Paraclete, Almunhamanna, and Ahmad," 253.

63. The Syriac Peshitta uses *ḥasīn* ("powerful") in Matthew, *ḥayltān* ("powerful") in Mark and Luke, and *qadmāy men*[*i*] ("before me") in John. But in any case, the hypothesis of Smith need not assume either a semantic or a philological closeness between the Syriac terms and the Arabic rendering.

to Jesus.[64] The ensuing mental leap from *aḥmad* to *Muhammad* and vice versa is itself not really problematic, since the first is a comparative and the second a participle of the same root ḤMD, which can both mean "praised" or "glorious."

On the whole, it seems much more satisfactory to trace aṣ-Ṣaff 61:6 back to passages such as Matthew 3:11; Mark 1:7; Luke 3:16; John 1:27, 30 rather than to Johannine Paraclete passages. It is not to be expected that the connection would have been preserved after Muhammad handed down the message of the Qur'an, since it had to be assumed that the revelation was entirely of divine origin. Some evidence in later authors establishes this connection almost incidentally: "Now Christ did not come after him but with him. Therefore, the one whom he meant by this is other than Christ. In fact, the one indicated here is the prophet [*an-nabī*] (May God bless him and keep him!)."[65] This affirmation is made both by Naṣr b. Yaḥya and by Shihāb ad-Dīn al-Qarāfī in their comments on John the Baptist's preaching, where he announced the coming of the Messiah in Mark 1:7 and Matthew 3:11–12.

Summarizing the Metadialogue on the Paraclete

The starting point of the Muslim argument that set out to demonstrate the preannouncement of Muhammad in the pages of the Bible is the qur'anic verse found in aṣ-Ṣaff 61:6. It was the rejection of the claim found in this verse by Jews and Christians that triggered, from very early on, a snowball reaction in Muslim texts, as may be seen already in *as-Sīra an-Nabawiyya* of Ibn Isḥāq, who died near the end of the eighth century.

Our survey of the historical development of the argument indicates that it was born in the context of polemics, upon the refusal of Christians to admit the occurrence of Muhammad's name in the pages of their Scriptures. From that point onward, aṣ-Ṣaff 61:6 gave birth to a deluge of creative arguments to prove its legitimacy, from the plain argument that it foreshadowed the coming of Muhammad to the argument that Christians stealthily substituted the original wording of the promise with another in order to dissimulate the clarity of the announcement.

64. Smith, "Did Jesus Foretell Ahmed?" 71–74. The author suggests that Mark 1:7 comes closest to the qur'anic reading.

65. Ibn Yaḥya, *An-Naṣīḥa al-īmāniyya*, in Sepmeijer, "Een weerlegging," 134. Same argument in al-Qarāfī, *Al-Ajwiba al-Fākhira*, 432.

Hermeneutical Keys in Building Bridges beyond Conflict

Given the Christian understanding of the finality of Christ and of his death on the cross, followers of Jesus are unable to carve a space for Muhammad in their view of the divine revelation, in a way that would be satisfactory to Muslims. Nevertheless, I am personally unable to accept the traditional narrative about Islam's prophet at historical face value in a way that permits me to use it as a polemical tool in my perception of Muhammad.

Using Deadlocks as Assets

What we are left with is the depiction in the Qur'an of a messenger, a *rasūl*—why less?—who was burdened enough for his Arab people, and devoted enough to God, to take the risk of giving up a life of potential wealth and comfort in order to bring the good news of the one God of Abraham, Moses, and Jesus to the world. This, for me, is the proper starting point for a conversation with my Muslim friends about their beloved prophet.

But finally, as well, the problem that arises if Christians accept the Muslim Paraclete claims for Muhammad is that it affects our understanding of pneumatology (the doctrine of the Holy Spirit) and through it our understanding of ecclesiology (the doctrine of the church). God's self-revelation would not be complete in the Christian theological scheme without the firm belief that Jesus's promises of the Paraclete were fulfilled on the day of Pentecost in Acts 2, which is also the event that marked the birth of the church.

Concluding Thoughts

Jesus promises that when the Father sends the Paraclete in his name, the latter will "teach you all things and will remind you of everything I have said to you" (John 14:26). He affirms that he will "send to you from the Father, the spirit of truth who goes out from the Father" and that this Spirit "will testify about me" (15:26). The promise of the Paraclete is part of Jesus's comforting words that "it is for your good that I am going away." For unless Jesus goes, the Paraclete "will not come to you; but if I go, I will send him to you" (16:7).

Thus, the day of Pentecost, which marked both the fulfillment of this Paraclete promise and the birth of the church historically, inaugurated for Christians the age of the Holy Spirit. The Spirit is hence the inspirer of the Christian Scripture and the continuing revealer of its meaning through the ages. It is the presence of the Holy Spirit with the disciples of Jesus through the ages that enables them to testify about him with truth and power. And most importantly perhaps, the presence of the Holy Spirit with and in Jesus's disciples is the mark of his own resurrected presence with them forever. The appropriation of the *paraklētos* as a recipient for the Holy Spirit since the earliest time of the birth of the church does not reflect a position of bad faith, which could be remedied through some exercises in exegetical gymnastics, to the benefit of prophetic preannouncements about Muhammad. The *paraklētos* for the church is the expression of God's continuing self-giving presence in and among his people through history.

Further Reading and Research

Cragg, K. *Muhammad in the Qur'an: The Task and the Text*. London: Melisende, 2001. By exploring "the soul in the *Sirah*," Cragg sets out to understand the significance of the Qur'an as addressed to and through Muhammad. Cragg carefully moves beyond the negative stereotypes of Muhammad often perpetuated by Christians employing this approach. Repudiating these approaches, Cragg demonstrates the profound insight that comes from engaging in his exploration by recognizing and respecting Islamic convictions about Muhammad.

Cragg, K. *Muhammad and the Christian: A Question of Response*. Oxford: Oneworld, 1999. Cragg crafts a deeply personal, yet careful scholarly answer to Muslim frustration at the lack of acknowledgement by Christians of Muhammad's prophethood. Cragg's response engages with the complexity and multifaceted significance of Muhammad for Muslims from a standpoint of commitment to Christian faith.

10 Beyond Conflict

In this final chapter, I take a fresh look at Islam and Muhammad within the framework of the Judeo-Christian tradition and consider the message of Muhammad from the perspective of salvation history. In closing, I attempt to bring the book full circle by looking at its implications for Christian-Muslim interaction at practical, theological, and spiritual levels.

Legitimate Ways for Christians to View Islam

My hope is that this book will make a positive contribution to the development of a more comprehensive biblical understanding of Islam. To my mind, this is one of the most important tasks that Christians have before them nowadays. Without a solid Christian theology of Islam, based on a biblical understanding of divine revelation, we remain at the mercy of our fluctuating feelings and moods, which tend to swing between highs and lows depending on the latest representations of Islam in the news media. As such, this book is merely one contribution within a much larger corpus still waiting to be written. Such a corpus will need to do justice to the Qur'an and the Muslim tradition, to the history of Christian-Muslim interaction, and to theology and biblical exegesis. I consider Miroslav Volf's *Allah: A Christian Response* (Harper-Collins, 2011), Veli-Matti Kärkkäinen's four-volume dialogical theology *A Constructive Christian Theology for the Pluralistic World* (Eerdmans, 2013–16), and Ida Glaser's *Thinking Biblically about Islam* (Langham Global Library, 2016) as trailblazing beginnings in the genre.

In the present book, I looked at obstacles and bridges in our understandings of God (chap. 3) and of Christ (chaps. 4–5) and considered some of the differences in our ways of understanding God's revelation through prophets and Scriptures from the perspective of the special place that Christ as the eternal Logos occupies in the biblical witness (chaps. 6–7). And finally, I looked at the way that Islam presented itself and its prophet historically and at some of the Christian responses to these representations (chaps. 8–9). My approach was historical and exegetical, woven into a theological framework of some key contemporary concerns.

In this closing chapter, I start with a simple definition of Islam, which I have used in my teaching over the past few years, embracing a more comprehensive understanding of the place and function of Muhammad, the Qur'an, and Muslims in our understanding of the religious phenomenon. As such, some thoughts in this chapter repeat ideas previously developed in the book and others push our boundaries of understanding further.

A Simple Definition of Islam

Having engaged with Islam's sources and with Muslims for over two decades, I present the following definition as a simple and straightforward way of understanding the phenomenon of Islam: Islam is a community, following its holy book, according to precedent. The *precedent*, in this definition, is Muhammad's own life; the *holy book* is the Qur'an that reflects the various stages of Muhammad's life; and the *community* is made up of the billions of Muslims inspired both by the Qur'an and by the life of their prophet throughout history. This framework is represented in figure 5.

Two Stages of Muhammad's Life

The Muslim tradition represents the life of Muhammad in two major phases. From the year when he received his first revelations in Mecca (the city of his birth), in 610, until the year of his migration to Yathrib (renamed Medina) with his early followers in 622, the sources represent him as carrying out a ministry of preaching, warning, and calling his people to the worship of the one God of the Judeo-Christian tradition. During the second phase, from 622 to his death in 632, he is represented as gradually establishing a political community, developing a set of rules that would grow into a full-fledged legal system, and carrying out wars of conquest and consolidation of political power, all under the continued inspiration and guidance of divine revelations.

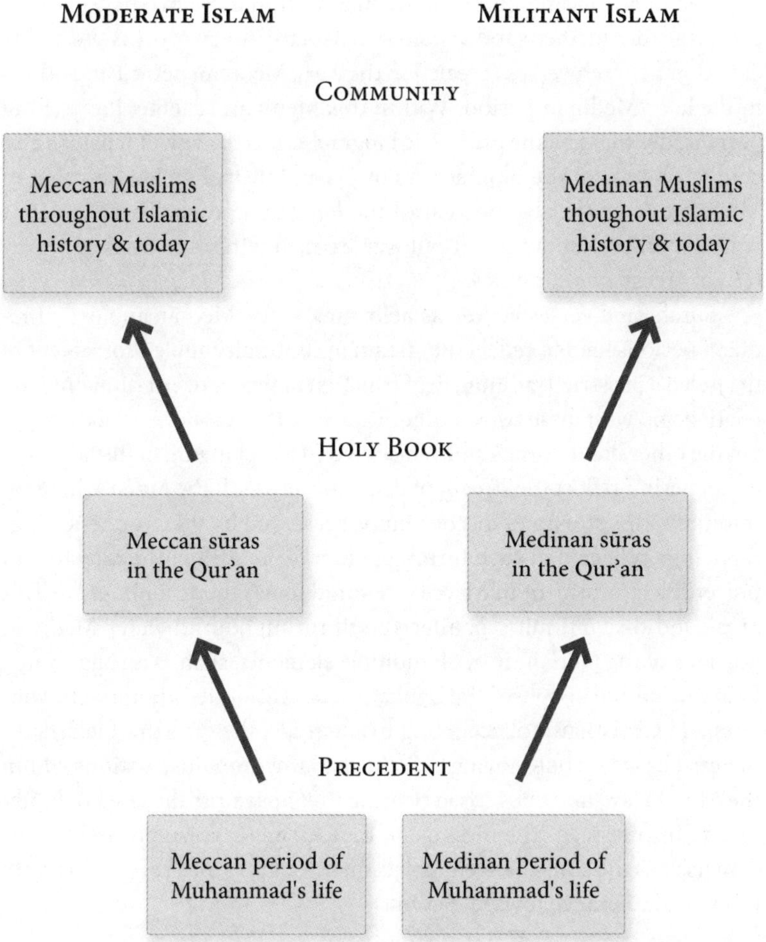

Figure 5. Mecca and Medina

The Meccan and Medinan Qur'ans

One of the primary hermeneutical tools that Muslim Qur'an interpreters have applied to their received text is a consideration of the *occasions of the revelation* of qur'anic sūrahs and verses (*asbāb an-nuzūl*). The process of interpretation, then, takes place within the established framework of Muhammad's life, with portions of the Qur'an considered to have been revealed in Mecca and others in Medina. Within these two periods, exegetes consider further subdivisions. Particularly noteworthy is the differentiation between verses revealed in the early Medinan period and others in the later Medinan period. Within this Medinan scheme, the turning point is identified by the prophetic biographers as the rise of tensions and conflicts between Muhammad's followers and the ruling Jewish tribes of Medina during the second year of the *hijra* to Medina. These tensions would soon break out into all-out war, exile, and in some cases annihilation of Jewish communities.

Sūrahs and verses viewed as belonging to the Meccan and early Medinan periods tend to reflect the stream of continuity and endorsement of the Judeo-Christian tradition, in affirmation of the nature of Muhammad's relationship with these two communities until the second year of the *hijra*. On the other hand, sūrahs and verses viewed as belonging to the later Medinan period reflect the stream of discontinuity with the Judeo-Christian tradition. This stream of discontinuity, preserved by the prophetic biographers, is reflected in such turning points as the shift in the direction of prayer from Jerusalem to Mecca—referred to as "the second *qibla*." This break and discontinuity manifests itself throughout the later Medinan portions of the Qur'an through multiple elements, such as an aggravated tone toward the people of the book, expressions of disappointment with Jews and Christians not accepting his message, the growth of legislative material based on but moving beyond and away from instructions within the Mosaic law, and calls to carry armed *jihād* against those who do not receive his message. The message of the Qur'an increasingly seeks to affirm itself as the seal—or even replacement—of previous revelations, with growing intolerance toward dissent.

Meccan and Medinan Muslims Historically and Today

A few years ago, I reviewed a book edited by Bruce Lawrence, entitled *Messages to the World: The Statements of Osama Bin Laden* (Verso, 2005). At the time I was studying this question of Meccan versus Medinan, and I therefore reviewed the book from the perspective of Bin Laden's qur'anic citations in his twenty-four public statements. I noticed that he consistently cited from those portions of the Qur'an assigned to the Medinan period by most of the Muslim exegetical tradition. From this schema of Meccan and Medinan themes, both within Muhammad's official biography and in the Qur'an, two types of Muslim groups emerge as somewhat distinct from each other through history and today. Some Muslims have been and continue to be inspired primarily by the message and paradigm of Mecca, whereas others emphasize and are inspired primarily by the message and paradigm of Medina. Individuals and groups whom I refer to as "Meccan Muslims" tend to abide by a moderate lifestyle, where primary emphasis is placed on the religious, moral, and spiritual dimensions of the Qur'an. On the other hand, individuals and groups whom I refer to as "Medinan Muslims" tend to manifest a more militant and often violent revolutionary lifestyle, inspired by the more politicized and militant dimensions of the Qur'an. Though Muslim scholars systematically refer both to Muhammad's two life periods and to qur'anic sūrahs and verses as Meccan and Medinan, reference to Meccan and Medinan Muslims is not common. But I have found these categories helpful in my attempt to understand diversity in Islam.

While this may sound rather theoretical and static, this distinction seems to make good sense of the diverse evidence found in the Qur'an. With this framework in mind, it becomes harder to label Islam as either peaceful or violent. In my view, labeling moderate Muslims as real Muslims and militant Muslims as usurpers is as unhelpful and inaccurate as labeling militants as the only true representatives of Islam and those who speak peace as hypocritical imposters. Islam is as diverse as any other religious or ideological system, and as in every group, it is the primary responsibility of moderates to engage extremists among them in dialogue about the most authentic expression of their beliefs.

Muhammad and Early Islamic History as Paradigm

In July 2005 Omar Bakri Muhammad, a Syrian-born Lebanese national, made the headlines of British newspapers as "Preacher of Hate," shortly after the London Underground bombing. When asked in an interview following the bombings whether, if he had known about the bombing conspiracy before it took place, he would have denounced the intending perpetrators, he flatly replied that he would never denounce a Muslim to a non-Muslim *kāfir* ("unbeliever") and commended the bombers for their action.

Bakri Muhammad, shortly after this, went on holiday to Lebanon, was arrested for forty-eight hours by Lebanese security forces, and then released. When he tried to return to the United Kingdom during the 2006 Israeli bombing of Lebanon, he was not allowed on the ship. In the course of a clampdown on *jihādī Salafī* groups in Lebanon in 2014, he was arrested by Lebanese Security Forces and charged with terrorism.

Omar Bakri Muhammad had lived in the United Kingdom since 1986 and had been on government benefit, as a political refugee, together with his wives and numerous children. A member of *Ḥizb at-Taḥrīr* and of *al-Muhājirūn* in the Middle East before coming to the United Kingdom, he had established in 1996 the official British branch of *al-Muhājirūn*. After 9/11, he called the perpetrators of the attack "the magnificent 19." British government pressure mounted on his movement until he disbanded it in 2004. At the time, he also declared the end of the "truce" between Muslims and Britain and its people. It later emerged that his party's website had, several years earlier, publicized a truce with Britain.[1]

What seems clear is that Bakri Muhammad interpreted the British government's crackdown on his movement after 9/11 as a declaration of war. The truce that he declared void mirrors an event that took place in Muhammad's military conflict with the people of Mecca. In the year 628 (seventh year of the *hijra*), Muhammad set out for a pilgrimage from Medina to Mecca, but he was prevented from entering the city by its people. After a process of negotiations in an area outside Mecca called *al-Ḥudaybiyya*, he agreed with them to a ten-year truce (*hidna*) when fighting would stop. According to the terms of the agreement, any free person from Mecca who chose to join Muhammad's community would be allowed to do so, whereas slaves would be prevented; while any person, slave or free, from Muhammad's community who would choose to return to Mecca would be allowed to do so. As it happened, the *Sīra* narrates that a group from a tribe allied to the Quraysh broke the *hidna* by attacking members of Muhammad's community in the course of its second year. At that point, Muhammad marched at the head of ten thousand men and was able to enter the city without a fight, after the governor Abū Sufyān opened the gates before him. These events, marked by what became known as "the truce of *Ḥudaybiyya*," represented a decisive victory and

1. To read more about Omar Bakri Muhammad, see en.wikipedia.org/wiki/Omar_Bakri_Muhammad (accessed January 5, 2017), as well as an interview with him dating from 2005, by Anthony McRoy, a London-based Religion journalist, republished by *Christianity Today* and available online at christianitytoday.com/ct/2005/105/22.0.html (accessed January 5, 2017).

became a major turning point in the destiny of Muhammad's emerging movement.[2]

The case of Omar Bakri Muhammad illustrates how the prophetic precedent represents the paradigm of behavior for militant movements within Islam. Bakri Muhammad adopted a strategy of conquest toward the West, modeled on his interpretation of certain events in Muhammad's life as providing a paradigm that is universally applicable for Muslims everywhere and at all times.

A Case for Meccan Islam

Militant Muslims are certainly not alone in adopting the prophetic paradigm as their rule of behavior. As a matter of fact, Muhammad's life represents the model that most Muslims seek to emulate in their own lives. But the issue of Meccan and Medinan is dealt with differently by Muslims, in line with the sort of Islam that they consider to be primary. The case of Sudanese reformer Maḥmūd Muhammad Ṭāhā (1909–85) is worthy of attention. In the 1930s, he became an activist with the Sudanese nationalist movement in its fight against British colonial rule, until he founded his own republican party (*al-Ḥizb al-Jumhūrī*) in 1945, working for an independent democratic Sudan. After a period of imprisonment as a result of his activism for women's rights, he went into a period of isolation and Sūfī practice, until he reemerged in 1951 with a new vision of Islam. In his new teaching, Ṭāhā reversed the chronology of the classical view of revelation, considering the Medinan period, with its heavy emphasis on law, as temporal and specific to seventh-century Arabia and secondary to the Meccan period, whose spiritual message he considered as primary and universal. It is the universal message of Mecca, in Ṭāhā's view, that could adapt to the contemporary world and address the requirements of democracy and human rights. After being accused of apostasy on more than one occasion, he was imprisoned and eventually executed in 1985.[3]

2. Details of these events and an English translation of the text of the treaty from *As-Sīra an-Nabawiyya* of Ibn Isḥāq may be read in F. E. Peters, *A Reader on Classical Islam* (Princeton: Princeton University Press, 1994), 87.

3. See the article by Annette Oevermann, "Ṭāhā, Maḥmūd Muḥammad," in *Encyclopaedia of Islam*, 2nd ed., ed. P. Bearman et al., 2nd ed. (Leiden: Brill, 1954–2005), 10:96–97. See also Mahmoud Mohamed Taha, "The Second Message of Islam," in *Liberal Islam: A Sourcebook*, ed. Charles Kurzman (Oxford: Oxford University Press, 1998), 270–83.

ʿAbdullahi Aḥmad an-Naʿīm, current professor of Islamic law at Emory University in Atlanta, is one of the inheritors of Ṭāhā's thinking. Born in Khartoum, in Sudan, in 1946, he was a member of his reform movement from 1968 until it was suppressed in 1984. After the execution of his teacher in 1985, he left Sudan and eventually joined the Emory faculty in 1995. He argues for the universality of human rights and considers that Sharīʿa must be viewed as transitory and not applicable at a national level today.[4]

Although the examples of Ṭāhā and an-Naʿīm do not represent the mainstream qur'anic exegetical method, they represent, in my opinion, an interpretation of the Islamic tradition that is more promising for Islam's future than the traditional understanding (described in chap. 2). Though Ṭāhā's systematic reordering of the Qur'an's Meccan and Medinan portions pushed the envelope of the traditional understanding quite far, the focus on the universal nature of the Meccan message—as opposed to the more temporal and historically bound message of Medina—is a way of thinking that I encounter increasingly in my conversations with progressive Muslim scholars, even though it is often not systematically spelled out in so many words. Muslims can in fact subscribe to this view without it demeaning the equal value of the Medinan period in the overall reception of the Qur'an, similarly to the way that Christians view certain parts of the Old Testament. No Christian, for instance, continues to practice the prescriptions of the Mosaic law in detail, beyond the Ten Commandments, despite the firm endorsement of Jesus's words, "Do not think that I have come to abolish the Law or the Prophets; I have not come to abolish them but to fulfill them" (Matt 5:17). We have no difficulty relativizing such material by relegating it to the past, viewing it as an intrinsic part of God's progressive revelation. Muslims too should have no difficulty maintaining their belief in the revealed nature of the Medinan Qur'an, even as they view some of its portions as no longer relevant for Muslims today. It too can be viewed as part of God's progressive revelation to Muhammad, fitting a particular time in the history of a Medinan Muslim community under extreme duress. I expect this hermeneutical angle to become increasingly popular among Muslim scholars globally, and this issue is well worth pursuing in interfaith conversations between Christians and Muslims.

4. ʿAbdullahi Aḥmad an-Naʿīm, "Sharīʿa and Basic Human Rights Concerns," in *Liberal Islam: A Sourcebook*, ed. Charles Kurzman (Oxford: Oxford University Press, 1998), 222–38.

Muhammad in the Context of Dialogue

Having established this particular framework for our understanding of Islam, how may we view the person of Muhammad and his role in the overall metanarrative of biblical salvation history? Is it possible to move beyond the traditional boundaries of our understanding of God's salvific plan by revisiting our linear understanding of chronology and Muhammad's place in this system?

Abraham, Moses, and Muhammad

I briefly return to Patriarch Timothy I's discourse about Islam's prophet in his reported dialogue at the court of Caliph al-Mahdī. From the perspective of behavior as a military leader, and of his role as lawgiver, Timothy was able to assert that "Muhammad walked in the path of the prophets" of the Old Testament, such as Abraham and Moses.

Opinions are divided about the appropriateness of Timothy's statement. Some read in it a confession of a defined prophetic role for Muhammad, whereas others argue that the patriarch was not in a position to say less than this in the restrictive context of the caliph's court.[5] In light of Timothy reporting on this exchange in private epistolary accounts, both in Syriac and in Arabic, I argue that the claim that he made his statement because he was under the pressures of a live debate at the court, and for fear of reprisal, does not stand scrutiny. Supposing that he felt obliged to put down in writing a record of his conversation in Arabic in a way that accommodates Muslim sensibilities, there would certainly have been no reason to force him to put it on record in such a way in Syriac as well. In his position as patriarch of the Church of the East, he was well aware that preserving a written record of such a statement about Muhammad, particularly in the Syriac language, would carry lasting echoes within his church, and therefore I don't believe that we can read it as mere rhetoric. On the other hand, it must be noted that Timothy never affirmed the

5. See the recent interaction between a number of scholars, including myself, with Harley Talman's article, "Is Muhammad Also among the Prophets?" *International Journal of Frontier Missiology* 31.4 (Winter 2014): 169–90. In particular, see the sharp disagreement of Ayman Ibrahim and Talman's response to it in *International Journal of Frontier Missiology* 32.4 (Winter 2015): 202–7.

belief that Muhammad was a prophet, adopting instead a formula that seems deliberately vague. What he affirmed quite simply is that in his opinion, given the official accounts of Muhammad's life, he would view him as having lived a similar lifestyle, and pursued a similar mission, to some of the prophets of the Old Testament.

Though such a statement would not be satisfactory if it issued from a Muslim theologian, it represents a significant model for Christians in conversation with Muslims. It is respectful, open, and honest. It allows for further discussion, exploration, and elaboration. From such a starting point, can we view the role of Muhammad as a sort of precursor of Christ for his people, similarly to the way that Abraham and Moses were instrumental in preparing for the coming of Jesus? In the qur'anic witness, these two great figures are presented as models both for Muhammad and for his people.

Abraham, in the Qur'an, models the man who is willing to stand alone against his polytheistic culture, people, and family in response to God's call. Āl-ʿImrān 3:67 tells us that "Abraham was neither a Jew nor a Christian, but he was one who turned away from all that is false, a monotheist who submitted to God; never an idolater." This affirmation is echoed again in verse 95, where people are called to "follow the creed of Abraham, a monotheist. He was not an idolater."

A more developed account of how Abraham came to believe in the one Creator God is found in al-Anʿām 6:74, which describes how Abraham took a lone stand against his people: "Remember when Abraham spoke to his father Azar, and said, 'How can you take idols as gods? I see that you and your people are clearly lost.'" The Qur'an then describes how he searched for the true God, observing that the stars, the moon, and the sun, though they shine brightly, eventually set and disappear, and therefore could not be God, as his people believed (verses 76–78). Al-Anʿām 6:78–79 contains his faithful confession: "My people, I disown all that you worship other than God. I have turned my face to him who brought into existence the heavens and the earth, and I have turned away from all that is false. I am not one of the idolaters." He courageously continues to argue against his ancestral worship, affirming that their gods can neither harm nor benefit him, until the Qur'an concludes in al-Anʿām 6:83: "Such was the argument we gave to Abraham against his people. We raise in rank whoever we will. Your Lord is all wise, all knowing." Later in the same sūrah (verse 161), Muhammad is himself invited to adopt Abraham as his model: "Say, 'My Lord has guided me on to a straight path through an ever-true faith—the way of Abraham, who turned away from all that is false and was not one of the idolaters.'" Turning "away from all that is false" and being "not one of the idolaters" is the dual mantra that the Qur'an echoes through its pages with regard to Abraham as the paradigm of the man who stands against idol worship.[6]

Sūrat al-Anbiyā' 21 contains a parallel narrative about the challenge that Abraham raised against the idolatry of his people (verses 52–70). It narrates that Abraham destroyed all their idols except the largest one, while they were away. When they came back, they inquired about who had committed this sacrilege, and when Abraham was found out and his people questioned him, he invited them to ask their largest idol: "Ask them if they are able to speak" (verse 63). "And they intended to harm him, but we made them the greatest losers" (verse 70). Here the narrative of Abraham contains a promise to Muhammad that God will protect his prophet and make him victorious over his enemies. This is explicitly stated in al-ʿAnkabūt 29:24: "The only answer of [Abraham's] people was 'Kill him or burn him,' but God saved him from the fire. In that there are signs for people who believe."

In Sūrat at-Tawba 9, the paradigm of Abraham serves as a consolation for those in Muhammad's early community who are unable to turn family members away from idolatry. They are informed that it is not their responsibility to pray for the forgiveness of those who do not respond positively to their message. "Abraham's prayer that his father would be forgiven," verse 114 affirms, "was due to a promise that he had given his father. However, when it became clear to him that his father was one of God's enemies, he renounced him, even though Abraham was tender-hearted, tolerant."[7] How different the interest of the Hebrew Scriptures for the Abraham narrative is from the primary focus of the Qur'an. The Bible retains no detail about the nature of Abraham's relationship with his father or his people. Genesis 12:1 briefly reflects the idea that Abraham left his people and his father to follow God's call: "The LORD had said to Abram, 'Go from your country, your people and your father's household

6. This double description is found in an-Naḥl 16:120: "Truly, Abraham was equal to a community in himself; he was devoted to obeying God. He turned from all that is wrong—and he was not among those idolaters."

7. Abraham's intercession for his father, mentioned here, is a reference to ash-Shuʿarā' 26:86: "Forgive my father, for he has been of those who were misguided." This sūrah and Sūrat aṣ-Ṣāfāt 37 also contain parallel narratives about Abraham's destruction of his people's idols.

to the land I will show you.'" But no further information is provided about Abraham's father or ancestry. The Abraham narrative in Genesis, like the Qur'an, focuses on his faithfulness, but his faith manifests itself primarily in connection with his trust in God's promise of a son, who will ensure for him a large number of descendants. It has little if anything to do with the rejection of idolatry that the Qur'an focuses on. The Abraham narrative of the Qur'an reminds us more of the character of Gideon in the Bible than it does of biblical Abraham. Careful study of the qur'anic Abraham concludes that he seems to be modeled on the paradigm of Muhammad, more than Muhammad is modeled on the paradigm of Abraham.

The New Testament also preserves the memory of Abraham multiple times, but primarily as a model for a faith that believes in God's promises against all odds. Romans 4:18 tells us that "against all hope, Abraham in hope believed and so became the father of many nations," and in Galatians 3:9 we read that "those who rely on faith are blessed along with Abraham, the man of faith." Abraham becomes the channel of blessing for all believers in Jesus who were not born as Jews, as Paul affirms that Christ "redeemed us in order that the blessing given to Abraham might come to the Gentiles through Christ Jesus, so that by faith we might receive the promise of the Spirit" (Gal 3:14). As a man who put his trust and faith in God against all hope, we read in Genesis that this was "credited to him as righteousness" (Gen 15:6). The expression is repeated several times in New Testament epistles (Rom 4:3, 9; Gal 3:6; Jas 2:23), so that Abraham becomes the new paradigm of faith for the emerging Christian community.

Reference to Moses is most prominent in the Qur'an, with his name mentioned more than any other.[8] His challenge of Pharaoh's sorcerers is a narrative that is repeatedly recounted. Moses is presented as the model of the faithful leader who leads his people out of the grip of unrighteous Pharaoh (al-Baqara 2:50; al-A'rāf 7:103–37; Yūnus 10:75; Hūd 11:96–97). The righteousness of Moses is affirmed constantly against the unrighteousness and disobedience of the Israelites, who keep leaning toward idolatry and whom he repeatedly brings back to the worship of the one God through many miracles and signs (al-Baqara 2:51–52; al-A'rāf 7:138). But above all, Moses in the Qur'an is the first prophet to come to his people with "a

8. The Moses narrative is spread throughout the entire Qur'an. References in this section represent only a part of these verses, which is sufficient to cover the principal themes of the narrative.

book" as Scripture. He is the giver of the law, with clear prescriptions on relational and cultic behavior (al-Baqara 2:53; al-Anʿām 6:91, 154; al-Isrāʾ 17:2), and the Qurʾan makes the unique affirmation that "God spoke directly to Moses" (an-Nisāʾ 4:164; al-Aʿrāf 7:144). As a carrier of Scripture, he will be followed by Jesus, who will bring the Gospel (al-Baqara 2:87).

The most prominent feature about Moses in the Qurʾan is the way that he is used as a rhetorical device to bring out the wickedness of the Jews. We are told that the Israelites rebelled by choosing "to worship a calf" (al-Baqara 2:51; an-Nisāʾ 4:153; al-Aʿrāf 7:148). Then they made the unfathomable and presumptuous request to "see God clearly" (al-Baqara 2:55; an-Nisāʾ 4:153). After they are sent the manna from heaven as food in the desert, they complain that they "will not put up with just one kind of food" (al-Baqara 2:61), and the same verse informs us that as a result, "humiliation and misery struck them, and they incurred the wrath of God because they persistently rejected his messages and killed prophets contrary to all that is right. They were transgressors." The Qurʾan somberly summarizes the hopelessness of the Jews in verse 74, before issuing a strict warning to Muhammad's followers about them: "Then, after that, your hearts were hardened. They were as hard as stone or harder. For there are rocks from which streams gush forth, and some from which water flows when they split open, and others that fall down in awe of God. He is not unaware of what you do."

The Qurʾan presents the Jews as a people who made a solemn pledge with God, but then condemns them "for breaking their pledge, for their refusal to acknowledge God's messages, for unjustly killing their prophets, and for saying, 'Our hearts are sealed'" (an-Nisāʾ 4:155). Two verses later we read the famous claim of the Jews that they have killed Jesus, followed with the swift rebuttal that "they did not kill him, nor did they crucify him, though it was made to appear as if it had been so" (an-Nisāʾ 4:157). The Israelites enter into a sharp argument with Moses about the promised "holy land," complaining that they will enter it only after Moses and his Lord go forward and chase out of it the "ferocious people" there (al-Māʾida 5:20–25). As a result, God pronounces his judgment that "the land is forbidden to them. They will wander aimlessly for forty years, on the earth," and he comforts his prophet: "Do not grieve over those who disobey" (al-Māʾida 5:26). If Abraham is Muhammad's model for taking a strong stance against idolatry even in opposition to his family, Moses is the model to encourage Muhammad to persevere in faithfulness, despite the persistent rejection of his leadership by his own people.

Both Abraham and Moses, then, in the Qur'an, are presented as exemplars of righteousness, as men who led their people out of idolatry and into the worship of the one God, with Moses being prominent in the role of lawgiver and community organizer. In summary, the qur'anic representation of Abraham and Moses becomes the paradigmatic blueprint of Muhammad's own self-understanding. This means that by understanding the function of Abraham and Moses in the Qur'an, we arrive at one of the most accurate understandings of the way that the original qur'anic message intended to portray the role and function of Muhammad. What seems to emerge, however, is that the Qur'an shaped the biblical characters of Abraham and Moses in order to fit retroactively the representation of Muhammad that it wished to portray, rather than adopting the biblical representations of Abraham and Moses as models for Muhammad. This certainly provides some interesting insights regarding the Qur'an's integration of biblical prophets into its construction of the faith it refers to as *al-Islam*—the position of surrender and submission to God. I have barely scratched the surface on this important issue, and I would argue that this conversation could represent a fascinating starting point for Christian-Muslim conversation, in our search for mutually enriching common ground.

The Two-Times Theory

From a normative linear chronological perspective, Christians have a hard time arguing that Islam's prophet functioned as a precursor of Christ, given that he came over five hundred years after the time of Jesus. By his calling his people out of paganism and into the worship of the one God, however, we may view his role as an important one in preparing the hearts of his people by aligning them with the Judeo-Christian worldview. To a certain degree, Greek philosophers such as Socrates, Plato, and Aristotle had a similar function in their ability to arrive at the belief in one ultimate being despite the polytheistic Greek culture in which they lived. Socrates paid for it with his life, and his fate is sometimes compared to that of Jesus. These developments in the Greek world played an important role, as the Greco-Roman culture and linguistic idiom became the main vehicles of Christianity, both in recording the text of the New Testament and in expressing its theology during the most formative centuries of its history. But how can we ascribe to Muhammad a role of precursor to Christ's message when he lived several centuries after Christ? We may be able to come closer to such a view by revisiting our understanding of time.

In Galatians 4:1–5, the apostle Paul explains:

> What I am saying is that as long as the heir is a child, he is no different from a slave, although he owns the whole estate. He is subject to guardians and trustees *until the time* set by his father. So also, when we were children, we were in slavery under the basic principles of the world. But *when the time had fully come*, God sent his Son, born of a woman, born under law, to redeem those under law, that we might receive the full rights of sons.

In previous sections of his epistle, Paul implied that "living under the law of Moses" made the Jews like "children." Here he says that even though they were heirs of God's promises, so long as an heir is a child, he/she is no different from a slave. But *at the fullness of time*, God invited (invites) the world into "full sonship." If we ask ourselves what effect this "fullness of time" had on the Mosaic law in the Pauline understanding, we find that it brought it to fulfillment as Christ inaugurated in his own person the primacy of grace. The law of Moses ripened culture up to the time when it matured and gave way to the kingdom of God inaugurated in Christ.

Another passage referring to this sort of cultural time is Hebrews 1:1–3:

> In the past God spoke to our forefathers through the prophets *at many times* and *in various ways*, but *in these last days* he has spoken to us by his Son, whom he appointed heir of all things, and through whom he made the universe. The Son is the radiance of God's glory and the exact representation of his being, sustaining all things by his powerful word. After he had provided purification for sins, he sat down at the right hand of the Majesty in heaven.

Through the prophets, God spoke "at many times" and "in various ways." May we not ask, here as well, according to these three verses, at what *time* and in what *way* God spoke through his Son? What I suggest is that these two passages allow us to consider a different definition of time. The "fullness of time," in the process of salvation history, differs from linear chronological time. We may more aptly speak about this as cultural or moral time. What God needed in order to bring about salvation to his people through his Son was not additional chronological time, but rather the time to prepare them culturally and morally for his encounter of humanity in Christ. Could we, then, consider that Muhammad might have had this function of preparing the polytheistic people of Arabia for such a moral and cultural time? The main problem with this hypothesis is that the Qur'an's representation of Jesus differs somewhat from the way that the New Testament presents him. Though little in the Qur'an about Jesus contradicts the New Testament presentation, several key components of his role and function remain absent from the pages of the Qur'an, most notably his role as savior, as the ultimate manifestation of the self-giving and redeeming God. But here too, as with Abraham and Moses, the gaps need not be taken as making constructive interfaith conversation hopeless. What is important is to bring out these differences and then to take them as starting points for theological dialogue.

The Status of Muhammad for a Christian

As affirmed previously, my understanding of the finality of the cross of Christ, and of God's salvific act through his Son, does not allow space for a further universal revelation or redemptive act. Allowing for this, in my view, injures the redemptive finality of the cross. But if a preacher or evangelist is able to function as a messenger of salvation for people, can we not consider that historically Muhammad came with a similar intent? The title *nabī* ("prophet") in its fully developed theological sense in Islam may be more than what the Bible could allow for a person even of such magnitude as Muhammad. And the title *rasūl* ("messenger"), likewise, in its more developed Islamic meaning, came to be understood as one who brings a new Scripture to his people. But *rasūl* in its more primary linguistic sense of "a person who is sent," as someone who comes to his people with a message to prepare them for God's salvation, is more admissible from a biblical perspective. Perceiving Muhammad as a *rasūl* in this sense is certainly not satisfactory from a Muslim perspective, but it may be an adequate starting point in conversations between Christians and Muslims about the role and place of Muhammad within the Judeo-Christian tradition. In order to avoid any confusion, however, I do not use the word *rasūl*—even in its primary sense—as I do not wish to be misunderstood, either by Muslims or by Christians, who may otherwise see in my statement an embrace of the Muslim confession of faith. In the next section, therefore, I will use the word *messenger* rather than *rasūl*, hoping that the more comprehensive English term will avoid confusion.

Muhammad—a Bridge to Christ?

The concept that we are left to wrestle with, from the preceding exploration, is the relationship of a messenger in this primary sense to the question of access to salvation. If we hold on to the biblical notion that a messenger functions as a *channel*, rather than as *the* locus of salvation, then we are moving toward some resolution of this tension. The New Testament teaches that Christ—rather than Christianity or any other religion—is the way to God and to his salvation. According to the New Testament witness, Christ was not simply a channel for God's salvation but its very locus. I stretch the theological boundaries of my thesis to the possibility of affirming that Muhammad, as a messenger and proclaimer of the God of the Judeo-Christian tradition, may function as a bridge to Christ. Some will object that the presentation of Christ in the Qur'an turns people away rather than closer to the Christ of the New Testament. But what I argue in this book is that if we look at the representation of Jesus in the Qur'an without the burden of the entire exegetical *tafsīr* tradition, we will discover that he is far closer to the New Testament witness than the later Muslim tradition has allowed.

I pointed in the preceding chapters to some of the problems in the traditional Muslim exegetical conclusions derived from the Qur'an about biblical questions. Properly understood in the context of the Judeo-Christian tradition, however, the Qur'an emerges as viewing itself as a book "with the truth to confirm what is available of other revelations" (āl-ʿImrān 3:3), and one that was made "easy to understand in your [Muhammad's] own [Arabic] language that they might remember" (ad-Dukhān 44:58). The Qur'an, from this perspective, is a book that intended itself as a sort of lectionary—a *qeryānā* in Syriac—to be read hand in hand with the Bible (see chap. 1). And if a lectionary is never to be read separately from the Scripture to which it is related, then the Qur'an can find its fulfillment in the New Testament portrayal of Christ, rather than being itself the fulfillment, as has been held by the Muslim tradition.

I am aware that these final paragraphs are provocative and that they will even sound offensive to some Muslims. But as I said in my introduction to this book, my primary target audience has been the church and the student of Christian theology in the twenty-first century. For potential Muslim readers, though I have made my utmost to be respectful in my attempt to approach Islam authentically and legitimately, I also warned that my conclusions would likely differ from the traditional Muslim ones. My goal was to help followers of Christ arrive at a more comprehensive understanding of the Qur'an, of Muhammad, and of the Muslim tradition from a biblical perspective. This book should help Christians appreciate Islam and give them a desire to develop more friendships with Muslims in order to have deeper conversations. My hope is that this book will be a helpful foundation, not just for fruitful conversations, but also for peacebuilding.

A Call to Awakening for People of Faith in the Twenty-First Century

Judging from the opening eighteen years of this new millennium, I expect the twenty-first century to be one of major social, political, and religious transition. Though world religions have played a major part in war and conflict throughout history, this reality has entered our living rooms and psyches perhaps in more gruesome ways than before as a result of satellite television and the ability of social media to draw every citizen into the conflicts through live online debate. As global citizens become increasingly conscious and moved by the intimate link between religious belief and militancy, people of all faiths may have to start playing a far more active role as peacemakers if religions are to have any positive role in the shaping of our societies in the coming decades. If we do not rise to this unprecedented challenge in the most robust ways, we will have failed in our most fundamental divine calling to be agents of God's reconciliation and transformation in the world.

In 2015 and 2016, we witnessed a degradation of fundamental values of human decency at a global scale. The rise of ISIS in the summer of 2014 stunned most people and triggered a global reaction. In the Muslim world, there was an outcry against the horrors committed by the group. Numerous conferences continue to be organized by Muslim organizations and countries to condemn ISIS behavior as un-Islamic. We have witnessed unprecedented calls for reform of the Muslim religious discourse, for the revision of school curricula, and for the centralization of legal authority as a means of reining in the disparity of *fatwas* ("legal religious rulings") that have gone completely out of control. For the first time since the abolition of the Ottoman Caliphate in 1924, we have heard the clearest statements thus far for the abandonment of the idea of the necessity of a centralized caliphal authority that would rule over the global Muslim community. This was accompanied by unequivocal calls for the promotion of civil society, within which Muslims would live peacefully and satisfactorily as part of existing democratic systems. These mainstream voices expressed their clear position against the Islamist struggle for the establishment of Islamic law (Sharīʿa) as a substitute for civil law, which had been a central theme throughout the twentieth century.[9]

The reaction to ISIS in the Western world, on the other hand, was dramatically different. Popular fear gave way to an astonishing rise of rightwing paranoia across Europe, North America, and Australia. These societies, which seemed to be moving toward greater maturity and unity in diversity throughout most of the twentieth century, have regressed over the past decade and a half since September 11, 2001, and considerably more rapidly over the past three years. Today the loudest voices are not for unity and the embrace of diversity, but for self-protection and self-preservation. We are falling prey to a discourse of racism, bigotry, and exclusion, where our base egotistic instincts have far more control over our behavior and decisions than our better God-given natures. In the following concluding sections, I come back to the key passage of Scripture that I reflected on in the introduction and consider its implications for disciples of Jesus who are called to a new revolutionary lifestyle that will challenge the current status quo. Micah 6:8 encapsulates God's fundamental driver for transformed human behavior and for the sort of public policy that can lead to peace globally:

> He has showed you, O man, what is good.
>   And what does the LORD require of you?
> To *act justly* and to *love mercy*
>   and to *walk humbly with your God.*

Imagining a New Future

In my first chapter, I reflected on the general implication that adopting mercy, humility, and justice (in line with Mic 6:8) as a way of life could have on conflict and peace. In these closing lines, I want to reflect on

9. I document the developments since November 2014 on the Institute of Middle East Studies blog at imes.blog.

practical ways that these values can affect relationships between Jews, Christians, and Muslims.

Based on the Bible's teaching against slander, as followers of Jesus we must strive toward balance and truth in our understanding of Islam and Muslims. We want to resist the propagation of slanderous caricatures of Islam, as much as of a utopian and idealized representation that fails to recognize the harm experienced by many at the hand of violent men acting under the banner of Islam. Too many self-proclaimed and self-styled experts on Islam have emerged in our circles since September 11, 2001. They have been received and their teaching embraced and idealized in our churches simply because their discourse fed into our phobias and confirmed some of our fearful suspicions.

Not all evangelicals will suddenly become well-informed experts on Islam. However, it is our duty to ensure that we encourage many in our communities to become experts so that they might inform and lead us. In the immediate term, we need to ensure that we surround ourselves with scholars who have a profound and balanced comprehension of Islam, interfaith, and East-West issues. In the longer term, we also need to identify the greatest challenges and opportunities in our relationship with Islam, and we need to get ready and properly equipped to face these in a way that will contribute to building peace and to alleviating conflict.

Evangelical churches worldwide are invited to explore their misgivings about Islam and prejudices about Muslims. They are invited to set apart "prophets" among them, who will dedicate time for an authentic study of Islam, and people who will explore their neighborhoods to identify Muslim communities, find out about their needs, and find ways to minister and be good neighbors to them. Muslims today, particularly in contexts where they are minorities, need to have positive experiences with their Christian neighbors. In these days of massive migration and global refugee crises, this will help them integrate better in their communities and avoid living in ghettos and environments that breed segregation and extremism.

A Call to Social Action

No doubt the most tragic phenomenon of our time is the massive forced migration that refugees are being subjected to as a result of the regional wars in the Middle East and North Africa. In such times of upheaval, our basic instincts of self-preservation drive us inward into places of exclusion, whether at the individual, communal, or national levels. Our fears lead us to suspicion of those who are different from us and to the building of walls of separation. We develop complex arguments based on moral judgment in order to justify such behavior. Arguably this is exactly what ISIS was betting on as it began to lose the war on the military stage. What religiously violent groups need in order to recruit large numbers into their ideological ranks is not so much victories on the ground, but rather the progress of the us-versus-them mentality. Fear is the best recruiter into the ranks of extremism because of its great capacity for the justification of violence.

Therefore, the victory over religious extremism will not be won on the battlefield of guns and heavy military hardware, but on that of knowledge and rectification of information. And the best way to get to know the other is by moving *toward* them rather than retreating *from* them in judgment. Therefore, God's call to mercy through his prophet Micah is a call to social action. As evangelicals, we need to engage in genuine work of mercy and compassion among Muslim communities worldwide.

Numerous churches in Lebanon have miraculously understood this in recent years. They have flung their doors open to refugees and demonstrated compassion to levels unseen before. Refugees, regardless of their religious backgrounds, have been flocking into church buildings, where they have found love, compassion, and community. No institution can understand and practice the compassion of God demonstrated in Jesus as the church can. The body of Christ globally is invited to follow this example. The most effective missionaries today are those who already have a career with hard skills before they take up the missionary calling. Muslim communities need to be served by real people with real jobs and real lives, and yet who are able to live differently through the realities of life by the power of Christ.

Followers of Jesus are transforming the human tragedy around them, and they are being transformed profoundly in the process. The more we delay our instinct to reach out to refugees, by means of false justifications of self-preservation, the more we are giving space to fear and prejudice and losing the battle against religious extremism.

A Call to Political Activism, Peacebuilding, and Courage

The rise of ISIS and of other violent ideologies does not, of course, emerge from a vacuum. To identify summer 2014 as a significant turning point at the start of the twenty-first century must not become an attempt at identifying a scapegoat for all our current ills. ISIS is not an isolated heresy. It is the manifestation of a developing ideology that is to be understood in significant part as one of the outcomes of the wars in Afghanistan, Iraq, Palestine, and Sudan and other major conflicts of the twentieth century. The phenomenon of religious extremism is the tip of the iceberg of a long history of conflicts, classical colonialism, and neocolonialism and of the struggle for hegemony, of which political powers have been guilty both East and West throughout history. Since this is a book primarily addressed to Christians, it is appropriate in the closing chapter to direct my critique and assessment primarily to myself and to my community.

I am not revealing anything radical by affirming that one of today's major sources of anger, frustration, and bitterness in the Muslim world is the Palestinian issue. This is not a localized conflict anymore. It has erupted into major conflicts globally and can convincingly be shown at the root of the tragedy of September 11, 2001. Just as it is the source of numerous wars, I believe it is also the key to the resolution of today's most troubling conflicts, from Afghanistan to Iraq and Syria, and all the way to intercommunal conflicts within the societies of Europe and North America.

Christians globally need to educate themselves about the history, theology, and politics of this issue,[10] but perhaps even more importantly, they need to educate themselves about the plight of the Palestinian people. They need to meet and build relationships with Palestinians wherever they find them. They need to walk through the narrow alleys of the colossal and inhumane prisons that Palestinian camps in Lebanon, Jordan, and Syria have become. And they need to listen to Palestinians and pay careful attention to their feelings as they express their plight.

In the midst of this history, people of faith are called to be agents of reconciliation, and reconciliation begins with confession rather than with a search for who is to blame for starting a conflict. At the same time, to focus on reconciliation does not imply that we must forgive and forget. The forgive-and-forget approach leads to the repression of hurt, only for it to come back and manifest itself in the form of a worse conflict later. True reconciliation is achievable only through forgiveness, and deep for-

10. It is worth mentioning the writings of Colin Chapman, Gary Burge, N. T. Wright, Stephen Sizer, Salim Munayar, Sami Awad, and others on the Israeli-Palestinian issue, as well as on the emergence and development of Zionism, dispensationalism, and Christian Zionism.

giveness is possible only after a minimal level of justice has been achieved toward the rectification of a situation of injustice.

The church of Jesus Christ is uniquely positioned to understand the depth and plausibility of this process. The real significance of the cross is in that, through the willingness of the only perfectly innocent man in history to lay down his life, reconciliation was achieved between human beings and their Creator through the cry of this man on the cross: "Father, forgive them, for they do not know what they are doing" (Luke 23:34).

The struggle for justice and reconciliation is therefore a call to political activism, hand in hand with peacebuilding. Followers of Christ today cannot stand idle in the face of injustice. But the restoration of justice that our Lord taught us is achieved only through forgiveness and release in the face of oppressors. This is the only process through which victims can liberate themselves from the inclination toward revenge and the perpetuation of the cycle of violence through self-victimization.

Our Lord left us these powerful words: "Peace I leave with you; my peace I give you. I do not give to you as the world gives. Do not let your hearts be troubled and do not be afraid" (John 14:27). Jesus's invitation for us to be peacemakers is therefore a call to courage and to confidence that the peace that we can bring to the world is the kind that no one else can bring.

A Call to Worship

Much conflict today emerges from human arrogance. All of us experience this at a personal level in our relationships with people. But this also applies in our relationships as communities and countries with others. As Christians, and perhaps even more particularly as evangelicals, we have adopted an arrogant attitude to other religions and even to other Christian denominations. We do this, forgetting that our spiritual identity is not that we are Christians or evangelicals or Baptists, but that we belong to Christ. From this standpoint of being *in Christ*, we do not consider ourselves to be in a position of competition with other religions or worldviews or philosophies. Our message is not one of putting down others or proving the superiority of our own system or worldview. It is simply an invitation to all to a relationship with God as Father, by being in Christ, regardless of which religion or ethnicity or society we were born into. We need to reevaluate our missional approaches in the Muslim world and among Muslim communities worldwide by reexamining our own identity as followers of Jesus.

At a global level between countries also, a politics of humility that acknowledges the other rather than denying them could potentially lead to the resolution of long-lasting conflicts. Our human history is filled with stories of nations and peoples subjugating others. Our modern history preserved a strong and often bitter aftertaste of colonialism, often extending into postcolonial attitudes toward immigrant communities or expressed again in the foreign policies of powerful nations toward those it looks down upon as needing their brand of democracy or freedom or culture.

Prejudice, then, seems to be growing into one of the great ills of our time, and religious people seem to be among those most prone to falling into this sin. Religions have a tendency to build a sense of pride in their faithful. One of them instills the conviction that its adherents are God's "chosen people." Another one affirms that its adherents are the "greatest nation that God has ever created." A third one affirms so vehemently that its adherents have been "saved by grace" that they can easily become judgmental about all others who do not seem to be living by their standards. But these are all travesties of religions' original intent. Chosen people, the greatest nation, and those saved by grace should understand their unique position before God as a calling to be a blessing to others, rather than a source of condemnation. Religious people who fall into the sins of pride and prejudice have fallen away from the presence of God.

The message of Micah contains a call to humility. As we cease to compare ourselves with other human beings and start to look to God as our model, we can only "walk humbly with our God." Micah's message is an invitation to worship. It is only as we respond to God's invitation into his presence in worship that our deep humanity begins to get restored. As we respond to global crises with fear, we retreat and build walls, and with this we fall into the grave sins of idolatry and worship of self. But as we respond to crises and fear by entering into the presence of God in worship, our hearts are turned to the destitute, to the oppressed, and to our fellow human beings. We abandon judgment for compassion and despair for hope.

God, through his prophet Micah, invites his church in this twenty-first century to practice mercy, justice, and humility, as we respond to his call to social action, peacebuilding, and worship. My hope is that the present book offers some resources for people of faith as they seek to come closer together before God by bridging the chasms of misunderstanding between them that have resulted from an often-turbulent history.

Bibliography

Note: qur'anic commentaries in Arabic may be found online at altafsir.com.

Abū Qurrah, Theodore. *Al-Qawl fī Ta'annus Allāh al-Kalima* (Treatise on the Incarnation of God the Word). In *Vingt traités théologiques d'auteurs arabes chrétiens (ix–xiii siècles)*, edited by Louis Cheikho, 108–20. Beirut: Imprimerie Catholique, 1920.

———. *Les oeuvres arabes de Théodore Aboucara évêque d'Haran*. Edited by C. Bacha. Beirut: Alfawaïd, 1904.

Abu Zayd, Nasr Hamed. *An-Naṣṣ, as-Sulṭa, al-Ḥaqīqa: al-Fikr ad-Dīnī bayna Irādat al-Ma'rifa wa Irādat al-Haymana* (Text, Authority, Truth: Religious Thought between the Desire for Knowledge and the Desire for Hegemony). Casablanca/Beirut: al-Markaz ath-Thaqāfī al-'Arabī, 1997.

———. *Ishkāliyyāt al-Qirā'a wa Āliyyāt at-Ta'wīl* (Problems of Reading and Methods of Interpretation). Casablanca/Beirut: al-Markaz ath-Thaqāfī al-'Arabī, 1994.

Accad, Fouad. *Building Bridges: Christianity and Islam*. Colorado Springs: NavPress, 1997.

Accad, Martin. "Corruption and/or Misinterpretation of the Bible: The Story of the Islamic Usage of *Taḥrīf*." *Near East School of Theology Theological Review* 24.2 (2003): 67–97.

———. "Did the Later Syriac Fathers Take into Consideration Their Islamic Context When Reinterpreting the New Testament?" *Parole de l'orient* 23 (1998): 13–32.

———. "The Gospels in the Muslim Discourse of the Ninth to the Fourteenth Century: An Exegetical Inventorial Table (Parts I–IV)." *Journal of Islam and Christian-Muslim Relations* 14 (2003): 1: 67–91, 2: 205–20, 3: 337–52, 4: 459–79.

———. "The Interpretation of John 20.17 in Muslim-Christian Dialogue (8th–14th Cent.): The Ultimate Proof-Text." In *Christians at the Heart of Islamic Rule*, edited by David Thomas, 199–214. Leuven: Brill, 2003.

———. "Loving Neighbor in Word and Deed: What Jesus Meant." In *A Common Word: Muslims and Christians on Loving God and Neighbor*, edited by Miroslav Volf et al., 157–61. Grand Rapids: Eerdmans, 2010.

———. "Muhammad's Advent as the Final Criterion for the Authenticity of the Judeo-Christian Tradition: Ibn Qayyim al-Jawziyya's *Hidāyat al-Ḥayāra fī Ajwibat al-Yahūd wa an-Naṣāra*." In *The Three Rings: Textual Studies in the Historical Trialogue of Judaism, Christianity, and Islam*, edited by Barbara Roggema, Marcel Poorthuis, and Pim Valkenberg, 271–36. Leuven: Peeters, 2005.

Accad, Martin, and John Corrie. "Trinity." In *Dictionary of Mission Theology: Evangelical Foundations*, edited by John Corrie, 396–401. Downers Grove, IL: InterVarstiy Press, 2007.

Adang, Camilla. *Muslim Writers on Judaism and the Hebrew Bible: From Ibn Rabban to Ibn Ḥazm*. Leiden: Brill, 1996.

ʿĀmirī, Abū al-Ḥasan Muhammad al-. *Kitāb al-Iʿlām bi-Manāqib al-Islam* (On the Merits of Islam). Edited by A. Ghorab. Cairo: Dār al-Kitāb al-ʿArabī, 1967.

Anonymous. "Gregory of Nazianzus." In *New World Encyclopedia*. Available online at newworldencyclopedia.org/p/index.php?title=Gregory_of_Nazianzus&oldid=977736 (accessed February 19, 2016).

Aulén, Gustaf. *Christus Victor: An Historical Study of the Three Main Types of the Idea of the Atonement*. Translated by A. G. Herbert. London: SPCK, 1950.

Bāqillānī, Abū Bakr Muhammad b. aṭ-Ṭayyib al-. *Kitāb Tamhīd al-Awāʾil wa Talkhīṣ ad-Dalāʾil* (The Book of Establishment of First Principles and Summary of Proofs). Edited by R. J. McCarthy. Beirut: Bibliothèque Orientale, 1957.

Baṣrī, ʿAmmār al-. *Kitāb al-Burhān* (The Book of Proof). In *Kitāb al-Burhān; wa Kitāb al-Masāʾil wa al-Ajwiba (Apologie et Controverses)*, edited by Michel Hayek, 19–90. Beirut: Dar el-Machreq, 1977.

Bat Ye'or. *Understanding Dhimmitude*. New York: RVP, 2013.

Bearman, P., et al. *Encyclopaedia of Islam*. 2nd edition. 12 vols. Leiden: Brill, 1954–2005.

Boraine, Alex. *A Country Unmasked: Inside South Africa's Truth and Reconciliation Commission*. Oxford: Oxford University Press, 2001.

Boubakeur Ḥamza, Si, trans. *Le Coran*. Paris: Fayard, 1972.

Bouyges, Maurice. "'Aliy Ibn Rabban at-Tabariy." *Der Islam* 22, no. 2 (1935): 120–21.

———. "Nos informations sur 'Aliy . . . at-Tabariy." *Mélanges de l'Université Saint Joseph* 28 (1949–50): 69–114.

Brueggemann, Walter. *The Prophetic Imagination*. 2nd edition. Minneapolis: Fortress, 2001.

Bukhārī, Muhammad al-. *Ṣaḥīḥ al-Bukhārī*. Translated by Muhsin Khan. Available online at sunnah.com/bukhari.

Campenhausen, Hans Freiherr von. *The Formation of the Christian Bible*. Translated by J. A. Baker. Philadelphia: Fortress, 1972 (original German 1968).

Chomsky, Noam. *Failed States: The Abuse of Power and the Assault on Democracy*. New York: Metropolitan, 2006.

———. *Hegemony or Survival: America's Quest for Global Dominance*. London: Penguin, 2003.

"A Common Word" document. Available online at acommonword.com/the-acw-document.

Crain, Jeanie C. *Reading the Bible as Literature: An Introduction*. Cambridge: Polity, 2010.

Crone, P., and M. Cook. *Hagarism: The Making of the Islamic World*. Cambridge: Cambridge University Press, 1977.

Cumming, Joseph L. "Did Jesus Die on the Cross? The History of Reflection on the End of His Earthly Life in Sunnī Tafsīr Literature." May 2001. Available online at faith.yale.edu/reconciliation-project/resources (accessed January 3, 2017).

———. "Ṣifāt al-Dhāt in al-Ash'arī's Doctrine of God and Possible Christian Parallels." May 2001. Available online faith.yale.edu/reconciliation-project/resources (accessed January 3, 2017).

Eliade, Mircea, ed. *The Encyclopedia of Religion*. 16 vols. New York: Macmillan, 1987.

Fisk, Robert. *The Great War for Civilization: The Conquest of the Middle East*. New York: Knopf, 2005.

———. *Pity the Nation: The Abduction of Lebanon*. 4th edition. New York: Nation Books, 2002.

Gabel, John B., Charles B. Wheeler, et al. *The Bible as Literature: An Introduction*. 5th edition. Oxford: Oxford University Press, 2005.

Gaudeul, Jean-Marie. *Encounters and Clashes: Islam and Christianity in History*. 2 vols. Rome: Pontificio istituto di studi arabi e d'islamistica, 2000.

Ghazālī, Abū Ḥāmid al-. *Ar-Radd al-Jamīl li-Ilāhiyyat 'Īsa bi-Ṣarīḥ al-Injīl* (Une réfutation excellente de la divinité de Jésus-Christ d'après le texte même de l'évangile). Edited and translated by Robert Chidiac. Paris: Librarie Ernest Leroux, 1939.

Glaser, Ida, with Hannah Kay. *Thinking Biblically about Islam: Genesis, Transfiguration, Transformation*. Carlisle: Langham Global Library, 2016.

Goddard, Hugh. *A History of Christian-Muslim Relations*. Amsterdam: New Amsterdam Books, 2000.

Goldziher, Ignaz. *Muslim Studies*. 2 vols. London: Allen & Unwin, 1971 (original German 1890).

Griffith, Sidney H. "Disputes with Muslims in Syriac Christian Texts: From Patriarch John (d. 648) to Bar Hebraeus (d. 1286)." In *Religionsgespräche im Mittelalter*, ed. Bernard Lewis and Friedrich Niewöhner, 251–73. Wiesbaden: Otto Harrassowitz, 1992.

Guillaume, Alfred. *The Life of Muhammad: A Translation of Ibn Ishaq's Sirat Rasul Allah*. Oxford: Oxford University Press, 2002.

Guillaumont, A., and others. *The Gospel according to Thomas: Coptic Text Established and Translated*. Leiden/London: Brill/Collins, 1959.

Gundry, Stanley N., Dennis L. Okholm, and Timothy R. Phillips, eds. *Four Views on Salvation in a Pluralistic World*. 2nd edition. Grand Rapids: Zondervan, 1996.

Guthrie, A., and E. F. F. Bishop. "The Paraclete, Almunhamanna, and Ahmad." *Muslim World* 41 (1951): 251–56.

Ḥamidullah, M., trans. *Le Coran*. Paris: Le Club Français du Livre, 1959.

Hayner, Priscilla B. *Unspeakable Truths: Transitional Justice and the Challenge of Truth Commissions*. 2nd edition. Abingdon: Routledge, 2010.

Hick, John, and Brian Hebblethwaite, eds. *Christianity and Other Religions: Selected Readings*. Philadelphia: Fortress, 1980.

Holy Bible: New International Version. Grand Rapids: Zondervan, 2011.

Hoyland, Robert. "The Correspondence of Leo III (717–41) and 'Umar II (717–20)." *Aram* 6.1 (1994): 165–77.

Ibn al-Ḥajjāj. *Ṣaḥīḥ Muslim*. Translated by Abdul Hamid Siddiqui. Available online at sunnah.com/muslim.

Ibn Anas, Mālik. *Muwaṭṭa' Mālik*. Available online at sunnah.com/malik.

Ibn Ḥazm, Abū Muhammad 'Alī b. Aḥmad. *Kitāb al-Fiṣal fī al-Milal wa al-Ahwā' wa an-Niḥal*.Cairo: Al-Qahira Publishers, 1900.

———. *Rasā'il Ibn Ḥazm al-Andalusī*. Edited by Iḥsān ʿAbbās. Beirut: Al-Mu'assasah al-ʿArabiyyah li ad-Dirāsāt wa al-Nashr, 1981.

Ibn Isḥāq, Ḥunayn. *Kayfiyyat Idrāk Ḥaqīqat ad-Diyāna* (How to Discern the Truth of a Religion). In *Vingt traités théologiques d'auteurs arabes chrétiens (ix–xiii siècles)*, ed. Louis Cheikho, 143–46. Beirut: Imprimerie Catholique, 1920.

Ibn Isḥāq/Ibn Hishām. *As-Sīra an-Nabawiyya*. Edited by M. as-Saqā, A. al-Abyārī, and A. Ḥ. Shalabī. Cairo: Muṣṭafa al-Babī al-Ḥalabī, 1936.

Ibn Qayyim al-Jawziyya, Shams ad-Dīn Muhammad b. Abī Bakr. *Hidāyat al-Ḥayāra fī Ajwibat al-Yahūd wa an-Naṣāra* (Arabic text). Edited by Aḥmad Ḥijāzī as-Saqā. Cairo: al-Maktaba al-Qayyima, 1980.

Ibn Qutayba, Abū Muhammad ʿAbdallāh b. Muslim. *Kitāb al-Maʿārif*. Edited by Saroite Okacha. Cairo: Dār al-Maʿārif, 1960.

———. *Kitāb Ta'wīl Mukhtalif al-Ḥadīth*. Cairo: n.p., 1908.

———. *Kitāb ʿUyūn al-Akhbār*. Cairo: Dār al-Kutub al-Misriyya, 1925–30.

Ibn Taymiyya, Taqī ad-Dīn Aḥmad. *Al-Jawāb aṣ-Ṣaḥīḥ li-man Baddala Dīn al-Masīḥ*. 2 vols. in 4 parts. Cairo: Nile Press, 1905.

Ibrahim, Ayman. "A Response to Harley Talman." *International Journal of Frontier Missiology* 32.4 (Winter 2014): 202–7.

Jāḥiẓ, Abū ʿUthmān ʿAmr b. Baḥr al-. *Al-Mukhtār fī ar-Radd ʿala an-Naṣāra*. Edited by M. A. Sharqāwī. Beirut: Dar al-Jil, 1991.

Jones, L. Bevan. "The Paraclete or Mohammed: The Verdict of an Ancient Manuscript." *Muslim World* 10 (1920): 112–25.

Juwaynī, Abū al-Maʿālī ʿAbd al-Malik b. ʿAbdallāh al-. *Textes apologétiques de Ǧuwainī (m. 478/1085): Shifā' al-Ġalīl fī l-Tabdīl; Lumaʿ fī Qawāʿid Ahl al-Sunna*. Edited and translated by M. Allard. Beirut: Dar El-Machreq, 1968.

Kärkkäinen, Veli-Matti. *A Constructive Christian Theology for the Pluralistic World*, vol. 1: *Christ and Reconciliation*. Grand Rapids: Eerdmans, 2013.

Kaskas, Safi, trans. *The Qur'an: A Contemporary Understanding*. Fairfax, VA: Bridges of Reconciliation, 2015.

Khalidi, Tarif. *The Muslim Jesus: Sayings and Stories in Islamic Literature*. Cambridge: Harvard University Press, 2003.

Kindī, ʿAbd al-Masīḥ b. Isḥāq al-. *Risālat ʿAbd Allāh b. Ismāʿīl al-Hāshimī ila ʿAbd al-Masīḥ b. Isḥāq al-Kindī Yadʿūhu bihā ila al-Islam, wa Risālat ʿAbd al-Masīḥ ila al-Hāshimī Yaruddu bihā ʿAlayhi wa Yadʿūhu ila an-Naṣrāniyya* (The Letter of ʿAbd Allāh b. Ismāʿīl al-Hāshimī to ʿAbd al-Masīḥ b. Isḥāq al-Kindī, Inviting Him to Embrace Islam, and the Letter of ʿAbd al-Masīḥ to al-Hāshimī in Response to Him, Inviting Him to Embrace Christianity). Edited by W. Muir. London: W. H. Allen, 1885.

Kittel, Gerhard, and Gerhard Friedrich, eds. *Theological Dictionary of the New Testament*. Translated by Geoffrey W. Bromley. 10 vols. Grand Rapids: Eerdmans, 1965–74.

Kraft, Charles. "Pursuing Faith, Not Religion: The Liberating Quest for Contextualization." *Mission Frontiers* (September–October 2005). http://www.missionfrontiers.org/issue/article/pursuing-faith-not-religion.

Küng, Hans. *Islam: Past, Present, and Future*. Translated by John Bowden. Oxford: Oneworld, 2007 (originally 2004).

Kurzman, Charles, ed. *Liberal Islam: A Sourcebook*. Oxford: Oxford University Press, 1998.

Lazarus-Yafeh, Hava. *Intertwined Worlds: Medieval Islam and Bible Criticism*. Princeton: Princeton University Press, 1992.

———. *Studies in al-Ghazzâlî*. Jerusalem: Magnes Press, Hebrew University, 1975.

Lecomte, Gérard. *Ibn Qutayba (mort en 276/889): L'homme, son oeuvre, ses idées*. Damascus: Presses de l'Ifpo, 1965.

Lewis, A. S., and M. D. Gibson. *The Palestinian Syriac Lectionary of the Gospels: Re-edited from two Sinai Mss. and from P. de Lagarde's edition of the "Evangeliarium Hierosolymitanum."* London: Paternoster House, 1899.

Luxenberg, Christoph. *The Syro-Aramaic Reading of the Koran. A Contribution to the Decoding of the Language of the Koran*. Berlin: Schiler, 2007.

Masson, D., trans. *Le Coran*. Paris: Gallimard, 1967.

Michel, Thomas. *A Muslim Theologian's Response to Christianity*. Tehran: Caravan, 1985.

Mingana, Alphonse. "The Apology of Timothy the Patriarch before the Caliph Mahdi." *Woodbrooke Studies* 11 (1928): 1–162.

Nau, F. "Un colloque du patriarche Jean avec l'émir des Agaréens et faits divers des années 712 à 716." *Journal asiatique* 11.5 (1915): 225–79.

Osborne, Grant R. *The Hermeneutical Spiral*. Downers Grove, IL: InterVarsity Press, 1991.

Payne Smith, R., and J. Payne Smith. *A Compendious Syriac Dictionary*. Oxford: Clarendon Press, 1903.

Peters, F. E., ed. *A Reader on Classical Islam*. Princeton: Princeton University Press, 1994.

Putman, Hans. *L'église et l'Islam sous Timothée I (780–823)*. Beirut: Librairie Orientale, 1975.

Qarāfī, Shihāb ad-Dīn al-. *Al-Ajwiba al-Fākhira ʿan al-Asʾila al-Fājira.* Cairo: Wehbeh Publishers, 1987.

Rassī, al-Qāsim b. Ibrāhīm ar-. *Ar-Radd ʿala an-Naṣāra.* In Ignazio Di Matteo, "Confutazione contro I cristiani dello zaydita al-Qāsim b. Ibrāhīm." *Rivista degli Studi Orientali* 9 (1922): 301–64.

Reynolds, Gabriel S. *The Emergence of Islam.* Minneapolis: Fortress, 2012.

Rippin, Andrew. *Muslims: Their Religious Beliefs and Practices.* 2nd edition. New York: Routledge, 2003.

Ryken, Leland. *How to Read the Bible as Literature.* Grand Rapids: Zondervan, 1985.

Saadi, Abdul Massih. "The Letter of John of Sedreh: A New Perspective on Nascent Islam." *Journal of the Assyrian Academic Society* 11.1 (1997): 68–84.

Saeed, Abdullah. "The Charge of Distortion of Jewish and Christian Scriptures." *Muslim World* 92 (Fall 2002): 419–36.

Sahas, D. J. *John of Damascus on Islam: The "Heresy of the Ishmaelites."* Leiden: Brill, 1972.

Schacht, Joseph. *The Origins of Muhammadan Jurisprudence.* Oxford: Clarendon, 1950.

Sepmeijer, Floris. "Een weerlegging van het Christendom uit de 10e eeuw: De brief van al-Hasan b. Ayyub aan zijn broer ʿAli." PhD thesis, Vrije Universiteit Amsterdam. Kampen: van den Berg, 1985.

Shehadeh, Imad. *Al-ʾāb wa al-ibn wa al-rūḥ al-qudus ilāh wāḥid, āmīn: ḍarūrat at-tafiaddudiyya fī al-wiḥdāniyya al-ilāhiyya* (The Father, Son and Holy Spirit, One God, Amen: The Necessity of Diversity in Divine Unity). Beirut: Dar Manhal al-Hayat, 2009.

Sizer, Stephen. *Christian Zionism: Road-map to Armageddon?* Downers Grove: IVP, 2006.

Small, Keith E. *Textual Criticism and Qurʾan Manuscripts.* Lanham, MD: Lexington, 2011.

Smith, Percy. "Did Jesus Foretell Ahmed?" *Moslem World* 12 (1922): 71–74.

Solomon, Sam, and E. al-Maqdisi. *A Common Word: The Undermining of the Church.* Charlottesville, VA: Advancing Native Missions, 2009.

Sourdel, D., ed./trans. "Un pamphlet musulman anonyme d'époque ʿabbâside contre les chrétiens.'" *Revue des études islamiques* 34 (1966): 1–33.

Ṭabarānī, Ibrāhīm aṭ-. *Le dialogue d'Abraham de Tibériade avec Abd al-Raḥmān al-Hāshimī à Jérusalem vers 820.* Edited by G. B. Marcuzzo. Rome: Institut Oriental et Université Pontificale du Latran, 1986.

Ṭabarī, Abū Jaʿfar Muhammad b. Jarīr b. Yazīd aṭ-. *Tārīkh ar-Rusul wa al-Mulūk* (A History of Prophets and Kings). Edited by Muhammad Abū al-Faḍl Ibrāhīm. Cairo: Dār al-Maʿārif, 1960.

Ṭabarī, ʿAlī b. Rabbān aṭ-. *The Book of Religion and Empire*. Translated by Alphonse Mingana. Manchester: Manchester University Press, 1922.

———. *Kitāb ad-Dīn wa ad-Dawla*. Edited by Alphonse Mingana. Cairo: Maṭbaʿat al-Muqtaṭaf, 1923.

———. *Kitāb ar-Radd ʿala an-Naṣāra* (The Book of the Refutation of Christians). Published in I. A. Khalifé and W. Kutsch's "Ar-radd ʿala-n-nasārā." *Mélanges de l'Université Saint Joseph* 36.4 (1959): 115–48.

Takrītī, Abū Rāʾiṭa at-. *Min Qawl Abī Rāʾiṭa at-Takrītī* (From the Sayings of Abī Rāʾiṭa at-Takrītī). In *Vingt traités théologiques d'auteurs arabes chrétiens (ix–xiii siècles)*, ed. Louis Cheikho, 146. Beirut: Imprimerie Catholique, 1920.

Talman, Harley. "Is Muhammad Also among the Prophets?" *International Journal of Frontier Missiology* 31.4 (Winter 2014): 169–90.

Tartar, Georges. "Jésus a-t-il annoncé la venue de Muhammad? Exégèse du verset coranique 61/6." *Parole de l'orient* 16 (1990): 311–28.

Thatcher, Oliver J., and Edgar Holmes McNeal, eds. *A Source Book for Medieval History*. New York: Scribner, 1905.

Thomas, David R. "The Bible in Early Muslim Anti-Christian Polemics." *Islam and Christian-Muslim Relations* 7 (1996): 33–34.

———. "Tabarī's Book of Religion and Empire." *Bulletin of the John Rylands University Library* 49 (1986): 1–7.

Villa-Vicencio, Charles, and Wilhelm Verwoerd, eds. *Looking Back, Reaching Forward: Reflections on the Truth and Reconciliation Commission of South Africa*. London: Zed, 2000.

Wāḥidī, al-. *Asbāb an-Nuzūl* (The Occasions of the Revelation). Available online at altafsir.com/AsbabAlnuzol.asp?SoraName=2&Ayah=144&search=yes&img=A.

Yale Response to "A Common Word." Available online at faith.yale.edu/common-word/common-word-christian-response.

Yaʿqūbī, Aḥmad b. Abī Yaʿqūb al-. *Tārīkh*. 2 vols. Edited by M. T. Houtsma. Leiden: Brill, 1883.

Zaehner, R. C. *The Bhagavad Gita*. Oxford: Clarendon, 1969.

Index of Names

ʿAbdo, Muhammad (d. 1905), 46, 138
Abū Hurayra, 134
Abū Qurrah, 179–80, 269, 270, 273–74
Abu Zayd, Nasr Hamed, 41–42
Accad, Fouad, 36–37, 58, 188–90
Afghānī, Jamāl ad-Din al-, 138
ʿĀmirī, Abū al-Ḥasan Muhammad al-, 238, 299–300, 301
Ashʿarī, Abū al-Ḥasan al- (d. 936), 57, 126, 244
Ayoub, Mahmoud, 71
Azharī, al-, 91

Bakri, Muhammad Omar, 327–29
Bāqillānī, Abū Bakr Muhammad b. aṭ-Ṭayyib al- (d. 1013), 122, 166, 174, 182, 222, 238
Barth, Karl, 10
Basil the Great, 105
Baṣrī, ʿAmmār al-, 269, 271–72, 273
Bayḍāwī, al- (d. 1286?), 46, 137, 224
Bouyges, Maurice, 235–36
Brueggemann, Walter, 22, 23

Cragg, Kenneth, 71
Cumming, Joseph, 57–58

George, Timothy, 76–77
Ghazālī, Abū Ḥāmid al- (d. 1111), 123, 177, 182–83, 222

Glaser, Ida, 323
Gregory of Nazianzus, 120
Gregory of Nyssa, 105

Hariri, Rafic, 29
Ḥasan b. Ayyūb al-, 87, 161, 222

Ibn al-Anbāri, 311
Ibn al-Munabbih, Wahb, 133, 199, 200, 312
Ibn Ayyūb, al-Ḥasan, 296, 304; and accusation of taḥrīf, 222, 249; Jesus and monotheism, 87, 89; Jesus not divine, 122, 126–27, 161, 162, 180–82; Jesus as a prophet, 164, 165–66, 167, 200, 254; use of the Gospels in, 211, 212, 252, 283
Ibn Ḥazm, Abū Muhammad ʿAlī b. Aḥmad (d. 1064), 122, 317; and accusation of taḥrīf, 93, 191, 222, 233, 239–41, 246, 256, 257, 258, 280, 283; genealogies of Jesus and taḥrīf, 242–44, 245, 246, 247; Jesus not divine, 127–28, 177; Jesus as a prophet, 164, 166–67, 254–55; temptation of Jesus and taḥrīf, 211, 252–54
Ibn Hishām (d. 833), 52, 113, 264, 314, 315, 318
Ibn Isḥāq (d. 768), 52, 113, 133, 264, 312, 314, 320

Index of Subjects

Abraham, 14, 17, 150, 168, 283, 331; in Qur'an, 51, 152, 155, 156, 193–94, 332–34, 335, 336
abrogation, principle of, 52–56, 280
Arab Spring, 4–5, 23, 29

Bible: asbāb an-nuzūl ("occasions of the revelations"), xxv, 47–51, 53, 55, 68, 111, 113, 149, 267; authenticity of for Muslims, 277; as hermeneutical tool, 325–26; Muhammado-centric reading of, 288–315; Muslim accusations against, 217–18, 219–23, 234, 248–55; reliability of text, 220, 234, 236–37, 257–58

Christ. *See* Jesus
Christianity: and a call to action, 342–46; doctrinal development in early, 115, 119–20, 184–86, 125–26, 214; and legitimacy of violence, 279–81; and polemics against Islam, 131–32, 265, 268–75, 278, 282, 290–92, 296, 320; and a theology of Islam, 323–27; understanding of the Paraclete in, 232, 290–92, 297, 321–22
Christian-Muslim encounter, xxiii, xxiiin1, xxiv–xxv, xxvii–xxix, 3–4, 7–8, 16, 24, 30, 50, 67–68, 70–71, 73–74; centrality of sacred texts in, 64–65, 214–15, 240–41; kerygmatic approach to, 9, 14–16, 17, 215; starting points for theological dialogue in, 100 104, 142–45, 183–84, 185–86, 215–16, 258–60, 286–87, 321, 336, 338; understandings of God in, 82–98
Christology, 81, 90, 109, 110, 141, 173–77, 231
conflict and religion, 2–3, 5–7, 25, 29, 259
conflict resolution, 108, 145, 341; and humility, 25–26, 345–46; and justice, 27–28, 29, 33, 344–45; and religious extremism, 342–44
Council of Chalcedon (451), 96, 178
Council of Nicea (325), 116, 125, 185
crucifixion: historicity of rejected by Islam, 57, 58, 140, 302, 310; Qur'anic view of, 128–38

Docetism, Docetic, 38, 61, 120, 158

exegetical tradition: Christian, 47–49, 59–63; in Christian-Muslim encounter, 67, 68 ; Muslim, xxv, xxvii, xxviii, 46–59, 64, 73–74, 80, 89, 91–92, 110–14, 132–39, 141, 169–71, 214–15; Muslim, on Paraclete passages, 124–25, 277, 278, 288–317;

Muslim, on taḥrīf, 223–30, 233–34, 256, 284

God: Christian understanding of, 57, 76–79, 80–81, 103, 104–5, 144–45; Islamic understanding of, 57, 76–79, 80–81, 82–98, 104–5, 144–45; Muslim critique of Christian doctrine of, 92–98, 99–100; self-giving nature of, 81, 128, 216, 144, 145, 287, 322, 338
Gospels, 39, 260; genealogies of Jesus in and taḥrīf argument, 239, 242–45, 246–48; Islamization of, 206–13, 214, 316; and Jesus's identity, 266–67; Muslim exegesis of, 63–64, 67, 85–90, 92–93, 99–100, 109–10, 131, 141, 158–73, 174, 178–82, 191, 227; Paraclete passages in, 289–316; preannouncement of Muhammad in, 195, 299, 300, 302–4, 309, 319; prove Muhammad a prophet, 275–78, 295; testimony of as corrupt or misinterpreted, 233–38, 248–55, 257; and title "Son of God" in, 28, 125, 126–28, 175–77; used to support Qur'an, 111, 120–25, 192, 281–84, 289. *See also* Injīl

ḥadīth (Islamic tradition), 49–50, 112, 138, 155, 264–65, 301; Bible as a corrective of, 191, 202–6, 214, 237–38; transmission of, 134, 137, 156, 315–16
Hebrew Scriptures (Torah): and accusation of taḥrīf, 226–27; Christocentric reading of, 39, 231, 265, 288; early Christian attitude toward, 206; and legitimate use of violence, 280; Muhammado-centric reading of, 293
hermeneutical principles, 40–43, 59–60, 126; Christian, 38, 45, 46, 64–65; for Christian-Muslim dialogue, 67–70, 160–61; Muslim, xxv, 35, 36, 37, 42–43, 55–57, 64–65, 111, 149–50; reading Christian into Qur'an, 36–38, 39. *See also* Scriptural interpretation; tafsīr
historical-critical method, 47–49, 56
homoousios, 125, 143

incarnation, 179, 231; biblical understanding of, 116, 142–45, 158, 178; Muslim rejection of, 76, 83, 94, 141, 145, 236
Injīl: as authoritative document, 191, 198–202, 319; as a corrective of ḥadīth, 191, 202–6, 214, 238; Islamization of, 206–13, 295, 316; Qur'anic view of, 192–97; and ṭaḥrīf, 219–23. *See also* Gospels
Islam: character of, 11, 43, 72, 81, 90–92, 93, 119, 155, 324; confirms/corrects/fulfils Judeo-Christian tradition, 39–40, 73–74, 126–38, 141, 150, 153, 157–73, 175–77, 178–82, 278–86, 288–315; interpretation of Qur'an, 44–57; legitimacy of violence, 279–81; Meccan and Medinan streams of, 14, 50–51, 55, 325–27, 329–30; polemical engagement with Christianity, 131–32, 139–40, 211, 214, 265, 274–75, 278–85; positive approaches to Bible, 198–213, 215, 220
isnād ("line of transmission"), 49–50, 137, 170; biblical, 131, 234
ISIS, 340–41, 343–44

Jacobites (miaphysite), 96, 116, 169, 178
Jesus: biblical identity and role of, 39, 266–67, 270, 339; divinity of denied by Muslims, 94, 97–98, 102, 113–14, 115–16, 119–25, 178–82, 208–9, 210; proves Muhammad's prophethood, 150–57, 297; in Qur'an and Muslim theology, 85–90, 115, 150, 157–73, 82–84, 149; and religious traditions, 18–20, 21–22; a starting point for Muslim-Christian dialogue, 100–101
Jews: and accusation of corrupting/

Index of Scripture References